MAKING THE AMERICAS

Series advisory editor: Lyman L. Johnson, University of North Carolina at Charlotte

MAKING THE AMERICAS

The United States and Latin America

from the Age of Revolutions to the

Era of Globalization

THOMAS F. O'BRIEN

UNIVERSITY OF NEW MEXICO PRESS 〰 ALBUQUERQUE

LIBRARY OF CONGRESS CATALOGING-IN-PUBLICATION DATA

O'Brien, Thomas F., 1947–
Making the Americas : the United States and
Latin America from the age of revolutions to the era of globalization /
Thomas F. O'Brien.
p. cm.
Includes bibliographical references and index.
ISBN 978-0-8263-4200-3 (PBK. : ALK. PAPER)
1. Latin America—Civilization—American influences.
2. Latin America—History.
3. Latin America—Relations—United States.
4. United States—Relations—Latin America. I. Title.
F1408.3.O27 2007
980—dc22

2007004234

Book and cover design and typography by Kathleen Sparkes
Book is typeset using Adobe Jenson Open Type Pro 11.5/14, 26P
Display type is Trajan Pro

❧

TO

DIANE,

SARAH,

DANIEL,

MATTHEW,

AND WENDY

❧

CONTENTS

❧

INTRODUCTION

ɕ ɕ

For more than half a century, the United States has been leading a worldwide process of transformation that has profoundly influenced the lives of people around the globe. This American mission of globalization, which stresses economies open to U.S. trade and investment, republican political institutions, individualism, competitiveness, and consumerism, has in fact been shaped by a centuries-long project of transformation in Latin America. Furthermore, the responses of Latin Americans to the American initiatives, including embracing consumer goods, reconfiguring the meaning of such products to accommodate the needs of local cultures, as well as rejecting some of the economic and political aspects of the American project in popular protests and revolutionary upheavals, prefigured many of the reactions of other cultures to the process of globalization. Yet just as these hemispheric interactions were taking on their greatest global significance, the academicians most concerned with their study seemed trapped by theoretical sterility and mired in circular debates.

☙

In 1992 historian Michael Hunt summarized the condition of diplomatic history this way:

> Our remarkably sustained exercise in self-reflection and self criticism over the last two decades was a defensive response

to the pointed criticism, if not the wounding indifference directed at diplomatic topics by an historical profession in transformation. Social historians flogged diplomatic history, and political history more generally, for seemingly old-fashioned methods and concerns, especially the tendency to identify with the political elite and to ignore the links between policy and the patterns of privilege and power within American society and culture. The new cultural history added its own charges: epistemological naiveté and an impoverished sense of the importance of language for an understanding of both historical evidence and historians' discourse. Those with a strong theoretical bent consigned diplomatic historians to the role of hewers-of-wood and the drawers of water in their world of international relations theory.[1]

Hunt's words succinctly captured the crisis in the study of international relations during the closing decades of the twentieth century. The field had been passed by in a profession newly empowered by approaches such as cultural and social history and by focusing on issues of gender and race. Despite the crisis that he described, Hunt concluded that this "travail" had in fact renewed the discipline. Hunt's conclusion was quite accurate, for even as he wrote, other scholars, many of them not trained strictly as diplomatic historians, were bringing fresh new approaches to the issues of international relations.

❧

As early as 1982, Emily Rosenberg's *Spreading the American Dream* explored not only the economic but also the cultural aspects of U.S. expansionism. Although much of Rosenberg's work focused on the role of the state, she also gave considerable attention to the effects of corporate activity in areas such as communication and transportation, as well as the initiatives of groups such as philanthropists and missionaries. William Roseberry's *Anthropologies and Histories* further expanded the analytical approaches to international relations in a set of provocative essays that explored topics ranging from anthropological debates about culture to dependency theory. One of those essays addresses the concept of Americanization both in terms of its cruder and long-discredited usage earlier in the twentieth century and a far more nuanced contemporary use of the idea to understand the complexities of interactions among cultures in the Western Hemisphere.[2] Roseberry's work marked the increasing influence of anthropological theories and approaches employed by historians, especially in the analysis of culture as a force in history. At the same time, examinations of race and gender, as well as subaltern studies, were taking on a growing significance in the history profession. The rich array of new analytical perspectives, which themselves were the source of much of the criticism of diplomatic history, were soon being applied by scholars to the history of international relations, especially in the Americas.

My own work, *Revolutionary Mission*, inspired in part by Rosenberg and Roseberry, examined the role of American business in Latin America. Rather than focusing on issues such as theories of the corporation or the specific effects of U.S. investments on economic development, the book examines the attempts of corporate executives and managers to transform their Latin American workforces, disciplining their employees to the rigors of wage labor and modern industrial work methods, encouraging American values such as individualism and competitiveness, and promoting consumerism as a lure into the world of full-time wage labor. At the same time, the work examines various forms of resistance by Latin Americans to the American agenda, culminating with the rise of populist, nationalist political movements in the 1920s and '30s that challenged the project of transformation pursued by corporate America with the endorsement of Latin American elites. The book offered one alternative to the focus on state interactions that had dominated the study of inter-American relations throughout the decades, but it was one of only several such new approaches that scholars were already generating in the 1980s. Much like my own analysis of corporatist agents of Americanization, Marcus Cueto's edited volume, *Missionaries of Science*, presented a series of studies by young scholars that traced the activities of the Rockefeller Foundation in Latin America. The essays in that collection explore the various foundation programs that employed American models to reform Latin American public health services and agriculture.[3] But other new approaches were moving farther afield from this type of institutional focus.

Gail Bederman's *Manliness & Civilization* explored Theodore Roosevelt's contribution to the construction of raced-based masculinity; Amy Kaplan's "Black and Blue on San Juan Hill" examined the projection of that construction of manhood into U.S. foreign policy. Mary Renda's *Taking Haiti* picks up many of these ideas about manhood and race as she traces the Americans' paternalistic mission in that island nation and the consequences for both occupiers and occupied as well as the formulation of American imperial culture. Gil Joseph's edited volume, *Close Encounters*, offers a series of essays that apply cultural perspectives to an array of interactions between imperial America and its southern neighbors. In perhaps the richest of the new works of scholarship in this vein, Luis Pérez in *On Becoming Cuban* studies Americans' influence on an emerging Cuban identity in a variety of encounters ranging from military occupation to missionary schools and popular culture. Pérez also delves into the resonance of Cuban culture within American society.[4]

In the course of less than two decades the study of inter-American relations has evolved from a crisis-ridden field derided for its theoretical sterility to an arena featuring lively scholarly debate among diplomatic historians over the material versus the ideological roots of U.S. foreign policy; at the same time, other scholars have marshaled a series of analytical tools from gender and race to culture and subaltern history to explore new and fascinating aspects of the history of the Americas. Even before the recent explosive growth in studies applying cultural history to the field of international relations, in fact soon after Hunt authored his article, the diplomatic historian Steve Rabe noted that the time had come to attempt a synthesis of the literature on international relations. Certainly that statement is all the more meaningful as an array of new perspectives have emerged in recent years. The area of inter-American affairs has benefited most from the resurgence in the study of international relations and represents the logical focal point for an attempt to craft a synthetic interpretation. In short, this work owes an enormous debt to a host of talented scholars who are employing both conventional and innovative approaches and who have contributed so much to our understanding of the American mission.

The central argument of this work is that over the past two centuries the people of the United States have envisioned themselves on a global mission of reform. Confident of the superiority of their free-market economy, competitive individualistic society, and republican political institutions, they set out initially on a mission to share these ideas and institutions with their neighbors in the Western Hemisphere. In the process, Americans formed, shaped, and reshaped perceptions of Latin Americans that strongly suggested that their neighbors were in urgent need of American reforms. Although early relations between the United States and its neighbors were marked either by ignorance or by belief in a shared commitment to the ideals of the Enlightenment, such optimism gave way by the middle of the nineteenth century to an American perception of Latin Americans as effeminate (and therefore irrational) inferior races, possessed of exotic cultures far removed from the manly, rational culture of the United States. At the same time leaders of the United States believed the American mission would stabilize their own society. During the nineteenth century Americans looked first to territorial and later to commercial expansion as the means of stabilizing the restless forces of a free market society increasingly populated by immigrants, who seemed to reject some of the fundamental values of the early republic. As a result, the United States launched itself on a path of territorial and then commercial hemispheric expansion designed to enhance domestic economic growth and in the process restore social stability. By the end of the nineteenth century the drive for overseas markets led to the creation of a civilizing American empire in the circum-Caribbean.

Convinced of their racial superiority and of their obligation to reform the inferior races of the region, American Marines, businesspeople, clergymen, and Washington bureaucrats attempted to reshape countries such as Cuba into model versions of their own republic, complete with republican political institutions, public-works systems, mass education, and free market policies. Imperialists like President Teddy Roosevelt believed that these endeavors would offer an invigorating challenge to American males who might otherwise sink into a lethargic state as a result of the comforts offered by their own modern culture. Central to these endeavors and often damaging their idealized goals of reform were the creation of privileged positions for U.S. economic interests and a patriarchal attitude toward the subordinated populations.

Although the elites of larger Latin American countries might be troubled by American occupations of Caribbean nations, they shared the Americans' disparaging attitudes toward the mixed-race populations of the region, and the American agenda of Progressive-era reforms closely approximated their own positivist strategies to modernize their societies. They embraced central aspects of the American project, particularly the promise of dramatically more efficient production methods. American-driven productivity improvements would allow the ruling classes of Latin America to resolve productivity problems arising from the repressive methods by which they had long exploited the labor of their own populations. Those conditions created a golden age for corporate America in the region as large U.S. businesses came to dominate Latin American mining, agriculture, and power generation in the first decades of the twentieth century. At the same time, Protestant missionaries, private philanthropists, American economists, and labor leaders found welcoming audiences among the elite and segments of the middle class, who embraced them as agents of modernization. This is not to say that these proponents of Americanization acted in lockstep, but they did share common values and visions about the American mission. Contrary to the hopes of the agents of Americanization, U.S. technology and capital, while generating economic growth, did not ensure prosperous societies with relatively equitable distributions of wealth. The missionaries of Americanization did not address the acute disparities in economic, social, and political power in Latin America. Those disparities would frustrate attempts to craft societies in which most citizens would share to some degree in economic growth. Furthermore, the formidable increase in material production that drove this golden age also proved its undoing.

As U.S. bank loans and investments generated vast new outpourings of agriculture and mining products into the world market, they contributed to a global crisis of oversupply that sent prices for goods such as sugar and copper spiraling downward by the late 1920s. Surplus production contributed to the onset of the Great Depression. The economic crisis caused enormous suffering in Latin America and undermined the claims of Americans and local elites that they were creating an age of perpetual prosperity. Even before the onset of the Depression, Latin Americans had begun shaping national identities formed in part by their rejection of U.S. economic domination and the series of U.S. military interventions in the circum-Caribbean. Those emerging identities and the impact of the Depression served as catalysts in the formation of multiclass alliances in Latin America that rejected U.S. domination, berated the elite for subordinating national interests to their alliance with the Americans, and demanded state action to confront the economic crisis and ease the suffering of the popular classes. The nationalist populist movements of the era set an agenda for Latin American politics for the next half-century while creating a formidable challenge to the American mission. A new coalition of social forces in the United States would address that challenge.

The election of Franklin Delano Roosevelt marked a realignment of social and political forces in the United States. Under the umbrella of the New Deal, capital-intensive industries, big labor, and the federal government forged an alliance that would resuscitate the national economy and reshape the American mission to Latin America. The alliance partners backed a program of state-funded economic stimulation and the creation of a social safety net for workers. At the same time it sought to revive the global economy as the state worked to promote international trade and investment that would benefit capital-intensive industries whose technological advances gave them a significant advantage in the global economy. As a vitally important region for U.S. trade and investment Latin America was deeply affected by these initiatives that reasserted the dominant economic position the United States had achieved there by the 1920s. At the same time, attempting to adapt to the popular mobilizations and nationalist impulses that had swept the region while securing access to Latin American resources in anticipation of a new world war, Washington depicted itself as a partner in the development of Latin America.

During and immediately after the war, the growing domestic and international economic role of the state and confidence in American productivity refined U.S. foreign policy. Washington now presented itself as the source of reconstruction in Europe and Japan and of development for the rest of the world. Americans argued that adoption of U.S. technologies would improve productivity, thus ensuring economic growth that would penetrate down through the layers of these societies, eliminating the need for radical restructuring of power relationships. During the 1950s modernization theorists further refined these ideas in their application to third world countries such as in Latin America. With modernization theory, agents of the American mission abandoned racist explanations of underdevelopment, replacing them with arguments that traditional cultural values and relationships in these societies erected roadblocks to development that could be dismantled with American assistance. Working through its own institutions as well as multilateral agencies, the American state would pursue that goal. The United States would be a partner in progress with Latin Americans, providing through state, corporate, and philanthropic programs the technologies, capital, and training to propel their societies into modernity. The Rockefeller Foundation's agricultural programs in Mexico gave clear expression to the strategies and goals of this modernization mission. The foundation encouraged the adoption of hybrid crop seeds along with intensive use of irrigation and fertilization to expand agricultural output and thus provide inexpensive foodstuffs to a growing urban, industrial population. American technology would seemingly be applied in an objective and impartial manner to remove a roadblock to development. In fact, while increasing output, the program also favored large commercial farmers, who were in the best position to exploit the new technology, giving them an increasing competitive edge over small peasant producers.

Despite this reconfiguration of the American project, the modernization mission retained the male centeredness and patriarchal vision inherent in the earlier civilizing mission. President John F. Kennedy and his successors saw themselves as members of a tough-minded brotherhood dedicated to preserving the dominant position the United States had achieved regionally and globally. The persistence of earlier perceptions of Latin America as a collection of volatile yet exotic locations became apparent in the flourishing tourist trade in the casinos and bordellos of Latin American cities such as Havana and Tijuana. The view that Latin America consisted of a series of exciting but dangerous societies contributed to the American emphasis on maintaining order and stability, which would outweigh concerns about social and economic equality. That emphasis not only reflected persistent stereotypes, it also ensured that the American alliance with Latin American elites, and thereby acute inequalities in economic and social power, would remain intact. That concern with maintaining order and vested American economic interests, as well as the long-standing U.S. policy of excluding other major world powers from the region fed the vehement anticommunism that was part and parcel of the modernization mission in its purest expression, the Alliance for Progress.

Under the Alliance for Progress the agents of the American mission from state officials to corporate executives, labor leaders, and foundation directors acted with exceptional harmony, as modernization theory provided a paradigm that guided programs, which were diverse in their mechanics but shared common goals. Yet despite the various development initiatives stressing increased American corporate investment, promotion of more efficient agricultural methods, improvements in education, and the encouragement of community activism, the alliance failed to trigger the era of self-sustaining growth predicted by modernization theorists like Walt Rostow. What economic growth did occur was insufficient to spur national development, and disparities between rich and poor continued to grow. Another central tenet of the American mission as reconfigured by Latin Americans prompted increasing popular resistance to American initiatives.

By the end of World War II, the American exhortations regarding the creation of democratic political systems had resonated throughout the region. Yet Latin Americans, conscious of the deep-seated inequalities that marked their own societies, struggled for a democracy not merely of representative government institutions, but a democratic order that would actively seek to create more equitable social and economic relations. That interpretation of democracy ran directly contrary to the American insistence on preserving existing power relationships while relying on the trickling down of benefits from economic growth to resolve inequities. Increasing popular unrest received additional inspiration with the Cuban Revolution, which led many Latin Americans to question the effectiveness of nationalist populist movements and to seek more radical solutions to economic underdevelopment as well as social and political inequalities. The revolution also inspired a series of guerrilla insurgencies that would periodically challenge established regimes and U.S. influence in the region throughout the next three decades. In the midst of the cold war, and with increased American investment in Latin American manufacturing that made these corporations ever more vulnerable to social unrest, Washington proved intolerant of popular mobilizations. The leaders of the American labor movement played a significant role in the anticommunist crusade by the U.S. government as they intensified their efforts to foster business-friendly unions, combat popular mobilizations, and destabilize regimes that Washington considered hostile to its interests. The United States intervened covertly and overtly to halt challenges to the status quo and allied itself with military dictators who were now reimagined as agents of modernization.

By the mid-1970s a long night of dictatorial rule and widespread abuses of human rights had descended on most of Latin America. Although these regimes continued to pursue nationalist economic policies, they provided a far more welcoming environment for U.S. multinationals than had their civilian predecessors. The military shattered unions and forced down wages while easing restrictions on the repatriation of profits by foreign corporations. As a result U.S. investment flourished during this era. At the same time, American ideas about consumerism permeated the region more widely with the growth of television networks that served up large doses of U.S.-produced programming and advertising. At another level of popular culture, the growing tourist industry provided a venue in which Latin Americans and Americans could fashion "authentic" folk art that fit Americans' preconceived notions of primitive cultures and allowed them to experience and purchase the exoticism of those societies, as a counterbalance to the supposedly artificial creations of their own modern culture. The Rockefeller and Ford Foundations pursued programs to train Latin American technocrats, who would manage the process of modernization in their own countries, within the framework of U.S.-conceived ideas about capitalist development led by American corporate investment. The Rockefeller Foundation had also continued its program of agricultural modernization now known as the Green Revolution, spreading its influence beyond Mexico into much of South America.

American modernization projects coupled with military regime policies that repressed labor as a means of attracting foreign investment exacerbated the social and economic inequalities in the region. The growing popular discontent with the worsening conditions erupted into armed rebellions in Central America at the end of the 1970s that would be met with massive violence.

The election of Ronald Reagan marked the fracturing of the alliance that had emerged under Franklin Roosevelt. In an increasingly competitive global economy, even capital-intensive U.S. corporations could no longer maintain their social pact with labor that ensured rising standards of living. An alliance of the state and corporate America would now pursue an antilabor agenda at home while employing U.S. military might to reassert American power in an ever-more-competitive world environment. With both covert actions and military aid, Washington fought to topple the Sandinista government in Nicaragua and defeat the revolution in El Salvador, both of which drew much of their inspiration from the example of the Cuban Revolution. Despite apparent success in those endeavors, U.S. actions alienated leading Latin American countries while the end of the cold war robbed Washington's anticommunist rhetoric of its power to rally the Latin American elite and middle class to the U.S. cause. Meanwhile, economic issues were overshadowing the bloody conflicts in Central America.

Awash in petrodollars generated by oil-producing nations in a time of soaring petroleum prices, U.S. banks threw themselves into a lending frenzy in Latin America reminiscent of a similar financial bubble in the 1920s. In 1982, rising interest rates and slowing economic growth in developed countries brought the spending spree to a shuddering halt, threatening the economies of the region and the world financial system. International bankers and the International Monetary Fund (IMF) eventually arranged write-downs and reschedulings of the massive debt, but insisted in return on structural reforms that included slashing government social welfare expenditures, reducing trade and investment barriers, and privatizing state enterprises. The so-called Washington consensus was not entirely unwelcome in Latin American government circles. Many policymakers, such as leading economists in Chile, had been trained in neoliberal economics under programs jointly sponsored by the U.S. government and private foundations.

In the aftermath of the debt crisis most Latin American governments embraced some version of the neoliberal policies promoted by the United States. Regimes in the region slashed funding for social services, rolled back regulations that inhibited international economic interactions, and sold off many of the state corporations that had been created in the aftermath of the Great Depression. Not surprisingly liberalization of trade and investment policies prompted a surge of U.S. economic activity in the region. During the 1990s U.S. investment in and trade with Latin America soared. Latin Americans seemed to embrace American culture as U.S. consumer goods spread throughout their societies and Hollywood dominated both TV programming and the cinema. American-inspired Pentecostalism attracted millions of new converts. Yet that seeming triumph is in fact part of a far more complex process. As in the past, Latin Americans' responses to the specific elements of the American mission have varied significantly.

The process of globalization has mobilized diverse constituencies of Latin Americans, who see the process as increasing foreign domination of their economies and intensifying the exploitation of the poor as it strips the state of its social welfare functions. While Latin Americans often embrace American consumer culture, they also reconfigure the material products of that culture to incorporate them into their own systems of meaning. So too, Pentecostalism, despite its American origins, now draws its energy from local social forces, providing the poor with perspectives and values that aid in coping with the process of globalization. Encounters with Americans can also have contradictory effects, such as in the tourist industry, which draws locals into the market economy while also providing many of them with the means to maintain long-standing community rituals and practices. But the most profound effects of the American mission may ultimately unfold in the home of that mission. Despite the periodic bursts of Latin American economic growth, which American technology and capital have contributed to, the American mission has failed to stimulate long-term economic development. Even during the globalization boom of the 1990s, a growing number of Latin Americans fell into poverty. In fact the American promotion of free market forces in societies marked by acute disparities of wealth has worsened the condition of millions and millions of Latin Americans as they fled the process of agricultural commercialization that undermined their rural way of life, only to encounter urban centers with few job opportunities and states with a diminishing commitment to the poor. Exposed to the dream of perpetual prosperity by the American mission, hundreds of thousands of Latin Americans flee their homelands each year to search for the fulfillment of that dream in the land of its birth. In the process they are profoundly transforming the home of the American mission.

The American experiences in Latin America, especially the goals and strategies of the mission as well as Latin American responses to it, offer insights into America's global project of transformation during the past half century. Americans' belief in the superiority of their economic and political systems as well as their culture launched them on a transformational endeavor in Latin America and shaped a similar mission to the world. From the jungles of Vietnam to the deserts of Iraq, the United States has not hesitated to intervene militarily to turn back perceived threats to its influence and to protect its economic interests. Those occupations as well as more modestly conceived initiatives have also sought to create American-designed political institutions along with market economies while encouraging American values such as individualism and competitiveness. These strategies were first developed and refined in places like Nicaragua and Cuba during the first half of the twentieth century. At the same time, the ways in which Latin Americans have variously rejected, embraced, and reconfigured elements of the American mission have prefigured equally complex reactions to the American mission from people around the globe.

Hopefully this work will provide readers with a new and more nuanced understanding of how the people of the Americas have shaped their history and how those experiences have shaped the American global project.

CHAPTER ONE

FROM ENCOUNTERS TO EXPANSION, 1776–1861

ON OCTOBER 3, 1839, NEW YORKER JOHN L. STEPHENS SET SAIL FOR British Honduras to assume his new post as the U.S. diplomatic representative to the Confederation of Central American States. The position itself owned a rather unhappy history. Of the eight previous appointees, four had died before or shortly after reaching Central America, three never occupied the post, and one brave soul, who held the position for five years, committed suicide shortly after learning that his appointment in Central America was being extended. Stephens, however, seemed ideally suited to the job. On the advice of his doctor, the young attorney had abandoned New York in 1834 to tour Europe and the Middle East. Upon his return to Manhattan he published two highly successful accounts of his adventures, making him the best-known travel writer of his day. With a serious interest in archaeology, he culled what information he could from the meager writings on Central American ruins, and now he eagerly looked forward to the prospect of exploring the "lost cities" of the Maya.

On October 30, the brig on which he had sailed safely deposited Stephens in the port city of Belize where he began his trip to Guatemala City, the capital of the fragile confederation. From the first, Stephens enthusiastically embraced Central America, comparing the humble port with its simple wooden structures to the likes of Venice and Alexandria. Growing up in a society where racial distinctions were strictly drawn, Stephens came to grips with the obvious racial amalgamation in Belize by concluding, "I hardly knew whether to be shocked or amused at this condition of society."[1] However, his Protestant moral rectitude left him offended by the willingness of so many poor Central Americans to opt for the practical arrangements of common-law marriage, rather than the formal bonds of a church-sanctioned union.

Stephens experienced considerable hardship on his journey toward Guatemala City, enduring seemingly endless hours on muleback over dangerous mountain trails, through drenching rain, and in debilitating tropical heat. Yet these challenges in no way deterred him from sidetracking from the direct route to the Guatemalan capital in order to visit the ruins of Copán. Even though much of the city's grandeur remained hidden beneath dense forest growth, Stephens was overawed by the majesty of this ancient Mayan center, later writing, "The beauty of the sculpture, the solemn stillness of the woods disturbed only by the scrambling of monkeys and the chattering of parrots, the desolation of the city, and the mystery that hung over it, all created an interest higher, if possible, than I had ever felt among the ruins of the Old World."[2] However, the American adventurer expressed a far less positive view of the region's current inhabitants and their knowledge of the ruins, noting, "When we asked the Indians who had made them, their dull answer was, 'Quien sabe? (Who knows?)'"[3] Yet his disparaging attitude toward the contemporary indigenous population in no way dimmed his enthusiasm for Mesoamerican archaeology. His descriptions of ruins in Central America and in the Yucatan helped stir scholarly and popular interest in the subject. But Stephens's other mission, that of diplomacy, would prove far less successful.

When the American diplomat arrived in the region, the Confederation of Central American States was already in its death throes, wracked by a civil war that pitted the confederation president, General Francisco Morazán, headquartered in El Salvador, against the Guatemalan Rafael Carrera. Stephens found himself a diplomat in search of a government to accept his credentials. In the process, he experienced firsthand the acute political instability that characterized the region. In this tumultuous period, Stephens's sympathies lay with the Liberal faction, in no small measure because "they had thrown off the yoke of the Romish Church, and in the first enthusiasm of emancipated minds, tore away at once the black mantle of superstition which had been thrown like a funeral pall over the genius of the people."[4] However, the American diplomat's principal dealings were with Rafael Carrera, who was emerging as the dominant political figure in Guatemala.

Like most Latin Americans of his time, Carrera held no particular opinion about the government that Stephens represented because he had only the vaguest notions about the United States itself. Stephens, however, had very strong opinions about the popular forces that propelled Carrera to power. They were "barbarians" and "fanatic Indians."[5] As far as Stephens was concerned, Carrera and his allies, who enjoyed the support of the indigenous population, "were consorting with a wild animal which might at any moment turn and rend them in pieces."[6] In turn, the conservative elite, who supported Carrera, were highly suspicious of the U.S. government, certain that Texas's secession from Mexico was just the first step in U.S. territorial aggression that would engulf Mexico and eventually Guatemala.[7] Not surprisingly, Stephens parted on less than friendly terms with the de facto regime in Guatemala and proceeded to El Salvador in hopes of finding the confederation government. The closest he would come to that goal was an interview with the confederation's vice president, whom he encountered on his trip into El Salvador. But by then the confederation was collapsing and was about to splinter into separate states.

With no government to accept his credentials, Stephens sailed off to Costa Rica and then trekked across Nicaragua. His new, self-appointed mission was to explore a possible route for a canal that would connect the Atlantic and the Pacific. Since 1825, various groups in Central America and the United States had attempted to launch plans for a canal across Nicaragua. But despite those efforts, little or nothing had been accomplished. Stephens gained access to the work of a British naval officer, who had surveyed the possible canal route. As a result, his book on his travels in Central America provided the most thorough assessment of the canal route yet available in the United States. But Stephens was not simply a cool-headed analyst. He was a thoroughgoing promoter of the canal. The prospect of an American-built canal funneling American merchants to Pacific ports from South America to China drove Stephens to a euphoric depiction of the proposed canal, claiming "it would be glory surpassing the conquest of kingdoms to make this greatest enterprise ever attempted by human force entirely our own work."[8] Stephens's specific dream of a canal would not be fulfilled in his lifetime, but his entrepreneurial energies helped create an important alternative to an isthmisian canal. In 1848, Stephens joined with New York capitalists William Aspinwall and Henry Chauncey to form the Panama Railroad Company. Serving as vice president of the corporation, Stephens went to the isthmus to oversee the construction. After an enormous toll in lost lives, the rail line was successfully completed in 1855. However, Stephens did not live to see his dream of a rail connection between the seas fulfilled. He apparently contracted a tropical disease during his work on the railway and died in New York in 1852. By the time of Stephens's death, thousands of Americans were already crossing and recrossing both Panama and Nicaragua as the two easiest routes between the east and west coasts. That activity was only a small part of what had become a growing number of interactions between North Americans and their Latin neighbors since the American Revolution.

Exchanges between intellectuals in the Americas and the tales of New England whaling men returning from the Pacific coast of South America in the late eighteenth century gave way in the first half of the nineteenth century to increasing trade, the declaration of a virtual U.S. guardianship over the Western Hemisphere in the Monroe Doctrine, the growing belief by white Americans in their racial superiority, the seizure of vast stretches of Mexico's territory driven by the American conviction that territorial expansion was crucial to domestic stability, the developing American commitment to a civilizing mission in the Western Hemisphere, the rush of Americans across Central America to California, the pioneering ventures of entrepreneurs such as William Wheelwright in Chile, and the invasions of American mercenaries or filibusters seeking to seize control of nations in the circum-Caribbean.

Latin Americans, in return, offered a range of responses to their encounters with North Americans, envisioning the United States as a paragon of republican virtue, enthusiastically embracing American technology and business practices while denouncing U.S. territorial aggrandizement at the expense of Mexico and the violent actions of the filibusters. During these decades American and Latin Americans had begun a series of interactions that would profoundly influence the history of the Americas and the world. The roots of that process and Latin American reactions to it extended back to the colonial past.

MISSION TO THE AMERICAS

The United States and the Latin American nations were born in the Age of Revolutions that swept the Atlantic world during the late eighteenth and early nineteenth centuries. Yet the peoples who occupied the Western Hemisphere and would soon share this formative experience knew precious little about each other. With the exception of Mexicans, Latin Americans still did not see their destinies as being inextricably linked to the actions of the United States. Initially, what little Spanish, Portuguese, and English colonists knew about each other did not bode well for future relations. For the Spanish and Portuguese (Brazilian) colonists, their rare encounters with English colonists usually came in the form of privateering attacks on their ships and port cities. Furthermore, even the more peaceful inhabitants of Britain's North American colonies were known to be heretical adherents of Protestantism. As for the residents of English colonies, they readily accepted the Black Legend that portrayed Spaniards as fanatical Roman Catholics, who spared no act of brutality in their conquest and treatment of the indigenous inhabitants of the Western Hemisphere. As exaggerated as these stereotypes may have been, the fact remained that distinctly different societies were emerging in the British and Spanish colonial systems.

The colonists, who populated the shores of North America, had fashioned societies of small agrarian producers. Having destroyed or driven off the indigenous population, less than 2 percent of white settlers were subject to indentured servitude, with black slaves replacing them as the principal form of bound labor, particularly in the southern colonies. Eighty-five percent of the white male population became farmers, while most of the rest found employment as craftsmen, day laborers, or seamen. Even while British rule persisted, these colonial communities had developed individualistic, competitive cultures with notable degrees of religious freedom and political participation. To their south, a dramatically different set of societies was emerging.

Spain had conquered a series of densely populated Indian empires stretched along an axis running from Mexico to Chile. After destroying indigenous leadership and institutions, the Spanish imposed their own administrative superstructure and initiated a massive religious conversion of the population. A small group of Spanish colonists ruled over societies comprised largely of Indian and mixed-race people. A patrimonial order and an elaborate racial hierarchy marked these societies. Despite the destruction of the old imperial structures, and the imposition of Christianity, much of what was indigenous society and culture survived in the form of peasant villages with their communal practices and landholdings. These villages became the key source of labor for the silver- and gold-mining enterprises that underpinned the colonial economy. A variety of forced-labor practices controlled the villagers, who worked in the mines and on the landed estates. At the pinnacle of this social, economic, and political hierarchy, the Spanish crown maintained an uneasy truce between its colonists and the large subjugated population whose labor and land they exploited.

Despite dramatically different social systems and cultures, as well as often negative perceptions of their neighbors, the colonists of the Western Hemisphere did begin to gain some limited knowledge of each other. The eighteenth-century European Enlightenment with its emphasis on human reason and individual freedom as the underpinnings of all knowledge and effective social institutions found an attentive audience among elites throughout the Western Hemisphere. Benjamin Franklin's reputation as a scientist was second only to that of Isaac Newton in Latin America, and the American Philosophical Society eagerly acquired the writings of scientists from Spain's colonies. Indeed, political philosophers in the Americas began to stress the homogeneity of the Western Hemisphere as a pristine environment in which the Enlightenment ideas of rational thought and democracy would flourish as they never could in the decadent societies of Europe.[9] On a more practical level, economic interests drew the two regions closer together.

✿

On March 23, 1793, young boys raced through the streets of Nantucket, Massachusetts, anxious to be the first to bring the glad tidings that one of its sailing vessels had just safely returned from an eighteen-month voyage. The arriving vessel, the *Beaver*, captained by Paul Worth, was a slow-moving, often malodorous whaling ship. The rugged Nantucket whaler enjoyed the distinction of being the first American ship of her kind to sail from a U.S. port to the new whaling grounds off the Pacific coast of South America. Worth had enjoyed a highly successful hunting season, returning with hundreds of barrels of whale oil that helped to light the lamps of America and fuel the economic growth of the northeastern states. The *Beaver* opened the way for a steady stream of New England ships rounding the Horn by the early 1800s in search of whales and seals.[10] The New England whalers found another lucrative enterprise in the form of smuggling. Insisting that supply shortages forced them to enter South American ports, the crafty New Englanders exploited these visits as opportunities to violate Spanish bans on trading with foreigners. While the New England whalers undertook contraband trade as a sideline activity, their mercantile counterparts pursued it as a full-time enterprise.

The United States's official position of neutrality during periods of European warfare, especially the 1790s, had allowed its merchants to supply the needs of European, especially Spanish, colonies starved for supplies by wars between their mother countries. Even in peacetime, the Spanish colonies offered significant opportunities. Although technically a closed-mercantilist-trading system, the Spanish empire in the Western Hemisphere operated with sievelike efficiency. Contraband had become a way of life for colonies whose economic needs often could not be adequately met by Spain, even in peacetime. Merchants from Boston to Baltimore played an increasing role in this process, providing much-needed goods and essential transport services at times when war in Europe effectively cut off the Spanish colonies from the mother country. Most of this activity was centered in the Caribbean region, but American merchants ventured as far south as Buenos Aires and Valparaiso to exploit the opportunities.[11] North American merchants, sea captains, and their crews were fast becoming a familiar if not frequent sight in some of the largest colonial ports to their south. Now rather than a few scholarly interchanges between members of their respective elites, several thousand American captains, merchants, whaling men, and general seamen were seeing and being seen in Latin America. Crewmen shared their experiences with sea shanties, telling of the dangers of the hurricane-wracked Caribbean and the furious waves and high winds of Cape Horn, while also recounting their few moments of pleasure on shore with "Rosita, Anna and Carmen too, They'll greet ye with a hulla-baloo, and soon ye'll know what they can do." They also recalled the charms of "Them Dago gals we do adore, They all drink wine and ask for more."[12] North Americans were already envisioning Latin America as a largely untamed, dangerous wilderness, inhabited by dark temptresses. The themes of wilderness, danger, and exotic females would reoccur time and again in the encounters between North Americans and Latin Americans. As for the reaction of Latin Americans to their occasional guests from the sea, they found them to be a generally noisy, often inebri-ated, and sometimes violent lot in need of restraining by local authorities. But for those who led these early voyages, the merchant adventurers of this time, Latin America soon took on significance beyond the opportu-nity for large profits in smuggling ventures. American merchants carried not only cargo but also ideology to the south.

In colonial America, much of the population shared the vision of preachers like Cotton Mather, viewing their scattered outposts as the rebirth of a pure Christian society that would be a shining light for the rest of the world to follow. Indeed, Mather's friend Judge Samuel Sewall went so far as to imagine Mexico transformed by American Protestants into a "New Jerusalem."[13] In time that concept of an ideal society to be spread to other cultures came to include not only the characteristics of Christianity but also what were conceived of as distinctly American values, includ-ing individualism and popular sovereignty. As children of the American Revolution, many of the merchants who visited Latin America at the turn of the century were ardent advocates of revolutions like their own that would sweep away the deadening hand of European colonialism and with it the benighted preaching of the Catholic Church.

In November 1801, Richard Cleveland, a merchant from Salem, Massachusetts, sailed from Europe with his fellow New Englander, William Shaler. Their principal purpose was to take advantage of the skyrocketing prices for goods in Chile and Peru as a result of the war in Europe that disrupted Spain's trade with her colonies. They harbored a second goal of a more political nature. Shaler included in his luggage Spanish translations of the Declaration of Independence as well as copies of federal and state constitutions. In the port of Valparaiso, Cleveland and Shaler took the opportunity to socialize with Creoles—those Spanish colonists who had been born in the New World. Warming to their hosts' tales of discontent with Spanish rule, Shaler recounted stories of the American War for Independence and assured his audience that freeing themselves from Spanish rule would enhance the wealth of the region by liberating it from the oppressive Spanish economic regimen. When Cleveland and Shaler departed they left their hosts with copies of the political documents they had brought along.[14] Cleveland and Shaler, much like many other U.S. merchants at the time, firmly believed that political liberation would bring with it free trade, benefiting both the new republics as well as their own balance sheets. Theirs was a sincere political crusade in which they could also see a considerable economic reward for themselves and their countrymen.

The activities of Richard Cleveland and other U.S. merchant adventurers marked an important new phase in the emerging relationship between their own country and the people of Latin America. Not only did they gain firsthand knowledge of the region, but also they reasserted the missionary zeal of Cotton Mather with their own plans for a conversion, in this case in the political thinking of Latin Americans. That desire to share the benefits of their revolution and its rationalist solutions to political and economic problems was often driven by the belief that their neighbors were in need of reform and uplift. After describing his and Shaler's propaganda efforts among the Creoles of Valparaiso, Cleveland had gone on to note, "The native inhabitants are generally amiable, hospitable, indolent, and ignorant."[15]

As much as Americans hoped to see a series of independent states emerge, they were not above casting covetous eyes upon the Spanish territories. They believed that their individualistic, competitive society depended on continued territorial expansion to relieve the economic tensions and social conflicts that were inevitable parts of such a system. After his adventures in Chile, Shaler spent several years engaged in trade along the coast of California. He later published an account of his stay, describing the wonders of the Spanish territory and the ease with which it could be seized.[16] Eventually the ambitious merchant would go beyond making suggestions and support schemes to separate Texas from Mexico. The merchants' promotion of revolutionary causes, their doubts about the qualifications of Latin Americans for citizenship in an economically robust republic like their own, and their desire for territorial expansion would have important consequences for relations between the United States and Latin America. Latin Americans, meanwhile, continued to hold very positive views of the United States.

Between 1808 and 1825, the people in Spain's Western Hemisphere empire rose in rebellion against their colonial masters. Although in some instances colonial control crumbled quickly, Spain soon counterattacked and reoccupied most of its rebellious colonies, setting the stage for a protracted series of struggles for independence. Those efforts to throw off the burden of European colonial domination encouraged a sense of community between the people of the United States and those now struggling for liberty. Independence leaders expressed admiration for the achievements of North Americans in the years after the American Revolution. Simón Bolívar, for example, observed in 1819 that "the people of North America are a singular model of political virtue and moral rectitude."[17] In fact many Latin American intellectuals looked to the United States as a utopian ideal. But unlike Samuel Sewall's conception of Mexico as a land to be transformed into a Christian utopia by North American Protestants, Latin American intellectuals envisioned the United States as a fully realized utopia they hoped to imitate.[18] North Americans could readily identify with the efforts of Latin Americans to free themselves and create independent nation-states. But the territorial ambitions of U.S. leaders weighed heavily in North American responses to the struggles for independence.

Presidents Thomas Jefferson and John Adams both viewed Spanish possessions, including Florida, present-day Texas, and the island of Cuba, as regions that should and would be incorporated into the United States. Florida particularly influenced U.S. policy. With many of its colonies in open rebellion, Spain made it clear to the United States that it would break off all negotiations to resolve border disputes, including those regarding Florida, if the United States supported its rebel colonies. As a result, the U.S. government steered clear of explicit support for

Latin American independence until Spain ceded Florida to the United States in 1819.

Even with the resolution of the Florida issue and the eventual recognition of the Latin American states, many American leaders harbored dark views of their neighbors. John Adams, who still embraced the biases of the Black Legend, went to great lengths to differentiate the American Revolution, driven, he believed, by the quest for liberty, from the Latin American revolutions, motivated, he argued, by Napoleon's occupation of Spain, which forced Latin Americans to choose self-governing regimes. Indeed, Adams asserted that under Spanish rule, "there was no spirit of freedom pervading any portion of this population, no common principle of reason to form an union of mind."[19] Not only did Adams cast doubt about the similarities between the two peoples and their revolutions, but he also stated, "There is no community of interests or of principles between North and South America."[20] In fact the greatest concern that shaped U.S. policy, beyond the acquisition of Florida and commercial relations, was the fear that the upheavals in Latin America might prompt one of the major European powers to intervene in the region, giving it a foothold in the Americas that would threaten U.S. interests. And it was Adams who would eventually craft a policy to address those concerns. But by then Latin Americans were becoming increasingly aware that their neighbors to the north were not the close allies that they had once envisioned.

As much as Simón Bolívar had expressed his admiration for the people of the United States, he was also careful to distinguish important differences between the systems of government in the Americas. He specifically rejected the U.S. model of government as ill suited to the needs of Latin America.[21] Like other leaders he also became increasingly wary of the ambitions of North Americans. Meanwhile, interactions between North America and the emerging nations to the south had intensified during the struggles for independence, and those interactions gave further evidence of U.S. ambitions as well, reinforcing perspectives that had begun emerging among leaders on both sides.

As Spain's colonies began their long struggles for independence, the U.S. government dispatched agents to represent its interests in the region. These representatives included special agents sent on specific missions, consuls, and agents for commerce and seamen, who were consuls in all

but name. Although promoting trade was their most important assign-
ment, many of these representatives took on political activities as well.
One of them was William Shaler, Richard Cleveland's partner in his
trade and liberation venture. Appointed by President James Madison as
an agent for commerce and seamen to Veracruz, Mexico, Shaler failed
to gain admission to Mexico, and after filling the same post in Havana,
Cuba, for more than a year, he transferred to a post in Louisiana in 1812.
There he linked up with several adventurers from both Mexico and the
United States, who hoped to take advantage of the independence struggles to detach Texas from Mexico. His enthusiasm for these ventures
eventually earned him a reprimand from Secretary of State Monroe.
U.S. caution was not because of any hesitancy to acquire territory—quite
the contrary. The concern was not to alienate Spain and thereby frustrate
continuing U.S. efforts to acquire Florida.[22]

Another ambitious American, Joel R. Poinsett, represented U.S.
interests in Chile and later in Mexico. While in Chile, Poinsett, on his
own initiative, drafted a constitution based on the U.S. document, which
his hosts politely declined to implement. Nearly a decade after Shaler's
misadventures Poinsett accepted an appointment as the U.S. envoy to
Mexico. Involving himself in local politics, he worked closely with the
opposition Liberals who seemed more closely aligned with his Jeffersonian
ideals than did the ruling Conservatives. Eventually his intense involvement in the internal politics of Mexico led to a bitter public outcry that
forced his recall. During this and his earlier appointment in Chile,
Poinsett had meddled in his host country's internal politics, certain that
his actions would help bring about the liberal democracy that he believed
lay at the core of his own nation's success. But as Poinsett's experiences
demonstrated, Latin Americans might well envision the United States as
a utopia, but they did not necessarily accept attempts by North Americans
to re-create that utopia in their own societies. It was a lesson that innumerable American missionaries, intent on reshaping Latin America's politics, economies, and religious beliefs would relearn throughout the next
two centuries.[23]

Part of the reason for such reactions stemmed from the fact that as
encounters between North Americans and Latin Americans intensified
by the 1820s, some very real differences between their respective societies
and cultures became inevitable sources of friction. One glaring difference

was the issue of religion. American emissaries, from Shaler to Poinsett, were convinced that Catholicism represented a superstition-ridden cult that held Latin Americans back from embracing the liberal progressive ideas of the United States. But for Latin American Conservatives, religious tolerance represented a threat to the complex multiracial hierarchy of their societies, which they believed were held together by the dominance of a state-sanctioned religion.[24] One such critic, Fray Melchor Martínez of Chile, offered an insightful interpretation of the sources of U.S. territorial and ideological expansionism as well as a ringing denunciation of its influence in Latin America. With his image and understanding of the United States shaped by the New England merchantmen and whalers who had visited his homeland, Martínez claimed:

> The Republic of Boston . . . recognizing and fearing the weakness of its existence, is making its great effort to enlarge its boundaries and to extend its system as the only method for providing for stability and permanence. To this end it puts into action all imaginable means, without hesitating at the most iniquitous and immoral in order to attract the Spanish colonists to its depraved designs. Freedom of conscience and freedom of the press assist it in publishing and spreading subversive and seditious principles and maxims, which always find reception among the majority of men ruled by ignorance and malice.[25]

Nor was the issue of religion the only point of controversy.

In the decades immediately following independence in Latin America, constitutions were honored more in their breach than in their enforcement, as individual strongmen, or caudillos, toppled republican regimes. Even more fundamentally, liberal experiments in social and economic reform typically gave way to seriously distorted versions of such transformations. The Latin American elites' versions of liberal reform, which included attacks on communally held property and communal rights, set off a decades-long struggle over two very different definitions of democracy. The communally rooted interests of the popular classes clashed directly with the individualistic, free-market notions of elite liberalism. In the midst of that struggle there was a widespread retreat from the liberal reform ideals of the independence movements to practices that closely approximated those of the Spanish crown in the late eighteenth century, namely, accelerating the process of privatizing rural lands, but in a manner largely advantageous to indigenous and Creole elites.[26] Meanwhile, the leaders of the United States were pursuing their own agendas in terms of their policies toward the region.

In 1823 President James Monroe promulgated the doctrine that now bears his name, although it was essentially the work of his secretary of state, John Adams. Despite its warning to foreign powers not to attempt further colonization or intervention in the Western Hemisphere, and subsequent claims by the United States that it represented a first step toward Pan-Americanism or the forging of a Western Hemisphere community, Latin Americans generally recognized it as a document in which the United States laid claim to Latin America as falling within its sphere of influence. In effect, it gave official expression to an earlier claim by Thomas Jefferson that the United States would be the arbiter of the region's future. The American government could not back up such an assertion, but U.S. leaders knew that the British had made clear their intention to use their considerable military and naval might to prevent other Great Powers from interfering in the Western Hemisphere. By making a pronouncement independently of Great Britain, Monroe and Adams kept open the possibility of further territorial acquisitions in the hemisphere and laid down the justification for future U.S. interventions in the region.[27] But such attempts to project U.S. power into the region could not stem the decline of U.S. economic ties to Latin America.

While Latin America captured nearly 30 percent of American exports in 1821, it barely accounted for 21 percent of those goods in 1836. Great Britain, by contrast, maintained a dominant position in the region's trade. However, the British held sway over what were an increasingly stagnant set of international economies in Latin America. The region's largely peasant population lived outside the money economy, and the highly skewed distribution of wealth restricted urban markets as well. Those realities, combined with the decline of war-induced demand and the destruction brought by years of combat, gave the lie to giddy dreams of commercial fortunes to be easily earned in Latin America. Indeed, the postindependence years threatened chaos in both the economic and social systems of the region.

By midcentury the ruling classes in Latin America were engaged in pitched battles among themselves for political control. The classic political contest pitted Conservatives against Liberals in most of these nations. A core difference over the future of the region's societies informed the political battles. The central issue concerned the pace and timing of liberal reforms designed to eliminate the corporatist privileges of such institutions as the Catholic Church and to open economies more fully to private enterprise and market forces. Although Conservatives did not consistently oppose the opening of their economies to free-market reforms, they were very much concerned that a rapid process of change would undermine the fragile stability of the multiethnic hierarchies that characterized their societies. This conflict often came to focus on Liberal efforts to reduce the power of the Catholic Church by eliminating its control of education and by stripping it of its considerable landholdings—policies that Conservatives felt certain would cripple the church and undermine its role as the principal force for social order. Combined with the economic destruction wrought by the wars for independence, the elite's internecine warfare destabilized Latin American states and left these regimes as inviting targets for both internal rebellion and foreign intervention.

Although Latin America's rulers had managed to keep in check the masses of Indian peasants, mixed-race mestizos, and black slaves during the struggles for independence, popular resistance would challenge the new oligarchic republics. At the heart of this resistance lay popular protests over attempts by the new states to strip peasant villages of communal landholdings in order to open them up to commercial development and the increased exploitation of labor through a variety of devices including tribute and forced labor. The assault on village landholdings represented not merely a threat to the economic well-being of millions of rural residents but an attack on the material underpinning of their societies and cultures. Peasant villages were not egalitarian communities. Considerable stratification, albeit restrained by local customs and practices, characterized peasant societies. Nor did pure economic self-sufficiency typify rural villages. Long before the arrival of the Spanish, the market forces of local barter and long-distance trade had become commonplace in Latin America. Nevertheless, peasants did place restraints on market forces and their tendency to accelerate social stratification. They also prioritized community interests and cooperation over individual ambition and competition. Peasants often sought to protect their values and interests through protest movements grounded in ethnic or regional identity. Furthermore, the intricately stratified peasant societies had varying levels of interaction with the dominant Creole culture. These conditions created a variety of interests and ambitions that found expression in a dizzying array of power relations that surfaced during times of rebellion.[28]

While diverse in its forms, motivations, and outcomes, popular resistance did have a common impact—it impeded the elite's plans for change. Peasant wars, populist caudillos, and more subtle forms of peasant resistance to commercialization battered the oligarchy's agenda and challenged its control of the countryside. In a few cases, social conflict in Latin America would prompt local powerbrokers to seek external intervention to salvage themselves and their programs. At the very least, popular resistance and intraelite conflict shackled market forces and left the region's enfeebled leaders ill prepared to resist waves of expansionism that swept across the United States into Latin America.

Expansionist America

Unlike Latin American elites, the ruling class of the United States could look back with considerable satisfaction on its nation's development during the first half of the nineteenth century. Its society was rapidly evolving from an agrarian order marked by small family farms in the North and large commercial plantations in the South into a vibrant industrial society. At the same time, a once weak federal government had successfully imposed centralized rule while maintaining its limited role in the national economy envisioned by its liberal founders. And yet American society remained volatile, even turbulent, as industrialization transformed the North, plantation expansion displaced Native American populations and subjected ever more human beings to the scourge of slavery, and commercialization of agriculture raised the entry price to those seeking to become free farmers. The competitiveness and fluidity of this society created profound uncertainties for tens of thousands of individuals who often found themselves cast adrift on a restless sea of social and economic change.

Increasingly impersonal and harsh working conditions, social differentiation, and wealth concentration prompted a profound restlessness in many Americans. Much of America's newly emergent working class adopted a migratory pattern of life in order to barter their skills for better wages. Others moved west seeking in the land an alternative to the harsh realities of nascent industrialism.[29] Even before the coming of the industrial order, the freeholder society of the North had generated pressures for westward expansion. As a result of population growth, men and women without a landed inheritance had migrated west aspiring to climb from laborer/tenant status to that of freeholder. But as industrialization added to the numbers of Americans looking westward, commercialization of rural America made the dream of owning a farm increasingly difficult to realize. Much of that problem stemmed from other fundamental changes in the national economy.

International trade had been one of the key elements in building the fortunes of colonial America's mercantile elite, and it remained a vitally important factor in the decades immediately after independence. However, much of that business consisted of the carrying and reexport trades highlighting America's role in moving goods between other countries during times of war and past the barriers of colonial exclusion. Yet with the end of the Napoleanic wars in 1815 came long-term peace and the reinstitution of strictures on colonial commerce. These changes along with declining prices for wheat and flour plunged the United States's reexport and carrying trades into a steep and prolonged decline. In response, eastern merchants sought new opportunities to invest capital domestically, including land speculation.[30] Waves of land speculation during the first half of the nineteenth century helped trigger sharp increases in land prices. That process along with the adoption of new technologies as essential parts of small commercial farms made farm making an increasingly expensive proposition and led many aspirants to freeholder status to champion territorial acquisition in order to lower the cost of land.

At the same time that eastern merchants were driving land speculation and infrastructure improvement in the West, planters dealing with the relative inefficiency of slavery as a labor system became advocates of territorial acquisitions, viewing the addition of new, virgin lands as the primary means of boosting productivity in cotton. New western territories were sought by the eastern merchants, who helped finance the expansion of the plantation system, though for them the main goal was to achieve footholds on the west coast of North America from which they could more readily exploit markets in Asia.

As economic change created a consensus for territorial expansion, often termed Manifest Destiny, it also encouraged a social mentality conducive to an aggressive foreign policy. During the early nineteenth century, the United States earned a reputation as a land of opportunity where ambitious individuals could make their way up the social and economic ladder. Yet this open, competitive society also had a darker side. America's freewheeling capitalist economy periodically suffered sharp, often devastating downturns. Panics in both 1818 and 1837 caused widespread business failures followed by years of severe deflation. For both working- and middle-class people the emerging industrial economy held great opportunity but also considerable risks and perils. Workers faced an ever more impersonal workplace. Those who sought escape by acquiring land found it increasingly difficult to do so due to rising prices. A middle class consisting of shopkeepers and other small-businesspeople, lacking the relative security that professional careers would later offer, faced the continued uncertainties of the unpredictable business cycles that could quickly reduce a prosperous business to an economic ruin. In this environment, American ambition and competitiveness often reached extremes as American society threw off numerous individuals willing to take the most extraordinary risks and invest in the most outlandish schemes in order to carve a place for themselves in this enterprising, volatile world. Some of these individuals would become the agents of Manifest Destiny.

By the beginning of 1819 Moses Austin, once a highly successful businessman from Durham, Connecticut, found himself in desperate circumstances. The War of 1812 and the crushing blows of the depression of 1818–19 had left much of Austin's business empire in ruins. Facing outright bankruptcy, Austin conceived of a plan to secure the right to settle American colonists in Spain's Texas territories. Given the deep-seated and not ill-founded suspicions that Spaniards harbored regarding American territorial ambitions, the scheme obviously grew out of Austin's desperation. Austin benefited from a recent change in Spanish policy that now encouraged colonial authorities to make extensive land grants. But the American entrepreneur passed away a few months after he secured permission to bring American colonists to Texas, leaving his son Stephen to fulfill his dream. Stephen's plans soon faced a new challenge as Mexico declared its independence from Spain, forcing Austin to spend a year in Mexico City securing confirmation of the earlier Spanish concession from the new government. During the next decade Austin settled as many as two thousand families in Texas. At this same time he engaged in large-scale land speculation, acquiring more than eighty-seven million acres of Texas property, making him the largest landowner and one of the wealthiest men in Texas. Stephen Austin had embraced the high-risk, desperate venture of his father and used it to rebuild the family's fortunes and social position. But the North American economy remained a rough and tumble, no-holds-barred struggle that could bring ruin as quickly as it brought riches. And just as his success seemed assured, Austin faced a dire threat from competitors.[31]

A group of business and professional people from New York and Boston with the backing of several private banks formed the Galveston Bay and Texas Land Company in 1830. The company's organizers sold more than ten million acres to eager colonists and investors, feeding the intense land hunger that gripped their fellow citizens by offering lots at a fraction of what they would cost in the United States. The Galveston Bay Company, however, feared a measure that Stephen Austin supported that would make Texas a separate state within Mexico. A provision of that measure would cancel the types of contracts under which the Galveston Bay Company had been doing business. The company worked assiduously to gain influence in the Mexican government, contributing to a decline in Austin's influence. The shifting balance of power among the Americans became clear when Austin was arrested in Mexico City at the beginning of 1834 and spent the next eighteen months in jail. Although no absolute proof exists that the Galveston Bay Company had prompted the arrest, Austin left prison fully aware of the danger the company represented to him and convinced that only separating Texas from Mexico could salvage the situation. Austin now openly threw his support to Texas independence.[32] The subsequent war with Mexico made Texas an independent nation that eventually joined the Union as the twenty-eighth state.

A number of factors brought on the Americans' conflict with Mexico including cultural differences and Mexican policies to ban further immigration and restrict trade. Yet American hunger for land and the conflicts among U.S. land speculators clearly played a central role in bringing

on Texas secession. Those forces were the products of an individualistic highly competitive free-market society that offered the possibility of
sudden riches and the dangers of total ruin. In this environment many
Americans like Moses and Stephen Austin were willing to undertake
highly speculative business ventures. That reality and the land hunger
driven by rising prices in the United States helped fuel continuing efforts
to expand the territory of the United States even at the expense of its
southern neighbor. Those expansionist projects had taken on an ugly
racist tone by the time Texas was admitted to the Union.

During the course of two centuries the American people had believed
themselves on a mission, which at times was conceived of as a Christian
crusade of spiritual renewal and at other times a political mission to
spread republicanism. Those inspirations remained very much a part of
the American sense of mission by the mid-nineteenth century, but by
then many Americans had developed a dark vision of other people in the
world, especially their southern neighbors in the Western Hemisphere.
Influenced in part by racist thinking in Europe, while at the same time
seeking justification for their enslavement of Africans and their elimination or mass displacement of Native Americans, many people in the
United States came to see themselves as part of a superior Anglo-Saxon
race with its roots traceable to England and Germany. According to
these ideas, white Americans sprang from this Anglo-Saxon race that
possessed innate qualities that made its members exceptionally well
suited for self-government and activities that would generate material
prosperity. By contrast many Americans viewed other races as inherently
inferior, incapable of achieving the self-governing political system and the
economic development that characterized the United States. From these
beliefs American racists concluded that they were destined to displace or
dominate the inferior races with whom they shared the hemisphere.

As conceived of in the mid-nineteenth century, American racist
views served a number of purposes within U.S. society. For frontier
settlers, the idea that they were part of a superior Anglo-Saxon race
that was destined to displace or destroy the Native Americans of the
West provided a powerful justification for their campaigns against
Indian settlements. So too Southerners found comfort in racist views
that seemed to explain away the enslavement of millions of blacks that
contradicted the egalitarianism of the American republic. Furthermore,

American society of the early nineteenth century witnessed the giving way of the social hierarchies of the early republic to a new order dominated by those who had fought their way up through an open, competitive, and often volatile social and economic environment. For a people immersed in such upheaval and uncertainty, racism offered the security of a racial hierarchy. No matter how fortune might treat them, white Americans could always take comfort in their supposed superiority over Native Americans and blacks. That vision of inferior races came to include all Latin Americans, but in particular the United States's nearest neighbors, the Mexicans.[33]

War with Mexico

By the 1840s many Americans had developed extremely negative opinions of Mexico and her people. One traveler to California described Mexicans as marked by "the dull suspicious countenance, the small twinkling, piercing eyes, the laxness and filth of a free brute, using freedom as a mere means of animal enjoyment . . . dancing and vomiting as occasion and inclination appear to require."[34] James Buchanan, who served as President James K. Polk's secretary of state during the war against Mexico and later as president of the United States, concluded in regard to Mexico's control of Texas that "our race of men can never be subjected to the imbecile and indolent Mexican race."[35]

At the same time that many Americans held these negative views of their immediate neighbors to the south, they also continued to share that fascination with Latin women that had characterized the Yankee sailors who had ventured into Latin American ports. They viewed Mexican women as dark-skinned temptresses, unfettered by the inhibitions that restrained Anglo women. These perspectives blended racial stereotypes with prevailing sexist beliefs that while men were the agents of civilization destined to conquer and tame nature, women represented a part of nature and were therefore subject to the civilizing control of men. American imperial designs on Mexico found justification in a perspective that viewed Mexicans as an inferior and effeminate race that destined them to be dominated by superior, masculine Anglo-Saxons.[36] Midwestern farmers, eastern merchants, and southern slaveholders saw themselves as energetic, competitive, individualistic entrepreneurs, who were destined to tame the "wilderness" of Mexico and displace its corrupt and effeminate race. Not surprisingly, Mexican opinions of Americans by this time were not much more favorable.

Prior to the secession of Texas, most Mexicans, like most Latin Americans, knew little about their northern neighbor. Mexicans certainly had some fear of Americans as Protestant heretics, but that was more than balanced in the years after independence by the belief that the United States served as an admirable model of liberal government institutions in the Americas. However, due to the secession of Texas, this limited and relatively balanced perspective gave way to a far more negative and even hostile attitude. Texas's admission to the union in 1845 confirmed for most Mexicans that the separation of Texas from Mexico resulted from a deliberate U.S. policy. The increasingly racist perspective from which many Americans often viewed Mexicans only exacerbated this hostility. Although members of Mexico's elite shared much of the Americans' disparaging attitude toward their own indigenous and mixed-raced populations, they were appalled to learn that American racists held them in the same contempt at they did the humbler classes of Mexican society. They returned that contempt with expressions of disdain. Manuel de Gorostiza, a noted playwright and diplomat, who had once been the Mexican minister to the United States, held a less than laudatory view of those paragons of American individualism and initiative—western frontiersmen. Writing in 1840, he argued:

> Let us consider the character of those who have populated
> the lands adjoining our border. Who is not familiar
> with that race of migratory adventurers that exist in the
> United States, composed of the most restless, profligate
> and robust of its sons, who always live in the unpopulated
> regions, taking land away from the Indians and then
> assassinating them? Far removed from civilization, as
> they condescendingly call it, they are precursors of
> immorality and pillage.[37]

Gorostiza's larger topic was the continuing threat to Mexico from American control of Texas, and in the years leading up to the war with the United States, Mexican political figures frequently promoted the idea of an armed expedition to recapture their lost province. Yet Mexico proved woefully unprepared to undertake any substantial military venture against the United States.[38] Increasing instability marked the first two decades after independence as social conflict and economic decline tore at the fabric of Mexican society. Like most of Latin America, Mexico's colonial legacy included a hierarchal social structure that subordinated both Indians and other ethnic groups. After independence, the state moved away from the paternalistic policies of the Spanish crown, opening these groups to increased exploitation of their labor and growing losses of community lands to ambitious local elites. That process helped set off decades of rebellion in the Mexican countryside as popular forces fought to retain their land and protect their rights. These problems found few resolutions from a state governed by an ever-more-fractious elite divided by personal, regional, and ideological conflicts. As a result, Mexico could not formulate and carry out a coherent policy to counter the aggressive American designs on its national patrimony.

Mounting tensions between the two countries resulting from American territorial ambitions and Mexican animosity toward the United States finally led to a confrontation between Mexican and U.S. forces in the disputed border region between Texas and Mexico in 1846. That encounter triggered a full-scale invasion by American forces across Mexico's northern border followed by a landing of troops at Mexico's Gulf port of Veracruz. But U.S. forces soon found themselves facing a formidable challenge from guerrilla bands. These partisans, some operating with government approval, others fighting independently, harassed U.S. forces, ambushing supply convoys and engaging American troops in hit-and-run firefights. Although the U.S. Army defeated government forces and occupied Mexico City, it became increasingly apparent that the guerrilla war waged by Mexicans would preclude a long-term occupation of the country. The challenge from popular forces also pressured President James Polk, an ardent expansionist, to limit his territorial ambitions in Mexico. In fact, the Polk administration found itself working to prop up the Mexican state, which was itself beleaguered by popular rebellion. As for the Mexican government, it felt pressured to reach a settlement with the Americans so that it could turn its attention and resources completely to the suppression of domestic uprisings. As a result, popular rebellion in Mexico pressured the warring states to sign the Treaty of Guadalupe Hidalgo in 1848. The peace agreement stripped Mexico of one-half of its national territory and added such areas as New Mexico, Arizona, and California to the U.S. national domain. Yet this settlement frustrated the expansionists' most vaunted ambitions of seizing all of Mexico.[39] In the longer term, the expansionist coalition would founder on the issue of race.

Even many of the most ardent Midwest expansionists opposed the addition of new slave territories at the time of the Mexican War. For freeholders, the spread of slavery to the new territories would threaten the promise of cheap lands with which to compete in the market economy. For slave owners, exclusion would rob them of a basic solution to slavery's productivity problems and threaten the balance of power in the U.S. Senate. During the 1840s and '50s free farmers in the Midwest became a major market for industrially manufactured tools and served as suppliers of grain and meat that fed the growing food-processing industry. The new industrialists of the North allied themselves with the free farmers to oppose slavery's territorial growth. The growing conflict between the slave society of the South and the free farmer and industrialist groups of the North shattered the expansionist coalition and paralyzed the central government. It now fell to private interests to exploit expansionist opportunities created by Latin American upheavals. One such opportunity arose during the occupation of Mexico.

Although the Polk administration had supplied weapons to the state of Yucatan to suppress a growing rebellion by Mayan Indians, that assistance failed to crush the insurgents. President Polk was anxious to stabilize Mexico to ensure the transfer of its northern states to the United States, but he soon rejected a plea from the central government to send troops to the Yucatan because it would require approval of a treaty that he knew Congress would never ratify. Instead, assistance came in the form of a mercenary expedition launched from New Orleans.

On December 23, 1848, a column of several hundred American mercenaries approached the village of Tihosuco in the Yucatan. Leading the group was Lieutenant Joseph A. White, who like most of his men had recently been released from the U.S. Army after the war with Mexico. At the behest of the Yucatan state government, White had recruited his band of mercenaries in New Orleans. Despite the relatively low pay and promises of modest homesteads being offered by the Yucatecan government, White easily recruited his regiment from among the thousands of army veterans milling about Southern towns, searching for work. In the intensely competitive and turbulent environment of America in the 1840s, the mission also appealed to the belief that one's fortune could be made through some dramatic venture, much like Moses Austin's desperate gamble in Texas. The adventure, as with future such expeditions, also appealed to American males' image of themselves asserting their responsibility to dominate and therefore "civilize" the world around them. Furthermore, the American mercenaries conceived of their venture as a mission to save the white race from the ravages of barbaric Indians. On that last point, the American mercenaries would come to regret their assumptions about the inferiority and "femininity" of "races" like the Maya.

On Christmas Day, Lieutenant White's force launched a frontal assault on the barricades set up by the Maya to block their approach to Tihosuco. Although the mercenaries quickly overran the Indian positions, they soon found themselves besieged as the rebels launched flanking maneuvers, subjecting the Americans to a withering cross fire. In the end the mercenaries' casualties stood at nine dead and sixteen wounded. Many of White's men abandoned the expedition after the battle, and by mid-March virtually the entire regiment had returned to New Orleans. The fighting skills of the Maya and the Americans' inability to adapt to the guerrillas' tactics had dashed the mercenaries' hopes for quick rewards and a victory of Anglo-Saxons over the "weaker" races of Latin America.[40] Yet the disappointing results of the campaign did nothing to halt a surge in such mercenary adventures, known as "filibustering campaigns," which erupted in the years before the Civil War. Cuba, which had remained within the Spanish empire, proved the most inviting target for the filibusters.

Cuba had attracted U.S. interest ever since the eighteenth century. Its sugar plantations provided a natural market for New England products such as fish and lumber; its sugar fed a growing market in the United States. That trade flourished even when Spain had banned such exchanges, and as Spain slackened those restrictions, Cuba became one of the United States's most important trading partners. Its size, location, and excellent harbors gave the island strategic significance to the United States. Leaders of the new North American republic, such as Thomas Jefferson and John Adams, had coveted the Spanish colony and confidently expected the island to become part of the United States.

Acquiring Cuba remained a popular national goal, and in 1848 President Polk made an unsuccessful offer of $100 million to purchase the island from Spain. In the drive to acquire Cuba, the conflation of imperial ambitions and male visions of subordinated females once again became apparent. As one advocate of acquiring Cuba put it:

> [Cuba] admires Uncle Sam and he loves her. Who shall forbid the bans? Matches are made in heaven, and why not this? Who can object if he throws his arms around the Queen of the Antilles, as she sits, like Cleopatra's burning throne, upon the silver waves, breathing her spicy, tropic breath, and pouting her rosy, sugared lips? Who can object? None. She is of age— take her Uncle Sam![41]

But the effort to add the Spanish colony to the United States was becoming less a broad national campaign and more a crusade by Southern slave owners. Southerners initially feared that Spain, under pressure from Great Britain, would abolish slavery in Cuba and create conditions conducive to a slave revolt in their own country. Later Southerners came to prize Cuba as a slave territory that could help balance the growing number of free states. The increasingly Southern orientation of the campaign to acquire Cuba became apparent during the filibustering expeditions of Narciso López.

López, a former Spanish military officer and colonial administrator, turned against his mother country and became an advocate of Cuban independence. Fleeing to the United States, López enjoyed the support of Cuban slave owners, who opposed Spanish trade restrictions and feared that Spain would abolish slavery on the island. Operating out of New Orleans, where his activities enjoyed the support of a number of prominent Southerners including John Quitman, the governor of Mississippi, López launched an invasion of Cuba in 1850, with six hundred mostly American mercenaries. After seizing a town in central Cuba, the filibuster had to beat a hasty retreat in the face of a determined Spanish counterstrike and a lack of popular support for his cause. Undeterred by this failure, López launched a second expedition the following year. Once again, the filibuster failed to rally local backing. His invasion collapsed, and the Spanish executed him and several of his lieutenants.

Despite the dismal outcome of López's expeditions, the enthusiasm for filibustering only seemed to intensify. Many of the people who had supported López played leading roles in a series of mercenary ventures during the 1850s. John Quitman, for example, signed on to lead yet another invasion of Cuba. However, after several years of fund raising and organizing, Quitman abandoned the venture, in part due to the opposition of President Franklin Pierce, who feared that support for a Southern proslavery enterprise would further undermine his political position in the North. But the filibusters found a new target in Central America.[42]

By the 1850s, John L. Stephens's speculations about the benefits of a transit way across Central America had become a reality. With the U.S. seizure of vast territories in the West and Southwest, and the gold rush in California, finding fast, safe passage to the West became an urgent national priority. Central America presented itself as the most logical site for such a route. In 1848 the U.S. Senate approved a treaty with the government of New Granada (Colombia) giving the United States the right to establish a transit way across the Panamanian Isthmus. The American government also provided subsidies for carrying the U.S. mail to George Law's United States Mail Steamship Company and William Aspinwall's Pacific Mail Steamship Company, which provided steamer service between the Atlantic and Pacific coasts of the United States and ports in Panama. These measures increased traffic across the isthmus and provided incentives to begin construction of the Panama railway. The success of the Panamanian transit way soon attracted competition from shipping magnate Cornelius Vanderbilt. Vanderbilt established his transit route across Nicaragua, allowing him to move freight and passengers between the east and west coasts of the United States.[43] But Vanderbilt's enterprise would eventually run afoul of an American of more modest circumstances, but with larger ambitions in Nicaragua.

William Walker of Tennessee typified many middle-class Americans of his time, as he first tried his hand at traditional professions to make his way in the world but eventually turned to high-risk adventures in an attempt to secure his place in America's often chaotic marketplace society. Trained as a doctor, Walker quickly gave up the idea of practicing medicine, turning first to the law and then to journalism. In 1853, Walker abandoned these conventional pursuits to lead an ill-fated filibustering expedition to separate the state of Sonora from Mexico. Two years later, at the invitation of Liberal rebels fighting to overthrow their Conservative government, the American filibuster sailed to Nicaragua with less than seventy men. Walker's small force helped turn the tide of battle for the Liberals and earned him the position of commander-in-chief of the army. The American mercenary eventually used his position to oust the new Liberal president and install himself as Nicaragua's new ruler after an election of dubious validity. Walker saw himself as the agent of a superior Anglo-Saxon race destined to dominate the inferior people of Central America. Not surprisingly, prominent Southerners such as Jefferson Davis became some of the strongest backers of Walker, who in turn encouraged that support by reinstituting slavery in Nicaragua.[44]

Despite his early successes, Walker had managed to accumulate a powerful array of enemies in a very short time. Neighboring Central American governments strongly suspected that Walker intended to add their countries to his domain. Great Britain, which was still contending with the United States for power and influence in the region, worked to rid the area of the American mercenary. Walker had also run afoul of Cornelius Vanderbilt by siding with two former partners of the entrepreneur, who had seized control of the transit way from him. At the same time, with the United States more divided than ever over the issue of slavery, President Franklin Pierce could not offer consistent support for his regime. By early 1857, Walker's position crumbled under the combined assaults of several Central American armies, and he was forced to flee to the United States. Walker made three more attempts to invade Nicaragua with the last effort ending in his execution by a Honduran firing squad.[45]

By the time of Walker's death, Americans were rapidly moving toward a civil war that would tear their society asunder for the next five years and bring an end to expeditions such as Walker's. Americans' obsession with territorial expansion, driven by racist beliefs, the search for cheap farmland, and efforts to protect and expand the institution of slavery had ended in a series of bizarre attempts at personal empire building by individuals like Qutiman and Walker, who were seeking to secure their place in a volatile marketplace society. Such individuals envisioned Latin America as an exotic, yet threatening environment that could bring fame and fortune to those who tamed it. One individual who articulated that vision was Joseph W. Fabens.

Fabens served as a U.S. consul in several different Latin American ports, eventually becoming the U.S. commercial agent at the port of San Juan del Norte, Nicaragua. While there, Fabens threw his support to Texas entrepreneur Henry Kinney's thinly disguised filibustering expedition to Nicaragua. When it became apparent that William Walker had gained the upper hand in the country, Fabens shifted his allegiance to Walker and took a position in his short-lived regime. Several years earlier Fabens had been on the Isthmus of Panama, which was already bustling with the comings and goings of thousands of American adventurers seeking transit between the East Coast and California. Here at the outer reaches of American influence, Fabens captured the environment both real and imagined that drew Americans like himself to Latin America:

> There seemed to be a great breaking up of the accustomed
> forms of life, a disappearance of old land-marks; and I found
> myself inwardly asking if in this lack of the sanctities of home
> the quiet intercourse of friends and all that is tranquilizing and
> enobling in literature, science and art, there was no danger that
> somehow in this rude and unavoidable intermingling of the
> purest and vilest characters might become confounded, and
> the soul wanting its accustomed food, lose something of
> its better nature, and allow "climbing impurity to stain the
> empyrean [heavens]!"[46]

If Fabens had some forebodings about the moral corruption that sprang from unfettered American expansionism, he remained no less certain than his fellow adventurers about the ultimate positive effect of their expeditions, asserting that "it was not until Anglo-Saxon enterprise strode over it [the Isthmus of Panama] that the world saw upon its front the nascent lineaments of a great empire."[47] Although Fabens and other filibusters saw themselves and other Americans as involved in a great civilizing mission, Latin Americans now viewed them in a very different light.

During the late 1850s a firestorm of anger swept Latin America in response to the U.S. annexation of Texas, the invasion of Mexico, and the plague of filibusterers that had been visited upon Central America and the Caribbean. A Bolivian newspaper characterized the United States as another Rome, bent on conquest and annexation. A Costa Rican diplomatic message described U.S. expansionist activities as "atrocious acts" "infringing every principle of the rights of man and society."[48] Yet as anti-American feelings reached a fever pitch, the U.S. drive for territorial expansion was subsiding, and Americans were exploring new methods of exercising influence and control while still fulfilling their self-ordained civilizing mission.

THE BUSINESS OF CIVILIZATION

From the moment that William Aspinwall secured a government subsidy for his Pacific Mail and Steamship Company he began entertaining the possibility of building a railroad across the Isthmus of Panama. In 1850, Aspinwall established the Panama Railroad Company that built the rail line, which cost John L. Stephens his life. Much like their territorial expansionism, Americans viewed this achievement in terms of male/female relations and as further testimony of their superiority, and their mission to subdue and civilize nature, now through business enterprise and technology. *The New York Mirror* referred to the opening of the railway as "the most sublime and magnificent nuptials ever celebrated upon our planet, the wedding of the rough Atlantic to the fair Pacific." The newspaper went on to note, "The stupendous enterprise of uniting the two oceans which embrace the greater portion of the globe, we are proud to say, was conceived and executed by our own citizens in the frowning face of obstacles none but Americans could have overcome."[49]

The railway proved an instant success, with tens of thousands of North Americans crossing the isthmus each year thanks to the rapid transportation it provided. Along with this infusion of American technology appeared other outcroppings of American culture. Enterprising U.S. citizens built hotels, saloons, and restaurants at the terminal points of the railway to provide passengers with the food, drink, and services they were accustomed to at home.

A number of areas of friction quickly developed between Americans and Panamanians. The efficiency of the railway deprived boatmen and muleteers of their livelihoods, and Panamanians, who lacked necessary skills and were unaccustomed to full-time wage labor, saw jobs with the railway going to immigrants, especially Jamaicans. The railroad company also had designs on the working-class neighborhood of La Ciénega that lay outside the boundary of the existing city of Panama. American law enforcement proved another source of discontent. One observer reported that the railway company's Isthmus Guard headed by former Texas Ranger Ran Runnels "have cleared the Isthmus of robbers and kept thousands of unruly laborers in wholesome subjection." This was accomplished with "[w]hipping, imprisonment, and shooting down in emergency. . . . The Company . . . has the power of life and death on the Isthmus, without appeal."[50] In short Panamanians were subject to a law enforcement system operated by and for the interests of a foreign corporation. Many of the Americans who traveled through Panama were not the best representatives of their own society. U.S. Navy Lieutenant James Melville Gilliss, traveling across the isthmus on his way to Chile, commented that many of his fellow citizens in Panama were "drunken vagabonds," who considered it their right as Americans "to trample on any weak and unresisting creature."[51] Conflict between Americans and locals also derived from fundamental cultural differences.

Americans continued to hold deeply disparaging attitudes toward people of color that seemed to intensify in their contact with Panamanians. Carrie Stevens Walter, who traveled through Panama as a child, recalled the locals as "fierce-looking, dusky natives, from whom we children shrank half in fear."[52] In turn, locals perceived the Americans as carriers of disease because so many of them died soon after arriving on the isthmus. Sharp differences on the issue of market forces and material culture also separated Americans from Panamanians. The competitive, hard-driven, individualistic, materialistic values of Americans clashed continuously with the community-oriented culture of Panamanians. These clashes at a variety of levels between the two societies soon erupted into violence. On the evening of April 15, 1856, Jack Oliver, an inebriated American, abused a local fruit peddler in the city of Panama, triggering a violent response. Hundreds of local residents poured into the streets, attacking American travelers and an array of American-owned businesses including hotels and the railway station. Approximately twenty people, mostly Americans, died before the violence subsided.[53] Yet most encounters between Americans and Latin Americans had far less dire consequences.

In Cuba, interactions with Americans led to a growing realization by Cubans that the colonial system could not cultivate but only constrain development of an economy increasingly being shaped by American influences. The sugar trade had rapidly drawn the two economies together during the first half of the nineteenth century. American trading houses provided new sources and methods of financing for Cuban planters, and they came to serve as business training programs for the ambitious children of the Cuban bourgeoisie. Many well-to-do Cubans sent their children to the United States to be educated. American technology also had a powerful influence as steam-powered equipment transformed production methods in Cuban sugar mills, American equipment provided six hundred miles of railway by midcentury, U.S.-built steamers linked the island to its northern neighbor, and the first telegraph system was introduced by an American. With U.S. technology came American engineers, machinists, and technicians to operate the new machinery. Perhaps the most obvious American influence came in popular culture.

In the 1860s Cuban students returning from universities in the United States brought with them the game of baseball. Cubans quickly adopted baseball as their own national sport with the first professional team being formed in 1872 and the first professional league created six years later. Aside from finding sheer joy in the game, Cubans found in the sport a means of participating in the type of healthy, competitive activity linked to American modernity, in contrast to what many viewed as the inhumanity and violence of Spanish bull fighting.

Not surprisingly Spanish colonial officials became intensely suspicious of the growing American presence. They feared that U.S. influence, especially in education, was instilling values subversive to colonial society. In fact, American values that highlighted the ultimate limitations of the colonial system helped Cubans redefine themselves and their society—a redefinition that did not include a colonial future.[54] In Mexico, the reactions to American business activity were heavily influenced by that country's past experience as a target of U.S. territorial ambitions.

Charles Stillman arrived in Matamoros in 1828 to market goods from his father's firm in New York. During the next quarter-century Stillman built a business empire in northeastern Mexico that included cotton exporting, mining ventures, ranches, and farms.[55] By the 1850s American businessmen such as Stillman enjoyed the support of Mexican Liberals who were rising to power at that time. President Benito Juárez viewed U.S. trade and investment as important elements in promoting

From Encounters to Expansion, 1776–1861 ❧ 47

Mexico's development. Yet some Liberals including President Juárez and his successor Sebastian Lerdo de Tejada remained painfully aware that American ambitions had cost Mexico dearly in the past two decades. They pursued a cautious approach to American investment initiatives, especially the building of railroads. President Lerdo cancelled five of six outstanding contracts for the construction of railroads connecting the United States and Mexico and also vetoed a reciprocal trade treaty. The unwillingness of Lerdo and other moderates to open Mexico fully to such investment would eventually lead to the ousting of Lerdo by an alliance of radical Liberals led by General Porfirio Díaz and U.S. business interests.[56] While American investments and their effects were largely confined to the circum-Caribbean before the Civil War, a few farsighted Yankee entrepreneurs ventured further south, most notably the American railroad builder, William Wheelwright.

Arriving in South America in 1823, Wheelwright soon developed a vision for the future development of the Southern Cone of the continent, a future that would be built on a transportation grid of transcontinental railroads, steamships, and telegraph lines. Wheelwright himself made prodigious efforts to fulfill that dream. He founded the Pacific Steam Navigation Company in 1840 to link Peru, Bolivia, and Chile, later extending steamer service to Panama. The American entrepreneur helped improve the water-supply system and installed electric lighting in Chile's main port of Valparaiso, built the country's first railroad, and developed the port of Caldera. During the 1860s, Wheelwright became the guiding force behind the Central Argentine Railway Company. Yet despite Wheelwright's impressive accomplishments, he was one of only a handful of U.S. investors who had a significant impact in South America before the Civil War. Even Wheelwright's American enterprises depended on capital from London because of a lack of support from the nascent capital markets in the United States.[57] Ultimately, British capital and technology would dominate the region's economies until the end of the nineteenth century. Yet Wheelwright's ventures and vision clearly reflected a continued belief by Americans that they were destined to play the pivotal role in the development and general uplift of Latin America. It was a belief common not only to entrepreneurs but to those in government as well.

During the 1850s, the U.S. military launched a series of ambitious expeditions in South America, but unlike the American invasion of

Mexico a decade earlier these were not combat actions with territorial ambitions. In the course of the decade, U.S. naval officers carried out six expeditions to the continent, gathering a dizzying array of data about topography and climate, as well as economic and political conditions. Although described as scientific expeditions, the underlying goal of these sorties was to counter European economic competition by exploring the possibilities for waterway and railway development by Americans.[58] For example, Lieutenant James Melville Gilliss's astronomical expedition to Chile provided a wide-ranging report on Chile that explored its potential for development and stressed the opportunities that would be created by a transcontinental railroad linking it to Argentina. For Gilliss, the country held enormous potential that could be tapped with the application of American energy and capital.

Gilliss took particular interest in the city of Concepción and its port of Talcahuano. Given its rich resource endowment in terms of land and minerals as well as an excellent deep-water port, Gilliss believed the area lacked only a few ambitious capitalists in order to lead South America in diversified economic growth.[59] Yet for all of his optimistic visions of Chile's future development with American assistance, Gilliss also revealed the continuing cultural gap that separated North Americans from their Latin American neighbors. Gilliss denounced what he viewed as the corrupt and superstitious practices of the Catholic clergy, concluding that the church controlled education not to open minds but to reinforce its superstitious doctrines. As for Chile's rural peons and urban workers, he considered them the most bigoted part of the entire population, who took easy offense at any "fancied insult to their religion."[60]

At midcentury, Americans still held to a long-standing view of themselves as playing a central role in the development and uplift of Latin America, yet they also harbored deep racially and culturally driven biases toward Latin Americans that had intensified since independence. But for the immediate future, despite the ambitions of entrepreneurs and the optimistic plans of naval officers, Americans would have few opportunities to act on their hopes or their biases regarding Latin America. The Civil War and postwar developments would focus American attention inward for the next two decades before a new wave of ambitious political leaders, energetic entrepreneurs, and idealists would initiate another, more intense era of encounters with Latin Americans.

❧

In the short century that stretched from the American Revolution to the Civil War, relations between Latin Americans and North Americans had undergone radical change. The limited knowledge and sometimes idealized perceptions that people in the former Spanish, Portuguese, and British colonies had about one another had given way to intensifying interactions and not infrequent animosity. Many Americans came to view their neighbors as inferior, incapable of self-government, and desperately in need of U.S. influence. Such ideas helped justify U.S. territorial expansion into Mexico and subsequent raids into Central America and the Caribbean by filibusters like William Walker. At the same time, Americans continued to harbor images of Latin America as a mysterious, sometimes dangerous, often exotic environment that dated back to the impressions of eighteenth-century sailors and merchants. As for Latin Americans, their views of Americans and reactions to them had also evolved.

Although independence leaders such as Simón Bolívar had praised their northern neighbor as a paragon of republican virtue, that image had been seriously tarnished by the aggressive territorial expansion of the United States and the disparaging attitudes many Americans held toward their southern neighbors. Guerrilla warfare in Mexico during the U.S. invasion and the attacks on the U.S. railway in Panama offered two striking examples of popular resistance to U.S. aggression and influence. Yet Cubans who had been even more intensely exposed to Americans were embracing U.S. culture as a progressive force that would help them shape their modern identity. Furthermore, Latin American elites would soon come to see positive potential in their relations with the United States.

CHAPTER TWO

THE ROAD TO EMPIRE, 1861–1899

ON MAY 31, 1863, A SAD PARADE OF HORSES, WAGONS, AND COACHES carried President Benito Juárez and the national government from Mexico City north toward the mining center of San Luis Potosi. Juárez fled from the capital to avoid capture by an invading French army. Mexico's decision to declare a moratorium on its national debt and the imperial ambitions of Napoleon III had triggered the invasion. Despite a courageous resistance by the Mexican people, the French would soon occupy the capital and impose a foreign sovereign upon the nation, leaving Juárez to organize a long and grueling resistance from the north. Although French aggression represented the most blatant violation of the Monroe Doctrine since its declaration nearly four decades before, the Lincoln administration could do little to prevent the occupation of Mexico and would do even less to drive the French out. Lincoln had offered a loan to enable Mexico to pay the interest on its debt, but the U.S. Congress rejected the credit extension. With the federal government fighting for its survival in 1863 and fearing any action that would tempt France or other European powers to back the Confederacy, Washington would hardly raise its voice against the occupation, and in fact cut off Juárez's purchase of arms in the United States, dealing a serious blow to the resistance. U.S. influence and interest in Latin America had fallen to its lowest ebb since the founding of the republic. And yet, over the next three decades rapid changes in the United States and Latin America would lead the North Americans to launch an imperial project in the Western Hemisphere.

The Civilizing Mission

While the precise effects of the Civil War on the country's economic development remain a matter of debate, the war certainly facilitated the process of industrialization that had begun early in the nineteenth century. The role of the national government in the economy remained small by modern standards, but during the war the northern interests that controlled the federal regime instituted land-grant policies, higher tariffs, and easier immigration standards that encouraged railroad development and resource exploitation, protected U.S. manufacturers, and helped ensure a growing supply of labor for industry. When peace came, the nation was poised for a period of dizzying economic growth during which extraordinary new levels of agricultural production and industrial output would transform the United States into the world's leading economic power.

Between 1860 and 1890 America's industries increased their output fivefold, raising their share of the nation's production of commodities from 32 to 53 percent. By the end of the century, big business emerged as a dominant feature of the economic landscape as large, corporately owned, and bureaucratically managed enterprises asserted their power. Easier immigration standards and economic growth attracted a flood of European workers to labor in American industrial plants, with nearly forty-five million new Americans reaching U.S. shores in these decades. With the number of industrial workers expanding from 1.5 million to 5.9 million, they accounted for one-quarter of the national labor force.[1] Striking changes also altered the face of the West.

Land grants to railroad companies helped spur a vast expansion of the national rail network, with forty-one thousand miles of rail added during the 1870s and another seventy thousand miles built in the following decade. Land allocated to farmers, combined with railways that allowed them to reach major markets with their products, and the use of barbed wire and increased mechanization of farming activities, spurred dramatic increases in agricultural production. Both corn and wheat output more than doubled by the end of the century.[2] Yet for all this dizzying economic success, social unrest and even rebellion shook American society.

The successful expansion of industrial capacity and agricultural output, along with the rapid extension of rail networks in both the United States and other parts of the globe, created an overabundance of industrial and agricultural products, driving down prices for these goods in a great depression of prices that stretched across the closing decades of the nineteenth century. This threat to profits drove companies to seek ever-greater production efficiencies with the introduction of technologies that would reduce the need for skilled labor, through efforts to gain greater control over the job activities of workers, and by the simple expedient of cutting wages. Those measures in turn sparked strikes and violent confrontations between workers and capitalists that shook the nation. In the West, the relentless advance of farmers and miners infringed on the reservation lands set aside for Native Americans, triggering armed conflicts and a military campaign by federal forces that would finally end with the massacre at Wounded Knee.

Meanwhile farmers grew increasingly frustrated with their inability to earn a living from their crops in the face of declining prices during this era. They targeted eastern banks, railroad companies, and big business in general as the sources of their predicament, founding the Populist Party in 1890 to challenge the economic elite and the two-party system. The great price depression triggered a campaign by desperate white farmers in the South to drive African Americans from the lands they worked as tenants. The Republican Party abandoned African Americans who would face a rapid erosion of their political rights. Racists, now cloaking themselves in the mantle of science, claimed that blacks were losing the traits of civilization, which they had allegedly acquired as slaves. In the urban North, the waves of immigrants from southern and eastern Europe with cultures distinctly different from that of their new homeland resisted the changes reshaping the American workplace, creating another threat to social stability.

Despite the efforts of women's rights advocates, America remained a male-dominated society in which men viewed women as emotional creatures in need of the protection and beneficent influence of males. Elite and middle-class males viewed their own "manly" qualities as those essential to the proper development and management of society. Yet as the benefits of material progress penetrated America, members of the elite such as Theodore Roosevelt expressed concern about the feminization of the male gender that might result from this overly civilized society. In fact they feared that the unrest in society stemmed in part from the inability of feminized males to control and manage their own civilization. With the stunning economic growth of the late nineteenth century had come a host of ills for which Americans now sought solutions.

Political leaders such as President Grover Cleveland, intellectuals such as Josiah Strong and Henry Adams, and eventually business groups such as the National Manufacturers Association would press for the securing of foreign markets to solve the nation's greatest economic problem—a vast overabundance of goods resulting from the country's ever-expanding industrial capacity. As a result, the U.S. government adopted a more aggressive foreign policy, particularly in regard to Latin America, which was seen as one of the most promising overseas markets for American business. Yet the new U.S. foreign policy was not driven solely by the need to expand foreign markets.[3]

American businessmen who sought to sell their wares in Latin America and elsewhere believed themselves to be on a dual mission of profit and civilization. They were confident that American technologies such as sewing machines and telephones would have an uplifting effect on the people in foreign markets, providing them with a share in the benefits of their own consumer civilization. Americans were supremely confident in the civilizing effects of their culture. Indeed within their national borders Americans had launched a large-scale program of uplift for Native Americans during the 1870s, establishing boarding schools to teach their children English and otherwise inculcate them with the values of "civilized" white society. The darker-skinned people of Latin America appeared to be an even larger group of benighted souls, who could benefit from American civilization whether in the form of consumer goods, education, or the disciplines of the American workplace. Of course that perspective reflected many Americans' belief that the darker-skinned people of Latin America, much like Native Americans and African Americans, were inherently inferior and required the paternalistic influence of the superior white race. A sure sign of that inferiority was what some Americans perceived as the inherent effeminacy of Latin Americans. Before the end of the century the American civilizing mission would take on a more aggressive quality as leaders such as Theodore Roosevelt would wield U.S. military might in an ongoing campaign to rescue the unfortunate masses of Latin America from their own degeneracy.[4] Meanwhile, Latin American elites had fashioned a similar political philosophy, promoting economic growth and attempting to ensure tight control over their own people.

By the mid-nineteenth century, the Liberal elites of Latin America were searching for solutions to the social, economic, and political chaos that had wracked their societies since independence. Increasingly, Liberals looked to the ideas of the French intellectual August Comte and his positivist philosophy that called for the scientific analysis of society's problems and the empowerment of the state to carry out rational policies that would resolve those difficulties. Critical to Comte's vision was his assertion that social order was essential to human progress, and that human progress must reinforce that order. For Liberals such as Juan Bautista Alberdi of Argentina and Justo Sierra of Mexico, these ideas offered the hope that they could continue to pursue their dreams of material development while reining in the unrest that had shattered their hopes for progress. In fact, by the last quarter of the nineteenth century, governments that emulated the values of positivism, such as the regimes of Porfirio Díaz in Mexico and Antonio Guzman Blanco in Venezuela, had emerged in the region. As Argentine intellectual and future president Domingo Sarmiento described it, positivist politicians like himself saw their societies as divided by a struggle between barbarism and civilization. In that struggle the positivists created state apparatus to suppress peasant rebellions and other popular uprisings that had disrupted their model of development. For the Latin American positivists their societies' popular masses must be held in check, by draconian measures if necessary, while the elite pressed ahead with an agenda of material progress. Only when the state had educated the larger population would the masses be fit to participate fully in their national life, and even then many positivists believed that only significant infusions of European blood through large-scale immigration could sufficiently whiten their own populations to make them responsible members of modern society. Over time, positivists credited their regimes with accelerating economic growth, creating national educational systems, encouraging European immigration, and upgrading the military.

While the positivist regimes of the late nineteenth century did spur considerable economic growth and relative social and political calm compared to past turbulence, those achievements had their limitations. Economic growth largely resulted from the increased exploitation and export of the region's agricultural and mineral resources. Much of the improvement stemmed from improved rail and port facilities and marketing provided in no small part by British investments, merchants, and the British merchant marine. But production methods on plantations, haciendas, and mines remained largely unchanged as labor-repressive methods forced large numbers of workers to toil in environments where technologies were little changed from earlier in the nineteenth century. If the explosive growth in exports was to continue, Latin American regimes would have to incorporate foreign technologies that would enhance productivity. These developments in Latin America converging with the new expansionist thrust from the United States would shape relations in the Americas during the second half of the nineteenth century. Among the first Americans to take advantage of the policies pursued by the Liberal elites were U.S. entrepreneurs.

Entrepreneurial Initiatives

On a sunshine-filled day in mid-January 1866 sixteen-year-old Edwin Atkins stood on the deck of the steamship *Eagle*, drinking in the sights of Havana harbor from the fortifications of Morro Castle to the red-tiled roofs and iron-grilled windows of the old colonial city. The young Bostonian had survived nearly a week of seasickness to arrive at this destination, but he was not one of the American tourists who had begun to winter in the Cuban capital. Atkins's father had been involved in the sugar trade with Cuba for nearly twenty years. Within three years the younger Atkins would return to the island to begin learning the business under the tutelage of Ramón de la Torriente, his father's principal business associate in Cuba.[5]

In the decades that followed, Atkins repeatedly visited the island to oversee his interests, which typically included not only purchasing sugar but also financing the annual crop for local planters. In 1882 Atkins entered the production side of the sugar business when he foreclosed on the plantations of the Sarría family. As Atkins himself explained, he became the most important U.S. sugar grower on the island by applying American business practices that stressed efficiency.[6] At the same time, despite their New England upbringing, Atkins and his wife Katharine readily adapted to the role of Southern slave owners when it came to their relations with the Afro-Cubans who labored on their estates. Atkins described a typical holiday scene on his plantation, Soledad:

> We the owners, sat upon a kind of throne constructed by the
> negroes and surrounded by the Spanish flag and coat-of-arms.
> The negroes brought us little presents of chickens, eggs, bananas
> and so on. As the procession filed in front of us, many of the
> older African Negroes would kneel and kiss our hands and
> feet, asking our blessing. . . . Those negroes addressed us as
> father and mother, and always called me master. They really
> considered themselves as our children; and while they would
> always steal any property of the estate, they would never,
> under any circumstances, touch any personal property which
> they seem to look upon as sacred.[7]

More generally, Atkins's views reflected the common perception among many Americans that people of color represented an inferior type of human being who were best dealt with by a firm hand and paternalistic attitude. Atkins's venture into sugar production also marked a common course followed by U.S. businessmen in Latin America after the Civil War—using their mercantile ventures to establish backward linkages into the production processes of local economies.

Trade remained the most important form of U.S. economic ties to Latin America in the decades after the Civil War. U.S. exports to the region grew from $64 million in 1880 to $132 million in 1900.[8] That increase was made possible in part by the growth of the U.S. industrial base, which could now provide finished goods in exchange for the primary product exports of Latin America. The Singer Sewing Manufacturing

Company was selling its machines through local agents in more than a half-dozen Latin American countries. By the mid-1880s the Tropical American Company was marketing telephone equipment in eight different Latin American countries, and the Edison interests were building lighting systems in the largest South American nations. Within a decade Standard Oil was marketing its petroleum products in Mexico and Cuba.[9] With the growth in trade, a number of merchants followed the lead of Edwin Atkins and invested directly in the region.

In Honduras, the Valentines, a family of New York merchants, secured mining concessions to establish the Rosario Mining Company in 1880. Sam Weil, a New Orleans merchant conducting business in the Nicaraguan port of Bluefields, followed a similar course to establish mining operations in that Central American country. Michael and William Grace incorporated the merchant firm of W. R. Grace and Company in Peru in 1867. In the next two decades the Graces, like Edwin Atkins in Cuba, foreclosed on sugar estates to directly enter the production process. But perhaps the most dynamic area of development for U.S. business was communication and transportation.[10]

In their effort to link their economies more closely to industrial powers such as Great Britain and the United States, the Latin American elites sought foreign development of international communication and transportation links. One American pioneer was James A. Scrymser, whose International Ocean Telegraph Company laid the first cable between Florida and Havana, Cuba, in 1866. Driven out of his own firm in the mid-1870s by the American financier Jay Gould, Scrymser proceeded to set up a series of new companies including the Mexican Cable Company and Central and South American Cable Company. Through these enterprises Scrymser laid a series of land and undersea cable lines across Mexico, through Central America, and down the coast of South America to Peru by 1882. In 1890 he extended the lines to Chile, and then purchased landlines to link the system to Argentina and Uruguay, creating a communication web that now provided rapid information transfers between the United States and most of Latin America. For American businesses the cables represented an important advance in their competition with British and other European interests in Latin America. They now could gain easy access to vital, current information about exchange rates, commodity prices, general market conditions, and advance warning of political events that might affect economic conditions. The cables linked to news services such as the Associated Press and Reuters and through them to newspapers would also bring new immediacy to the encounters between Americans and Latin Americans who could now read up-to-date accounts of happenings in each other's countries.[11] Transportation networks proved an equally pressing concern for Latin American elites. Railroads represented an immediate and concrete solution to the region's transportation needs, and such investments would also lead to additional direct investments in local production processes.

Henry Meiggs, a contemporary of William Wheelwright, had been involved in railroad building in both Chile and Peru. Before his death in 1877 Meiggs accepted a project to build a rail network in Costa Rica, which he turned over to a nephew, Minor C. Keith. A booming coffee industry had developed in Costa Rica's central highlands, but a sparsely populated tropical Caribbean coast separated the coffee producers from their major markets in the United States and Europe. The rail network would solve that problem. As a subsidy for construction costs, Keith received land grants from the government, which he soon converted to banana plantations. He extended his banana investments through Central America and into Colombia before acquiring the Boston Fruit Company in 1899 to form the United Fruit Company, a firm that would have a profound influence on the region's future.[12]

Although British holdings in Latin America still dwarfed U.S. interests, American ventures in transportation and communication proved that U.S. technology could rival or surpass British investments as a spur to the economic growth sought by Latin American elites. Furthermore, U.S. businesspeople had demonstrated a willingness to enter directly into the production process and upgrade output with improved technology and management techniques, something British interests had rarely done. U.S. investors clearly saw themselves as important agents of economic growth and more generally as a civilizing force in Latin America. However, changes brought by American entrepreneurs frequently stirred local animosity toward the U.S. presence.

Communities of small banana growers along the Caribbean coast of Central America developed highly contentious relations with United Fruit and other U.S banana companies, or *fruteras*. The planters sought to maintain their access to the free market that would ensure the highest price for their product while the fruteras attempted to enforce contracts that would ensure a fixed price for the fruit that they purchased from the planters. U.S. mining enterprises tried to eliminate *gambusinos*, the independent contractors who worked mines for their owners in return for a percentage of their production. American companies wanted to replace the gambusinos with wageworkers and thereby reduce their production costs. In turn, the wage labor force in American mines and banana plantations faced intensified supervision and longer hours of work as the U.S. companies sought to increase profit margins. Nor did Americans hesitate to express their disparaging attitude toward Latin Americans. Those attitudes and increasingly stressful work conditions fed a simmering resentment among small producers and workers who became the target of American production initiatives, but most of that discontent would not burst forth to the surface until after the turn of the century. Meanwhile other Americans were arriving in Latin America intent upon their own mission of uplift, but with more altruistic goals.

Missionaries

In the early morning hours of February 19, 1873, John W. Butler, a young Methodist Episcopal missionary standing on the deck of a steamer as it entered the harbor of Veracruz, Mexico, took inspiration from the sight of the planet Venus, which seemed to rest on the rim of the snow-capped volcano Mt. Orizaba. Butler saw the appearance of Venus as an omen for the coming of a time "when the smile of Him who is 'the bright and morning star' shall rest on the heart of redeemed Mexico."[13] Butler, like dozens of other American Protestant missionaries, would devote most of his adult life to spreading the gospel among Mexicans. By 1891 those efforts had won them more than sixteen thousand communicants or converts and as many as fifty thousand adherents who participated in some aspect of the missionary programs. Protestant missionaries were also active in Cuba, Brazil, Chile, Peru, and Guatemala. The inspiration for the Protestant missionary ventures in Latin America was rooted in a long tradition of religious Evangelicalism in American history.

In response to the rationalism of the Enlightenment of the eighteenth century and the social turbulence of the nineteenth century, Protestant clergymen had instituted a new wave of Evangelical revivals to reassert what they believed to be the fundamental principles of Christianity and to reinspire their flocks in the face of the challenges and uncertainties of modern society. Particularly influential was a New Englander named Samuel Hopkins and his ideas about unreserved consecration to God. The individualistic character of Hopkins's doctrine had a profound influence on early missionaries to Latin America, who viewed their primary objective as the conversion of each individual soul.[14] In fact, as their emphasis on individualism suggests, the missionaries were as much purveyors of American cultural values as they were messengers of Christianity. Out of self-interest and conviction they pressed for religious pluralism, arguing for the end of the Catholic Church's privileged position as the state-sanctioned church in Latin America and the secularization of the church's landholdings. They also urged the creation of public school systems to counter the church's monopoly on education and trumpeted the importance of free speech. One missionary in Mexico went so far as to urge American immigrants to set up reading circles to discuss topics dear to the American spirit of civic activism such as good roads, home hygiene, and city sanitation.[15]

Not surprisingly the missionaries came to view Latin American Liberals as their allies and protectors, especially in Mexico where the Liberal constitution of 1857 finally made it possible for Protestants to proselytize. Liberals and American Protestants did indeed share a number of common views, particularly in regard to diminishing the power of the Catholic Church and promoting liberal political institutions. Furthermore, Liberals tended to see Protestant missionaries, much like Americans in general, as purveyors of modern ideas and practices that would benefit their societies. In turn, the Protestants' admiration for Liberals, especially in Mexico, was just short of idolatrous. John Butler referred to President Porfirio Díaz as a "remarkable man" and concluded that Mexico's prosperity at the end of the nineteenth century was due in large measure "to the efforts and incorruptible character of her noble president, Porfirio Díaz."[16]

By the 1890s a new wave of missionary activism surged forward, driven in part by the Young Men's Christian Association's Student Volunteer Movement that spoke optimistically of evangelizing the entire world in one generation. At the same time Protestant missionaries frequently echoed the ideas of Anglo-Saxon superiority although those views were tempered by the belief that religious conversion combined with exposure to American values could ameliorate the effects of racial inferiority. In fact missionaries' projects now reflected the influence of the Social Gospel, which coupled the salvation of souls with the reformation of society. This approach gave new emphasis to social activism on the part of the missionaries, particularly the expansion of educational programs that would reach out to new and potential converts.[17] Primary and secondary schools offered exposure to Protestantism as well as training in academic disciplines, especially mathematics, science, and English, which were often lacking in Latin American institutions. Missionaries also provided a steady dose of American values as they urged on their pupils the importance of promptness, cleanliness, and the competitive spirit.

Although these missionaries would never win over large numbers of converts in the nineteenth century, their activities did have real attraction for and influence on Latin Americans. Even those not interested in the Protestant faith might well send their children to a missionary school for the opportunity to expose them to the benefits of an American-style education. Others saw in their conversion not merely a personal spiritual decision but the moral validation of new values that they wished to adopt, including concepts of individualism, competition, and personal freedom. Such values may explain the tendency for Protestant missionaries to find their greatest success among members of the middle class. In Cuba, still under Spanish colonial rule and the power of a Catholic Church dominated by Spanish clergy, conversion to Protestantism could also represent another way of defining a distinct Cuban identity and asserting Cuban cultural if not political independence.[18] At the same time, most Latin Americans were not receptive to or even tolerant of Protestants. In Mexico and Cuba, Protestants experienced considerable hostility toward their activities. Property owners were loath to rent facilities to the missionaries. Angry crowds sometimes disrupted their services and desecrated their churches. While the missionaries believed that the Catholic clergy instigated these incidents, at times the aggressive tactics of some missionaries also contributed to the problems.[19] Yet on the whole, the Protestants' mission and impact was a pacific one that sought the salvation of souls and the inculcation of Christian and American values. That same pacific quality did not distinguish the policies of their government in its relations with Latin America in this era.

BUILDING AN EMPIRE

The ventures of U.S. businesspeople and the sacrifices of Protestant missionaries formed part of a renewed American commitment to Latin America in the closing decades of the nineteenth century that found its most striking expressions in the policies of the U.S. government toward the region. During this period Washington began forcefully asserting that it possessed the right to protect its vested interests in the region and claiming a paternalistic responsibility for the well-being of the people of Latin America. In reality its ability to act effectively on such claims was largely limited to the Caribbean and the nations that bordered it. Yet it did not prevent successive U.S. administrations from involving themselves in the affairs of South American countries as well. A variety of factors drove and influenced U.S. policy at this time.

William Seward, as Lincoln's secretary of state, laid out a vision of American empire as a largely commercial venture dominating the Western Hemisphere with a few island military bases that would protect U.S. commercial and strategic interests in the region. Presidents James Garfield and Grover Cleveland would take vigorous action designed to implement Seward's vision. Policymakers acted with particular urgency by the 1890s because of their belief that expanding overseas markets offered the one viable solution to widespread social unrest prompted by years of falling prices and the economic depression of the late nineteenth century. U.S. leaders strongly seconded by U.S. business interests became certain that only overseas markets could relieve the problems of oversupply created by American industrial might, and they viewed Latin America as an important part of that solution. That perspective dovetailed nicely with the ideas of the naval strategist Alfred Thayer Mahan, who argued for a modern navy as essential to the extension of American influence. A revised version of Americans' self-conceived mission to Latin America also played an important part in this new policy.[20]

While men like Richard Cleveland and James M. Gilliss had believed that political documents like the U.S. Constitution and the ingenuity of a few U.S. capitalists could rescue Latin Americans and put them on the course of republican government, Americans in the late nineteenth century held a far more pessimistic view of their neighbors' prospects and the degree of assistance they might require. American racists, now garbed in the raiment of pseudoscience argued forcibly that the experience of

African Americans and Native Americans in the United States proved the inherent inferiority of nonwhites. Furthermore, efforts to educate Native American children demonstrated a new American conviction that only long-term intervention by Anglo-Saxons committed to civilizing such people could possibly lift them from the depths of human decline. Americans soon fused such ideas with a disparaging attitude toward the effects of European colonialism to shape a renewed U.S. mission to Latin America that would require a new assertiveness and a commitment to an aggressive strategy of civilizing its supposedly benighted people. Although policymakers, businesspeople, and missionaries might differ over the precise terms and goals of that mission, they could generally agree that they were all participants in this great undertaking whose purposes could variously be served by trade and investment, conversion and education, as well as diplomatic and military interventions. Those policies also gave vent to American concerns about masculinity. The new imperial mission would ensure the continued vigor of American males. If they no longer had Western frontiers to explore and subjugate, they did have the macho mission of subjugating and civilizing Latin Americans. Nor would the Americans' aggressive new policies be entirely unwelcome in the region.

The Liberal regimes that dominated Latin America had already welcomed American businesspeople and missionaries, seeing them as important assets in their positivist projects that stressed economic development while asserting authoritarian control over their populations until the great task of civilizing them could be accomplished. But many states also saw benefits to be derived from a more assertive U.S. government strategy toward the region. European colonial possessions and European, especially British, economic dominance meant that Latin American statesmen often found their nations the target of European diplomatic pressure and military interventions to resolve claims involving repayment of international debts and territorial disputes. Given U.S. ambitions in the region, Latin American leaders would appeal for American support in these disputes knowing full well the Americans' desire to diminish European influence in order to enhance their own.

Jousting between the United States and Great Britain over their competing interests in Latin America, especially the circum-Caribbean, dated back to before the Civil War. George Squier, who like John L. Stephens pursed a multifaceted career as a diplomat, entrepreneur, and archaeologist, was appointed diplomatic envoy to Central America in 1849. During his tenure he not only secured a treaty for the Vanderbilt transit way across Nicaragua, but he also spent a good deal of his time challenging British interests in the area. At stake were London's control of British Honduras (present-day Belize) and the protectorate it claimed over Miskito Indians living along Nicaragua's Caribbean coast. The British and the Americans had intense interest in building a canal across Nicaragua, a right that Squier's treaty had secured for the United States, but that could be effectively vetoed by British domination of the country's Caribbean coastal region known as Mosquitia. The Clayton Bulwer Treaty of 1850 forestalled conflict over these issues by pledging both sides to avoid territorial acquisitions in the region and to cooperate in any future canal venture.

By 1895 the Americans had renewed their interest in building a canal, but not as a joint venture with the British. Nicaraguans, who were increasingly frustrated by the British protectorate, turned to the United States for support when they once more challenged London's influence. The United States gave its reluctant backing to the Nicaraguans, suspicious of how the Nicaraguan government might treat U.S. business interests established in Mosquitia under the British protectorate. Meanwhile, Great Britain, already reconsidering its role in the region because of other pressing international concerns, surrendered its claim to the protectorate. However, Nicaragua's President José Santos Zelaya would learn more than a decade later he had ousted the British only to replace them with another powerful and far more aggressive force—the Americans. Meanwhile the United States and Great Britain became locked in another dispute in the region, which raised the real possibility of war between the two countries.[21]

Venezuela and Great Britain had feuded for decades over the boundary line that defined Venezuela's eastern border that separated it from British possessions. At stake were valuable mineral rights and the control of trade routes in northern South America. Venezuelan appeals to the United States for assistance resulted in President Grover Cleveland issuing a strongly worded message to the British affirming an aggressive interpretation of the Monroe Doctrine and in effect demanding that the British submit the dispute to a U.S.-initiated arbitration process. British Prime Minister Lord Salisbury rejected the basic premises of Cleveland's argument, and for a time war appeared to be a distinct possibility. However, Salisbury eventually opted for arbitration, concluding that concessions to the Americans, who shared common interests with the British, would benefit Britain far more than open hostility.[22]

The Nicaraguan and Venezuelan incidents along with U.S. involvement in domestic conflicts in Chile and Brazil demonstrated a new strategy by the United States designed to diminish European and especially British influence and assert the paramount importance of the United States in the region.[23] The increased involvement of the U.S. government would facilitate the efforts of businesspeople and missionaries in the area. But the event that truly defined the new imperial mission in its fullest scope came in 1898 when the United States intervened in Cuba.

With the exception of Mexico, there was no Latin American society where the United States had greater interest or deeper involvement than Cuba. Trade with Cuba had been an important part of America's international commerce since the colonial era, and now entrepreneurs such as Edwin Atkins had entered the Cuban economy directly. Presidents from Thomas Jefferson to James Buchanan had tried to buy Cuba, and Americans had enthusiastically supported the filibustering expeditions of Narciso López. However, since the days of López, the U.S. policy had essentially accepted Spanish rule as a guarantee against a more powerful European nation securing control of this economically and strategically significant island. The United States posited acceptance of the status quo on the assumption that Spain would not harass American business interests and could maintain order in Cuban society. But while Washington might be willing to accept continued Spanish rule on the island, an increasing number of Cubans were not.

Although Narciso López's expeditions had failed to rally Cubans to topple the Spanish colonial regime, that did not mean that Cubans were accepting of Spanish rule. The long-standing hostility between Cuban-born Creoles and Spanish-born *peninsulares*, who dominated the colonial bureaucracy as well as the island's international trade, continued to fester during the 1860s. Furthermore, Spain imposed protectionist tariffs that seriously damaged commerce with the island's foreign trading partners including the United States and continued to reject Creole demands for the reform of the colonial administration. Mounting discontent erupted in a rebellion in 1868 that would shake the island for nearly a decade. The Creole elite's refusal to rally popular forces with radical measures such as the abolition of slavery doomed the uprising. Ironically, it was the colonial regime that initiated the abolition of slavery during the 1880s, but Spanish reforms failed to quell the demands for Cuban independence.[24] In 1895 with appeals for American support, Cubans once again launched a rebellion against Spanish rule that would challenge the basic assumptions of recent U.S. policy.

War in Cuba

In the early morning light of January 19, 1897, twenty-year-old Adolfo Rodriguez strode out onto an empty field outside Santa Clara, Cuba, with a cigarette nonchalantly dangling from his mouth. The Cuban peasant was flanked by two Catholic priests and a detachment of troops who were to form his firing squad. Young Adolfo had joined the rebellion at its outbreak and fought for independence until captured by the Spanish in December 1896. Convicted of insurrection and condemned to death, he fell before a fusillade of bullets without the slightest expression of fear. The famed war correspondent, Richard Harding Davis, reported the young Cuban's sacrifice, and thanks to the availability of cable service and the popular press, Adolfo quickly entered Americans' consciousness as a symbol of Cuba's tragedy.[25]

Stories like Adolfo's as reported by the press in the United States helped create public sympathy for, even frenzy over, the plight of Cubans and the atrocities inflicted by the Spanish counterinsurgency campaign. Yet it is unlikely that those concerns played a pivotal role in the decision by President William McKinley to go to war. Of far greater importance to that decision was the aggressive and expansive policy that the United States had been conducting toward Latin America as it inserted itself into the international wrangling between Great Britain and several Latin American countries. The United States clearly intended to exercise far greater influence in the region to protect and expand its strategic and business interests. The independence war in Cuba became a major challenge to that strategy.

Cuba held enormous economic and strategic value for the United States. By 1894, Cuba accounted for 6 percent of U.S. international trade, and U.S. investments totaled $50 million. The largest island in the Caribbean with excellent harbors could potentially provide the United States with naval facilities from which to extend its power in the Caribbean and offer protection for the transoceanic canal that American planners now envisioned running across Nicaragua. However, as the Cuban insurgency raged on into 1898 without a conclusive outcome, it threatened these real and potential U.S. interests in several ways. First, the rebels' use of a scorched-earth policy that burned cane fields and destroyed plantations damaged U.S. investments, disrupted Cuban trade, and created economic uncertainty in the United States, which was just recovering from nearly five years of business depression. U.S. entrepreneurs involved in the Cuban trade warned President McKinley that the rebellion was costing them $100 million a year in business. Leading American capitalists such as John Jacob Astor, William Rockefeller, and J. P. Morgan reluctantly agreed that the administration must act to end the conflict. Edwin Atkins urged the annexation of Cuba, although he hoped it would be accomplished peacefully because the Spanish government had continued to provide his plantations with protection that allowed them to operate even in the midst of war. A second issue that prompted business interests and political leaders to urge action was the nature of the rebellion itself.[26]

The insurgency that erupted on the island proved to be more than a political struggle for independence. The uprising drew its greatest support from the middle and lower echelons of Cuban society—petty bourgeois groups such as lawyers and teachers, and destitute planters, workers, and peasants. Furthermore, many of those who would fight in the liberation army were people of color. These groups transformed the rebellion from a simple struggle for independence into a revolution seeking to topple both the Spanish colonial administration and the Cuban Creole elite who had actively cooperated with it.[27] The revolution represented a direct threat to the Cuban elite and their American allies such as Edwin Atkins. The Cubans and Americans, who saw a very real threat emerging to their interests if the revolutionaries should oust the Spanish, urged U.S. annexation of the island.[28]

For the administration in Washington the Cuban rebellion demanded intervention for a number of reasons. The tacit understanding with Spain had broken down because the declining colonial power could no longer guarantee U.S. economic and strategic interests on the island. U.S. merchants and investors were demanding their government take a hand to end the turmoil as were U.S. capitalists with larger interests, who feared the ripple effects Cuban turmoil could have on the national economic recovery. The potential for social revolution rose like a specter to haunt both Cuban and American elites, threatening to bring to power radical social forces largely comprised of Afro-Cubans. For all the public outcry over Spanish war atrocities and the sinking of the battleship *Maine* in Havana harbor in February 1898, William McKinley's decision for war was driven principally by these larger concerns.

In his message to Congress, McKinley made it clear that the United States would act to restrain both sides in the conflict. The U.S. military would not go to Cuba to bolster the rebel cause; indeed, the president made no mention of Cuban independence in his address. Americans would quickly attempt to reduce Cubans to spectators in their own liberation struggle. By terming the intervention the Spanish American War, Americans sought to conjure a new reality that excluded the Cuban people from their own history. Americans would soon be describing Cubans as an uncivilized, decadent rabble ill equipped to govern themselves. That effort represented both an attempt to justify and ensure a dominant role for the United States in shaping Cuba's future and the projection of domestic issues and values into the creation of the new American empire.[29]

Both then and now Teddy Roosevelt and the Rough Riders' charge up San Juan Hill captured the essential reality of the U.S. intervention in Cuba for most Americans. Brave young Americans drawn from the Western frontier and the classrooms of Ivy League colleges fearlessly risked their lives to end the rule of the pitiless Spanish oppressors in Cuba. In sharp contrast with the sympathetic depictions of Cuban rebels at an earlier moment, at San Juan Hill Americans employed rapid cable service and the mass media to marginalize Cubans' agency in their own liberation. The noted American author Stephen Crane in his firsthand account of the battle for the *New York World* denounced the Cuban rebels for their failure to fight alongside the heroic Americans. Crane neglected to mention that a U.S. decision to exclude the Cubans from military operations accounted for their absence. As for the hero of the day, Teddy Roosevelt, his account of the events included a description of his confrontation with African

American soldiers. As these troops, whose white officers had been killed in the assault, moved to rejoin their own regiment, Roosevelt drew his revolver and threatened to shoot the first man who continued down the hill. Roosevelt's account reflects the subordinated state of African Americans in the United States and the racist perceptions that helped maintain that subordination. In Roosevelt's version of events African Americans needed white officers in order for them to function effectively, and according to Roosevelt, they readily accepted their resubordination to white authority after his gun-wielding confrontation with them. These arguments display a striking similarity to the ones that American occupiers would soon make about Cubans. The Americans had a very definite agenda of their own in Cuba that required the marginalization of most Cubans.[30]

Roosevelt's charge up San Juan Hill not only provided an opportunity to assert the perspective that people of color were incapable of self-direction much less self-governance; it also offered a striking symbol of the role of American manhood in the new imperial venture. As a young state assemblyman in Albany, New York, Teddy Roosevelt's high-pitched voice and fashionable clothes had earned him derisive comments about his masculinity from the local press. Roosevelt soon remade that image through his exploits as a hunter and rancher in the American West. The ambitious Roosevelt fused racist ideas about the inferiority of people of color with concepts of American manhood to argue that the more manly American race must take on a mission to civilize the darker-skinned, effeminate, and inferior races of the world. Indeed, Roosevelt and others saw such a mission as essential to the maintenance of American manhood that would no longer be forged through civilizing exploits in the fast-disappearing wildernesses of the American West.[31] Cuba would quickly become the testing ground for these ideas that linked racial superiority, manliness, and a civilizing mission.

AMERICANIZING CUBA

Just after dawn on December 20, 1899, a handful of Cuban officials serving the U.S. military occupation government motored out into Havana harbor to meet the coastal steamer bringing General Leonard Wood to the island's capital. Wood, who had served as the senior military commander of the Rough Riders and then as military governor of

Santiago Province, had arrived to assume the post of military governor of Cuba. His appointment was not merely a product of his experience and accomplishments as a military officer. With the assistance of
his longtime friend Teddy Roosevelt, Wood had conducted a relentless
campaign to undermine the reputation of his predecessor, General John
Brooke, and had gone so far as to hire a professional public relations
agent to publicize his candidacy for the post.[32] Yet Wood was more
than a scheming, ambitious bureaucrat. He sincerely believed that the
occupation represented a golden opportunity for the United States to
reform Cuba and its people. As Wood later explained, he attempted to
create "a republic modeled closely upon the lines of our great Anglo-
Saxon republic."[33] In many ways Wood sought to apply rational reform
principles to Cuba, and in so doing he would establish the blueprint for
the United States's civilizing mission in the circum-Caribbean for the
next three decades.

Among the most visible of Wood's reforms was a massive $15 million
public works program of port upgrades, sewer projects, drainage of
swamplands, street improvements, repair of public buildings, as well as
the construction of new hospitals and schools. These expenditures represented efforts to restart the Cuban economy as well as improve health and
sanitation on the island. The school buildings were part of a larger educational project that saw the opening of thirty-eight hundred such facilities
and the enrollment of more than two hundred fifty thousand students
by 1902. But the school buildings, as well as other initiatives, represented
more than bricks and mortar; they translated into a concerted effort to
Americanize Cubans.[34]

As a part of educational reform, the occupation government had
U.S. textbooks translated into Spanish for Cuban schoolchildren, and it
sent thirteen hundred Cuban teachers to the United States for training.
Wood clearly saw educational reform as a vital tool for the revival of what
he described as "a race that has been steadily going down for a hundred
years and into which we have got to infuse new life, new principles and
new methods of doing things."[35] To that end, the general launched a
similar Americanization project in the Cuban judicial system. Deeming
the Spanish-created court system corrupt and inefficient, Wood sought
advice on judicial reform from U.S. Supreme Court Justice E. D. White,
installing a system of trial by jury and generally revising the judicial code

to reflect U.S. legal concepts.[36] Among the most cherished of those ideas
was the protection of private property.

From the outset, Leonard Wood had sided with the propertied
classes of Cuba as pillars of stability, and like so many future U.S. imperial administrators, he felt that stable financial and business conditions
were essential to progress in Latin American societies. To that end, the
occupation government in 1899 declared a moratorium on collection of
debts, which saved many Cuban sugar planters who had suffered severe
losses during the insurgency. As much as Wood and later imperial agents
were defenders of private property, they were also advocates of a major
role for U.S. capital in the reconstruction and future prosperity of Latin
American economies. When Wood allowed the debt moratorium to
lapse in 1902 without creating local lending institutions that would help
indebted sugar growers survive, he sounded the death knell for much of
the island's planter class. The bankruptcy of Cuban plantation owners
opened the door for U.S. investors to acquire wide swaths of the island's
productive land. Wood struck another blow for U.S. interests when
he instituted special court procedures that allowed for the breakup of
communally held estates that controlled substantial landholdings on the
eastern end of the island, thus creating new opportunities for U.S. corporations to purchase and expand sugar plantations. By 1906 U.S. citizens
had spent $50 million acquiring 4.5 million acres or about 15 percent of
Cuba's land.[37] The general also became a leading advocate of a reciprocal trade agreement with Cuba that was eventually ratified in 1903. The
treaty would lower duties on Cuban sugar imports in the United States
and provide further encouragement for U.S. corporations to invest in
the island's agricultural sector. Wood predicted that with such a treaty,
"the Island will, under the impetus of new capital and energy, not only be
developed but gradually Americanized and we shall in time have one of
the richest, most desirable possessions in the world."[38] For Wood, U.S.
corporations would serve as partners in the civilizing mission, bringing
economic prosperity and with it political stability while contributing to
the larger project of Americanization.

As Wood's reference to Cuba as a "possession" indicated, he was not
a proponent of Cuban independence. Indeed the McKinley administration, fearing that an independent Cuba might prove unwilling to do
Washington's bidding, had prodded Republican Senator Orville Platt to

propose an amendment to the Cuban constitution that curtailed Cuban sovereignty by effectively requiring prior U.S. approval of foreign treaties and loans, the leasing of naval bases such as Guantanamo Bay to the United States, and permitting U.S. intervention to maintain order on the island.[39] Even with the Platt Amendment providing the United States with extraordinary controls over the new Cuban government, Wood remained doubtful of any course that granted the island even a circumscribed form of independence. On board a U.S. cruiser bearing him home after the transfer of power to the Cuban government, Wood lamented, "The general feeling among the Cubans was one of intense regret at the termination of American government."[40] Wood's reluctant departure marked not the end but only the beginning of the American empire in Latin America.

⧉

America's new imperial enterprise with its mission of civilizing Latin America had begun in earnest with the occupation of Cuba, and in the decades ahead the lessons learned in Cuba would be applied in a number of other Latin American countries. In the early decades of the twentieth century the American government leaders, businesspeople, missionaries, and private philanthropies would all play their roles in fulfilling the mission of the new empire. Theirs would continue to be a venture influenced by images of Latin America as a frontier in need of civilizing influences and by values regarding race and gender that would presume the need for an energetic American mission of uplift in the region.

As the initiatives of individual adventurers and entrepreneurs in Latin America gave way to larger corporate interests, Americans came to focus on commercial interactions and investments. Corporate and political leaders as well as American missionaries increasingly saw themselves on a civilizing mission to people burdened by their own racial heritage. At the same time, Americans continued to harbor images of Latin America as a mysterious, sometimes dangerous, often exotic environment. As for Latin Americans, their elites had come to see positive potential in their relations with the United States. Latin American Liberals and American Protestants shared a number of common values. The United States was becoming an important trading partner and a source of industrial technologies and work methods that promised to resolve productivity problems in Latin American economies. Furthermore, the United States came to serve as an important counterweight to British influence in the region. As a result, Americans found themselves being welcomed warmly by Latin American rulers at the turn of the century. Together the two groups would seek to modernize the region while maintaining social stability. But that alliance would itself become an important source of popular discontent and unrest that would one day challenge the Americans and their civilizing mission.

CHAPTER THREE

THE CIVILIZING EMPIRE,
1899–1917

In the early morning darkness of October 4, 1912, Major Smedley Butler and a contingent of three hundred U.S. Marines positioned themselves at the bottom of Cayotepe Hill outside of Masaya, Nicaragua, ready to attack the forces of General Benjamin F. Zeledón that were entrenched at the top of the promontory. At Butler's signal, the marines began an assault coordinated with that of a second marine contingent, and soon they dislodged Zeledón and his troops. Butler's attack effectively brought an end to a rebellion by Liberal forces against the Conservative government, which the United States had installed in Nicaragua and backed with loans from U.S. bankers such as Brown Brothers. Butler's role in these events was not new to him for he had already played a pivotal role in the creation of an American empire in the circum-Caribbean. As a young second lieutenant he had been part of the U.S. invasion force in Cuba and had led the marine unit that played a critical part in the toppling of Nicaragua's Liberal regime in 1910. Yet Butler himself had a less than glowing opinion of his erstwhile Conservative allies. Nor did he think very highly of the mission his government had sent him on. As he wrote to his wife shortly after the battle:

> After resting on the Coyatepec . . . I took my battalion down the hill and through Masaya back to our train. . . . As I came through Masaya, about 400 Federals [government troops] were proceeding joyfully to get very much intoxicated and loot the town in the way of celebrating their victory—a victory gained at the expense of two good American lives, all because Brown Brothers, Bankers, have some money invested in this Heathenish country.[1]

Despite his disparaging attitude toward the Nicaraguans he was fighting to keep in power, and his cynical assessment of U.S. policy there, Butler did not abandon his career as a soldier of American imperialism, serving in places such as Panama, Mexico, and Haiti. In many ways, Butler's career and his perspectives capture the dynamics of the empire, which the United States created in the Caribbean Basin during the first three decades of the twentieth century. Beginning with the invasion of Cuba in 1898, the United States committed itself to a course of intervention in nearby Latin American nations driven in part by economic and strategic concerns but also convinced that it bore the responsibility to civilize the people of the region.

That civilizing mission, which would impose strict standards of financial accountability, reform governmental institutions, upgrade public works, and improve public health and educational facilities was deemed necessary by Americans because of what they perceived to be the inferiority of Latin Americans. The pervasiveness of such sentiments is suggested by the frequency with which popular journalists expressed them without fear of censure or rebuke. For example, journalist Herbert Briton Whitaker, while reporting on the Mexican Revolution, claimed, "Under all his bombastic talk, the veneer of civilization we have imposed upon him, the Mexican is still a savage. . . . Fickle, irresponsible, treacherous, his purposes are as water, his intent is written on shifting sand."[2] As a result, U.S. protectorates were marked by a strong element of paternalism, evidenced in Smedley Butler's continuing commitment to the American imperialist mission. At the same time U.S. politicians, steeped in the tradition of limited government, were loath to have the state assume the sole responsibility for this civilizing mission. U.S. policy included a major role for corporations and banks as part of the reform mission. That effort combined with economic factors that were already drawing increasing corporate investment into the region marked the period as one of intensifying state intrusions into Latin America as well as explosive growth in American business involvement. At its height, this era of imperialism did much to advance Americans' self-conceived mission in Latin America as well as shape the perceptions Latin Americans held of their intrusive northern neighbors.

IMPERIAL EXPANSION

Although Americans at the beginning of the twentieth century viewed themselves as missionaries of civilization to the world around them, American society itself remained a place of rapid, unsettling, and even chaotic change. Throughout the early decades of the century, countervailing forces of rapid social and economic transformation that heralded the emergence of a modern society clashed with efforts to restrain those forces and bring them under the control of political authorities, business elites, and the new professional classes.

When the value of manufactured goods exceeded the value of agricultural goods produced in 1900 by 100 percent, the United States had statistically emerged as an industrial society. In 1913, when the United States produced twice the manufacturing output of its nearest rival Germany, the country had established itself as the world's leading industrial power.[3] These phenomenal leaps in economic output derived from the structure and process of American capitalism. The concentration of capital in ever larger corporations with rationalized management structures fueled the increasing mechanization of production processes and the application of new technologies such as electricity. Increased mechanization signaled an intensified control of the workplace by supervisors and managers anxious to break down the casual worker-controlled production methods of the past. New management and production strategies deskilled workers, breaking their labor processes down into simpler functions, which could then be replicated by machines or carried out by unskilled laborers—a process typified by continuous process, or more simply, assembly-line manufacturing.

Working people reacted sharply to strategies that diminished the need for traditional skilled workers and translated into a loss of worker control and very often lower wages. Many working people would turn to Samuel Gompers's American Federation of Labor (AFL) and its philosophy of business unionism, that is, negotiating with management for improved wages and working conditions. Others chose more radical alternatives such as anarcho-syndicalism that pursued a course of militant resistance and sought to affirm labor's control over the workplace. The huge influx of immigrants, who brought their own customary work practices and often did not share the Protestant and English language culture of earlier American workers, further increased unrest among the working class. In the face of mounting labor militancy in the first two decades of the twentieth century, business leaders, much like their contemporaries in Latin America, presented themselves as the harbingers of order and progress struggling against the unruly forces of barbarism represented by the working class. The new middle class of professional engineers, lawyers, social scientists, and business managers joined the cause of the business elite because they saw their own futures tied closely to the maintenance of an orderly society marked by a meritocracy that would reward professional achievement.[4] Yet despite the consensus that often marked the policy initiatives of the "better classes" American society remained wracked by unrest including racial conflict.

During the last two decades of the nineteenth century black Americans experienced a deterioration of the gains they had achieved during the era of Reconstruction that followed the Civil War. Although the federal government had ensured southern blacks access to public office in the years after the war, Republican leaders stopped short of a massive redistribution of land that would have provided African Americans with a material underpinning to their newly won rights. By 1900, white elites had rolled back gains made by African Americans and imposed Jim Crow laws that mandated racial segregation. These developments were justified with the principles of scientific racism, which argued that demonstrable physiological differences marked superior from inferior races within humankind. Those beliefs along with political considerations led even the party of Lincoln to abandon blacks in the South and to accept the segregation of southern society, while touting the healing of the nation's wounds from its separatist conflict of the

nineteenth century.[5] Renewed doubts about the male-dominated char-
acteristic of that past posed yet another challenge to conceptions of an
idealized American past.

For middle-class men, turn-of-the-century America held a number
of challenges to their self-conceived role in their society. Doubts arose
about nineteenth-century conceptions of ideal middle-class men as
assertive and even aggressive individuals, who readily assumed the task
of protecting and guiding the emotional and less responsible sex as well
as the lower classes. Middle-class womens' movements demanded access
to higher education and the professional positions that men monopo-
lized. An ever-more-restless working class seemed loath to accept the
guidance of their social betters, and the growth of big business threatened the well-being of those who still made their living as independent
entrepreneurs. Such challenges led to a redefinition of American middle-
class manhood in the early twentieth century.

Professionalism provided part of that image as middle-class males
defined themselves as calm, rational professionals, who could reform
and manage society in the face of the forces of disorder. In addition, this
ideal of manhood was clearly defined as belonging to the white race in
opposition to nonwhite races with their presumed feminine qualities of
irrationality and irresponsibility. On a broader scale white males envisioned themselves as the leaders of a great mission to bring the benefits of American civilization to the nonwhite masses of the globe. The
idea of the American male's civilizing mission meshed seamlessly with
the increasing strategic and economic significance of Latin America for
the United States to make the region the principal target of that civilizing mission. American males would assume the paternalistic role of
bringing order out of the chaos of these primitive societies, introducing
them to the benefits of modern capitalist development. At times that
mission would have to be carried out with the use of force, but employing
violence against primitive societies would in fact give appropriate vent to
the controlled aggression of civilized men honing the hard edge of their
maleness as forecast by the memorable spokesperson for manliness and
imperialism, Teddy Roosevelt.[6]

The civilizing mission offered a host of opportunities for a variety of American males to assert those qualities that for them defined
their manhood. Teddy Roosevelt most notably among politicians built

his career on precisely the images that fused manhood and a civilizing mission to inferior races. Smedley Butler was one of many military
officers who fashioned their own images as true American men in the
imperial adventure. A host of U.S. capitalists such as Minor Keith of
the United Fruit Company and Daniel Guggenheim of the American
Smelting and Refining Company and innumerable midlevel professionals built their fortunes in the process of bringing American business
practices and technology to the region. But the mission did not remain
the exclusive preserve of politicians, military men, and capitalists. Other
professionals also joined in the great imperial venture.

In contrast with the nineteenth century when Americans' awareness of their hemispheric neighbors was largely confined to travelers'
accounts such as those penned by John L. Stephens and occasional cable
dispatches in newspapers about a diplomatic crisis or natural disaster, a
flood of images and information about the region now entered the public
consciousness. Explorers like Hiram Bingham, who claimed to have
discovered "the lost city of the Incas," boasted the professional aura associated with academic institutions. These insitutions sought to explore
and define Latin American civilizations both ancient and modern in
terms of modern science, demonstrating how American science could
seemingly peel away the mysteries that supposedly shrouded Latin
American societies and their past.

A number of professional authors such as Samuel Crowther, Nevil O.
Winter, and Earl Chapin May made their careers writing corporate histories and travel accounts that depicted the exotic and primitive nature
of Latin American countries, while extolling the virtues of companies such as United Fruit and Anaconda. Similar perspectives permeated newspaper accounts of U.S. interventions in countries such as
Nicaragua and Haiti, as U.S. journalists defined those ventures in terms
of America's responsibility to stabilize and reform its neighbors. Many
correspondents reporting on the Mexican Revolution cast their stories
within classic stereotypes. The novelist Jack London, although well
known for his socialist views and writings, described Mexicans as "half-
breeds" and went on to explain, "They are what a mixed breed always
is—neither fish, flesh, nor fowl. They are neither white men nor Indians.
Like the Eurasian, they possess all of the vices of their various comin-
gled bloods and none of their virtues."[7] But some journalists did offer

an alternative vision of such events, although the images they presented of Latin Americans may have been no less stereotypical.

Traveling with the forces of Pancho Villa in northern Mexico in 1914, John Reed, who would win international acclaim for his sweeping accounts of both the Mexican and Russian Revolutions, reported the following conversation between two peons:

> "It is said," remarked the old man quaveringly, "that the United States of the North covets our country—that the Gringo soldiers will come and take away my goats in the end . . ."
>
> "That is a lie," exclaimed the other, animated. "It is the rich Americans who want to rob us, just as the rich Mexicans want to rob us. It is the rich all over the world who want to rob the poor."
>
> The old man shivered and drew his wasted body nearer to the fire. "I have often wondered," said he mildly, "why the rich, having so much, want so much. The poor, who have nothing, want so little. Just a few goats. . . ."
>
> His compadre lifted his chin like a noble, smiling gently, "I have never been out of this little country here. . . . But they tell me that there are many rich lands to the north and south and east. But this is my land and I love it. For the years of me, and my father and my grandfather, the rich men have gathered the corn and held it in their clenched fists before our mouths. And only blood will make them open their hands to their brothers."[8]

Both Reed in his description of the Mexican Revolution and fellow correspondent Carlton Beals in his account of the Nicaraguan revolutionary Augusto Sandino's war against U.S. Marines provided positive, even romanticized versions of these struggles, depicting the rebels as humble but heroic figures fighting against the exploitation by their own ruling class and greedy Americans.[9] The idealism of journalists like Reed and Beals was shared by another group of Americans whose values and views of Latin America differed sharply from these anti-imperialist correspondents.

The early twentieth century marked the high-water mark of missionary activities by mainstream Protestant churches in Latin America. Although their central goal remained that of saving souls, the missionaries now were imbued with the ideals of the Social Gospel that emphasized not merely individual salvation but also the reform of society as a whole. These same ideas transformed the Young Men's Christian Association (YMCA) from an evangelical organization to one that emphasized social services and athletics. The Y would open a number of branches in Latin America, seeking to spread the Social Gospel of service as well as American ideals about physical culture, competitiveness, and individualism. Joining these organizations by the end of World War I were private foundations, especially the Rockefeller Foundation, which sought to bring the benefits of American civilization to Latin Americans through programs promoting public health and improved medical training.

American activists in the civilizing mission approached their work from a variety of ideological perspectives and through an array of institutional structures from the U.S. military to missionary organizations. Not surprisingly their goals and plans would clash at times, but more striking are the common perspectives they shared about their paternalistic civilizing mission to the lesser races of Latin America and the common values they shared in carrying out that mission. Over time those perspectives and values found reinforcement in the American media from travel books to film travelogues and Hollywood epics that stressed the view of Latin America as an exotic and uncivilized environment. Further reinforcement came at times from Latin American elites, who often shared the Americans' disparaging views of their own populations.

During this period, free-market economic policies and positivist political regimes dominated the economies and political systems of Latin America. Agricultural crops such as coffee, wheat, and sugar, and mining products from silver to copper poured forth from the region's economies into the major markets of the United Sates and Europe. These exports elicited a deluge of manufactured imports from the industrialized world that could meet both consumer needs of the elite and middle class, as well as provide the building blocks of railroad networks, highways, port facilities, and utilities. With state coffers filling from taxes on international trade, the positivist regimes of the period built more powerful state apparatus especially professionalized and heavily armed military establishments that would ensure the maintenance of internal order. They also financed public works projects and expansion of public education, although such initiatives were largely confined to urban areas and primarily benefited the elite and middle classes.

The regimes of the era had a strong authoritarian character, but they did make some concessions in terms of political participation to an expanding middle class of professionals, shopkeepers, and white-collar employees. But such concessions usually came in reaction to popular protests and violent uprisings. Some of the larger South American governments also made the first halting efforts to address the social question— in essence the emergence of an ever-growing working class that manned the port facilities, railroads, mines, and plantations that formed the core of their export economies. Although the working class in the manufacturing sector remained small and relatively insignificant at this time, those who labored at the ports, railroads, and mines had the potential to choke off the exports that fed national economies. Workers in these sectors were already busy forming labor organizations that ranged in type from fairly traditional mutual-aid societies and trade unions that assisted workers through cooperative associations or in negotiations with management to anarcho-syndicalist movements that advocated direct actions such as general strikes to topple the state and establish workers' control. In Latin American countries like Mexico, where domestic- and foreign-controlled commercial enterprises were infringing ever more rapidly on peasant-controlled lands, unrest also stirred in the rural sector. Although labor unrest was most commonly met with repression, there were the first halting efforts to craft labor laws and confront the horrendous living conditions in working-class slums. However, with elites generally viewing their own workers and peasants as racially unfit for the task of creating a modern society, repression would remain the most common form of addressing the social question. Social stability, especially in the export sector, was essential if the region's rulers were to succeed in their effort to attract U.S. investments.[10]

Although Latin American elites controlled much of their own export production, especially of agricultural products, these groups came to rely heavily on U.S. investment and technology to underpin their early-twentieth-century economic miracle. Despite the modern facade of booming Latin American urban centers, the basic labor practices, which produced the export boom, remained largely unchanged from the late nineteenth century. Whether through service tenantry in which agrarian workers gained access to land in return for service on the landlord's estate, private forms of labor indebtedness such as debt peonage that required peasants to repay debts with their labor, or state labor drafts that forced rural residents to work on public works projects, the elites employed coercive methods including police powers to gain access to and exploit labor. In the absence of a free labor market, and because of oppressive working conditions and low wages, peasants and workers were little inclined to work energetically and often sought to evade or escape forced-labor conditions. The systems of labor exploitation proved highly inefficient with high costs of enforcement representing a constant drag on attempts to accumulate capital in order to improve efficiency.[11] In light of these conditions U.S. corporate investment frequently served as a solution to these problems, bringing capital and technology to bear on the problem of productivity. For this reason Latin American elites usually welcomed U.S. investors as allies in their continuing drive to expand economic growth while retaining order in their societies. Just after the turn of the century, a monumental example of American technological capacity began to take shape across the Isthmus of Panama.

THE IMPERIAL STATE

John L. Stephens's dream of an American-built canal across Nicaragua appeared to take a major step closer to reality in 1887 when the Maritime Canal Company secured a concession from the Nicaraguan government to build a canal across its territory. However, after a four-million-dollar investment the project collapsed due to corruption and political unrest in Nicaragua. Ultimately, it was the French who began excavating for such a waterway through Panama in 1883. However, in 1888 with less than 40 percent of the work completed, the French, falling victim to financial difficulties and the effects of disease and death on their workforce, halted the project. In the years that followed, American interest grew more intense as imperialists, Teddy Roosevelt foremost among them, dreamed of a canal that would extend U.S. naval and mercantile power throughout Latin America and into Asia.

The U.S. government began clearing the diplomatic way for a canal through Panama in 1901, signing a treaty with Great Britain that abrogated the Clayton Bulwer Treaty of 1850, which had essentially required that any canal represent a joint effort by the two powers. The following year the Roosevelt administration negotiated a treaty with Colombia for canal rights through its province of Panama, only to have it rejected by a specially convened Colombian congress. When an uprising occurred in Colombia's historically rebellious isthmian province, Roosevelt rushed U.S. forces to Panama to prevent the Colombian government from suppressing the uprising and then quickly signed a canal treaty with the new Republic of Panama.

If the Panama railroad had created a series of outposts of American society in Panama, the canal project turned a ten-mile-wide swath of the country, known as the canal zone, into a miniature U.S. territory. For the six thousand white U.S. citizens who lived in the zone, the Isthmian Canal Commission provided bachelor-quarter hotels complete with American meals and phonographs blaring ragtime. Married couples enjoyed modern apartments or freestanding homes equipped with modern conveniences such as electricity, along with access to commissaries stocked with U.S.-manufactured consumer goods. Country clubs and movie theaters provided leisure-time entertainment. The YMCA offered facilities with services ranging from bowling and billiards to gymnasiums. By 1910, thirty-nine churches representing an array of Christian denominations dotted the canal-zone landscape.[12] But these re-creations of American material culture were dwarfed by the enormous excavation that was being driven through the heart of the zone and Panama itself.

The canal excavation bore stark witness to the enormity of American industrial might and the ability of Americans to project that power overseas, mastering the most challenging of natural environments. So awe-inspiring was the sight of the excavation that until the canal opened in 1914, thousands of tourists visited Panama each year simply to view the spectacle. At the nine-mile-long Culebra Cut, the largest excavation site, trains brought six thousand workers in each day, six days a week, as drilling, blasting, and repair crews worked round the clock to advance the colossal project. Soaring above the laborers and the sounds of drilling and dynamite explosions, stood ninety-five-ton steam shovels capable of moving thousands of cubic yards of earth each week. Teddy Roosevelt himself visited the site and struck a commanding pose in the cab of one of the great shovels, testifying to a new aspect of American manliness, the cool command of powerful technology. Aside from its ultimate benefits to U.S. naval and maritime traffic, the canal sent a compelling message throughout Latin America about the power of U.S. industrial machinery and techniques and the determination and aggressiveness of the humans who commanded this technology.[13] In addition to replicating U.S. material culture, the canal project also mimicked the race relations of the United States.

The vast majority of the forty-five to fifty thousand people who worked on the canal project at its peak were West Indians. Under U.S. rule, strict policies of racial segregation and discrimination prevailed in the zone. The Isthmian Canal Commission excluded blacks from all white-designated hotels and churches as well as the YMCA clubhouses, while commissaries and hospitals had separate sections for blacks. Single black workers were housed in crude barracks, while married couples for whom no housing was provided usually found shelter in shantytowns built of boxes and scrap lumber. When on the job, West Indians found themselves addressed with racial epithets by their white supervisors.

These realities of the canal zone were captured by Harry Franck, a young American writer who in the process of crafting a series of travel books centered on his own globe-trotting adventures took a position in the Canal Zone Police Force for a few months in 1912. On the one hand Franck extolled the wonders of the YMCA, noting, "Uncle Sam surely makes life comfortable for his children wherever he takes hold. It is not enough that he shall clean up and set in order these tropical pest-holes; he will have the employee fancy himself completely at home." But as for the zone's workforce, Franck concluded, "There can be no question of the astounding stupidity of the West Indian rank and file, a stupidity amusing if you are in an amusable mood, unendurable if you neglect to pack your patience among your bag of supplies in the morning."[14] The commission euphemistically designated white workers as gold employees and blacks as silver employees. That distinction translated into substantially lower wages for those on the silver payroll. Diseases and a variety of industrial accidents took thousands of lives among the West Indians, who worked on the excavation that was carried on in a pestilence-ridden tropical environment.[15] The canal thus sent two powerful images through Latin America, one of industrial might and the other of a society marred by institutionalized racism. Meanwhile, the construction of the canal gave the United States a new and vital stake in the circum-Caribbean that made regional political unrest and a continuing European presence in the region all that much more unacceptable to American imperialists.

In an address to Congress at the end of 1904, Teddy Roosevelt announced a reinterpretation of the Monroe Doctrine. Termed the Roosevelt Corollary, the doctrine asserted a policy of preventive intervention that would permit the United States to intrude in Latin American countries threatened by European governments because they had failed to pay their international debts. For Roosevelt, the policy served to further limit the European presence in the region and provided justification for using financial controls as a means of carrying out the civilizing mission. Only a month later, the Dominican Republic granted authority to the United States to take control of its customhouses, which soon led to a financial protectorate over the small Caribbean country.[16]

Under Roosevelt's successor, William Howard Taft, Roosevelt's policies and the earlier initiatives of Leonard Wood in Cuba morphed into Dollar Diplomacy, a policy that sought to exclude European financial influence from the circum-Caribbean, stabilize, and modernize local societies by taking control of customhouses, asserting influence over government finances, as well as promoting U.S. loans and corporate investment. In effect, U.S. policy as applied to the circum-Caribbean had evolved from late-nineteenth-century visions of expanding U.S. markets and competing more effectively with Europeans to a more sophisticated approach that would use both state initiatives and private enterprise to circumscribe European influence, build U.S. economic control while finding outlets for U.S. capital and products, civilize and thereby stabilize local societies, and in the process create a more secure environment for the strategically important Panama Canal.[17] At the same time, the policy gave expression to Americans' belief in their innate superiority over their neighbors to the south. Carrying the benefits of Progressive policies to Latin America, they could fulfill their paternalistic mission of lifting up the lesser races of the Western Hemisphere with sound government, rational policies, and the initiatives of U.S. capitalism. One goal that the new policy would not achieve was the avoidance of further military interventions like the Cuban occupation. In fact, U.S. forces would soon be imposing control in Nicaragua, the Dominican Republic, and Haiti.

Although Nicaragua's significance as a potential canal site had largely dissipated after the United States secured the Panama route,

U.S. involvement in the Central American country actually intensified. Nicaragua's president, José Santos Zelaya, had once been viewed as a typical Liberal ally of U.S. interests in the region, but the canal project intensified concerns about stability in Central America, and Washington came to view Zelaya's meddling in the affairs of neighboring states as a threat to that stability. Zelaya was hardly the only Central American leader to dabble in regional politics, but he further offended the United States when he began to renege on a series of business concessions made to U.S. interests and managed to alienate the United Fruit Company in its dispute with local banana growers. In the closing months of 1909, U.S. business interests such as United Fruit helped finance a Conservative rebellion against Zelaya's regime. When the U.S. broke diplomatic ties with his government, effectively throwing its support to the rebels, Zelaya resigned. However, his Liberal successor managed to drive off the rebels, finally surrounding them in the Caribbean port of Bluefields. It was at this point that Smedley Butler, who was forging his career as a soldier of U.S. interventionism, first entered the Nicaraguan scene. On May 31, 1910, Butler led a contingent of two hundred marines into the port and proceeded to occupy it for three months. The Conservatives, now able to collect customs revenues and receive shipments of arms, finally turned the tide of battle and forced the collapse of the Liberal administration.[18]

With the Conservatives now installed in power, the Taft administration quickly instituted its Dollar Diplomacy strategy, pressing a series of loans on the new regime from the financial houses Brown Brothers and Company and J. and W. Seligman and Company. These loans were guaranteed with customs revenues that would be under the supervision of a U.S.-appointed collector and the bankers' control of the national railroad company. The loans that would pay off an outstanding debt to a London syndicate and supposedly stabilize Nicaragua's currency were designed to meet the basic goals of Dollar Diplomacy—diminishing European influence, achieving economic growth while encouraging U.S. investment, and securing political stability.[19] But as Smedley Butler's subsequent expedition to Nicaragua in 1912 clearly demonstrated, stability was not one of the accomplishments of the policy, and the United States was drawn ever deeper into Nicaraguan affairs. Even when most of the U.S. forces from the 1912 intervention were withdrawn, a one-hundred-man marine detachment was left in the capital of Managua to maintain order. The Wilson administration gave a U.S.-run high commission control over both revenue collection and budgetary expenditures by the Nicaraguan government. Yet financial instability and political unrest continued to dog the U.S. experiment in nation building through financial controls. Meanwhile, the United States had taken on two additional such missions in the Caribbean.

The product of an eighteenth-century slave rebellion against French colonialism, the black Republic of Haiti had long represented a diplomatic conundrum for the United States. Haitians shared a common revolutionary and republican tradition with the United States, but as free, self-governing black people, they represented a challenge to the American history of slavery and to the twentieth-century reality of racial segregation. Despite official ambiguity, the U.S. government showed an increasing interest in Haiti as it intensified its campaign to sweep the European powers from the Caribbean. In Haiti, U.S. commercial interests competed with French, British, and German merchants for business. The French, through their majority position in the national bank, dominated the country's finances. However, an opportunity to refashion those power relationships emerged in 1915 when the country's recently ousted president ordered the murder of political prisoners held in the capital's jails and then was himself killed by an enraged crowd. In July, U.S. Marines landed and quickly occupied the country.

By the time of the occupation, personalist leaders, who were backed by peasant militias tied to them by kin relations, personal loyalty, or simply mercenary connections, dominated the political landscape. The marines focused on disarming these *cacos*, or peasant soldiers, by offering amnesties and monetary rewards. Those who resisted were hunted down by the marines, finally forcing the survivors to declare an armistice. The U.S.-occupation government installed a Haitian as a puppet president and then set about its program of reform and stabilization that included creation of a national police force under the guidance of the ubiquitous Smedley Butler; road building, public health, and education projects; upgrading the government bureaucracy; and in 1922 a $16 million loan from National City Bank.[20] Once again, the U.S. government had launched itself on a project to stabilize a Latin American society through the imposition of Progressive policies while at the same time reorienting the country's economy toward the United States by establishing control over its finances. A further inspiration for these policies no doubt sprang from Washington's dealings with Native American populations. Much like the system of Indian schools and the creation of Indian military units, U.S. education policies and the creation of the constabulary were designed to offer a degree of Americanization while at the same time employing subject people to police their own.[21] Meanwhile, the Dominican Republic, Haiti's neighbor on the island of Hispaniola, also found itself occupied by U.S. forces.

Less than a year after they had invaded Haiti, U.S. Marines occupied the capital of the Dominican Republic. Teddy Roosevelt's earlier financial intervention that had included a customs receivership and a $20 million bank loan had failed to create the type of stable political environment that the United States now insisted on seeing in Caribbean nations. Once again military occupation provided the basis for the now predictable array of U.S. reforms including improvements in education and public health, public works projects, and the creation of a U.S.-trained national constabulary.[22] Nor were the smaller countries of the circum-Caribbean the only targets of the United States's interventionist strategy.

In 1910 Francisco Madero, the scion of an elite family who had become increasingly embittered over the national regime's open-door policy toward foreign capital, challenged Porfirio Díaz for the presidency. When diverse groups rallied to Madero's cause, Díaz accepted the inevitable and fled into exile. But Madero proved incapable of holding together the array of forces that helped bring him to power, and after his assassination, contending revolutionary armies rampaged through Mexico. As early as 1911 President William Howard Taft summarized the concerns of Henry Lane Wilson, the U.S. ambassador to Mexico this way: "He feared that the forty thousand or more Americans would be assailed and American investments of more than a billion dollars would be injured or destroyed because of the anti-American spirit of the insurrection."[23] More than two and a half years later, as the revolutionary struggle still raged, and damage to U.S. property continued to mount, Woodrow Wilson considered an all-out military invasion of Mexico. Wilson became the first American president to confront the fact that widespread social upheavals such as the one unfolding in Mexico would represent a powerful challenge to U.S. dominance in the circum-Caribbean. But after giving serious consideration to invading

Mexico, Wilson dropped the idea. Frank Vanderlip, the president of National City Bank (later Citibank) with close ties to the administration, explained the reasons for this new caution:

> We were very close to war with Mexico a few days ago, but the situation there has improved somewhat. There is still a chance we will become involved, but the Administration is entirely awake to the reason for not becoming involved. Military authorities estimate that it would cost $1,000,000 a day and take two years to entirely subdue the country. It would be certain to be an unpopular venture after the first few months.[24]

The one-million-dollar-a-day figure alone would have been enough to give Wilson doubts about occupying Mexico. The occupation of Cuba had cost a mere one-half million dollars a month, and the annual cost of sending warships to trouble spots in Central America was only $1 million.[25] The outright invasion of Mexico simply represented too big a challenge in terms of the military commitment as well as the cost in dollars and political capital. Faced with that reality, Wilson opted for a strategy that had succeeded in ousting the Nicaraguan Liberals when U.S. Marines occupied Bluefields. In April 1914, U.S. naval forces occupied the Mexican port of Veracruz to prevent the delivery of weapons shipments to the regime in Mexico City that Wilson opposed. In a variation on the Bluefields operation, which had allowed the Nicaraguan Conservatives to rearm themselves, the U.S. occupation forces left a large cache of weapons and ammunition in Veracruz upon their departure. At the time of the U.S. departure, the Constitutionalists, a revolutionary faction that the United States favored, were advancing on the port. The Constitutionalist forces were thus able to secure the American weapons stash. Led by Venustiano Carranza and Alvaro Obregón, the Constitutionalists turned the tide of battle against more radical movements led by Pancho Villa and Emiliano Zapata.[26]

But despite repeated instances of U.S. intervention, the state was not the only or in many instances even the prime agent of the civilizing mission. The proponents of Dollar Diplomacy always envisioned corporate America as playing a central role in the mission to bring progress and stability to the region. In many cases, especially in South America,

U.S. corporations were having a more profound effect on local societies than any policy engineered in Washington.

THE GOLDEN AGE

At the end of the nineteenth century U.S. business interests in Latin America had largely focused on transportation, communication, and mercantile ventures. In a few instances such as Minor Keith's banana plantations and Edwin Atkins's sugar estates those activities had led to direct investments in the production process. But with the exception of Mexico, where U.S. capitalists took advantage of Porfirio Díaz's welcoming policies and the close proximity of valuable natural resources, direct investments in production represented a small part of U.S. activities in the region. That picture changed rapidly after 1900. In the United States, mammoth modern corporations now had control of or access to prodigious sums of capital along with some of the most advanced industrial technologies in the world. The potential of combining those factors with inexpensive labor in Latin America to produce low-cost inputs for industry, and the growing urban population, and a favorable investment climate in Latin America brought a surge of U.S. investment in mineral and agricultural production.

After World War I, agriculture, mining, and oil accounted for 60 percent of all U.S. investments in the region. In Cuba, U.S. corporations such as the Hershey Chocolate Company and the Punta Alegre Sugar Company had more than $600 million invested in the sugar industry and accounted for more than half of the island's sugar output by 1925. The United Fruit Company (UFCO) played the central role in banana production in the Caribbean Basin with 295 square miles of land under cultivation and another 3.5 million acres that it owned or leased for future development. In Central America, UFCO was joined by the Standard Fruit and Steamship Company and the Cuyamel Fruit Company, giving U.S. corporations a virtual monopoly on the banana trade.[27]

The Guggenheim Brothers of New York created a mining empire that stretched from Mexico to Chile. The Guggenheim-dominated American Smelting and Refining Company controlled smelters and mines in Mexico valued at $100 million by 1910. In Chile, the brothers acquired the Braden Copper Company and turned their Chuquicamata copper-mining property into the largest open-pit mine in the world. The Rockefeller family's Anaconda Mining Company held a major stake in Mexico thanks to its ownership of the Cananea mines. Anaconda acquired the Guggenheims' Chuquicamata mine for $70 million in 1923 when the brothers launched a bid to take over the entire Chilean nitrate industry. Smaller firms such as Phelps Dodge Corporation in Mexico and the Cerro de Pasco Corporation in Peru further extended and intensified the dominant position that U.S. mining companies achieved in Latin America.[28]

In the oil industry, Edward Doheny, who had helped launch the Los Angeles oil boom in the 1890s, developed the first commercial oil fields in Mexico. Standard Oil joined the competition for Mexican oil in 1917. By then Standard already controlled the most important oil fields in Peru through its subsidiary, the International Petroleum Corporation (IPC). Matching earlier moves by its European competitors, Standard also entered the Venezuelan oil industry in 1922.[29]

The investments of U.S. corporations in agriculture, mining, and oil played a critical role in Latin America's continuing export boom after the turn of the century. The $70 million that the U.S. fruteras invested in Central America boosted the total banana exports of Guatemala, Honduras, and Nicaragua by 300 percent by 1920. With U.S. corporations controlling more than 80 percent of the capital in its mining industry, Mexico increased its copper exports tenfold between 1890 and 1905. U.S. corporations invested $170 million in Chilean mining between 1912 and 1926, boosting its copper production by nearly 500 percent.[30] But U.S. investors were not the only nongovernmental emissaries of change to Latin America.

By the early twentieth century, emissaries of the U.S. Protestant denominations to Latin America had absorbed important elements of the Social Gospel. Spreading of the word involved more than individual conversion. Missionary efforts had to also address ignorance, ill health, and poverty. In Latin America, Protestant ministers would engage in a host of socially uplifting endeavors, opening schools and hospitals and setting up athletic programs. This crusade carried not just a Christian but a distinctly American message. As Jean Pierre Bastian has explained, "The missionary societies contributed (by means of their schools, social works and publications) to the diffusion of a new faith whose cultural matrix can be found in the *American way of life.*"[31]

American businesses developed close working relationships with missionaries, who seemed to offer a quick fix for workplace problems. The most immediate interest and concern of the business community were the educational activities of the Protestant churches. Beyond the obvious benefits of basic education, there was the larger importance of value-laden instruction carried out by American Protestant ministers, who as a part of their mission sought reconciliation between capital and labor. As much as conversion to Protestantism represented a deeply personal spiritual choice, conversion to American Protestantism also involved acceptance of strongly held American values. Protestant missionaries taught not only Christian values in their Latin American schools; they also taught thoroughly American values that stressed individualism, hard work, and the positive powers of the free market.

✎

The beginning of the twentieth century marked a high point in the American imperial mission. The United States had intervened in a number of circum-Caribbean countries including Cuba, Haiti, the Dominican Republic, and Nicaragua, using its military might to dislodge the remnants of European influence, promote U.S business interests, and launch campaigns of civilization focused on rationalized government procedures, improved education and public health, and the general promotion of market forces. That effort was not confined to the countries where the United States employed military force, nor was the responsibility shouldered solely by the state. U.S. companies enjoyed explosive growth throughout Latin America, rapidly gaining on and then replacing Great Britain as the most important external economic force in most of the region. U.S. businesses not only accelerated economic growth by improving productivity in key export sectors and through international loans, but also they engaged in their own civilizing campaign, disciplining Latin Americans to wage labor and modern industrial practices, promoting values of individualism and competitiveness, and even making a start on the promotion of consumerism. They were joined in this project by Protestant missionaries, who in their own way sought to advance the project of Americanization that lay at the heart of the civilizing mission.

Americans could well take pride in the achievements of this multi-faceted endeavor. U.S. Marines had restored order in several Caribbean republics and begun reforming government services. Schools and medical services had been upgraded. U.S. businesses had fueled export booms in both Central and South America. Corporations along with Protestant missions had encouraged the spread of market forces and encouraged values central to the development of modern capitalist societies. Furthermore, the U.S. mission had often prompted positive responses from Latin Americans. Elites welcomed both the spur to economic growth and modernization as well as the larger vision of a civilizing mission that meshed well with their own positivist policies. For workers, peasants, and middle-class employees, U.S. corporations could mean higher-paying jobs and opportunities for advancement. Furthermore, U.S. industrial products brought to Latin Americans in powerful new ways the images of a society of exceptional technological achievement and enormous material abundance where all were free to compete for a share of this wealth and the happiness that seemed an inevitable product of consumption. And yet the embrace of the American mission did not mean that all Latin Americans accepted that mission with unquestioning enthusiasm.

The American civilizing mission was the product of a male-dominated vision of societal development through rationalized state policies and the continued expansion of the modern capitalist system with consumerism playing a vital role in expanding markets and serving as a spur to individual ambition and hard work. Yet that mission also envisioned the core of its civilization as a white male Protestant society. Those who did not fit that image either in the domestic environment or overseas were deemed to be effeminate, racially inferior beings. They required the firm hand of discipline and training in a process of Americanization to be directed by the rational, self-disciplined white males whose responsibility it was to guide the less fortunate onto the road of progress. It is hardly surprising that many aspects of that vision would prompt hostile responses from Latin Americans.

CHAPTER FOUR

DEFENDING THE EMPIRE, 1917–1929

On August 15, 1920, Honduran banana planter Jacobo Munguía and twelve hundred machete-wielding workers occupied the Caribbean port of La Ceiba. The increasing power of U.S. fruit companies had driven small Honduran growers to desperation as they found themselves reduced to little more than contract employees while peasants struggled to adapt to their new status as wageworkers dependent on the banana companies. The striking planters and workers demanded concessions, particularly increased wages, from the Standard Fruit Company. When Standard refused, the workers launched forays into the surrounding countryside, burning bridges and company farms. As was typical in such situations, the frutera summoned a U.S. battleship to the Honduran coast to intimidate the strikers. But in the face of widespread popular support for the protestors and the refusal of the local military commander to act against the strikers, the gambit failed, and the company finally made a major wage concession to the workers. Throughout the 1920s Munguía would continue to harass the fruit companies, earning the title "Terror of the Coast."[1] When an Italian worker in the employ of Standard Fruit was murdered, a local satirical sheet offered a macabre twist on the U.S. civilizing mission, suggesting, "Let us civilize the foreigners as we did the Italian in true Honduran fashion."[2]

Meanwhile a local labor organization, the Sociedad Artesano, was rumored to have developed a hit list of frutera employees it planned to eliminate. United Fruit's response to such threats was to hire known murderer Gustavo Pinel to head its security forces. Pinel in turn protected and advanced the company's interests with tactics that included torture and murder. Allen Plummer, a Standard manager, captured the climate on the Honduran coast when he wrote, "You see we are here among the Hondurians, and they are quite treacherous, and often kill one another, and quite frankly the Americans are threatened."[3] Violence and the threat of violence had become a central element in the dialogue between the ever-more-powerful fruteras and the local population that struggled to maintain a degree of independence. The Hondurans' mounting resentment over the effects of the American corporate revolution and U.S. interventionism that marked these events converged into an increasing anti-Americanism that would spread through Latin America during the 1920s, confronting the agents of American empire with unforeseen challenges.

❧

Even as the United States emerged as the first fully modern society and economy, it faced an array of domestic and foreign challenges from labor radicalism to global war as well as threats to its empire in Latin America. Confronting those problems was a cadre of American professionals who employed the powers of a modern society, ranging from increased industrial productivity and modern marketing techniques to international financial mechanisms and the institutions of the modern American state.

During the first third of the twentieth century American corporations applied increased mechanization along with rationalized management techniques to work processes, thus achieving unparalleled increases in production and productivity. These developments displaced skilled workers and drove others into menial jobs within the new workplace. These dramatic changes spurred militant labor actions as workers struggled to raise their wages and protect their positions within the production process. The anarcho-syndicalist International Workers of the World (IWW), founded in 1905, espoused direct action such as strikes and demonstrations to achieve improved conditions for labor and ultimately to secure worker control of the production process. The IWW's cause won support among hundreds of thousands of workers. In stark contrast to Samuel Gompers's AFL, which was willing to work with corporate leaders, the IWW was viewed by business owners as a real and present danger to the U.S. free-enterprise system. Citing the IWW's refusal to support the U.S. entry into World War I, the federal government launched a massive crackdown, imprisoning more than 150 IWW leaders. Meanwhile, another radical threat emerged in the political system with the founding of the Socialist Party in 1901. The party's presidential candidate secured nearly one million votes in both the 1908 and 1920 national elections. After the triumph of the Russian Bolsheviks in 1917, communism offered yet another radical alternative to capitalist development. As threats to the national political and labor establishments mounted, violence against African Americans persisted.

Although the number of lynchings of blacks declined during the first two decades of the new century, these atrocities continued to provide a stark reminder of the power of racial hatred and racial stereotypes that depicted blacks as both childlike and submissive yet also violent and rapacious. The challenges, which blacks and new immigrants represented to the Protestant Anglo-Saxon American ideal, helped trigger the founding of the modern Ku Klux Klan in 1915 and fed its campaign of hate and intimidation against blacks, Catholics, and Jews. As for Native Americans, they continued to be subjected to an aggressive program of Americanization as thousands of their children were sent off to boarding schools for reeducation into white American society.[4] In the midst of these turbulent conditions, the new American middle class cringed at the threats to order and sought to stabilize society through reformism.

The new professional classes, which had emerged in the United States by the turn of the century, soon devoted themselves to a national agenda for reform. American middle-class males now defined their masculinity in terms of being rational, logical managers of their own and the nation's affairs. Often their goals found support from a wide array of groups in society such as the push for prohibition of alcoholic beverages, which appealed to social reformers concerned about poverty and violence, business elites preoccupied with worker efficiency, and religious leaders concerned about moral corruption.[5] In the political sphere the new middle class gave vent to its ideas through Progressivism. Progressives sought to develop rational policies administered by professional experts to improve health and education, upgrade government by reducing political patronage, and replace it with civil service standards as well as rein in some of the worst practices of big business. In general, Progressives believed that rational analysis and professional management could cure the ills of society and above all assure order and progress.

Consumerism offered another set of ideas that would give common purpose to Americans after the turn of the century. Department store pioneers like John Wanamaker and Marshall Fields developed modern marketing techniques that successfully promoted the idea that the consumption of market-generated goods and services provided the means to achieving human happiness. As large corporations came to dominate the economic landscape, and fewer and fewer Americans owned their own companies or worked their own land, they could take comfort in a new form of democracy, the equal right to desire and consume material goods. In fact consumerism would become one of the central features of what Americans defined as civilized society. Americans could share a sense of equal participation in a consumer society despite economic inequalities, and corporations would benefit from a vast broadening and deepening of the domestic market.[6] Much of the American reformist agenda would be marshaled to address challenges to the American mission in Latin America as the United States faced growing protests over both its overt interventions in the circum-Caribbean and the increasing power its corporations exercised in the region.

Professional economists, termed money doctors, such as Edwin Kemmerer, became a critical part of the reformist initiatives launched by the U.S. government. Operating at first as government agents and later as quasi-independent experts, they spent several decades seeking to secure the adoption of the gold standard for Latin American currencies and strict fiscal regulations for government finances, believing that these measures would open local economies more fully to the world market and bring order to their social systems. Other members of the new professions helped shape American activities in Latin America.

Another type of professional, union organizers like Samuel Gompers of the AFL, brought American-style business unionism to Latin America. Gompers believed that the focus on hours and wages of business union- ism would counteract the growing influence of anarcho-syndicalist and to a lesser degree communist ideas among Latin American workers. In addition, the social reform efforts of Protestant missionaries would now be complemented by the work of professional reformers as private philan- thropies, most notably the Rockefeller Foundation, extended their efforts to stabilize domestic society through educational and medical programs to Latin America. Major corporations such as General Electric and the Guggenheim enterprises responded to labor unrest with their own version of reform. Adopting a strategy of industrial welfare, some large compa- nies provided adult-education classes to "Americanize" their largely immi- grant workforces and offered health and safety programs to encourage a sense of corporate loyalty among their restless workers while cutting down on workdays lost to illness and accidents. They would find such strategies equally useful in dealing with their Latin American employees.

Some corporate leaders also contributed to the mission by offering their vision of a consumer utopia that could be created in Latin America by their enterprises. Although mining and agricultural companies remained the dominant forces in U.S. investment, corporations such as General Electric, International Telephone and Telegraph, and Coca-Cola now used the techniques of modern marketing to entice Latin Americans into the wonderland of consumer products. But the agents of the American mission would face severe challenges from a wide array of Latin American groups, including at times their longtime allies—the Latin American elite.

Clashes over economic interests could disrupt the corporate/elite alliance in cases such as Mexico, where the local bourgeoisie believed that their own government was giving unfair advantages to foreign investors. More generally, elites, especially in South America, became increasingly wary of U.S. assertions of power, with many fearing that the Americans would seek to spread their interventionist tactics from the circum- Caribbean to the nations of South America. Domestically, the alliance with the Americans would become the source of growing protests by middle- and working-class groups as well as peasants, who found them- selves exploited by U.S. corporations in their drive to wring profits from their Latin American investments. Those protests would grow louder and more militant when the region's surging production of primary products helped flood the world market in the late 1920s, driving down prices for everything from sugar to copper and causing widespread economic suffering. The protests and rebellions combined with economic decline would bring the golden age of U.S. investment and Latin American export growth to a sudden and dramatic end while unleashing social and political forces that would challenge the international alliance that had underpinned the economic growth and positivist regimes of the era. Some of the earliest challenges to the American empire erupted in the American protectorates of the circum-Caribbean.

CHALLENGES TO EMPIRE

In Cuba, where the imperial mission had begun, a fraudulent national election in 1905 triggered an armed rebellion leading to U.S. intervention in 1906. Full Cuban sovereignty would not be restored until 1909. Thousands of U.S. troops had been required to quell the uprising by Nicaraguan Liberals in 1912. Despite the initial pacification of cacos in Haiti, a new guerrilla insurgency erupted in 1919 and required more than a year of bitter combat in the countryside to suppress. Between 1917 and 1922 peasants in the eastern regions of the Dominican Republic carried on a guerrilla war against U.S. forces. The American-designed civil regimes in these countries were failing to provide the efficient and effective management their creators had expected of them.

Political corruption proved to be endemic in Cuba. Political figures used state revenues and concessions to assure political support while officeholders wielded the new apparatus of government such as the courts to ensure their reelection. The Nicaraguan Conservatives emptied the state treasury to pay off "war debts" allegedly owed to their leaders and corporate backers. They also proved adept at evading the intensifying U.S. efforts to enforce rigorous fiscal controls. Many of the reforms in Haiti and the Dominican Republic, especially education, fell victim to declining state revenues. The root causes of many of these failures can be found in the flaws that marked the imperial mission.

Despite U.S. protestations to the contrary, the interventions in the circum-Caribbean represented a direct threat to these societies' sense of nationhood and their national sovereignty. The military-occupation government in Cuba had deliberately restricted the franchise to exclude from power the most ardent advocates of immediate and complete independence for the island. And the Platt Amendment became an open invitation for political groups to redress imbalances in the political order by engaging in armed rebellions that would force the United States to intervene and reconfigure the power structure.[7] In Nicaragua, the United States spent nearly two decades maintaining in power the Conservatives, a distinct political minority. The marines' use of forced-labor gangs to build roads in Haiti helped trigger the caco rebellion while in the Dominican Republic the rapid expansion of U.S. corporate sugar estates set off the guerrilla uprising.[8] But the challenges to the U.S. mission derived from more than its attack on national sovereignty and its usurpation of ultimate economic and political power.

Embedded in the imperial project that utilized military force, financial controls, U.S. capital, and Progressive reforms to shape stable, pro-American nations with economies oriented to the United States lay a vision of a paternalistic Anglo-Saxon race bent on a civilizing mission to Latin America. Leonard Wood's description of his own duties as a mission to rescue the failing Cuban "race" captured the essence of the perspective carried by the agents of U.S. imperialism. That perspective empowered those agents, who ranged from marines to customs collectors to schoolteachers, with the belief that they represented father figures responsible for proper training and uplift of their wards, the Latin Americans. Such a concept legitimized a range of tactics from military force to educational programs that Americans could utilize to chastise and train their dependents. That perspective was vividly portrayed in a cartoon by a marine private that depicts a fully armed marine holding a Lilliputian-sized Haitian peasant in his hand and sternly lecturing him, "Listen Son! Do unto your brothers as you'd hav'em do unto you. Savvy?"[9]

Those ideals also reflected a sense of moral superiority on the part of these agents. Irving L. Lindberg, one of the U.S. officials charged with rationalizing the Nicaraguan government's finances, concluded that the "graft, extravagance, carelessness, extortion, and in some cases direct fraud" that marked the expenditure of state revenues confirmed his belief that Nicaraguans operated on "a different standard of ethics or honesty as compared with Anglo Saxon's." Even during their brief occupation of Veracruz, U.S. officials sought to impose strict controls on bordellos and to carry out a general cleanup of the city. Novelist Jack London, who visited Veracruz during the occupation, reported that the Americans had rid the streets of the "rif-raff" and the "able-bodied loafers."[10] In 1921 the United States sent Enoch Crowder to Cuba as a special presidential representative to institute a "moralization program" designed to ensure fiscal integrity and political stability on the island.

Such paternalistic perspectives, when combined with deep-seated racism, led many of the agents of imperialism to view Latin Americans as degraded, even dehumanized, beings. Not surprisingly, that perspective combined with the military power the Americans wielded led to abuse. Marines fighting the insurgency in the Dominican Republic committed a number of atrocities—murdering prisoners and shooting unarmed civilians including women and children. Yet U.S. military tribunals convicted few of the offenders, often dismissing eyewitness accounts because Dominicans were considered unreliable.[11]

For its military agents in Haiti, the American civilizing mission had become a quagmire of moral ambiguities. These paragons of American manhood found themselves haunted by fears of going native by establishing affectionate relationships with Haitian women that would surely lead them down the road to moral ruin. At the same time, the marines used force to suppress the first and second caco uprisings and to enforce corvée labor for road building. Operating in a context of racial bias and paternalistic attitudes, some marines engaged in gratuitous acts of violence against Haitians that ranged from shooting prisoners to rape.[12]

James Weldon Johnson, a noted poet who would become the first black man to head the National Association for the Advancement of Colored People, reported on the Haitian situation in a four-part series in the prestigious liberal journal, The Nation. Johnson provided a chilling account of American mistreatment of Haitians:

> Brutalities and atrocities on the part of American marines
> have occurred with sufficient frequency to be the cause of deep
> resentment and terror. Marines talk freely of what they "did"
> to some Haitians in the outlying districts. Familiar methods
> of torture to make captives reveal what they often do not know
> are nonchalantly discussed. Just before I left Port-au-Prince an
> American marine had caught a Haitian boy stealing sugar off
> the wharf and instead of arresting him he battered his brains

in with the butt of his rifle. I learned from the lips of American marines themselves of a number of cases of rape of Haitian women by marines. I often sat at tables in the hotels and cafes in company with the marine officers and they talked before me without restraint. I remember the description of a "caco" hunt by one of them; he told how they finally came upon a crowd of natives engaged in the popular pastime of cock-fighting and how they "let them have it" with machine guns and rifle fire.[13]

If the paternalistic views of Americans empowered the agents of imperialism, it also limited their vision and deeply flawed their civilizing mission, including its more humane and well-intentioned policies. Convinced of the inherent inferiority of their charges, American agents crafted reform programs that reflected that bias. The educational projects developed for Haiti placed the emphasis on vocational training, reflecting the belief held by U.S. administrators that Haitians, much like African Americans, were intellectually suited for no more than skilled labor.[14] Ignoring the realities of local environments, American agents insisted on imposing public works projects and bureaucratic structures that frequently could not be sustained by the national economy. Their economic strategies that often sought advantages for U.S. corporations over domestic and European competitors reflected a greater concern with U.S. profits than with the development of national economies. The denial of nationhood and national sovereignty, paternalistic perspectives imbued with racist attitudes and a sense of moral superiority, as well reforms drawn from U.S. experience and often serving U.S. economic interests triggered mounting popular animosity toward the U.S. protectorate policy by the 1920s. That animosity was not limited to the people of the circum-Caribbean.

U.S. officials never seriously considered using interventionist tactics to extend their civilizing mission to South America. Direct intervention in the nearby, relatively small nations of Central America and the Caribbean had proven quite manageable with costs of the Haitian and Dominican occupations running between one and one-half million dollars annually.[15] The potential costs of intervention farther south were another matter. As President Wilson's advisors had warned him, a full-scale invasion of a large country like Mexico could easily run to $1 million a day. Most of the nations of South America were large and lay at a considerable distance from the borders of the United States, factors that effectively precluded direct military intervention.

Since the 1880s the United States had pursued its diplomatic interests in South America through a series of regional conferences designed to seek consensus on key issues and of course to promote U.S. economic interests. This relatively benign policy of Pan Americanism stood in stark contrast to imperial endeavors in Central America and the Caribbean. And the ruling classes in Latin America could readily identify strong similarities between their own positivist policies and the Progressive strategies pursued by the United States at home and abroad. Furthermore, the Liberal elites of South America were as eager as their Central American and Caribbean counterparts to promote U.S. trade and investment. But at a series of Pan-American conferences after the turn of the century, South American nations voiced increasing criticism of U.S. interventionism and growing concern about the attempts of the United States to extend its power into the region. Argentina in particular pressed for Pan-American approval of the Calvo and Drago Doctrines, named after Carlos Calvo, an Argentinean expert in international law, and Luis María Drago, an Argentine diplomat. The doctrines established the principle of nonintervention and rejected the use of force to collect international debts.[16] Nor were such concerns limited to the political elite.

Latin American intellectuals, reacting to aggressive U.S. policies and racism, contrasted what they saw as the superior spiritual qualities of Latin American culture with the materialistic underpinnings of U.S. values. The Uruguayan author José Rodó first asserted this thesis in his book *Ariel*, published at the beginning of the century. The famed Nicaraguan poet Rubén Darío joined the chorus of critics with his poem "Roosevelt." The poem addresses Teddy Roosevelt as "hunter" confronting the U.S. president's self-styled image as a macho big-game hunter. In one stanza of his poem, Darío warns of the threat of U.S. imperialism and offers a vision of a common Latin American identity derived from both its indigenous and Spanish roots:

> You are the United States,
> future invader of our naïve America
> with its Indian blood, an America
> that still prays to Christ and still speaks Spanish

Darío posited a Pan Hispanismo rooted in Latin America's own multi-cultural past in opposition to the United States's Pan Americanism that essentially sought to promote U.S. economic interests in the region. Darío's criticism of U.S. imperialism and his extolling of Latin America's indigenous heritage became common themes of popular culture during the early decades of the twentieth century.[17]

Anti-imperialist and anti-American themes reverberated through popular consciousness as mass-circulation newspapers brought the stories and images of U.S. invasions to the urban inhabitants of Latin America. Populist political movements that appealed to the middle and working classes picked up on the growing popular anger at the United States. In 1924, Víctor Raúl Haya de la Torre, a Peruvian university student leader living in exile in Mexico, founded Alianza Popular Revolucionaria Americana (APRA), which in the next several decades would become one of the most noteworthy populist movements in the region. Like Darío, Haya de la Torre played on themes of the region's Indian past—the focal point of Indigenista movements, especially in Mexico and Peru, which extolled the achievements of Native American civilizations. These ideas held particular appeal for members of the expanding middle class who were often of mestizo or mixed-race origin.

Haya sought to design a political program that would appeal to a broad array of social groups that felt exploited by U.S. imperialists. Two of APRA's founding principles addressed the issue by directly calling for "Action against Yankee imperialism" and "Internationalization of the Panama Canal."[18] Although APRA's real political impact would be confined to Peru, Haya's themes of a Latin American identity rooted in its own past and opposition to U.S. imperialism became favorite topics of populist, nationalist, socialist, and communist movements that emerged in Latin America at this time. In fact, as Latin Americans began crafting a popular identity from Indigenismo and a sense of nationhood, the presence of the United States played an important role in this evolving identity. On the one hand, the American idea of limitless increases in material wealth struck a responsive cord among Latin Americans who were seeking to craft their own modern societies; on the other hand, they were also defining themselves through their opposition to what they perceived as crass values underlying U.S. culture and the threat of U.S. imperialism. That new popular identity would play an important role in determining interactions with the United States throughout the rest of the twentieth century.

Corporations and Americanization

Among the most frequent targets of Latin American nationalists were the U.S. corporate giants that now comprised an important part of the region's economies. Although agriculture, mining, and petroleum accounted for the bulk of U.S. investments by 1920, power and communication firms along with financial institutions were playing an ever-larger part in American corporate penetration of Latin America.

The General Electric Company (GE) formed the American and Foreign Power Company (AFP) to manage the power-generation enterprises it acquired in eleven different Latin American countries by the end of the 1920s. At the same time, the International Telephone and Telegraph Company (ITT) controlled telephone systems in ten Latin American countries including Cuba, Mexico, Brazil, Chile, and Argentina. The U.S. government showed a particular interest in promoting U.S. control of communication systems in the region. When James Scrymser's All-America Cables Company found its attempts to extend its cable lines up the Atlantic coast of South America blocked by a British monopoly, U.S. diplomatic pressure and legal challenges by Scrymser's company broke the monopoly in 1919. ITT later acquired All-America Cable and its vast Latin American communications network of cables. The government also gave support and encouragement to GE to create the Radio Corporation of America (RCA), which went on to dominate the market for radios in the region.[19] But even with some degree of state assistance, the enormous strides made by these corporations would have been impossible without the direct assistance of New York financial houses.

Banks such as J. P. Morgan and National City Bank along with a number of smaller institutions provided the capital that made the rapid corporate penetration of Latin America possible. Furthermore, they became the critical source of external financing for Latin American governments. When World War I fractured the financial links between Latin America and Europe, American banking houses found themselves in an ideal position to do business in the region. With their export growth providing additional revenues to support larger loan payments, Latin

American governments had borrowed $1.5 billion from U.S. institutions by 1929 to fund public works, cover government expenditures when export earnings slipped, and help compensate for profits repatriated to the United States by American companies.[29] But the impact of U.S. corporations cannot simply be defined in terms of the number of dollars invested or the growth in exports, for American firms also played a central role in altering technologies and work methods in Latin America.

The contributions of U.S. companies to this process of change varied depending on the type of industry. U.S. banana corporations remained essentially low-tech undertakings compared to ventures in mining, petroleum, power generation, and telecommunications. Nevertheless, as the fruit companies moved from simply purchasing bananas on the coast into the production process, they did generate considerable change. The fruteras built railroads, dug channels in rivers, and built port facilities equipped with modern electric machinery and radio communications to facilitate shipments of bananas. They also developed rationalized administrative structures within their operations and carefully engineered plans for the growing of bananas on plantations.

The Cerro de Pasco Corporation in Peru like other U.S. operations was already transforming mining in Latin America by introducing a system of carefully engineered shafts and tunnels to more efficiently extract ore and applying new mining technologies such as air-powered drills to improve productivity. The Guggenheims had gone a step further at their Chuquicamata mine in Chile by using huge steam shovels and vast chemical treatment plants to extract copper from low-grade ores. More technologically advanced companies also played their part.

General Electric's work in expanding electrical-generating capacity in Latin America had a highly positive impact on economic output. The fact that electric power could be introduced and precisely controlled at various stages of the industrial process meant tremendous increases in efficiency for everything from Cuban sugar mills to Andean mines. ITT and RCA provided striking improvements in the speed and immediacy of telecommunications. Not only could business and general information be disseminated more rapidly, but also radio would offer a new and immediate exposure to American popular culture. The magic of film technology exposed an increasing number of Latin Americans to a variety of compelling, but often conflicting, images of the United States.

On the one hand, U.S. films presented dramatic visual depictions of U.S. technical processes, the wealth of American society, and some of the appeal of its consumer culture. On the other, many U.S. films portrayed Latin America in a negative light—a world of petty dictators, loose women, and untrustworthy males. Hollywood often conveyed images of Americans in their own self-conceived role as paternalistic intruders in these backward societies. During the early 1920s U.S. moviemakers frequently depicted Mexican males as dishonest, violent, and cowardly individuals. The repugnant images so incensed the Mexican government that it began banning imports of films by companies that produced the offending footage. In 1922 the film industry reached an agreement with Mexico to cease producing such movies in return for a lifting of the ban.[21] But the changes that U.S. corporations brought to the region were not limited to advanced technologies and cultural images. Often U.S. companies had very direct and immediate impacts on the lives of Latin Americans, especially workers and peasants.

The degree to which U.S. enterprises sought to reshape the everyday lives of Latin Americans often depended on the type of endeavor involved. The fruteras, for example, primarily required unskilled labor for clearing forests and swamps and for planting and harvesting bananas. Managers mostly concerned themselves with securing a large labor force and disciplining employees to the harsh realities of plantation work. This in itself constituted a significant change for the rural residents of Central America, who clung to existing economic activities as subsistence peasants or small-scale commercial banana growers. For these people, work on the fruteras was usually treated as a temporary expedient to bring in cash that would help maintain their existing way of life. The fruteras utilized a task system for workers that paid them only after specific assignments were completed to prevent them from abandoning their jobs once they received their pay. The companies also utilized scrip (company currency redeemable only in company stores) to anchor the workers to the plantations. When such tactics failed to attract a sufficiently large workforce, they imported thousands of West Indians, who had already been exposed to wage labor on Caribbean sugar plantations. Initially mining companies pursued a somewhat similar strategy.[22]

The Cerro de Pasco Corporation tapped an existing system of *enganche* labor recruitment to man its operations. Under enganche, local merchants extended credit to peasants, giving them a claim on the peasants' labor as a form of repayment. On behalf of Cerro de Pasco, labor contractors brought in the indebted peasants and supervised their work in the mines. But Cerro de Pasco's modernization of its operations during the 1920s created the need for directly controlled, more experienced, more stable workers. The company began to create an ever-larger force of long-term wageworkers. The modernization process eroded the ability of Andean peasants to supplement their income with part-time work in the mines while it also created a permanent and more militant force of wage laborers.[23]

Utilities such as American and Foreign Power and ITT required a large number of skilled technicians, white-collar office workers as well as professionals such as engineers to staff their operations. For these U.S. corporations, the issue of labor revolved around effective control over workers, who were already accustomed to wage labor, but who like their American counterparts often challenged the growing control that modern corporations exercised in the workplace.[24]

In both the United States and Latin America workers resisted the long hours, close supervision, and harsh discipline that characterized modern industry. To counteract that resistance, companies instituted a variety of policies and institutions to create a permanent and stable workforce. Mining, petroleum, and agricultural companies built towns for workers that provided housing, stores, schools, and various forms of entertainment. The towns served not only to anchor workers to the job site; they also provided a series of venues in which the corporations could socialize their laborers into the modern industrial workplace. Schools provided elementary training in reading and mathematical skills that would enhance the performance of workers and their children. At the same time, schooling inculcated values such as hard work, corporate loyalty, and sobriety. Company-sponsored athletics achieved two ends: one, they offered an alternative to social drinking, which lowered worker performance, and two, they provided lessons in the benefits of competitiveness and individual achievement.

The company town had a clock looming over it to remind workers of the need for promptness and had distinct areas for sleeping, eating, and working to provide a graphic display of specialization of function. The town gave material expression to the corporate effort to Americanize local workers. U.S. mining companies went even further, attempting to use the camps to regulate the personal lives of their employees. In Chile, at the El Teniente mine, the Braden Copper Company sought to overturn the practice of common-law marriage among workers, requiring them to produce a certificate of marriage in order to cohabitate on company property. The company's welfare department encouraged women to create a typical American nuclear family supporting their husbands' hard work and raising children to be ideal employees of the future. For corporations like AFP, which dealt largely with white-collar and skilled workers, reforms focused on close supervision and strict standards of accountability. Their educational efforts for such workers included more advanced attempts at Americanization, such as offering self-help classes as well as mandatory training in English.[25]

As U.S. companies became ever more deeply involved in the production process and the creation of stable workforces, they exhibited increasing concern about regular attendance by their employees. Company-sponsored sports teams and films, along with the ban on the sale of alcohol in company towns, were designed to lessen social drinking by workers and reduce absenteeism. Mining companies launched extensive safety-training programs to reduce accidents. Even the United Fruit Company, which relied on unskilled labor, showed a particular concern for the health of its workers. At the company's Central American plantations, malaria, pneumonia, and tuberculosis killed more than five hundred UFCO workers in a single year. The company combated the problem with its own medical department, launching an antimalaria campaign and creating a series of hospitals and clinics at its plantations.[26]

Although most U.S. corporations focused on extractive and agricultural ventures, they did play a role in promoting consumerism in Latin America. Central to the task of these U.S. corporations was weaning Latin Americans away from subsistence agriculture and occasional paid labor to create a full-time wage-labor force. Company stores, among the few places where company scrip could be redeemed, provided an object lesson in the importance of wages and exposure at least to some rudimentary U.S. consumer goods. Over time the promotion of consumerism became essential to the creation of a committed wage-labor force. Only when workers accepted the premises of consumerism would they willingly embrace full-time wage work and exhibit ambition, which the quest for more and better material goods could inspire. As one champion of the UFCO noted in 1929, "[In Central America] our advertising is having the same effect as in the United States. . . . I have seen the insides of huts completely covered with American magazine pages. . . . All of this is having its effect in awakening desires."[27] By that time other corporations had entered the region with the primary purpose of generating consumer demand for their products.

GE was creating a vast market in electrical appliances and extended those activities into Latin America. Coca-Cola found a market in Latin America prior to World War I, but it was largely confined to clusters of Americans in places like the canal zone and Cuba. After the war, Coke began launching market initiatives in the circum-Caribbean including Mexico and Guatemala. Meanwhile Ford Motor Company entered Latin America when it opened its first assembly plant in Argentina in 1916 and was joined by General Motors a decade later. These and a variety of other U.S. companies began to promote the special appeal of consumerism, promising that the "good life" could be achieved by consumers who purchased their products. Through their participation in consumerism Latin Americans could take another step in creating modern, civilized societies.[28] Interestingly enough leaders of the U.S. labor movement aided corporate promotion of the wonders of market forces.

AGENTS OF AMERICANIZATION

Under Samuel Gompers's leadership, the AFL promoted business unionism that focused on bread-and-butter issues of hours and wages and eschewed controversial subjects such as the redistribution of economic and political power. Gompers was in fact an advocate of U.S. overseas economic expansion, certain that it meant higher wages for American workers. At the same time he was anxious to avoid a situation in which Latin American workers would provide low-wage competition for his members. During World War I, Gompers created the Pan American Federation of Labor (PAFL) in an effort to align the Latin American labor movement with the AFL.

Gompers's antipathy toward anarchism and socialism won him the strong support of Woodrow Wilson, who agreed to covertly bankroll the conference that created PAFL, and a newspaper, *The Pan-American Labor Press/El Obrero Pan-americano*, to spread Gompers's views among Latin American labor movements. With most of Gompers's attention focused on militant Mexican workers and their role in the Mexican Revolution, the newspaper began publication in San Antonio, Texas, in August 1918. Although PAFL managed to create a few affiliates in such U.S. protectorates as Cuba and the Dominican Republic, its overtly pro-American policies won it few supporters in the Latin American labor movement, and it soon began to lose influence in the region.[29] But there would be an important role for the AFL in the Mexican Revolution where Gompers would energetically oppose the growth of anarcho-syndicalism. Meanwhile, the corporate/AFL message of uplift through full participation in a market-driven society was reinforced by the efforts of Protestant missionaries and philanthropic institutions.

By the beginning of the twentieth century, most Protestants believed in the compatibility of Christianity and commerce. In fact Protestant missionaries were quite conscious of their role in the civilizing mission. They firmly believed that values such as self-discipline, thrift, and honesty, which they taught their converts, would prepare them for success in a market-driven society. They would thus assist those converts on the road to salvation and in the process create modern market societies with the same types of individual opportunities as their own modern Christian civilization.[30] The YMCA had wholeheartedly adopted the Social Gospel theme of reform with its educational and recreational programs, and it spread these ideas by creating facilities in such countries as Cuba, Mexico, and Peru. The programs of the Y helped inculcate values of individualism and competitiveness in young adults. The benefits of such training for U.S. business and U.S. interests in general were made abundantly clear by Delbert Haff, an official of the Phelps Dodge Corporation, who wrote that the Y "is creating a new and infinitely better young Mexican manhood. It is improving morals and physical standards. . . . Through its steadily increasing membership, [the YMCA] is actually Americanizing the Mexican youth."[31] Meanwhile, the Social Gospel had spawned a new and powerful disseminator of its ideas.

By the end of the 1920s, the Rockefeller Foundation had emerged as the dominant U.S. secular philanthropy in Latin America. The foundation grew directly out of the influence that the Reverend Frederick T. Gates had on John D. Rockefeller Sr. and reflected the principles of the Social Gospel. The foundation and other private philanthropies such as Carnegie and Ford also drew inspiration from Progressive reformers, who sought to do away with some of the most negative aspects of industrial corporations without radical upheaval in the existing capitalist order. Given their origin among the great corporate fortunes of America, it is hardly surprising that foundation managers mimicked corporate managers in striving for productivity improvements with their own efforts to rationalize social services and create a more efficient social order.[32] Their Latin American activities, such as the Rockefeller Foundation's campaigns to wipe out yellow fever in Veracruz and the Yucatan during the 1920s, represented not so much a defense of individual corporate interests as they did a concern for the stability of the international capitalist system and the growing role of the United States within it.[33] The Rockefeller Foundation expanded its Latin American public health initiatives throughout the 1920s, but by the end of the decade it began new programs specifically designed to upgrade medical schools.[34] The foundation attempted to create typical American professional institutions. At the same time, U.S. professionals were already hard at work reforming another aspect of Latin American societies.

The U.S. policy of Dollar Diplomacy in which the government regulated the finances of its overseas dependencies through guaranteed bank loans had spawned a group of private consultants on issues such as currency reform that included Charles A. Conant, Jeremiah Jenks, and Edwin Kemmerer. Their efforts helped define the new profession of economics and particularly the field of international finance.[35] Initially much of their work was carried out directly for the U.S. government, but by the mid-1920s the State Department, facing growing domestic and Latin American criticism over its interventionist policies in places like the Dominican Republic and Nicaragua, backed away from official endorsements of bank loans to Latin American governments. Yet Washington remained convinced that such loans promoted U.S. business in the region and maintained stability. Kemmerer provided an invaluable assist by undertaking a series of advising missions to countries such as Colombia and Chile that outlined reforms to be carried out in taxation, banking, and public administration that usually resulted in the hiring of U.S. economists to oversee the reforms. In turn, the reform program provided sufficient assurances to New York bankers to win additional financing for the governments involved.[36]

Economists like Kemmerer were more than financial technicians. They saw themselves as agents of the civilizing mission, an important part of which they believed could be accomplished through financial reform. Their basic strategy of creating stable international currencies and central banking institutions based on the gold standard would not only benefit New York banks but also open up the subject economies more fully to international market forces. In turn these specialists saw markets as moral forces that would instill the responsibility and discipline essential to a modern society.[37] Much like the "hunter" Teddy Roosevelt, new American professionals envisioned themselves as the rational, self-controlled male agents of civilization in Latin America. In her book *Financial Missionaries to the World*, Emily Rosenberg explains how economists like Kemmerer came to view themselves as manly reformers, instilling morality in other societies:

> Edward Kemmerer . . . exemplified this late Victorian "manly" ideal both in his professional career and in his role as an international financial advisor. . . .

> His conception of his own duties as a man clearly involved an income that could maintain dependents as well as nurture connections with other men in his upwardly mobile professional world. Indeed, a fear of monetary inflation and its consequences for social status were general concerns among new professionals. . . .

> Kemmerer's lifelong obsession with fighting inflation was thus closely linked to what he perceived to be the moral tenets of "manliness." Inflation, he believed, penalized hard work and savings while it rewarded careless people who made no provisions for the future. . . . He wanted to fashion a world of stable value, one which rewarded those who saved for the current and future support of dependents.[38]

Kemmerer did not believe that the people in former Spanish colonies exhibited the qualities of responsible males. After serving as an advisor to the U.S. occupation government in the Philippines, Kemmerer concluded, "Three centuries of Spanish rule 'had developed children, not independent self-reliant men.' Filipinos 'have yet to learn the lessons of political honesty, of thrift, and of self-reliance' and before achieving self-government had to embark upon 'the development of those sturdy moral values.'"[39] Most agents of Americanization shared Kemmerer's views, but there was not complete unanimity in their community.

Although the various groups that shared in the American civilizing mission had many common goals, it does not mean that their values were homogenous or that they always acted in perfect concert with one another. The AFL opposed corporations that remained vehemently antiunion and often criticized U.S. interventionist policies in places such as Mexico and the Dominican Republic. Some Protestant missionaries denounced the immoral behavior of U.S. entrepreneurs and managers in Latin America. Yet on the whole these agents of Americanization offered a fairly coherent and attractive vision of the American way to Latin Americans.

American corporate leaders along with their missionary, union, philanthropic, and professional allies offered an array of appealing possibilities to Latin Americans. U.S. productivity would improve efficiency and growth in their economies. American companies, missionaries, and philanthropies provided at least elementary education, health, and recreational services as well as popular entertainment and consumer goods. Economists like Kemmerer held out the prospect of a more stable, prosperous future under U.S. financial guidance. Not surprisingly, many Latin Americans welcomed the presence of these U.S agents. They were often captivated by the allure of the most modern of societies where there seemed equal opportunity for all to strive for and achieve a share in the "good life" of consumer bliss. Businessmen, labor leaders, missionaries, philanthropists, and economists presented a far more appealing version of the civilizing mission than did marine detachments and stiff-necked reformers like Leonard Wood. Yet among these influential groups, corporate America was quite capable of prompting just as much hostility as any U.S. expeditionary force.

RESISTANCE

Some of the grievances against U.S. enterprises had a familiar ring to Latin Americans because they involved loss of land. In Mexico, where U.S. companies acquired one hundred million acres of land during the three decades that Porfirio Díaz dominated the country, American corporations were now seen as spearheading the assault on peasant properties that had been going on throughout the Liberal era. In Central

America small growers and peasants resented the loss of land and the monopolistic control that the fruit companies had over the surviving independent planters. Even when loss of land proletarianized peasants, their longing for land did not subside. In 1923 when United Fruit workers went on strike in Guatemala, they seized farms belonging to the company and insisted they would not return them because they were the real owners.[40] For workers in mines and other industrial undertakings a different set of issues triggered their anti-Americanism.

As a part of the reform mission, U.S. mining companies sought to ensure ever-greater control over their workers in order to improve efficiency and thereby increase profits. By developing permanent workforces and employing phalanxes of timekeepers, supervisors, and engineers to monitor their labors, the corporations challenged the existing work processes in which gangs of miners worked together under the supervision of one of their own and the gambusino system in which the miners had taken a share of the ore in payment for their work. The companies' imposition of piecework systems instead of straight wages and the creation of complex pay scales designed to encourage competition among workers created further resentment. The workers viewed these devices, as well as social reforms including attempts to decrease social drinking, as attacks on their rights. In 1906 workers at the Cananea mine in Mexico went on strike over such issues. The local governor allowed Arizona rangers to cross the international border to enter his state, attack the workers, and crush the strike.[41] During the first three decades of the twentieth century these types of grievances would trigger a series of strikes against U.S. mining, petroleum, and shipping companies in Latin America. But the workers' resentment of American rationalization of the work process and wage issues were not the only triggers for such job actions and the growing anti-American sentiment.

The mission of corporations, churches, and foundations shared a common flaw with the larger civilizing mission of the American state—both private sector leaders and government policymakers believed in the fundamental inferiority of the people they had come to reform. Missionaries viewed Latin Americans as badly in need of moral regeneration and fit for no more than the vocational training programs prescribed for African Americans at home. The Rockefeller Foundation's efforts to upgrade medical systems reflected American biases about the inferiority of Latin American societies and a belief that the implementation of U.S. models represented the best solution for the region's problems.[42] But corporate managers far outdistanced their philanthropic colleagues in terms of the depths of their biases and the policies built on those prejudices.

The American corporate investment platforms from banana plantations to copper mines were as deeply imbued with American racism as the segregated Panama canal zone. Indeed many of the views that American managers held of their Latin American workers bore striking similarities to their views on African Americans. Cerro de Pasco managers could describe their workers as "sheep like" during periods of labor peace, but at times of unrest they denounced workers as violent and dangerous. Ralph Ingersoll, an engineer for the Phelps Dodge Company, expressed the most benign version of the American managerial viewpoint when he noted:

> It takes just four years to complete the Americanization of the
> Mexican—to teach him to bathe every day, to sleep in clean
> rooms with plenty of air, and to curb, in a measure, his ferocious
> appetite for spirits. Also it is an accepted fact that the results are
> highly satisfactory and that increased output goes hand in hand
> with physical and mental improvement.[43]

But there was nothing benign in the treatment generally meted out to Latin American workers. Latin Americans received a fraction of the wages paid to Americans employed at the same sites and doing the same work. U.S. companies much preferred to hire U.S. citizens for white-collar positions, even when Latin American professionals with U.S. university degrees were available. When they did secure employment, local professionals faced the same pay discrimination as their working-class brethren. Housing for married Latin American workers amounted to little more than shacks in most cases, while U.S. employees lived in bungalows with all the amenities of home. Local workers understood that they were to steer clear of the housing venues for American employees.[44] Nor were workers, peasants, and the middle class the only Latin Americans to take offense at their treatment by Americans.

The elites of Latin America shared many of the perspectives held by American agents of civilization. They too envisioned top-down policies that would ensure social stability and economic growth with an important role in the latter process for U.S. business. They also shared the Americans' disparaging attitudes toward their own mixed-race populations. Reflecting that consensus, governments from Mexico to Chile had fashioned policies designed to attract U.S. investment and loans. Yet if there was a consensus on certain aspects of the U.S. mission, there was by no means a whole-hearted embrace of the growing U.S. presence in the region.

Latin American elites often disparaged the crass materialism of Americans, contrasting it with what they felt were the more spiritual values of their own Hispanic culture, a position that had found resonance in the work of José Rodó. Latin American leaders had harshly criticized U.S. interventions and challenged U.S. ambitions to dominate the Western Hemisphere. There was also acute sensitivity to the economic domination that Americans often achieved. The Cerro de Pasco Corporation at one point found its operations blocked by Peruvian troops when it failed to reach an accommodation with a company controlled by prominent Peruvians. The Cerro de Pasco Corporation's problems would only disappear after it reached a $60 million settlement with the local firm.[45] In Mexico, members of the elite became restless in the face of competition from powerful U.S. companies that enjoyed vast capital resources and preferential treatment from the government in Mexico City. Resentment and fear of U.S. interventionism and the darker sides of U.S. corporate culture also stirred resentment among Mexico's peasants, workers, and middle class, thus launching one of the most powerful anti-American reactions in twentieth-century Latin America.

In 1911 revolutionary forces in Mexico toppled the United States's longtime ally Porfirio Díaz and plunged the country into years of armed conflict that jeopardized U.S. economic investments. Those events had prompted Woodrow Wilson to intervene in Veracruz in support of the Constitutionalist faction and against the groups led by Pancho Villa, Emiliano Zapata, and the workers' organization, the Casa de Obreros, which sought radical social and economic change and threatened U.S. interests. But even more moderate factions, such as the Constitutionalists led by Venustiano Carranza and Alvaro Obregón, did not prove entirely to the liking of the United States. The Constitution that they crafted in 1917 reflected the intense nationalism that helped drive the revolution as it created a strong central government and reestablished the nation's control of its subsoil rights that had been ceded to foreign companies. It also acknowledged the aspirations of peasants and workers. The Constitution, particularly Article 27, which reclaimed subsoil rights and opened the possibility of nationalization of U.S. property, became the central point of conflict between the United States and the new Mexican government.

When Obregón succeeded Carranza as president in 1920, the State Department refused to recognize his regime until it guaranteed U.S. property rights that existed before the revolution. Working in close association with the State Department, the International Committee of Bankers on Mexico, which represented large U.S. and European financial houses and corporations, blocked further credits to Mexico until the government recognized foreign property rights. In 1922 the committee reached an agreement with Mexico on its foreign debt, and the following year Obregón effectively assured the United States that Article 27 would not be implemented retroactively.[46] Diplomatic recognition followed soon after. The willingness of the corporate community and the State Department to reach an accommodation with Obregón derived largely from the awareness that his regime represented the one effective force against the mounting radicalism of Mexico's popular classes. Recognition brought a renewed flow of financing for the regime that would help bolster its efforts to combat popular unrest.

Despite the provisions of the 1917 Constitution, the revolutionary government did little to enact enabling legislation that would protect workers. Furthermore the regime seemed more interested in accommodating foreign bankers and corporations than in protecting workers and the national patrimony. During the 1920s, workers, usually with the support of local political figures, launched a growing number of strikes that shook Mexico, along with mounting job actions by white-collar employees and protests by consumers against rising utility rates. Although worker and consumer demands focused on economic issues, they also took a strong nationalistic tone, denouncing U.S. corporations and their exploitation of Mexicans. Furthermore, anarcho-syndicalists enjoyed increasing support in the labor movement especially among electrical, mine, and petroleum workers, who used anarchism's direct-action tactics to demand greater control over the work process. Mexican workers combined those ideas with a critique of the new revolutionary regime's willingness to accommodate U.S. interests to fashion a powerful message calling for social justice and presenting themselves as the true nationalists who would protect Mexico's wealth and curtail American corporate exploitation of Mexicans. Haunted by the fear of the labor movement and its message, U.S. government and corporate representatives proved anxious to support the new regime as their best protection. After Plutarco Calles succeeded Obregón in 1924, Calles made ever-greater efforts to bring the labor movement under state control and subordinate local political officials to Mexico City.[47]

Obregón and Calles enjoyed important support from the AFL in their struggle with radical labor movements. The conference that created PAFL in 1918 was held in Laredo, Texas, where Luis Morones of the recently formed Confederación Regional Obrera Mexicana (CROM) played an important part. Under Morones's leadership, the new Mexican labor federation would serve as a junior partner in PAFL and become an instrument of Mexican government policy, offering a business-union alternative to the expanding anarcho-syndicalist labor movement. Thus the AFL, with its covert funding from the Wilson administration, played an important part in U.S. efforts to curb the radicalism of the Mexican Revolution. The AFL would serve in that capacity time and again in Latin America in the decades ahead.[48] But if the United States had achieved a modus vivendi with the new rulers of Mexico, it was also clear that relations with Mexico had become far more complex than they had been during the Porfiriato. A whole range of social groups from the middle class and workers to the peasantry now wielded some degree of influence in Mexico, and whether through the mediation of the Mexican state or the direct actions of Americans, their nationalistic principles and their aspirations for a more equitable society would have to be addressed in some form. U.S. relations with other nations were becoming equally complex and problematic.

Although the marines had managed to suppress the peasant rebellion in the eastern region of the Dominican Republic in 1922, that did not mark the end of resistance to the U.S. occupation. Ever since the landing of the marines, Dominican nationalists had been campaigning in the United States, Europe, and throughout Latin America for an end to occupation. As a result, the State Department faced growing protests from governments and organizations in the Americas and Europe. The nationalists won the support of Samuel Gompers's American Federation of Labor, and by 1920 even most U.S. newspapers, which had heartily supported the occupation, now opposed it. In 1921, the United States made its first tentative offer of a gradual withdrawal. Continued pressures finally brought the installation of a provisional government in 1922 and the final U.S. withdrawal in September 1924.[49]

In the case of Haiti, the United States had encountered resistance not only from the armed cacos of the Haitian countryside but also from within the United States itself. James Weldon Johnson's articles in *The Nation* were only part of an ongoing campaign he and the NAACP waged against the U.S. occupation of the island nation. During the 1920s Johnson's efforts were complemented by a variety of anti-imperialist organizations in the United States. Those actions were further bolstered by Haitian political figures who lobbied for full independence. Despite these efforts and a long-standing commitment to leave Haiti by 1936, the American agents of empire, similar to Leonard Wood in Cuba, proved reluctant to prepare the Haitians for independence. That reluctance stemmed from the Americans' conviction that their black charges lacked the competence to manage their own affairs. W. W. Cumberland, who held the post of U.S. financial advisor to Haiti, reported, "In my four years experience in Haiti not a single Minister of Finance made *one single* constructive suggestion on any economic, commercial or financial subject."[50]

General John H. Russell, the U.S. high commissioner in Haiti, ran an authoritarian regime that repressed any serious signs of dissent. However, declining coffee prices that seriously damaged the national economy combined with local opposition to the U.S. occupation triggered a wave of strikes and protests during the closing months of 1929. During one protest, U.S. Marines opened fire on hundreds of angry peasants, killing at least twelve of them. The incident triggered new waves of criticism of the occupation both in the United States and overseas, which convinced the Hoover administration to speed the end of the Haitian occupation.[51] Washington finally withdrew from Haiti in 1934. But by then the United States had become embroiled in another and far-bloodier rebellion in its Nicaraguan protectorate.

For more than a decade after its initial intervention, the United States had unsuccessfully struggled to stabilize Nicaraguan politics by crafting a system that assured Conservative domination and Liberal exclusion. Finally in 1924 the Nicaraguan elite formulated a solution that held the promise of long-term stability. That year, a coalition of moderate Conservatives and Liberals succeeded in electing Carlos Solórzano as president. But the triumph was short lived as the hard-line Conservative Emiliano Chamorro rose in rebellion, ousting Solórzano in January 1926 and triggering a new rebellion by the Liberals. Damage to corporate investments and the danger that the U.S. reform program would collapse led the Coolidge administration to dispatch thousands of troops to Nicaragua in an effort to salvage those interests and shape the course of the Liberal-Conservative struggle in favor of the latter.

When Democratic senators and the United States press began to criticize this renewal of overt intervention, Secretary of State Frank Kellogg implied that Nicaragua might be the target of a Bolshevik plot, while Emiliano Chamorro suggested that his Liberal opponents were receiving support from Mexico and that both were acting in concert with Soviet Russia. With the interventionist part of the civilizing mission coming under increasing domestic criticism, the U.S. government and its Latin American allies now attributed the need for intervention to communist subversion, a message that would grow in intensity and frequency of use in the decades ahead.[52] In the short term, however, no justification could disguise the fact that repeated landings of marines had not resolved the conflict. Faced with that reality, the administration sent a special emissary, Colonel Henry Stimson, to negotiate a resolution. By May 1927 Stimson had managed to arrange a settlement, known as the Tipitapa or Espino Negro Accords, between the Liberal and Conservative forces. For Stimson, the agreement was the first step in his career as a major architect of the American empire and an icon to a generation of cold war statesmen. But to one Nicaraguan general, Augusto César Sandino, the accord offered renewed evidence of the ability of the United States to manipulate Nicaragua's elites and the nation's affairs.

Augusto Sandino, the illegitimate son of a moderately successful coffee planter, had fled his home after wounding a local politician during a violent argument. While in exile Sandino worked for several U.S. companies including the United Fruit Company in Guatemala and U.S. oil companies in Tampico and Veracruz, Mexico. His time in Mexico sensitized him to issues of U.S. domination and exposed him to the surge of Mexican nationalism during its revolution. Returning home when hostilities erupted between Liberals and Conservatives, Sandino carried with him a commitment to end U.S. interference in the affairs of his own country. When other Liberal generals accepted the U.S.-brokered peace, Sandino rejected it as another example of U.S. imperialism and the willingness of Nicaraguan politicians to accept the dictates of the State Department. He chose to return to where his career as a rebel had begun and to launch a new insurrection.

When he had first returned to Nicaragua, Sandino had worked for a few months at the U.S.-owned San Albino mine in the northern province of Nueva Segovia. Opting to join the Liberal uprising, he convinced several dozen of his fellow workers to join him and created his own rebel force. Now, having rejected the United States's latest intervention, he returned to Nueva Segovia to lead an armed insurrection. Sandino sought to rally followers around a set of ideas that combined anti-imperialism and nationalism with visions of a more just and equitable society. Those ideas had strong appeal to the peasantry of Nueva Segovia, who had been victimized by commercial coffee growers and mine owners. Themes of anti-Americanism and social justice would also appeal to workers in U.S. mines and plantations on the Caribbean coast.[53]

At first, the United States paid little heed to Sandino and began reducing its forces in Nicaragua after the Espino Negro Accords were reached. However, the guerrilla insurgency in Nueva Segovia soon forced Washington to reverse course and begin increasing force levels to nearly six thousand troops. Much as in the Dominican Republic, the marines, assisted by the U.S.-trained and -equipped Nicaraguan National Guard, faced a long, hard slog in the Nicaraguan countryside where both sides would engage in murderous acts of violence. As in the earlier occupations of Haiti and the Dominican Republic, the marines carried with them a paternalistic sense of mission, believing that they were obliged to bring stability and order to people of limited maturity who were prone to violence. And once again that perspective provided the justification for violence that included summary executions and torture. Although such acts only exacerbated anti-Americanism in the countryside, they did not prevent the marines from confining the insurgency to northern Nicaragua.[54]

Sandino's message of anti-Americanism and social justice resonated with the wageworkers of the Caribbean coast and the free peasants of Nueva Segovia, who had been faced with loss of land and rights. But it did not have the same appeal for the large majority of the country's rural residents, who lived in western Nicaragua. Most of these people had little if any exposure to Americans and either squatted on public or private lands or worked as tenants on large estates. Those realities, and the ability of the marines and Guardia to confine Sandino militarily, limited the influence of Sandinismo. However, Sandino's movement remained a major challenge to the United States and its mission. Sandino's ability to survive and resist raised doubts about the invincibility of the military machine that ensured U.S. domination in the circum-Caribbean. As the State Department's international economist William Cumberland reported:

> Formerly United States Marines were considered by the Nicaraguans as invincible. That reputation has for the moment been superseded by open contempt for the inability of American forces, with all modern equipment to capture the bandits adhering to Sandino, though the latter are greatly outnumbered.[55]

Sandino's influence extended beyond his own country and Central America. The U.S. effort to crush the Sandinista movement prompted bitter criticism of U.S. interventionism by delegates from a number of Latin American countries at the 1928 Pan-American Conference in Havana. The communist-supported Anti-Imperialist League campaigned on behalf of Sandino, as did the Peruvian populist Raúl Haya de la Torre. Within the United States anti-imperialist organizations also derided Washington for its ongoing military intervention in Nicaragua. In Washington, Senator John Blaine proposed an amendment that would prohibit the use of force to protect U.S. overseas investments, and Senator Gerald P. Nye denounced the administration for "helping to crucify a people in Nicaragua merely because Americans have gone there with dollars to invest." But Sandino's greatest challenge to U.S. interests lay in the vision that he expounded.[56]

In formulating his critique of U.S. imperialism and the inequities of Nicaraguan society, Sandino, much like Mexican workers before him, had depicted the United States and its domestic supporters as evil allies who had betrayed the nation. That vision represented a powerful alternative to the vision of U.S. agents of empire and Latin American elites.

Their shared mission of civilization was to be achieved by rapid capitalist development in a stable environment that would be assured by the exercise of force either by the elite or by the United Sates. Soon these alternative visions of Mexican popular nationalism and Sandinismo would sweep through the region, inspiring mass movements and political upheaval throughout much of Latin America.

The explosive growth in movements that would challenge the power of the United States and domestic elites was driven in part by a little-noticed economic trend at the time Sandino began his insurgency. The massive outpouring of capital and technology by industrial countries designed to improve the production and transportation of primary goods such as mining and agricultural products had succeeded far beyond expectations, and those products were now pouring into the world market at an astonishing rate. The prices of coffee, sugar, copper, and other staples of the Latin American economies were falling precipitously, and with them the ability of these countries to pay back the hundreds of millions of dollars they had borrowed overseas. That problem combined with a crisis in the international financial system would send the Great Depression sweeping across Latin America, collapsing economies, toppling governments, and triggering popular movements that combined the themes of nationalism, anti-imperialism, and the struggle for equality into a compelling critique of elite rule and U.S. dominance.

∾

By the early twentieth century there was already growing concern throughout Latin American societies that the American project contained within it the goal of U.S. domination. Those concerns helped spur anti-imperialism and a variety of literary as well as political attempts to redefine Latin American identity and Latin American nationalism, at least in part as a reaction against the power and materialist culture of the United States. Latin Americans from powerful elites to peasants reacted to the loss of economic opportunities when U.S. companies came to command critical sectors of their national economies, displacing local capitalists, overwhelming small entrepreneurs, subjecting workers to the rigors of modern industrial practices, and depriving peasants of land. Furthermore, no matter how idealistic some of the agents of empire might be, the American civilizing mission contained within it a vision of Latin Americans as racially inferior beings in need of uplift.

These mounting concerns helped trigger movements such as the Mexican Revolution and Sandinismo that merged concerns about social and economic inequalities with an anti-American nationalism that held both the elites and the United States accountable for those inequities and the losses of economic and political sovereignty that Latin Americans had suffered. In the 1920s the agents of the imperial mission found themselves under siege by revolutionary upheaval, guerrilla insurgency, and internal as well as domestic critics of imperialism. Those critics included Smedley Butler whose disparaging attitude toward U.S. businesses' role in the American empire intensified. He later wrote, "I spent 33 years and 4 months in active service . . . and during that period I spent most of my time being a high-class muscle man for Big Business, Wall Street and the bankers. In short, I was a racketeer for capitalism."[57] By then, a broad-based anti-imperialist movement had challenged the policy of intervention and protectorates. Anti-imperialism at home, unrest in Latin America, and the devastating blows of the Great Depression would force U.S. political and corporate leaders to rethink and reshape their version of the civilizing mission in order to survive the maelstrom that engulfed them after 1929.

CHAPTER FIVE

FROM DEPRESSION TO WAR, 1929–1945

O𝚗 𝚃𝚑𝚎 𝚊𝚏𝚝𝚎𝚛𝚗𝚘𝚘𝚗 𝚘𝚏 M𝚊y 7, 1933, S𝚞𝚖𝚗𝚎𝚛 W𝚎𝚕𝚕𝚎s, 𝚝𝚑𝚎 𝚗𝚎𝚠 U.S. ambassador to Cuba and a good friend of President Franklin Roosevelt, disembarked from a United Fruit liner in Havana harbor to be greeted wharfside by Cuban government officials. Given the location and Welles's patrician bearing, not unlike the ramrod posture of a military officer, the event might have been mistaken for a reenactment of General Leonard Wood's arrival more than three decades earlier. But the circumstances surrounding the two events could not have been more different. Wood had arrived as the all-powerful military governor of a conquered Cuba, intent on transforming it into a replica of his own Anglo-Saxon homeland. Welles arrived as the power structures that Wood had crafted were teetering on the brink of collapse, and the specter of social revolution was haunting the island's rulers. Sugar prices had fallen to historic lows, devastating the nation's principal industry and source of foreign exchange. The state was effectively bankrupt, salvaged only by emergency bridge loans from U.S. banks that allowed the regime of President

Gerardo Machado to meet payment obligations on the tens of millions of dollars it had previously borrowed. The collapse of sugar prices was also shredding the powerful economic bonds that the United States had forged with the island. Cuban exports to the United States had fallen 80 percent since 1924, and American imports had declined by more than 85 percent. Economic catastrophe combined with the oppressive policies of the U.S.-backed Machado regime triggered the formation of a series of middle-class opposition groups determined to topple the president from power. The regime's practice of murdering political dissidents prompted the creation of the student-based organization, ABC, which responded in kind by assassinating government political figures and senior police officials. Massive unemployment and the payment of starvation wages led to a strike by twenty thousand sugar workers that crippled nearly one-third of the mills in Cuba.[1]

Roosevelt had sent Welles on a mission to preserve U.S. economic dominance, salvage some version of the U.S.-crafted political order, and fend off the more drastic consequences of the social unrest that now swept the island. Yet both men knew that past U.S. practices, which would have already dictated military intervention, were no longer assured of success. A new, more subtle approach would be attempted and applied not only in Cuba but throughout the region. The island nation was by no means the only such challenge facing the United States in the 1930s. The devastating effects of the Great Depression were sweeping across Latin America, wrecking havoc with national economies and U.S. corporate investment, undermining faith in the U.S. civilizing mission, exacerbating existing anti-Americanism, and triggering upheavals similar to the one in Cuba. And even as policymakers grappled with these problems, new challenges arose as World War II accentuated the danger of growing fascist influence in Latin America. The years encompassing the Great Depression and the Second World War would witness a major restructuring of U.S. policies toward the region with the intention of preserving American dominance and pursuing an ever-more-ambitious version of the American mission. Along the way, U.S. intellectuals and policymakers would redefine the civilizing mission, downplaying assumptions about Latin Americans' racial inferiority and U.S. superiority. In their place they would substitute images of a partnership among the republics of the Americas in a common project of economic development and antifascism.

ॐ

The immediate causes of the global economic debacle that threatened the power of the United States in the Americas can be traced to the decade immediately preceding the Wall Street collapse. The United States emerged from World War I not only as the world's leading industrial power but as its financial center. The banking institutions of New York City such as National City Bank and J. P. Morgan, already important players in international lending, now became the decisive force in world finance. In the decade after the war, New York financial houses not only lent $1.5 billion to Latin American governments but also extended billions of dollars of credit to sustain Germany as it struggled to rebuild and pay off the huge war indemnities imposed on it by the victorious allies. Through the early twenties, this process seemed to fuel healthy growth in the world economy as more efficient production and transportation technologies allowed primary products producers to pour more and cheaper exports into the world market. But by the second half of the decade that flood of goods was forcing down world prices and endangering the ability of Latin American nations to make their debt payments. When the New York stock market crashed in October 1929, it set off a nationwide panic, triggering business failures and drying up foreign lending by banks. The loss of external loans set off a collapse in the German economy—one of the world's largest—and soon forced Latin American nations to default on their mounting foreign debt. The German collapse combined with the panic in the United States and the debt crisis in Latin America sent the world economy into depression. After 1929 the machinery of capitalist growth seemed to be grinding to a halt, threatening to undermine global economic and political stability.[2]

Although industrialized nations generally suffered less severely in the Great Depression due to self-sufficient economies that could meet both industrial and agricultural needs, the United States endured some of the worst blows of the Depression. In addition to the collapse of businesses and banks, American consumers, now an important force in the economy, began defaulting on an array of debt used to buy products ranging from cars to washing machines, exacerbating the effects of the Depression. Industrial production in the United States fell by one-third between 1929 and 1932, and the number of unemployed soared from 1.5 million to more than 12 million. Prospects for domestic recovery remained bleak, and there was scant hope on the international scene where global trade fell 60 percent and international lending 90 percent.[3] Little wonder that many people believed they might be witnessing the collapse of capitalism and the end of liberal political institutions. Millions of Americans threw their support to more radical political movements including the Socialist and Communist Parties and Senator Huey Long's populist movement. In the midst of this crisis, America's economic elites found themselves deeply divided over the course of action to rescue the nation's economic and political institutions.

Since 1896 a coalition of big business and the Republican Party had dominated the U.S. political scene. Corporate interests representing sectors such as the steel, textile, and shoe industries joined with the Republicans to shape national economic policies that emphasized minimalist government, a strong dollar, and high protectionist tariffs to safeguard the U.S. market for domestic manufacturers. However, by the 1920s fast-growing corporations in oil, electrical generation, and auto manufacturing began challenging this economic orthodoxy. Leaders of firms such as Standard Oil and General Electric recognized that unlike the labor-intensive firms that had long dominated the domestic economic terrain, their capital-intensive industries enjoyed technological advantages, which would allow them to compete successfully in global markets. High tariffs represented a major disincentive to such a strategy. Another point of contention stemmed from the fact that high labor costs of traditional industries led both these companies and the government to pursue antilabor policies. Leaders of capital-intensive enterprises, for whom labor represented a much lower portion of their costs, were more willing to seek some accommodation with unions. These differences over policymaking took on growing significance and urgency as the Depression threatened the foundations of American social and economic stability.

After the election of Franklin Roosevelt in 1932, a coalition of economic and political forces began to form around the president that would address the most pressing challenges of the Great Depression. Together the Democrats, executives from capital-intensive industries, and leaders of large labor unions ensured social stability through domestic social welfare and labor polices such as the Social Security system and the Wagner Act, which gave government support to collective bargaining. Influenced by Keynesian economics that stressed the expenditure of state revenues to promote economic growth, the federal government launched a broad-ranging program of public works projects to resuscitate the national economy. In addition, this coalition utilized reciprocal trade treaties and the federal Export Import (EXIM) Bank, which financed international commerce to pursue an aggressive internationalism designed to reinvigorate trade and promote the overseas interests of capital-intensive firms. As the initiatives indicate, these new policies also meant a dramatically expanded role for the federal government in both domestic and international affairs.[4] State powers were further enhanced when the government harnessed the economic might of the nation to fight a total war against the Axis powers between 1941 and 1945.

The key to the alliance that guided the United States through the Depression and war was its ability to articulate a social, economic, and political paradigm that focused on the concept of productivity. The stress on the ability to achieve ever-greater levels of economic efficiency welded the business-labor alliance together through the belief, as Charles Maier noted, "that the United States could enjoy productive abundance without radical redistribution of economic power."[5] Furthermore, efforts by business and government to combat the Depression and win the war not only brought business leaders into state agencies but also created a consensus on the use of interventionist planning as a critical means to achieve productivity improvements and to create a more stable form of capitalist development.[6] The broad alliance now had an ideology focused on a planned capitalist process, which would achieve economic growth and general prosperity while avoiding class conflict. It was an ideology that would be extended into foreign affairs as the basis for rebuilding Germany and Japan and would strongly influence the American mission to Latin America. Furthermore, the enhanced wartime powers of the federal government would not dissipate, but rather grow after 1945.

During this era the U.S. government took on the characteristics of what Emily Rosenberg has described as the "regulatory state." In addition to the creation of the EXIM Bank, the Roosevelt administration established the Office of Inter-American Affairs (OIAA) that engaged in activities ranging from propaganda to technical assistance, and later the Truman administration created the Point Four foreign-aid program.

With the state now playing an enhanced role in U.S. interactions with Latin America, the various agents of the American mission including businesses, foundations, unions, and missionaries exhibited numerous instances of close cooperation among themselves and a number of striking crossovers in terms of personnel especially between corporations, foundations, and government agencies. Although they hardly operated in lockstep, these agents of Americanization would demonstrate significant similarities in terms of their goals and the means they used to achieve them. The intensified attention that Latin America received from the United States was justified in the face of a series of Latin American challenges to U.S. dominance generated by the Depression, war, and labor militancy.

The Great Depression did not suddenly strike Latin America in 1929 because many of the region's economies had been suffering since the mid-1920s from declining prices for their exports and increasingly unmanageable debt burdens. But those difficult times hardly prepared these nations for the devastating blows of the global economic collapse. With prices for their export products going into free fall, the value of exports from many Latin American economies fell by 50 percent or more between 1928 and 1932. The prices of imports were also falling, but they did not decline as fast, thus severely curtailing the ability to import products and pay off foreign debts. After 1931, almost all Latin American governments defaulted on their international obligations.[7]

The massive unemployment and growing social unrest triggered by economic collapse undermined the liberal elite governments that had dominated national politics for decades. From El Salvador to Argentina, Latin American militaries toppled civilian regimes and imposed dictatorial rule. At the same time, the economic disaster gave new energy to populist and nationalist movements such as Victor Haya de la Torre's APRA movement in Peru and Getúlio Vargas's Estado Novo in Brazil. Although larger Latin American countries had already made some headway toward industrialization, they now sought to accelerate that process and decrease dependence on foreign goods by restricting imports and initiating government programs to promote industrialization. Such strategies did not exclude foreigners from establishing or investing in domestic industry, but many Latin American governments imposed new taxes and regulations on foreign corporations. The most striking example of the new economic nationalism came in 1938 when Mexico's president, Lázaro Cárdenas, nationalized U.S. and British oil companies. The effects of the Depression, the hostility of populist political movements, and the challenges of nationalist economic policies made the 1930s a difficult period for U.S. business in the region. Eventually recovery for local economies and improved prospects for American corporations came with the outbreak of World War II.

Depression, Rebellion, and Nationalism

As President Herbert Hoover struggled to cope with the unraveling of the national and international economies, he also had to address a Latin American problem inherited from the era of U.S. imperialist ventures in the circum-Caribbean. As of May 1929, the United States still had more than three thousand marines in Nicaragua to counter the threat from Augusto Sandino's insurgency. The U.S. forces and the American-trained National Guard had managed to confine Sandino to the northern reaches of Nicaragua, but they had not defeated him. At the same time, the financial burdens of the Great Depression and the mounting domestic and international criticism of the U.S intervention finally pushed Hoover's secretary of state, Henry Stimson, to announce that the complete withdrawal of U.S. forces would take place after Nicaragua's 1932 presidential election. With the departure of the marines, Sandino negotiated a ceasefire with the new president only to be assassinated by Anastasio Somoza, the U.S.-backed commander of the National Guard.[8] But well before Sandino's tragic end, Hoover and other policymakers had come to recognize the soaring costs of intervention. The Nicaraguan nationalist coalition of peasants and workers that had challenged both their own elite and the United States had proven a formidable opponent, costing the United States dearly in terms of lives and treasure. It was not the only such challenge that Washington faced in the region.

Peruvian President Augusto Leguía's resignation in August 1930 typified the changes sweeping Latin America as the Great Depression sent shock waves through the region's economic and political institutions. Through eleven years of autocratic rule, Leguía had served as a close ally of the Unites States, relying on American corporate investments and bank loans to fund economic growth. As that system was collapsing around

him, Peruvians mobilized to end his regime and attack the alliance that
had underpinned it. In the months after the president's resignation, tens
of thousands of workers at the Andean mines of the U.S.-owned Cerro
de Pasco Corporation went on strike, attacked company property, and
demanded radical changes in the way the corporation did business.

The workers' campaign, expressed in nationalist rhetoric, denounced
American exploitation of Peruvians and enjoyed widespread support
from elements of the middle class including many white-collar employees of the company, local merchants, and government officials. Much as
in Mexico and Nicaragua, the American mission had brought disparate groups together with a common sense of identity rooted in their
opposition to that mission. If these events had transpired in an earlier
time, and within the circum-Caribbean, they might well have triggered
U.S. military intervention. But with U.S. interests under siege in much
of Latin America, and often in South American countries that lay far
from American shores, the Hoover administration crafted an alternate
response. Secretary of State Stimson informed the Peruvian government that it would receive no help in resolving its debts to the financial
house J. W. Seligman unless troops were used to suppress the workers.
With Peruvian soldiers moving into the mining camps, the Cerro de
Pasco managers dealt a second and telling blow to the labor movement by
shutting down the mines for a month. Yet the suppression of the miners
hardly brought peace for U.S. corporate interests as oil workers attacked
Standard Oil's International Petroleum Company and female phone
operators struck against ITT in Peru.[9] By 1933 forces similar to those
in Peru were challenging U.S. predominance in the country where the
American imperial mission had begun more than three decades earlier.

The revolutionary forces that swept Cuba in 1933 brought out in
stark relief the nature of the challenge to U.S. dominance in Latin
America. Nowhere had Americans pursued their civilizing mission
with greater energy; nowhere had American penetration been deeper
or more profound. Leonard Wood had shaped Cuba's political institutions and Washington provided the all-important seal of approval
required for any Cuban regime to survive. Corporate America dominated the island's trade, international finances, and major economic
sectors. American culture from telephones and automobiles to baseball
permeated Cuban society. After President Gerardo Machado's hasty

departure from the island in August, a loose coalition of working- and middle-class groups struggled to topple the remnants of the old political order and challenged American hegemony on all fronts. Although American culture had contributed to Cubans' sense of national identity as they distinguished themselves from their colonial past, the revolutionaries gave expression to another aspect of that identity—a nationalism that rejected both U.S. economic and political domination, and American racism that relegated them to the status of second-class citizens in their own country.

On dozens of American-owned sugar plantations workers rose up and seized the properties, expelling the U.S. managers and raising the black and red flags of anarchism and communism. Workers at General Electric's AFP power plants organized unions and work stoppages and demanded greater worker control over the enterprise. Both AFP and ITT faced mounting consumer protests over their rates, which were considerably higher than those charged in the United States. Although some of the demands by workers and white-collar employees involved basic wage demands raised to a level of absolute necessity by the Depression, their agenda proved far broader than economic concerns. Both workers and employees gave vent to their deep-seated resentment of American economic domination and the demeaning attitude of U.S. managers toward Cubans, as well as their attempts to Americanize Cuban employees with required courses in English and policies designed to stress competitiveness. Workers also demanded greater control over their industries to fight job loss and the work-speed-up campaigns that were part of corporate productivity strategies.

President Ramón Grau San Martín, a reformist university professor who had come to power as a result of his membership in a civil military junta, was attempting to cope with these upheavals that shook the country. In an effort to mollify workers and the middle class, as well as address the desperate economic conditions in the country, Grau San Martín instituted a set of reforms, establishing the eight-hour workday, legalizing unions, requiring that Cubans comprise at least 50 percent of the workforce in every company, and ordering AFP to reduce its rates. When AFP refused to resolve differences with its workers, Grau San Martín seized the company's plants and placed the workers in charge of operating them.[10]

Although Cuba's small Communist Party proved slow in recognizing the revolution that was taking place around it, Ambassador Sumner Welles saw in the unfolding events a communist design and the worst kind of radicalism. In the ambassador's eyes, Grau San Martín and his government were communist sympathizers who were leading Cuba down the path of revolution. The events in Cuba sorely tested Welles and his mentor, the newly elected Franklin Roosevelt, who was determined to expand on Hoover's nonintervention strategy and who had already made reference to a "Good Neighbor Policy."[11] At Welles's suggestion Roosevelt refused to recognize the new government, assuring that there would be no short-term solution to Cuba's international debt crisis. Roosevelt rejected the ambassador's call for military intervention, but the president did agree to encircle the island with thirty U.S. warships. Welles then began courting Fulgencio Batista, the leader of the Cuban armed forces. He made it clear to Batista that the Grau San Martín regime would never receive diplomatic recognition and that the threat of U.S. military intervention still existed. Those warnings helped convince Batista to force Grau San Martín to resign in early January 1934, replacing him with a handpicked successor who quickly won U.S. approval and then signed a reciprocal trade agreement with the United States.[12]

The events in Cuba clearly defined the initial significance of the Good Neighbor Policy. The United States would forgo direct intervention in Latin American countries except under the most extraordinary conditions. But the United States was not abandoning its dominant position in the region or its efforts to enhance that position. Instead, new tactics had been tested and proven effective. The denial of recognition in Cuba amounted to an international financial blockade on the Grau San Martín regime—an expanded version of the financial pressure Hoover had placed on the Peruvian government. While no overt intervention took place, the threat of intervention helped push the military to act against Grau San Martín. And Welles's relationship with Batista demonstrated the tactic of winning over or pressuring key domestic actors to accomplish U.S. goals without resorting to military force. Yet, over time, the policy proved to be more than just a new set of tactics that accomplished the same goals as landing U.S. Marines.

In the face of the fraying of economic ties that had bound much of Latin America to the United States and the rising tide of Latin American nationalism, often expressed as anti-Americanism, the Roosevelt admin- istration showed considerable tolerance for the policies of nationalist regimes. The administration demonstrated restraint when the government of Mexican president Lázaro Cárdenas launched a land reform initiative that led to the seizure of U.S.-owned property. Washington also offered a relatively subdued response to the Bolivian government's nationaliza- tion of Standard Oil's interests in 1937. As Laurence Duggan, the State Department Political Advisor made clear, the administration expected corporate America to exhibit similar restraint in dealing with Latin American economic nationalism. He commented in regard to Chile where U.S. corporate interests faced mounting hostility in the 1930s that U.S. companies would have "to give sympathetic and intelligent consideration to the necessities and demands of labor and the Chilean government and to endeavor to work out harmonious solutions so far as possible before prob- lems reach critical phases."[13] The new approach was most severely tested in 1938, when Mexico nationalized U.S. oil companies.

Serious problems had been brewing between Mexican workers and U.S. petroleum firms since 1936. At the heart of the dispute lay two demands by the workers for a substantial wage increase and the incorpo- ration of almost all corporate employees into the union. When the petro- leum companies rejected these demands, the Mexican Supreme Court ruled in favor of the union. At that point the corporations announced their willingness to make the wage concessions but refused the demand on unionization, knowing that it would give the workers effective control over their operations. In March 1938, when the corporations defied the Supreme Court ruling, President Cárdenas nationalized them.

Initially, Washington took aggressive action, canceling its purchases of Mexican silver that had pumped vital U.S. dollars into the Mexican economy. But the administration soon drew back from that position. After three years of resisting corporate pressure for harsh measures against Mexico, Washington accepted an arrangement that offered the oil companies a fraction of the money they claimed they were owed, in return for guarantees of new U.S. financial assistance to Mexico.[14] Roosevelt's reluctance to exert intense pressure on Mexico stemmed in part from his anger over the exorbitant compensation demanded by the companies. But it also reflected a dawning realization that although Cárdenas and his predecessor had at times been denounced by American corporate executives and politicians as "Bolsheviks," the Mexican revolutionary elite actually shared much in common with their American counterparts.

Despite Cárdenas's nationalization of oil interests, his subsequent creation of a national oil company signaled his rejection of worker control and made it clear that the oil industry would be managed much like any modern corporation. As U.S. Ambassador Josephus Daniels noted, the oil workers "thereby saw vanish what they thought [had] been one of their principal points gained by developments in the last two years i.e. control of the industry."[15] Furthermore, Cárdenas categorically rejected similar attempts to assert worker control in U.S.-owned mining and electric power companies. The Roosevelt administration was discovering that economic nationalists in Mexico and elsewhere were asserting the right to tax, regulate, and in a few cases nationalize U.S. corporations, but they were above all else concerned with economic development and fully expected corporate America to play a part in that process. That continuing receptivity to U.S. trade and investment was crucial to Roosevelt's plans for economic recovery.

Reviving international trade and investment were critical parts of Roosevelt's efforts to lift the national economy out of the Depression and to aid the capital-intensive industries whose leaders had allied themselves with his New Deal. As a region where the United States had achieved a dominant position in trade and investment, and where Germany had been making serious inroads, Latin America was the logical starting point to launch that revival. In addition to creating the EXIM Bank, Washington negotiated a series of reciprocal trade agreements with Latin American countries. These initiatives were clearly designed to provide an advantage to U.S. business and reassert American economic power. For example, trade agreements and loans made after the fall of Grau San Martín bound Cuba more completely than ever before to the U.S. economy and extinguished Cuban nationalists' hopes for economic independence.[16] While larger nations in the region could resist such one-sided arrangements, most of them would find their economies tied far more closely to the United States than ever before. Meanwhile, the EXIM Bank, in addition to financing trade with Latin America, began extending development loans to Mexico and other nations. Although the new initiatives of the Roosevelt administration do not fully account for the change, the fact is that trade between the United States and Latin America doubled during the first four years of the Good Neighbor Policy. Improved economic ties and improved relations based on a greater tolerance for Latin American nationalism proved critical once war engulfed Europe.

The growing threat from Nazi Germany played an important part in influencing U.S. policy toward Latin America, even before war erupted in Europe in 1939. Roosevelt's relatively tolerant policy toward the Mexican and Bolivian oil nationalizations reflected in part a desire to maintain friendly relations with a region that would be a vital source of raw materials in the event the United States became involved in a European war. In anticipation of that need, the administration authorized the creation of government sponsored corporations that signed purchasing agreements with Latin American countries for strategic materials such as tin, copper, and rubber, assuring the United States of a steady flow of these products and guaranteeing prices for the producers.[17] Once the war erupted, most Latin American countries, cognizant of the importance of the United States to their economies, broke diplomatic relations with the Axis powers.

During the 1930s Brazil was able to take advantage of Washington's anxious efforts to secure its supply lines for raw materials from South America. Under Getúlio Vargas, the populist leader who ruled with the backing of the military, Brazil played Germany and the United States against each other as it negotiated trade agreements with both powers. However, after the war broke out, Washington upped the stakes by providing funding for Brazil's Volta Redonda steel plant, which marked a major step forward for Brazilian industrialization. From that point forward, Brazil tilted sharply toward the United States and would even send troops to fight alongside the allies in Europe.[18] But perhaps the most concerted effort to bind Latin America more closely to the United States can be seen in Roosevelt's creation of the Office of Inter-American Affairs (OIAA), and his appointment of Nelson Rockefeller, one of the heirs to the Rockefeller-Standard Oil fortune, to head that agency.

During a visit to Latin America in 1937, Rockefeller became convinced that U.S. corporations including Standard Oil had to adopt more progressive policies, addressing the needs of their workers and adjusting to the realities of economic nationalism. At the same time, Rockefeller remained convinced that Latin America's development depended on opening its economies more fully to global forces, especially the influence of U.S. companies. Such views harmonized with the basic principles of the Good Neighbor Policy, and Rockefeller had in fact proposed the creation of the OIAA to the president as a way of promoting pro-American values in Latin America. Although the OIAA did sponsor a certain number of cultural exchanges, it focused much of its attention on influencing the press, radio, and cinema in the region.

Using OIAA subsidized shipments of scarce newsprint as a bargaining tool, Rockefeller managed to insert pro-American stories and images in more than twelve hundred Latin American newspapers and magazines. The OIAA also banned the export of U.S. films that it considered potentially offensive to Latin American audiences and convinced producers to make deletions or changes in other movies. The agency also worked with filmmakers to craft images that would promote a sense of hemispheric solidarity; films such as Disney's *Saludos Amigos* and *The Three Caballeros* provided a scenic tour of Latin America and depicted comic dialogue between Donald Duck and a Brazilian parrot named Joe Carioca. In addition, the OIAA produced its own Spanish-language news and informational films. It supplied transcripts and short programs to radio stations throughout Latin America, as well as blanketing the region with shortwave radio broadcasts. Much of the radio programming, like the films, mixed samplings of American popular culture with pro-American and anti-Nazi messages. The agency encouraged U.S. corporations to continue advertising even when wartime shortages made it difficult for them to supply their products to Latin America. It also offered tax incentives to those firms whose advertising clearly supported U.S. war efforts. Not satisfied with simply beaming messages to Latin America through various mediums, the OIAA commissioned public opinion surveys to better understand the interests and reactions of local audiences to various forms of media and entertainment.[19] The federal government was now taking a much more direct role in spreading the ideas of the American mission by directly promoting the positive aspects of American values and popular culture. Nor did the OIAA limit its efforts to media messages.

Patterning his efforts after his family's foundation, Rockefeller offered technical assistance programs. Just as the Rockefeller Foundation did, the OIAA reviewed proposals from various countries and then contracted with private agencies or corporations to carry out the approved projects. In a direct mimicking of the foundation, the agency sponsored initiatives to improve food production and public health. Not all these efforts were strictly philanthropic in their intent. The OIAA sponsored studies on the production of tropical products such as rubber and geological surveys designed to map mineral deposits such as manganese and tin—products vital to the U.S. war effort.[20] The OIAA also reached back to past U.S. policy initiatives as it forged ties with the American Federation of Labor. Rockefeller, much like Woodrow Wilson, was anxious to promote business unions that would focus on wage and hour issues as opposed to the broader agenda including social and political concerns favored by most Latin American labor movements.

The range of the OIAA's activities under Rockefeller demonstrated the vastly expanded role of the state in promoting the American mission in Latin America. But beyond that, Rockefeller and many of those associated with him personified the convergence of interests among the various agents of that mission. Rockefeller's business background reflected the increased involvement of corporate leaders directly in state policymaking. For example, besides Rockefeller, William L. Clayton of the Texas-based Anderson Clayton Corporation, which dealt in Latin American agricultural products, not only assisted Rockefeller at the OIAA but also served as the assistant secretary of state for economic affairs. The influence of philanthropic agencies can be seen in the career of Albion Patterson, a Princeton graduate and Rockefeller protégé, who worked for the Institute for Inter-American Affairs (IIAA), a Rockefeller-inspired government corporation designed originally to support health services and agricultural development. After leaving the IIAA, Patterson went on to head U.S. government agricultural assistance missions in several Latin American countries. Throughout his government career Patterson consulted with Rockefeller Foundation officials and patterned his health and agricultural development programs along the lines of the foundation's practices. And Serafinao Romauldi, an OIAA staff member in its labor division, later served the AFL as an organizer and worked closely with the U.S. government to craft a probusiness labor federation in Latin America after the war. Yet while such career patterns reflect a convergence of interests, it is also true that these nongovernmental organizations also were actively pursuing their own versions of the American mission during these years.

Agents of the Mission

On January 11, 1932, Chile's working and middle classes staged a general strike, denouncing their own elite for conceding control of the nation's nitrate and copper wealth to foreigners and holding both groups responsible for the nation's desperate economic condition. The protestors demanded the immediate dissolution of COSACH, a joint venture between the Guggenheim Brothers and the Chilean government that now held monopoly control over the nation's nitrate industry. The dismantling of COSACH became the central theme of the next presidential election, and by early 1933 the new president, Arturo Alessandri, had set about dissolving the corporation. One American diplomat noted the positive effect of the process concluding, "We are no longer conscious of Chilean mobs howling for the blood of American industrialists."[21]

With COSACH already teetering on the verge of bankruptcy due to the effects of the Depression, the Guggenheim Brothers witnessed the demise of a scheme that they once believed would make them rich beyond their wildest dreams and the permanent decline of their once-powerful global mining empire. The Guggenheims' Chilean debacle typified the experience of many American corporate leaders as their enterprises were battered by both the effects of the Depression and the increasing rage of Latin Americans at their own elites and U.S. entrepreneurs who only a few short years earlier had promised a future of perpetual prosperity.

Economic statistics outlined the decline of U.S. business in Latin America during the Great Depression. The value of U.S. direct investments, which totaled $3.7 billion in 1929, stood at only $3 billion in 1940, despite several years of renewed economic growth. Beginning in 1931 Latin American governments defaulted on $1 billion in loans from U.S. financial institutions and private investors.[22] It would take two decades of wrangling, negotiations, and write-downs of the loans to resolve the problem. But even such numbers cannot convey the devastation inflicted on U.S. corporations and on Latin American societies.

The Phelps Dodge Company, one of the largest mining enterprises in Mexico, shuttered its operations in 1931, sending thousands of workers fleeing across the countryside in a desperate search for employment. Although Phelps Dodge would eventually reopen its facilities, dozens of other smaller U.S. mining companies failed completely. In Chile, the Anaconda and Kennecott copper companies, after investing more than

$200 million to develop their mines, saw the value of their production fall from $111 million in 1929 to $11 million in 1932. AFP's Latin American operations suffered from both the collapse of the consumer market for its products and exchange controls that made it nearly impossible to send profits back to the United States. The corporation staggered under millions of dollars of debt incurred to expand and modernize power-generation facilities. The United Fruit Company slashed its workforce and the wages of the laborers who remained.[23] American corporations, a key source of the export products that fueled local economies, had withdrawn into survival mode, reducing exports and leaving tens of thousands of workers and their families destitute.

In addition to the effects of the Depression, U.S. companies also faced growing resentment over their domination of key sectors of national economies, the low returns that many Latin American nations received from these investments, and the racist attitudes and poor treatment meted out by corporate managers to their Latin American employees. As a result, the companies faced increased regulation and taxation. Chile, for example, increased taxes on copper companies. Chile, Peru, and most large Latin American countries passed laws requiring that a minimum percentage of every company's workforce must be made up of local citizens. In 1936, Venezuela passed a labor law that required oil companies to provide housing, education, and health services to their workers. As demonstrated in Bolivia and Mexico, Latin American governments also proved willing to intervene and even expropriate U.S. holdings. This combination of factors had a particularly negative impact on U.S. investments in agriculture as the Cárdenas government sped up land reform, leading to the expropriation of large U.S. holdings in the agrarian sector. In Cuba, even after Batista's coup, the government imposed new regulations on sugar companies, and popular demands mounted for expropriation of the large U.S. sugar plantations. Those factors seriously discouraged new investments in the sugar sector. While agricultural holdings had accounted for 24 percent of U.S. direct investments in Latin America in 1929, that figure had shrunk to 12 percent by 1940, and agriculture ceased to be a major sector for U.S. corporate activity.[24] But the difficulties experienced by U.S. corporations did not mean that they entirely abandoned their focus on growth or their role in the American mission.

The collapse of smaller U.S. mining companies in Mexico enhanced the power of larger corporations such as ASARCO. The desperation of the unemployed also allowed mining companies to more aggressively discipline their workforces. In announcing layoffs in 1932 the Cananea Company specifically targeted union members, and Phelps Dodge in undertaking a new mining venture refused to hire experienced miners, who tended to be labor militants. In Chile, the Kennecott Corporation that now owned the El Teniente mine had experienced considerable difficulty in creating a stable and obedient workforce despite relatively high wages and social welfare policies designed to attract workers and instill values such as hard work and competitiveness. The Depression gave a major boost to those efforts as the collapse of the nitrate industry and deteriorating economic conditions in the countryside cut off alternative employment opportunities for the restless mine workers. With wages falling, Kennecott provided a monthly family bonus for married workers in a further effort to create a more settled and compliant workforce.[25] Thus even as U.S. enterprises endured the blows of the Depression and the mounting criticism of economic nationalists, they found ways to advance their interests and the American mission. The outbreak of the war and adaptations by the companies would give a substantial boost to both those efforts.

The war proved to be a blessing for U.S. corporations in Latin America, especially those involved in the production of minerals and petroleum that were vital for the war effort. Wartime demand boosted prices for these products and the government-owned Metals Reserve Company signed purchasing agreements with Latin American countries that assured steady prices. The company also provided financing to corporations such as Phelps Dodge to assist them in expanding their facilities and thereby their output. The U.S. government intervened more directly in the case of the airline industry. Washington distributed funds to Pan-American Airways to expand its facilities in Latin America. It also blacklisted German-controlled airlines in Latin America, helping to drive them out of the region, leaving Pan Am to extend its network and establish a dominant position. Although government officials stressed the wartime necessity of these measures, they were well aware that they were helping to enhance future U.S. corporate power in the region at the expense of both their European enemies and allies. The war also drastically reduced

Europe's role as a trading partner for Latin America. As a result, U.S. companies in such sectors as pharmaceuticals made considerable head-way in displacing their European competitors.[26] Yet improved conditions for U.S. business were not entirely the result of wartime demand or U.S. government policies.

During the war a generational change occurred among U.S. corporate managers as many of those who had run the companies during the golden decade of the 1920s retired or moved on. The new generation of executives had risen through the ranks as the companies were battered by the Depression and militant nationalism.[27] At least some of these new leaders drew the same lessons from their experiences as Roosevelt's advisors. Although they were still intent on pursuing profits and their civilizing mission, they were also aware of the need for a new sensitivity to Latin American nationalism and the cultural differences that separated them from their employees. Part of these efforts consisted of public relations strategies.

By the 1920s a group of young university-educated professionals, who envisioned themselves as leading agents of modernization, dominated American advertising. By spreading the word about technological breakthroughs and prompting consumer demand for new and more efficient products, they believed that they were accelerating the processes of efficiency and rationalization that were essential to making the United States the first modern society. At the end of the decade they were anxious to spread that modernizing energy into Latin America. By the early 1930s, America's premier advertising agency, the J. Walter Thompson Company, had followed major customers like General Motors into Latin America's largest urban markets including Buenos Aires, São Paulo, and Rio de Janeiro. Through newspaper and radio advertising, the agency spread positive images of U.S. corporations and the basic messages of American consumerism, namely that the consumption of American products could bring personal improvement and happiness and make individuals effective members of the modern world.[28]

Advertising also helped U.S. corporations promote their identification with their Latin American hosts and to stress the concept of solidarity within the Americas. AFP in Cuba, for example, translated the name of GE's advertising character from Ready Kilowatt to Listo Kilowatt. Taking a cue from the OIAA's encouragement of advertising stressing hemispheric unity in the face of the Nazi threat, Coca-Cola ads featured a map of the Americas and the motto "United today . . . United forever." Going beyond the minimum requirements of hiring a certain percentage of nationals to staff their companies, U.S. corporations such as Phelps Dodge and AFP began training Latin American professionals to assume responsible management positions. Although only a minority of U.S. firms regularly practiced such policies by the time of the war's end, their activities signaled a growing sensitivity to Latin American values and concerns and attempts by corporations to integrate themselves more effectively into their host societies. At the same time, such measures furthered the American mission as Latin American professionals, who had often sided with workers in the populist protests of the 1930s, were introduced to the advantages of the American career ladder and the benefits of corporate loyalty. In addition, campaigns such as Coca-Cola's that stressed solidarity put an inter-American face on U.S. consumerist values.[29] Meanwhile, interchanges at the level of popular culture were giving Americans and Latin Americans increased exposure to one another.

Between the great wars, Americans became fascinated by Latin American cultures. American intellectuals such as Lesley Bird Simpson and Frank Tannenbaum had developed an interest in Mexico and made frequent visits there by the early 1920s. In 1929, the Guggenheim Foundation gave fresh incentive to such endeavors when it established Latin American Exchange Fellowships to promote cultural exchanges between U.S. and Latin American artists and intellectuals. Between 1930 and 1932 twenty-nine Latin Americans, including ten Mexicans, became Guggenheim fellows, as did twenty-four Americans.[30] Tourism played an important part in the process of cultural transfers as improved transportation and enhanced tourist facilities such as hotels and cabarets drew millions of Americans to the region, especially the nearby nations of Mexico and Cuba. Pan-American Airways, for example, provided the speed and convenience of commercial air travel and enticed Americans south with an advertising campaign that included lavishly colored posters featuring lush tropical forests and quaint depictions of the region's inhabitants.

During the 1930s and '40s, two million Americans visited Cuba, while U.S. tourists to Mexico spent $38 million in 1930 alone. For tourists, these countries offered an opportunity to sample what they defined as the foreign and the exotic in a safe and comfortable environment. As American society cracked down on drinking, gambling, and prostitution, these societies also offered an opportunity for Americans to free themselves of domestic restrictions on their behavior. Many tourists were drawn to the architectural wonders of old Havana and the folk art of rural Mexico, but many others flocked to the proliferating racetracks, cabarets, and houses of prostitution. Havana in particular became known for its wild nightlife, and before the end of the 1940s, the American Mafia had cemented close ties with Cuban politicians that protected its casinos, bordellos, and activities in the drug trade. Tijuana, Mexico, had become famous for its gambling casinos, racetracks, and cantinas, many of which were financed by U.S. entrepreneurs.[31] Americans in fact were fashioning their own version of Latin American reality that reinforced earlier stereotypes of Latin American cultures as exotic, sensual, and perhaps dangerous. At the same time, Latin and especially Cuban rhythms permeated the popular music industry in the United States. Entertainers from Xavier Cugat to Desi Arnaz introduced music crazes ranging from rumba to the mambo, transforming popular music.[32] The American film industry played on this fascination with things Latin and offered its own version of hemispheric solidarity at the same time that it promoted U.S. values.

Besides the prodding from OIAA and the widespread popularity of Latin culture, U.S. film executives had another powerful motive for producing more Latin-themed films with positive images and stressing inter-American friendship. The war quickly wiped out most of their markets in Western Europe and Asia, leaving the Western Hemisphere an important foreign outlet. Latin performers such as Carmen Miranda and Desi Arnaz suddenly found themselves starring in a series of Latin-themed movies, while the studios also produced films such as *Juarez*, which depicted Mexican President Benito Juárez as a Lincolnesque figure. Yet despite their efforts to portray Latin Americans in a more favorable light, Hollywood filmmakers still maintained certain stereotypes. American films depicted performers such as Carmen Miranda and Desi Arnaz as personifications of a culture characterized by its exotic sexuality—an image not far removed from the imaginings of eighteenth-century New England whaling men. In these films, Latin American men proved no match for virile American males in the courting of Latin beauties.

Latin American audiences did not welcome these films with unquestioned enthusiasm. *Argentine Nights* nearly caused a riot when it debuted in that country, and critics objected that the heavy-handed theme of Good Neighborliness that permeated Hollywood products was little more than U.S. propaganda. Nevertheless, the U.S. films with their superior production values were, on the whole, highly successful in Latin America. Hollywood stars became the subject of regular coverage by newspapers and magazines, and Hollywood productions gave fresh impetus to American concepts of beauty and the wonders of consumerism.[33] Film companies were not the only private U.S. institutions that were integrating themselves more fully into Latin America.

The commitment and range of the Rockefeller Foundation's Latin American activities grew throughout this period. The foundation's eradication programs aimed at hookworm, yellow fever, and malaria continued into the 1930s, but by that time the philanthropy had changed the focus of its health projects. During the Depression years, the foundation shifted from eradication programs to support for scientific education in order to improve the training of doctors. That choice represented a concern for projects that would have a long-term impact and a belief that carefully conceived and managed initiatives, while modest in scope, could have a multiplier effect, transforming entire sectors of social infrastructure such as health care. Those beliefs would strongly influence the federal government's aid programs in the decades to come.

The foundation provided grants to a medical school in São Paulo, a physiological institute in Buenos Aires, a Peruvian facility focusing on the effects of high altitudes on human development, and a cardiology center in Mexico. That support included fellowships for doctors to study in the United States, funds for equipment purchases, as well as grants to support projects by leading scientists. However by the 1940s the philanthropy's priorities shifted once again, and it targeted much of its funding toward improving agricultural production, pouring more than $12 million into its program in Mexico and extending these initiatives into Colombia and Chile in the early 1950s.[34] The original Mexican program stressed the training of Mexicans in such techniques as crop rotation, the use of chemical fertilizers, and most importantly, the development and introduction of synthetic and hybrid strains of wheat and corn, launching what later became known as the Green Revolution.

The foundation's medical programs helped a number of Latin American doctors achieve international reputations in their fields of research and led to the development of important medical research facilities. The agricultural initiative to improve seed strains proved particularly effective in raising wheat yields in Mexico. Yet both programs suffered from major shortcomings due to their reliance on U.S. models. Although the United States prided itself on a health care system that included elite medical facilities, U.S.-trained Latin American researchers often found that they could not secure adequate monetary support and equipment in countries where an array of needs from infrastructure development to primary education placed enormous demands on existing resources. Furthermore, breakthroughs in medical research and doctors trained in specialized areas of medical research simply did not address the immediate needs of the vast majority of Latin Americans, whose most pressing health concerns included clean water and proper nutrition.

The foundation's agricultural programs that evolved from the U.S. land-grant college system and farm extension services focused on the potential and the needs of capital-intensive, commercially orientated farming operations. Although many Mexican wheat farmers fit that profile, the vast majority of Mexican farmers, who grew corn and worked small subsistence plots lacked the resources to acquire improved seed, fertilizers, and irrigation systems essential to the success of the Rockefeller program.[35] Despite the overly optimistic assessment of the challenges facing their strategies and the failure to take into account local conditions in their design of projects, the leaders of the foundation would remain convinced of the efficacy of their programs, and they would significantly influence Washington's own aid initiatives in the years ahead. Meanwhile, the other important group of philanthropic agents in the American mission had made considerable strides in integrating themselves into Latin American societies.

The evangelical congress held by Protestant denominations in Havana on the eve of the Great Depression marked a notable change in the missionary character of Protestant churches in Latin America. For the first time, the majority of the delegates were Latin Americans. Furthermore, the participants committed themselves to continuing the process of nationalizing the leadership of their churches. The congress also capped a decade of rapid growth among the Protestant denominations, with the total number of Latin Americans affiliated with Protestant churches approaching three-quarters of a million. Yet serious differences remained over the issue of nationalization, with some leaders opting for a strategy that would distance their churches from identification with the United States and in particular what they perceived as the rapacious behavior of U.S. corporations. Others were more concerned with combating the influence of communism and the dangers of class warfare. During the next several decades, mainstream Protestant churches would continue to adhere to the principles of the Social Gospel, seeking to reform capitalism while working to reconcile the interests of capital and labor. At the same time, they became ardent critics of leftist political causes and militant labor movements. That strategy largely closed off the possibility of conversions among the working class, but missionaries found other opportunities to pursue their work.[36]

Protestants focused particular attention on Latin American youth. The YMCA and YWCA enjoyed strong growth. By 1949 the Y's South American federation counted forty-two thousand members. That expansion resulted from the appeal of the Y's sports and educational programs, as well as financial assistance from American businessmen, who saw the Y as an important force for instilling young, middle-class Latin Americans with individualistic and competitive values that would prepare them for work in modern corporations while serving as an antidote for social unrest.[37] Protestant missionaries had also launched important initiatives among Latin America's indigenous population.

With their communities under increasing stress from the forces of modernization that challenged and disrupted existing values and social relationships, indigenous populations proved receptive to the new-world vision offered by Protestantism. Similar to their relationships with the Liberal regimes of the past, Protestant missionaries found willing allies among the nationalist populist regimes of the 1930s and '40s, who saw the missionaries' schools as an important means of incorporating rural communities into the nation-state when the resources of national educational systems proved inadequate. Most notable among these missionaries was William Cameron Townsend, the founder of the Summer Institute of Linguistics (SIL).

Townsend won the support of both Moisés Sáenz, the head of Mexico's rural education program, and President Lázaro Cárdenas. Cárdenas, who had been a part of the revolutionary government's long struggle to curtail the powers of the Catholic Church, which had long exerted a powerful influence on Mexican education, must have relished an opportunity to embrace the Protestant missionaries. But he and Sáenz were also impressed by Townsend's promise that his missionaries would create dictionaries for the wide array of Indian dialects and provide translated materials including the Bible to the nation's indigenous inhabitants. Anxious to integrate these groups into the larger national society, Sáenz and Cárdenas became ardent supporters of the institute, whose missionaries fanned out across rural Mexico and eventually into Central and South America. Townsend would also enjoy the support of leading American capitalists such as Nelson Rockefeller, who saw SIL as an important means of maintaining social peace as they sought to exploit the resources of rural Latin America.[38] Yet Townsend's successes could not hide serious divisions within the ranks of Protestant missionaries.

By the end of World War II, mainstream churches had made considerable advances in nationalizing their leadership, but serious divisions now existed over their degree of identification with the United States, their stand on social injustice and capitalism, and most importantly, the internal divisions between mainstream and Pentecostal Protestantism. Pentecostalism's emphasis on direct inspiration from the Holy Spirit, oral tradition, and popular participation that appealed to the working poor ran contrary to the culture of mainstream churches that stressed rational thought, written tradition, and guidance of the clergy while appealing to the middle class. Pentecostalism traced its origins to William Joseph Seymour, an African American preacher from Louisiana who in 1906 began preaching to working-class African Americans in Los Angeles about the wonders of baptism in the Holy Spirit that would find expression in the gift of speaking in tongues. In 1910 European immigrants who had converted to Pentecostalism in Chicago carried its message of rebirth in the Holy Spirit and a strict ascetic code of conduct to Brazil where it would enjoy its greatest successes during the twentieth century. The ravages of the Great Depression created an especially conducive environment for conversions by Pentecostals, who accounted for approximately one-quarter of all Protestants in Latin America by 1940. As their numbers grew, the Pentecostals found themselves the target of mounting criticism from the hierarchy of other Protestant denominations.[39] Meanwhile, the American Federation of Labor found itself facing its own internal and external challenges to its influence in Latin America.

After the effective demise of the Pan-American Federation of Labor during the 1920s and the devastating blows of the Great Depression, U.S. labor leaders largely confined their actions in Latin America to denunciations of communist and anarcho-syndicalist influences in the region's labor organizations. Furthermore, by the mid-1930s the U.S. labor movement no longer spoke with one voice on Latin America. The AFL, which continued to support allies such as conservative Mexican labor leader Luis Morones and his confederation the CROM, now faced a challenge at home from the Congress of Industrial Organizations (CIO), a rival labor federation that backed the radical labor leader Vicente Lombardo Toledano and his Confederación de Trabajadores de Mexico (CTM).

Differences between the two sides became apparent when the CIO gave implicit backing to Lázaro Cárdenas's expropriation of the oil industry in 1938, while the AFL denounced the expropriation as an unacceptable assault on private property and worked with U.S. business interests to undo the nationalization. Furthermore, the AFL sought to undermine Toledano's Latin American Confederation of Labor (CTAL), which the AFL saw as a direct challenge to its efforts to develop a network of probusiness union affiliates in Latin America. In cooperation with Nelson Rockefeller's OIAA, William Green and George Meany of the AFL invited a group of Latin American labor leaders to visit the United States. But the AFL's attempt to create an alternative to Toledano and the CTAL ran up against the Roosevelt administration's unwillingness to undercut the CTAL's anti-Nazi message and the support that Toledano enjoyed from the CIO.[40] However, after the war the interests of the two American labor federations would coalesce, and big labor would come to play a central role in pursuing the American mission during the cold war.

∾

The Great Depression brought the golden age of American business investment in Latin America to a crashing halt and threatened the complex network of ties that the United States had built with its southern neighbors as populist nationalists challenged the alliance between their own elites and the United States. Yet despite the economic and political damage, the United States was able to rebound from these setbacks. Under Franklin Roosevelt, Washington began to downplay the threat of overt intervention and to build more amicable relations with its neighbors to ensure access to Latin American resources in the event of war. When the war did come it helped U.S. corporations to rebound from their Depression-era losses. But most importantly, the Great Depression helped forge an alliance between the Democratic Party, capital-intensive industries, and big labor that ensured corporations the right to continually revamp the workplace in return for rising wages and a federal social safety net anchored in the Social Security system. That alliance relied on American productivity to fund these basic understandings, and it was Americans' faith in their ability to perpetually increase productivity that would underpin U.S. postwar foreign policy, reshaping the American mission to Latin America in the decades after 1945.

Americans' whaling ventures into the Pacific created some
of the earliest encounters between Americans and their
South American neighbors. Source: John R. Spears,
The Story of the New England Whalers. New York:
The MacMillan Company, 1908.

The American merchant adventurer Richard Cleveland, who brought American goods and American political ideas to South America in the early nineteenth century. Source: Richard J. Cleveland, *Voyages of a Merchant Navigator of the Days that are Past: Compiled from the Journals and Letters of the Late Richard J. Cleveland*. New York: Harper and Brothers, 1886.

John L. Stephens, diplomat, businessman, and adventurer, who introduced Americans to the wonders of Central American archaeology and helped launch the Panama railway. Source: *Harpers Monthly Magazine*, January 1859.

This nineteenth-century political cartoon depicts Americans' self-image as the male protectors of a feminine Cuba. Source: C. Jay Taylor, *Puck*, June 3, 1896.

Members of the U.S. 10th Cavalry who fought at San Juan Hill.
Source: National Archives.

General Leonard Wood,
who as the military
governor of Cuba
sought to Americanize
the island and its
inhabitants. Source:
National Archives.

A political cartoon depicting Great Britain's acceptance of
U.S. dominance in the Western Hemisphere at the beginning
of the twentieth century. Source: Homer Davenport, *Review
of Reviews*, January 1902.

President Teddy Roosevelt seated in the cab of one of the powerful steam shovels that carved out the Panama Canal. Source: Library of Congress.

The hut of a black worker on the Panama Canal
constructed from dynamite boxes. Source:
Harry Franck. *Zone Policeman 88*. New York:
The Century Company, 1913.

U.S. Marines checking a citizen of Veracruz for weapons during the U.S. occupation of the port in 1914. Source: Library of Congress.

A captured Haitian caco with two U.S. Marines. Source: National Archives.

Smedley Butler (front row, fourth from the left), the U.S. Marine officer involved in a series of American interventions in the circum-Caribbean. Source: National Archives.

A gospel tent used by Southern Baptist missionaries in Argentina in the 1920s. Source: Southern Baptist Historical Archives and Library, Nashville, Tennessee.

Sumner Welles and President Franklin Roosevelt meeting to
discuss the crisis in Cuba in 1933. Source: National Archives.

Fulgencio Batista, the Cuban military officer
whom Sumner Welles pressured to oust
Cuba's revolutionary government in 1934.
Source: U.S. Information Agency.

Augusto Sandino (center), the Nicaraguan revolutionary
who fought a prolonged guerrilla war against U.S. Marines.
Source: National Archives.

The Braden Copper Company's El Teniente mine in
Chile, one of the modern U.S. mining ventures that
dominated mineral production in Latin America.
Source: Library of Congress.

The Sears Roebuck store in Monterrey, Mexico, in 1954.
The sleek design of the store suggested that its consumer
products offered Mexicans ready access to the wonders of
modern society. Source: Library of Congress.

Vice President Richard Nixon with newly
inaugurated Argentine president Arturo Frondizi
during Nixon's 1958 trip to Latin America that led
to the stoning of Nixon's motorcade in Caracas,
Venezuela. Source: Library of Congress.

Fidel Castro and two of his followers during their armed
struggle against Cuban dictator Fulgencio Bastista.
Source: National Archives.

"— And His Father Lives Up There"

A Herblock cartoon depicting American fears in the 1960s that sharp disparities in wealth were driving revolutionary movements in Latin America. Source: Herblock Foundation.

Chilean workers rally in support of Socialist Salvador Allende during his unsuccessful bid for the presidency in 1964.
Source: Library of Congress.

The Hipermercado in Tucumán, Argentina, with its Statue
of Liberty logo suggesting that American freedom means the
freedom to consume. Source: Constance Classen.

An Otavalan Indian using a loom to create the textiles
that have found a ready market among U.S. tourists.
Source: Lynn A. Meisch. *Andean Entrepreneurs:
Otavalo Merchants & Musicians in the Global Arena.*
Austin: University of Texas Press, 2002.

A political cartoon depicting the influence that Venezuela's oil has given to its populist president Hugo Chávez. Source: Kjell Nilsson-Maki, www.Cartoonstock.com.

CHAPTER SIX

NATIONALISM, COMMUNISM, AND MODERNIZATION, 1946–1958

ON THE MORNING OF MAY 13, 1958, VICE PRESIDENT RICHARD M. NIXON deplaned at Caracas's Maiquetia Airport and proceeded by motorcade toward the Venezuelan capital. The vice president later recalled what happened next:

> Just as we reached the city limits, I heard a dull thud and thought for a moment that we had hit a chuck hole in the road. But then another and another followed and I realized that rocks were hitting our car. A moment later our driver slammed on the brakes. We had come upon an ambush. . . . A mass of people rushed into the street from their hiding places, spitting, throwing rocks, waving placards, and shouting obscenities.[1]

Nixon and his party would endure two more assaults by rock- and pipe-wielding demonstrators before safely reaching the U.S. embassy. In arriving at an explanation for the violent demonstrations, the vice president ignored the fact that the Eisenhower administration had strongly supported the recently deposed dictator Marcos Pérez Jiménez and had awarded the strongman a Medal of Merit in a lavish Caracas ceremony just seven months earlier. Instead, Nixon concluded that communists had spearheaded the attacks on his motorcade. As a precaution, President Eisenhower dispatched two companies of airborne infantry and two companies of marines to Caribbean bases for a possible mission to the Venezuelan capital.[2] The vice president's visit to South America, with the primary purpose of attending the inauguration of President Arturo Frondizi of Argentina, was ending badly.

❧

Nixon's rude welcome to Caracas came almost exactly twenty-five years after Sumner Welles's arrival in Havana. During the quarter-century that elapsed between the two events, the United States had abandoned the imperialistic rhetoric of the civilizing mission, declaring Latin Americans partners in the battle against the Great Depression and Nazism. In more recent years, the United States had sought a hemispheric alliance against communism and promoted strategies of capitalist development, assuring Latin Americans that the process would provide them with material wealth comparable to that of the United States. But as the events in Caracas clearly illustrated, something had gone terribly wrong since the heady days of World War II when the United States rallied Latin Americans to join in the war of the Western democracies against fascism and applauded signs of democratic progress in Latin America itself.

The Second World War, deteriorating relations with the Soviet Union and intensifying Latin American nationalism, had powerful effects on Washington's policy toward its neighbors in the Americas during the 1950s. Emerging from the war, the United States was preoccupied with assuring continued access to Latin America's natural resources in the event of another world war. That concern evolved into the need to maintain access to these resources to fuel national economic growth and challenge the Soviet Union in the global contest known as the cold war. Initially, Washington saw Latin American nationalism as the greatest threat to that continued access. In February 1945, Assistant Secretary of State William Clayton delivered an address at an inter-American conference in Mexico City, calling for the lowering of tariff barriers between his own country and Latin America, the expansion of U.S. industrial exports to the region, and an enhanced role for U.S. corporations in the agricultural and extractive industries of Latin America. In effect, Clayton wanted to roll back a decade and a half of economic nationalism and return to the liberal development polices and U.S. investment activities of the 1920s. More specifically, the U.S. delegation unsuccessfully sought support for draft resolution number 98, which called for the end of economic nationalism "in all its forms."[3] In a reference to the same problem a report crafted in 1950 by George F. Kennan, the acknowledged architect of the U.S. policy of containment toward the Soviet Union, explicitly stated, "There is no part of the world where business relationships play a greater role in our foreign-policy problems than in Latin America."[4] In fact throughout the 1950s U.S. officials ranked economic nationalism ahead of communism on their lists of concerns about Latin America.[5] At the same time, American policymakers frequently saw nationalism and communism as essentially one and the same problem. As Gerald Haines has noted in his study of U.S. diplomacy in Brazil:

> American policymakers, not unlike their Brazilian counterparts,
> in general had a difficult time distinguishing nationalists from
> Communists and were more likely than not to simply lump the
> two together and condemn them both. They saw revolutionary
> nationalism as synonymous with anti-Americanism.[6]

The concern with communism would grow with the resurgence of leftist politics and labor militancy that soon gave birth to a strident anticommunism both at home and abroad. In Latin America popular militancy was triggered in part by economic conditions during and immediately after the war.

The Second World War brought a surge in demand and rising prices for Latin American exports, improving economic conditions and strengthening ties to the United States, the one industrialized economy that was not suffering material damage from the global conflict. Between 1941 and 1945, economic recovery and programs promoting industrialization brought 50 and 60 percent increases in the number of manufacturing workers in Mexico, Brazil, and Argentina. Growing urban workforces translated into larger and more militant labor movements that would press for greater economic benefits from their nations' rulers and the American corporations that controlled key sectors of the region's economies.

Inspired in part by the vision of World War II as a democratic crusade against dictatorship, urban workers, the middle class, and center-left political parties pressed for political freedom and progressive social policies. These forces for change enjoyed a brief period of success between 1944 and 1946, pressuring four dictatorial regimes into democratic changes and securing political reform from other governments that had relied on restricted political participation. In the new liberalized environment labor militancy increased sharply with waves of strikes occurring in the mid-1940s. Although their actual vote clearly left them as statistical minorities, communist parties in Cuba, Chile, and Brazil made remarkable advances in membership and voter support. Yet this springtime for Latin American democracy rapidly faded.

The traditional elite that still held sway in these countries soon responded. Seeing their political power threatened, anxious to create a stable labor environment to attract foreign capital, and taking advantage of the reemerging anticommunist militancy of the United States, the dominant classes struck back after 1946, rolling back political reforms, outlawing communist parties, and cracking down on independent unions as national governments asserted tight control over their labor movements.[7] Those actions meshed almost seamlessly with the actions of the U.S. government, which had become a harsh critic of democratic openings that gave vent to leftist political sentiments and popular nationalism. Viewing communism and nationalism as indistinguishable because of the threats they posed to their interests, Latin American and U.S. elites would join in a strident anticommunist campaign.

All U.S. presidents since Woodrow Wilson had been openly hostile to the Soviet Union. Roosevelt set aside that animosity while the Soviets assumed the primary burden of halting Hitler's expansionism. But soon after the war, U.S. policymakers became fearful of Soviet intentions in

Europe and of growing labor unrest at home. In the aftermath of the war, as Western Europe lay in ruins and anti-imperialist rebellions began to shake much of Asia and Africa, the Soviet Union appeared to threaten the United States and its Western allies. As unions mounted militant challenges to corporations, conservative politicians and corporate executives identified union demands as expressions of communist influence, and a hunt for communists in both government and labor was soon underway. A militant anticommunism would mark both domestic and foreign policies during the 1950s.

Washington proved ready to offer its support to almost any regime that defined its politics as anticommunist and proved willing to crack down on leftist political parties and militant unions. Both the Truman and Eisenhower administrations saw the Latin American armed forces as important allies in that effort. At the urging of the United States, the countries meeting in Rio de Janeiro in 1947 signed the Inter-American Treaty of Reciprocal Assistance, which established a permanent defensive alliance with a particular emphasis on mutual assistance in combating internal subversion. The following year, they created the Organization of American States, which provided for multilateral intervention to assist any member state threatened by communist aggression. The Mutual Security Act of 1951 served as the basis for long-term military assistance programs, supplying U.S. weapons and cementing close ties between U.S. and Latin American military officers. In time, Washington would look to its military allies as essential actors in the battle against communist subversion.[8] Such policies not only emanated from U.S. strategic and economic concerns; they also reflected the self-image of members of the American elite, people such as John Foster and Allen W. Dulles, who had long envisioned themselves as the manly figures charged with pursuing the American mission to the world.

The Dulles brothers dominated U.S. foreign policymaking during the 1950s, with John serving as secretary of state and Allen as director of the Central Intelligence Agency (CIA) under President Dwight Eisenhower. The brothers were the latest generation of an elite family that included their grandfather John Foster and their uncle Robert Lansing, both of whom served as secretary of state. Like many other members of that elite, the brothers established their professional reputations on Wall Street with both of them serving as partners in the distinguished law firm of Sullivan and Cromwell. The firm had played a central role in making the Panama Canal an American enterprise, and its clients included United Fruit and GE's American and Foreign Power Company.

The brothers were steeped in the traditions of the American elite that stressed the ideal of the heroic male, imbued with physical courage and dedicated to the aggressive defense of America and its Christian traditions. Each of the brothers upheld those traditions with John dismissing the idea that communism could simply be contained and calling on America to pursue a "spiritual offensive," in effect a Christian crusade against godless communism.[9] Allen immersed himself in the cloak-and-dagger operations of the Office of Strategic Services, the World War II predecessor of the Central Intelligence Agency, and then masterminded the CIA's covert actions designed to thwart Soviet aggression, especially in third world regions like Latin America. The brothers' dealings with Latin America would also reflect the long-standing paternalistic attitude of U.S. leaders toward the region. A 1953 document laying out the Eisenhower administration's Latin American policy listed a number of past and present presidents, including Cárdenas of Mexico, Perón of Argentina, and Grau San Martín of Cuba, and described them all as "immature and impractical idealists" who "lack the disposition to combat extremists within their ranks including communists."[10] In light of the perceived irresponsibility of Latin American leaders, the United States intensified its efforts to defend its interests in the Western Hemisphere.

The federal government rapidly expanded its functions to carry out its antinationalist, anticommunist crusade and to advance the interests of U.S. capitalism in response to the alternate vision of state-managed economies and socialist societies. Its efforts included increased funding for economic development through the Point Four program. In addition, the United States Information Service (USIS) used a variety of media initiatives to promote attitudes favorable to U.S. investment and the larger project of Americanization. When faced with more militant challenges to its interests, the United States could now turn to the newly created CIA. Washington also helped create an array of multilateral agencies such as the International Monetary Fund (IMF) and the International Bank for Reconstruction and Development (IBRD, later part of the World Bank).[11] The assistance provided by these multilateral organizations as well as Point Four was directed at promoting private enterprise rather than statist economic development.

In addition to building new federal and multilateral institutions, Washington substantially increased economic aid to Latin America in the years after the war. That funding, which totaled less than $200 million in 1950, exceeded $600 million in 1957. Working primarily through multilateral agencies such as the World Bank, the United States also loaned the region $1.5 billion between 1948 and 1955. These funds filled a void in financing due to the reluctance of U.S. banks to make large credit commitments to Latin American governments after the debt crisis of the 1930s. But at least until the mid-1950s, the size of those disbursements paled in comparison to the funds poured into the reconstruction of Western Europe. Even when the Eisenhower administration significantly increased aid to the region, Washington made it clear that Latin Americans must look primarily to U.S. corporate investment to promote economic development.[12] Yet what is most striking about this process is the convergence of policies and perspectives among the American institutions that had long been involved in Latin America. Not only state agents but also corporate executives, union leaders, foundation professionals, and missionaries shared a common ideology of modernization that incorporated faith in productivity improvement and the antinationalist, anticommunist militancy that marked the postwar years. That strategy was part of a reconfigured civilizing mission designed to promote capitalist development, while it also contributed to the campaign against communism and statist economic policies.

MODERNIZATION THEORISTS

American elites had begun redefining Latin America and the civilizing mission even before the outbreak of World War II. Their ideas, which would find expression in academic treatises and concrete policies after 1945, drew on several elements of the increasingly discredited civilizing mission. Agents of the earlier mission, from Leonard Wood to money doctors such as Edwin Kemmerer, had often drawn distinctions between their own society's command of technology and reliance on rational problem solving as opposed to the lack of technology and irrational thought patterns they believed characterized uncivilized societies. These distinctions, which had been informed by racist perspectives, had been tempered during the 1930s by the work of anthropologists such as Franz Boas and Margaret Mead, who argued that societal distinctions stemmed from differences in cultures that were themselves subject to change or modification. Modernization theorists now argued that the failure of underdeveloped societies to progress resulted from the traditional nature of their cultures, which led to the irrational use of resources. According to this view, developed Western societies had undergone a progressive series of changes that transformed them from traditional to modern—a path that could now be followed by less developed countries.

In his 1960 classic *The Stages of Economic Growth—A Non-Communist Manifesto*, Walt Whitman Rostow summarized the key concepts behind modernization theory and made clear its links to the struggle against communism. In that book, Rostow outlined the stages that societies pass through as they eliminate cultural and structural obstacles to development and finally achieve "takeoff," namely, self-sustaining growth or modernity. Modernization theorists also asserted that underdeveloped societies such as those in Latin America could be assisted through these stages of development by industrialized countries and by their willingness to adopt the values and institutions of modern capitalism. Two conceptualizations that had not changed from the ideas of the civilizing mission were the paternalism and male centeredness of modernization theory.

U.S. proponents of modernization strategies envisioned an essential role for the United States in propelling traditional societies through the process of development. Latin Americans might be conceived of as partners in the process, but they were to be directed and acted upon by external agents of change. Rostow himself argued that developed nations would have to guide childlike third world societies through the process of modernization.[13] Theorists and policymakers also continued to envision men as the agents who would break down traditional institutions and values, replacing them with an environment that encouraged the development of the self-actuating individual with rational problem-solving skills and a proclivity for creating and applying new technologies to improving productivity. If it was the uncivilized society that was once envisioned as possessed of feminine characteristics, it was now the traditional society that bore supposed feminine qualities such as irrationality and a lack of dynamism.

In another throwback to the civilizing mission, theorists such as Rostow argued that Americans were arriving at a consensus about how their society's major problems should be resolved. Soon they would be reduced to bickering over the details. To save themselves from such intellectual lethargy, Americans could launch themselves on the heroic task of modernizing the third world. In the thesis could be heard the echoes of Teddy Roosevelt's argument that the civilizing mission would restore flagging American manhood.[14] At the same time, as the subtitle to Rostow's book suggests, the modernization theorists envisioned their creation not only as a blueprint for development but also as a capitalist alternative to the communist vision of a workers' paradise.

In keeping with American ideas about the wonders of productivity, modernization theorists asserted that the wealth generated by their version of development would trickle down through the layers of society and make it unnecessary to redistribute economic or political power through revolutions. These ideas that stressed economic development and the preservation of existing power relations in third world countries meshed neatly with existing U.S interests in Latin America. In theory at least, U.S. leaders could propel Latin American economies forward while preserving their long-standing links to the region's elites that ensured both groups' continued dominance. Anticommunism and modernization theory merged into an ideological synthesis that shaped U.S. perspectives and policies on Latin America in the postwar era.

These ideas were encouraged and promoted by state actors and by the Rockefeller and Ford Foundations, which since the 1930s had provided funding for social science research to address the problem of achieving economic growth and development while maintaining social stability. A strong international element was added to these efforts after the war as the two foundations poured millions of dollars into the development of international relations and foreign area studies programs at leading U.S. universities. The foundations also promoted the application of modernization theory to Latin America and other third world areas as a means of spurring economic development while maintaining social stability and fending off the threat of communism. Those goals reflected the findings of foundation-sponsored foreign policy studies, and the view of U.S. policymakers that the postwar prosperity of the United States depended on continued access to overseas natural resources and the general expansion of U.S. corporate interests in an environment conducive to capitalist development.

Philanthropic interests linked up with academic and government initiatives in 1952 with the establishment of the Center for International Studies at the Massachusetts Institute of Technology that drew funding from Ford and the CIA. The center produced both studies of modernization in the third world and reports on that process in communist societies. A number of modernization theorists participated in the center's work, most notably W. W. Rostow.[15] Modernization theory as applied to U.S. relations with Latin America after 1945 provided a revised version of the civilizing mission, which philanthropists, intellectuals, business, government, and labor leaders could rally around.

THE MISSION OF MODERNIZATION

The convergence of views that now marked the alliance was personified by Nelson Rockefeller. The Rockefeller family had shaped the mission of its foundation along the lines of the Social Gospel, and the Rockefellers had been pioneers in promoting "scientific" approaches to labor relations. In turn, Nelson had an abiding interest in Latin America and firmly believed that the region's future depended on planned economic development driven by private enterprise and enlightened by progressive labor policies. He and his ideas had enormous influence on U.S. policy toward Latin America. As the director of the Office of Inter-American Affairs, Rockefeller adopted many of OIAA's programmatic goals and techniques directly from Rockefeller Foundation methods and had made a lasting impact on U.S. initiatives. That influence is best personified by Albion Patterson, the Rockefeller protégé who headed a U.S. government agricultural assistance mission in Chile.

Patterson's activities in Chile during the mid-1950s offer particular insight into the convergence of views on modernization. Patterson's rural development program for the area around the city of Concepción followed the Foundation's approach of seeking to implement an American-style extension service to provide assistance to local agriculturists. The Concepción region had been chosen because of its deep-sea port and the presence of steel mills, textile plants, and coal mines. Quite simply the city represented a booming industrial complex with a burgeoning population, which the local agricultural system could not adequately feed. For his development scheme Patterson had selected the precise location that Lieutenant James Melville Gilliss had chosen for his vision of capitalist development a century earlier. But in this case, informed by the theories of modernization, the strategies of the scheme were far more precise.

The U.S. government's rural project would replicate those of the Foundation in seeking to promote the development of large commercial agricultural enterprises that would utilize American technologies to produce food with maximum efficiency and meet the needs of industrial growth. If a philanthropic agency had set the form and goals for government efforts, it also shaped the value system of the project, and they were not values that assumed that the meek would inherit the earth. As Patterson himself explained:

> If the problem we are tackling in Chile is the immediate need
> for increased food production, we can't put any large part of
> our budget into giving the down-and-outer advice on nutrition,
> child care etc. Unless he produces more or the region around
> him produces more, he won't be able to follow our advice. Why
> involve the taxpayers of two countries in a subsidy for which we
> can write no termination agreement? Isn't it always in the end
> more humanitarian to be realistic than romantic?[16]

Patterson's version of the modernization mantra "planning and productivity" would be echoed by a generation of American policymakers.

A 1952 report on technical assistance to Brazil had explained in even more explicit terms the link between the ideology of productivity and the varied social service initiatives undertaken by the U.S. government in Latin America. The report's author noted:

> The productivity of Brazilians is low because of deficient diet,
> lack of training and poor health. In manufacturing for example,
> manpower productivity is estimated to be $1/7$ to $1/8$ of that of the
> United States. Only some 38 percent of the Brazilian children in
> rural areas are enrolled in the primary school grades, and in the
> vocational field such schooling is far from keeping pace with
> the demands of industry for skilled workers.[17]

Malnutrition, health problems, and poor education were perceived as obstacles to the all-important drive for modernization. The U.S. government helped set up and support Brazil's Special Service for Public Health and worked with it to establish health centers and well-water systems. Following the Rockefeller Foundation's example in Mexico, the United States nurtured the development of a Brazilian national agricultural extension service and provided support for vocational training.[18] Beyond the immediate goal of increased productivity, these programs sought to ensure stable capitalist development in Latin America.

A description of a U.S.-sponsored labor-training seminar in Mexico explained both its productivity enhancing purposes and the effort to cope with the social dislocations prompted by rapid modernization. As a U.S. official explained, "The purpose of the labor training is to equip Mexican labor to maximize its contribution in the rapid industrialization process now under way in that country and to strengthen the free and democratic labor organizations against the constant threat of Communist infiltration. . . . It [communism] tries to take advantage of the great and startling problems which rapid mechanization and industrialization causes [sic] in the minds of a labor force which only recently was still predominantly employed in agricultural pursuits."[19] These comments also illustrate how thoroughly development initiatives based on modernization theory dovetailed with anticommunist policies. U.S.-guided capitalist development in Latin America would seek to counteract the dislocations inherent in the process of modernization and thereby prevent communists from exploiting that instability for their own ends. The Rockefeller Foundation's mission of ordering and stabilizing the social order to protect the global expansion of capitalism and the creation of consumer societies challenging the communist ideal of a workers' paradise had become the avowed mission of the U.S. government.

Although American state functionaries did not carry out programs directly designed to promote a consumer economy in the region, they did serve as forceful advocates of American business in general. As was the case in the age of Dollar Diplomacy, the state used financial mechanisms to more fully incorporate Latin American countries into the U.S. economy. But now the United States had multilateral mechanisms at its command to assist in this process. In Chile during the 1950s, the U.S.

government, the IMF, the IBRD, as well as the Klein-Saks mission of private consultants pressed on Chile a stabilization plan that increased the country's dependence on foreign loans and enhanced the power of large U.S. corporations such as Anaconda and Kennecott. By contrast, this stabilization program, like other elements of the mission of Americanization, largely ignored structural inequalities such as inequitable land distribution patterns and tax systems that lay at the heart of the nation's underdevelopment.[20] At the same time, the American state also used more subtle methods to promote an environment favorable to U.S. business.

Although USIS programs in Latin American countries supported U.S. foreign policy as their primary activity, most program directors would agree with the one in Argentina, who in 1959 listed as his second objective "to produce understanding of efforts made by U.S. through economic cooperation, emphasizing the role which free enterprise plays in advancing the welfare of Argentina and Argentine people." Even more specifically the USIS mission in Mexico City sought "to lessen nationalistic fears [of U.S. investment]" and "to present the basis of the free enterprise ideology."[21] More importantly as the Mexican labor-training seminar made clear, U.S agencies made a concerted effort along with U.S. businesses to train and discipline workers in Latin America to make them an effective workforce for a modern capitalist economy.

Modernization theorists also believed that a fundamental impediment to the further development of traditional societies was their top-down paternalistic social order that discouraged local initiatives and self-reliance. Building from that premise, foundation and government development projects in the 1950s promoted the idea of self-help. As one foreign aid official explained, community development consisted of the plans and procedures, that would get local villagers and communities involved in improving their own economic and social conditions.[22] Community development programs, at least in theory, were designed to reverse the dynamics of highly centralized social orders and to prompt villagers to identify and solve their own problems with some outside technical assistance. In fact, projects such as the U.S.-sponsored initiative for the village of Chonin, Brazil, in the early 1950s exhibited many of the top-down Rockefeller techniques of careful surveying of the village's needs in agriculture, health, and education, and had imbedded within it the same preconceived notions about the ineffectiveness of folk medicine and the dire need for the adoption of new technologies.[23] Meanwhile, a once-important force in the American coalition was experiencing significant problems of its own keeping up with the process of modernization.

As of 1952, there were nearly four thousand Protestant missionaries working in Latin America. Social service activities, especially primary education, still represented an important part of their work, absorbing $8 to $10 million per year of their budgets.[24] Other elements of the coalition continued to work closely with the missionaries. In Chile religious groups such as the Seventh-day Adventists cooperated informally with the U.S. government's technical assistance programs for agriculture.[25] The corporate sector also continued to work with missionaries, entrusting them with portions of the educational institutions they created. But missionaries now played a relatively small role in the project of modernization. The reason for that reduced participation became abundantly clear in a study of the missions published by the National Planning Association in 1956.

Indicative of the changing realities, the study was funded by the Ford Foundation and written by Dr. James G. Maddox, who had worked for Nelson Rockefeller on projects in Venezuela and Brazil. Maddox focused on the technical assistance aspect of missionary activity in Latin America. In a portion of the conclusion with the telling title "The Efficiency Problem," Maddox noted that the curriculum of missionary schools was now sadly out of date, failing to provide training that would create productive artisans and farmers. As for mission medical institutions, they continued to emphasize curative medicine instead of preventive strategies, which were now the focus of foundation and government efforts. Maddox also stressed the need for the missions to train community leaders.[26] In short, the missionaries, once the ideological vanguard for the civilizing mission, had fallen badly out of step with the postwar coalition's efforts to create conflict-free capitalist societies through planned programs focused on productivity improvement. Furthermore, a new era and a new role for missionary activity were already dawning as Pentecostal missionaries took the lead in evangelization.

Pentecostalism in Latin America enjoyed a new wave of growth when Harold Williams, a missionary for Aime Semple McPherson's Four-Square Gospel, carried another American wave of inspiration to Brazil in 1953. This surge of Pentecostal enthusiasm employed distinctively American techniques, including tent revivals aimed at mass conversions and a stress on faith healing over the earlier emphasis on strict codes of conduct.[27]

Pentecostalism, with its focus on the absolute authority of the Bible in all areas of life and the significance of a highly emotional and personal experience of God, found a growing audience in rural areas among an ever-larger number of residents whose subsistence agricultural communities were disintegrating under pressures from expanding agribusiness enterprises and in the cities where many of these same people sought relief from their plight.[28] If Pentecostal missionaries were not advocates of the progressive reforms, which had formed the core of the Social Gospel, they would help many Latin Americans cope emotionally with the wrenching changes that the process of modernization would bring to their lives. U.S. corporations, now expanding with a new vigor throughout the region, were playing a pivotal role in that process of change.

CORPORATE AND LABOR MODERNIZERS

Although the war brought renewed growth and profits for many U.S. corporations in Latin America, American companies still faced major challenges to their interests. Latin Americans remained alienated by the racist attitudes that they still detected among many Americans and had become enamored of statist economic policies that seemed to have transformed the Soviet Union. Furthermore, economic nationalism appeared to be a hydra-headed challenge that threatened multinationals from a variety of directions. Although outright expropriation such as the Mexican oil nationalization remained the exception, economic nationalism had assumed a variety of threatening forms, including foreign-exchange controls, increased internal taxation, tariffs, mounting labor militancy, and increased labor legislation as well as policies promoting domestic industrialization by Latin American states. Those policies now had a new intellectual justification.

Raúl Prebisch, the Argentine economist who headed the United Nation's Economic Commission for Latin America (ECLA), directed a series of studies that concluded Latin American economies suffered from unfavorable terms of trade, selling low-priced raw materials for high-priced manufactured imports. Prebisch and his disciples proposed the strategy of Import Substituting Industrialization (ISI) that would raise tariffs to protect the development of heavy industries such as steel. That approach gave intellectual underpinning to ongoing efforts at state-promoted industrialization and invigorated calls for other nationalistic economic policies. Yet despite these challenges, most American corporations in Latin America would flourish in the postwar era.

Direct U.S. investments in Latin America grew rapidly in the post-war period. Totaling about $3 billion in 1940, they exceeded $8 billion by 1960 with 90 percent of that increase coming after 1945. The composition of corporate commitments had also changed dramatically, in part reflecting the realization that certain types of direct investments were fighting a rearguard action. Agriculture ceased to be a significant area of investment due to the increasingly risky environment faced by U.S. agricultural enterprises as Latin American governments continued to press for expropriations, increased taxes, and greater worker rights. Even United Fruit had seen the handwriting on the wall and began to shift from direct control of production toward marketing during the 1950s.[29] Public utilities facing nationalization and continuing foreign-exchange problems shrank from 25 percent of U.S. investments to 14 percent. Petroleum and mining soared from one-third of the total to more than 50 percent, with most of that resulting from expanded investments in oil. Most significantly for the long term, manufacturing, which accounted for less than 7 percent of the total in 1940, represented more than 18 percent of U.S. direct investment by 1960.[30] That development stemmed from a number of factors.

U.S. manufacturing companies were anxious to exploit expanding Latin American markets especially in the larger economies such as Brazil, Mexico, and Argentina. The environment for such investments in the region proved favorable despite the adoption of ISI. Latin American governments were quite willing, even anxious, to have U.S. and other foreign corporations circumvent their protectionist barriers by investing directly in their economies. They viewed such investment as a further spur to industrialization, although they remained committed to protecting those manufacturing sectors dominated by local capitalists. Even as the U.S. government encouraged ISI policies, Washington maintained its opposition to statist economic policies that gave the government direct control over much of the economy and might be used to exclude foreign investors. The United States, however, encouraged Latin American states to achieve self-sufficiency in those industrial sectors that would support their exports of primary products such as minerals and provide inputs for U.S. manufacturers operating in their economies. Yet the surge in U.S. investment despite the intensification of Latin American economic nationalism was not simply the product of government policies.

The enclave profile that typified most U.S. enterprises in Latin America through the 1930s had undergone significant modification by the 1950s. In response to nationalist pressures these corporations sought to integrate themselves more fully into local environments. Creole Petroleum, for example, was quick to point out that by the mid-1950s it was purchasing a quarter of its supplies and materials in Venezuela. In addition, the company supplied financing to local companies that provided the corporation with services such as hotels and ferryboats. Given its Rockefeller origins, it is not surprising that Creole invested $7 million in Nelson Rockefeller's Venezuelan Basic Economy Corporation and its experiments designed to boost agricultural production and food distribution in the country.[31] But perhaps the most interesting intersection between Creole and other institutions involved in the modernization mission was its effort at community development.

In an attempt to shed its enclave image, integrate itself more fully into the local community, and along the way reduce some of the costs of its company towns, Creole Petroleum launched its own Community Development and Integration Program in the early 1950s. The program evolved from the belief by company officials that "the tradition of local responsibility for local problems is not nearly as strong in Venezuela as for example, in the United States."[32] And as one company manager noted, its underlying assumption was "based on the world's experience that social progress is accelerated by the encouragement of individual initiative."[33] In other words, Creole would help overcome the obstacles to modernization inherent in Venezuela's traditional society by initiating community development programs that paralleled the efforts of the U.S. government. The company launched two community projects, one in Tamare and the other in Juidbana. In these communities the company would promote the development of educational and medical facilities, as well as stores and housing, but reduce its own role in the provision of these services. Rather than supplying company housing on a rental basis, the firm encouraged home ownership with financing for workers. By 1959, Tamare boasted a shopping center, movie theater, and other commercial facilities built and owned by local interests with Creole financing. But even more than in the case of the federal government's community development projects, it was clear here that the vision for these communities was strictly an American one, closely based on U.S. postwar suburbs and stressing the American belief in "democratic" capitalism, that is, a system in which large and small capitalist enterprise could coexist and bring general prosperity within the same social and economic order.[34]

But as much as some extractive industry enterprises like Creole might experiment with development initiatives based on foundation and government models, more widespread changes were being initiated by corporations in the fast-growing manufacturing and retail industries. Manufacturing within Latin America required increasing integration into local economies, with growing reliance on local manufacturers as well as local markets and financial networks. As a result, U.S. industrialists sought to upgrade and improve these parts of the local economy.

The GE manufacturing operations in Brazil represented a pioneering effort of this sort. The company over the years outsourced a variety of parts and subassemblies for products ranging from light bulbs to air conditioners. GE provided technical specifications for these components and supplied training and engineering advice to assist Brazilian enterprises in filling these orders. GE and other companies like it were carrying out a major transfer of technology and American production methods to the Latin American manufacturing sector.[35] Sears and Roebuck's Latin American operations had similar effects. In response to Mexico's ISI policies that restricted imports of consumer goods, the company helped finance a variety of local suppliers in clothing, furniture, and appliance manufacture. Although such efforts did not represent major technology transfers, the corporation did introduce aspects of American style and design to these local producers. More importantly, Sears made a significant contribution to the development of a consumer society, being among the first to place display advertising in newspapers and to introduce lighted display windows and open-rack displays of goods. Although hardly a pioneer in the Mexican credit field, Sears helped spread the practice of consumer credit. The retailer also went to great lengths to recruit and train Mexican employees while offering them benefits such as profit sharing.[36] Meanwhile, American labor unions sought to mold Latin American workers into cooperative members of the corporate community and carried out joint efforts with the U.S. government to mollify Latin American workers.

In response to Assistant Secretary of State William Clayton's 1945 address calling for a return to the liberal development polices of the 1920s, Latin American labor leaders, most notably Lombardo Toledano, rejected what they viewed as an attempt to undermine the process of industrialization in their countries in order to intensify U.S. domination of critical sectors of their national economies. But the AFL and CIO were united in their support of the so-called Clayton Plan. Leaders of the CIO made clear that they, as much as AFL figures, subscribed to the international economic policies of the alliance that now guided U.S. foreign policy. In accord with government and business, union leaders saw increased industrial exports as an essential part of maintaining domestic economic growth and job creation. Due to the CIO's support of this basic tenet of the alliance's economic policy, and what soon became a growing split within labor and political movements in the West over the issues of communism and the cold war, the federation would offer no serious resistance to the AFL's renewed offensive against Toledano and the CTAL in the postwar years. Any remaining differences between the two federations effectively disappeared when they merged in 1955 to form the AFL-CIO. Meanwhile, the AFL had reinvigorated its close ties to the federal government and became a major partner in the government's aggressive campaign against labor militants and the political left in Latin America.

Close cooperation between the federal government and the labor unions dated back to the war when Rockefeller's OIAA had worked with the AFL to offer an alternative to Vicente Lombardo Toledano's left-leaning CTAL. After the OIAA's labor liaison, Serafino Romauldi, joined the AFL, the State Department backed Romauldi and the AFL in their creation of the Organización Regional Interamericana de Trabajadores (ORIT). In turn the OIAA supported ORIT's work, subsidizing labor-training seminars. These training sessions were part of a much larger cooperative effort between the AFL-CIO, ORIT, and the U.S. and Mexican governments to secure control of major CTAL labor unions for the state-supported federation, the Confederación de Trabajadores de Mexico (CTM). The coalition succeeded in wresting control of the mineworkers and other key unions from the CTAL and building long-term relations with labor leaders through OIAA-financed trips to the United States.[37] Between 1953 and 1956, fifty-nine Mexican labor leaders visited the United States on such junkets. As one official explained in 1955, the purpose of one set of trips was "to gain the cooperation of union members for the productivity goal a number of editors and writers of major labor papers will soon study the adjustment of American labor to productivity problems in this country."[38] The positive effects of such trips became apparent in the case of one Mexican labor leader, Bernardo Cobos, who went to the United States on a four-month USIS grant to study labor education. When he returned, the CTM placed Cobos in charge of all of its worker education.[39] USIS with the support of ORIT and the CTM further aided the cause by publishing a biweekly report, "El Obrero," with international news on labor. But the information agency's principal mechanism for influencing labor was its film initiative, which promoted the advantages of bread-and-butter trade unionism. With the approval and support of its secretary general, Fidel Velásquez, the CTM circulated the films throughout the federation.[40]

The U.S. government and ORIT also attempted with less success to undermine Chile's left-leaning labor federation, the CUTCH. In 1952, Romauldi tried unsuccessfully to launch an anticommunist labor confederation in Chile. That same year, he led a delegation to Chile at the invitation of the Copper Mine Workers Confederation. Among the ORIT delegates was Paul K. Reed, an international representative of the United Mine Workers Union, who played a pivotal role in securing control of the Mexican Mine Workers Union for conservative progovernment labor leaders. In reporting on their visits to Chile's coal mines as well as the Kennecott and Anaconda copper operations, Reed and the others focused on two issues: levels of productivity and the state of management-labor relations. In the coal mines they made note of the outdated machinery and methods and the generally squalid living conditions of the workers. Giving expression to the American vision of high productivity, corporations with modern labor relations policies that would create a prosperous working class, and an environment safe for expanding U.S. investments, Romauldi concluded, "We noted that where cordial industrial relations were being practiced and grievances were speedily settled, productivity tended to rise and the average worker was generally free of anti-U.S. sentiments."[41]

USIS made a concerted effort to support the transformation of Chilean labor. Next to general support for U.S. foreign policy, the most important goal of USIS in Chile was "to demonstrate to [the] Chilean public and official circles the progressive and dynamic nature of the American economic system with particular emphasis on modern management practices and upon the advantages of a non-political, democratic labor movement."[42] USIS in Chile published a labor bulletin stressing the advantages of American trade unionism. The USIS developed the material "in close collaboration with the USOM [United States Overseas Mission] Labor Advisor, the Embassy Labor Attaché and Embassy Political Officers *and always in consultation with representatives of the large U.S. industries operating in Chile.*"[43] But problems with Latin American workers were not confined to the region itself. Many people whose lives were not improved by the project of modernization found an alternative in the United States itself.

People and Images

Ever since the United States had seized vast territories from Mexico in 1848, Mexicans had played a pivotal role in the economies of the American Southwest. Mexican workers helped build the railroad network of the region, and tens of thousands labored in agricultural enterprises from California to Oklahoma and Texas. In addition, the unstable conditions created by the Mexican Revolution prompted a quarter-million Mexicans to migrate legally to the United States between 1910 and 1920 while thousands more would find their own way across the border without legal sanction. By 1937 some 2.5 million Mexicans resided in the United States. The U.S. and Mexican governments sought to repatriate many of these immigrants during the Great Depression, but by the late 1930s the threat of war was creating a new demand for their labor.

The manpower requirements of the military and the needs of defense industries that attracted workers from lower-wage positions in agriculture and the railroads created a large new market for Mexican workers. During the war, the U.S. and Mexican governments established a state-supervised program for importing temporary laborers that brought several hundred thousand workers to the United States. Similar arrangements were continued into the 1950s. Between 1954 and 1959, 2.5 million contract workers entered the United States.[44] Mexican migrants shaped the early phase of a phenomenon that would intensify throughout the second half of the twentieth century. In ever-growing numbers, Mexicans and other Latin Americans would seek documented or undocumented entry into the United States, drawn by economic opportunity to the north and driven by weak economic growth and unstable conditions in their own societies. They would also share common problems of economic exploitation and racism in their new homeland. But a few Latin American immigrants enjoyed considerable success in the U.S. economy.

The extraordinary popularity of American baseball in Latin America, especially in the Caribbean and Central America, spawned a series of professional leagues, and after World War I the Cuban pitcher Adolfo Luque established himself as the first Latin American star of the U.S. major leagues. A handful of Cuban and Dominican players made it to the majors during the 1920s and '30s, prompting some African Americans to try and pass themselves off as Latinos in order to evade major league baseball's strict color barrier. Once Jackie Robinson broke that barrier in 1947, the door for Latin American talent opened wide, and more than seventy Latin American players made their debut by 1959, including stars such as Camilo Pascual, Oreste "Minnie" Miñoso, and Roberto Clemente.[45] But in the film industry the Latino presence had diminished.

The end of the war brought a drastic decline in Hollywood's generation of Latino-themed movies, and actors such as Carmen Miranda and Desi Arnaz soon found their film careers evaporating. Despite Hollywood's shifting focus, Latin America continued to account for 20 percent of the foreign market for U.S. films. As a result, studio heads avoided producing movies that resurrected the ugly stereotypes of the past. Films such as *A Medal for Benny*, *Viva Zapata*, and *The Salt of the Earth* presented sympathetic portraits of Mexicans and Mexican Americans. By contrast, in America's newest entertainment medium, television, Desi Arnaz's role in *I Love Lucy* reinforced old stereotypes about Latino males as vain, temperamental figures whose heavy accents made them the target of numerous jokes.[46]

Although American television often presented stereotypical images of Latinos, U.S. television programs began to penetrate a small but growing market in Latin America while Hollywood products continued to dominate the region's cinemas. U.S. films carried their own power-ful messages about modernity, especially the idea that participation in a modern society required a flourishing consumer economy. These images proved compelling for many Latin Americans and would play a role in how they defined themselves and their societies as modern. Yet if the ideal modern society meant a democracy of choice in which everyone had an opportunity to participate as a consumer, most Latin American societies did not meet that standard. As postwar labor militancy clearly demonstrated, disparities in income distribution provoked unrest among the working class, creating a major challenge for U.S. business and the U.S. government.

Challenging the American Mission

Despite the fact that the state, business, foundations, and labor unions had achieved a consensus on modernization as the ideology of the American mission and had been working more closely than ever to achieve the goals of that mission, the United States continued to face serious challenges to its position. During the war the United States had welcomed liberalization of the autocratic or dictatorial regimes that governed many Latin American nations, including the overthrow of the Guatemalan dictator Jorge Ubico in 1944. Latin Americans had begun to respond en masse to the American mission's message of democracy. Yet many new regimes with a base of support rooted in the expanding urban middle and working classes gave vent to an even more strident version of the popular nationalism that had swept the region during the 1940s. Furthermore, socialist, communist, and other leftist political movements achieved a larger voice in national politics.

Much of the discontent that arose during this democratic surge sprang from wartime conditions. The rapid growth in exports fueled an equally fast increase in foreign-exchange earnings that caused the money supply to balloon in Latin American economies. The increase in the money supply fed rising demand for products that were often in short supply due to wartime conditions, leading to severe inflation. At the same time, workers and white-collar employees were unable to secure wage increases comparable to rates of inflation, as employers and the state cracked down on work stoppages in the name of the war effort.

When wartime conditions eased, labor militancy soared as working people struggled to secure a living wage.

Through most of the region, traditional elites and the military still held ultimate power and had minimal tolerance for the realities of democracy. Furthermore, those same elites, concerned with maintaining postwar growth, soon learned that the U.S. government was sending the bulk of its economic recovery aid to Europe and expected Latin Americans to attract more private U.S. investment in order to ensure growth in the region. Attracting U.S. capital would require a docile workforce that would accept low wages. A reaction against democratic openings and especially leftist and nationalist political movements as well as militant labor unions soon triggered an assault on the process of political liberalization. The U.S. government would offer encouragement and support for that reaction.[47] Yet the antidemocratic tide did not sweep away anti-American sentiment.

The war and U.S. policies that had drawn Latin America more completely than ever into the U.S. economic system also stirred nationalistic resentment among Latin Americans, who argued that U.S. purchasing agreements had kept the prices of their exports artificially low. Increased American investment led to increased criticism of the dominant position that U.S. corporations enjoyed in key sectors of national economies. Despite the efforts of some U.S. corporations to adopt more positive attitudes toward Latin Americans, workers still experienced racist attitudes among some of their managers and were often treated as second-class citizens. More generally the process of modernization generated increasing unrest within Latin American societies and growing resentment toward the American version of development.

During the postwar period the concentration of wealth within Latin America remained extreme with the top 20 percent of income earners receiving 60 percent of national income versus the 45 percent that was typical in developed countries. The share of the bottom 20 percent of earners was only 3.7 percent, while inflation created a general problem for the middle and working classes. Annual population increases of 2.5 percent or more placed serious strains on government resources, and the disintegration of many peasant communities sent a flood of migrants toward urban areas where slow job growth meant most of them would not find full-time employment.[48] These conditions and continuing resentment of corporate America, which was the engine of American modernization strategies, stirred new militancy among middle- and working-class people, who struggled against North American bias and the erosion of their standard of living. Anxious to defend U.S. economic interests and wary of militant labor and political movements that they often perceived as evidence of communist infiltration, U.S. policymakers would strike out aggressively at these threats to American hegemony.

The degree to which the United States reacted to challenges to its postwar position depended on the perceived nature and extent of the threat. For example, the United States had been unfailingly hostile to what it viewed as Argentina's pro-Axis military government during the war and had tried unsuccessfully to undermine General Juan Perón's bid for the presidency in 1946. Perón, with strong backing from organized labor, fashioned a nationalist populist regime marked initially by extensive strikes and later by the nationalization of U.S. companies in the telephone and electric industries. Although the State Department was incensed by Argentine labor militancy and chagrined by the nationalizations, U.S.-Argentine relations improved markedly by the beginning of the 1950s. In part this reflected a realistic assessment by American officials about the prospects for U.S. utilities in Latin America. In his 1950 memorandum, George Kennan had noted, "I think we should recognize that foreign ownership of public utilities and other enterprises whose operations have a direct effect and significant impact on the daily lives of peoples, is by and large a thing of the past."[49] For his part, Perón made clear his own staunch anticommunism and by 1949 was bringing the unions under tight centralized control. Furthermore, Peronist economic policies provided for compensation for all nationalized U.S. investments, and Perón expressed his desire to encourage further U.S. investment. Perón might well represent a populist form of economic nationalism that would affect some U.S. interests, but Peronism obviously did not constitute a radical challenge to the American mission.[50] Elsewhere in the region Washington identified more serious threats of just that type.

In the closing months of 1946 Gabriel González Videla of the centrist Radical Party played on nationalist and populist issues in a successful campaign for the Chilean presidency. Once in office, the new president forged a coalition government that included the conservative Liberal Party and the Communist Party. González Videla continued to speak in sympathetic terms about the plight of Chilean workers and hinted at the possibility of nationalizing the copper industry. But his coalition soon came under intense pressure from a power struggle that pitted Chilean workers and the Communist Party against González Videla as well as U.S. corporations and the State Department. Despite efforts by U.S. copper companies to integrate Chilean workers into their enterprises with policies promoting the nuclear family, education, and competitive athletics, blue- and white-collar employees deeply resented their status as second-class citizens excluded from mining camp facilities for American workers and the damage to their standard of living wrecked by inflation.

After the settlement of a strike at El Teniente, workers remained deeply dissatisfied and job actions spread throughout the copper, nitrate, and coal industries. The Communist Party gave strong backing to these labor actions and sought to organize campesino unions in the countryside. The El Teniente strike and subsequent labor actions, along with the growing militancy of the Communist Party, brought external pressure on the Chilean president. The heads of the U.S. copper companies and State Department officials made it clear that this unrest would make it impossible for the corporations to expand their investments in Chile and would prevent Chile from securing new and badly needed loans from U.S. institutions such as the EXIM Bank.

Faced with U.S. pressure and the internal challenge from the communists, González Videla expelled the Communist Party from his government in late 1947 and declared a state of emergency in those provinces where the coal, copper, and nitrate industries were located. The government arrested union and Communist Party leaders, sending many off to concentration camps in the northern desert. The State Department quickly secured a $4 million credit from the EXIM Bank so that Chile could pay for badly needed coal, and the country's international financial transactions soon returned to normal. After the government passed the Law for the Defense of Democracy, which outlawed the Communist Party, Anaconda announced a plan to invest $130 million in its Chuquicamata mine. Although González Videla had been motivated by the obvious communist challenge to his authority, he had a particularly strong incentive to carry out a harsh crackdown to ensure badly needed international financing and renewed foreign investment.[51]

But the United States would save its strongest measures to deal with a perceived communist threat closer to home.

The 1944 Guatemalan Revolution created an opening for democracy that allowed workers for the United Fruit Company and its subsidiary, the International Railway Company of Central America, to successfully press for better hours and pay. With the election of Jacobo Arbenz in 1950 the company faced new challenges as the president used a new agrarian reform law to expropriate most of UFCO's vast landholdings, offered support to militant actions by its workers, and began building a highway that would undermine the railway's transportation monopoly. In addition, a government-appointed mediator concluded that workers at AFP's Guatemalan electric company were due a 40 percent pay increase. In neighboring Honduras, where banana workers had also begun to mobilize, leading to a massive two-month-long strike in 1954, U.S. diplomats detected the influence of Guatemalan diplomats.

The Eisenhower administration was certainly influenced by UFCO's and AFP's calls for help and was convinced that Arbenz's actions comprised part of a larger anti-American conspiracy formulated by the president's communist advisors. But they saw an even larger threat inherent in Guatemalan policies. A year before the toppling of President Arbenz, a National Security Council report on the possibility of an antitrust suit against UFCO had explained the importance of countering Guatemala's actions. As the report noted, "In Latin America generally, nationalization of the United Fruit Company properties would further stimulate the already serious movement for similar action against the U.S. companies, which have properties with the established value of $5 billion in Latin America including strategic industries in the fields of mining and petroleum."[52] In light of these considerations the administration set in motion the CIA covert operation that ended Guatemala's all-too-brief experiment in democracy in June 1954.[53] Ernesto Che Guevara, an Argentine medical student and government sympathizer, witnessed Arbenz's downfall and then fled to Mexico where he would join the cause of the young Cuban Fidel Castro. Together Castro and Guevara would launch a revolution in Cuba, the birthplace of America's civilizing mission.

In the years that stretched from the end of World War II to the toppling of the Arbenz government, the United States had dramatically reshaped its mission to Latin America. The civilizing empire had given way to the mission of modernization. Americans, who once viewed their neighbors as uncivilized and racially inferior, had reimagined Latin Americans as constrained by traditional cultures that impeded them on the journey to modernization. In the process of that reformulation, the agents of the American mission including the state, corporations, foundations, and labor unions had increasingly coalesced around a strategy that would promote capitalist development while maintaining social stability and fighting economic nationalism and communism. The state in particular took on a greatly enhanced role in that process as it added an array of national and multilateral agencies to promote modernization while combating ideological challenges to that mission.

Yet as much as modernization theorists had pushed aside rigid racial causation in favor of images of partnership and modifiable cultural differences while crafting precise strategies for the American mission, they continued to perceive that task as a paternalistic endeavor of uplift in which the United States and its brand of capitalism must play an essential role. Whatever their altruistic aims, the agents of the American mission consistently sought to bind Latin America more closely to their economic system and refashion its people in their own image. At the same time, the agents of this mission remained convinced that the productivity imbedded in their version of modernization made radical restructuring of social and economic power relationships unnecessary.

Although Latin Americans responded positively to the mission of modernization, they remained selective in the integration of American ideas and values into their own cultures. Cognizant of the acute disparities between rich and poor in their societies, many Latin Americans concluded that democracy must translate into economic as well as political equality. They embraced the U.S. wartime encouragement of democracy, but many Latin Americans used it to give vent to worker militancy and to support leftist and nationalist political movements. While welcoming efforts by the United States to reinvigorate the global economy and the basic tenets of modernization theory, they conceived their own modernization strategy that pressed for a far-larger role for the nation-state in development and for greater control over foreign enterprises. As its actions in Chile and Guatemala made clear, the United States, concerned with combating communism and nationalism and determined that it would design and direct Latin America's development, crushed the most radical challenges to its reconfigured mission. But those actions would enflame, not extinguish, popular resentment toward the Colossus of the North, leading to new and dangerous turbulence in Latin America during the 1960s.

CHAPTER SEVEN

DEFENDING THE MISSION OF MODERNIZATION, 1959–1969

As the professional gunfighter Chris Adams rode into the sunbaked village only the town elder emerged to welcome him. The old man explained the timidity of the local peasants by noting that his people were farmers who were "afraid of everything." But other villagers soon appeared to greet Chris and his six companions. In fact, it had been the younger peasant leaders who had crossed the Rio Grande and implored Adams and his mercenary colleagues to come to their rescue. The peasants looked to this small band of Americans to protect them from the bandit chief Calvera and his henchmen, who regularly pillaged the town and murdered innocent citizens. In a final deadly confrontation with Calvera, the Americans liberated the villagers and redeemed themselves.

The Magnificent Seven's classic tale of violence, liberation, and redemption played out on cinema screens across the United States in 1960 while another band of Americans was undertaking a similar mission of liberation in Latin America. In Washington DC, Richard Bissell, the head of the CIA's covert operations branch, and a handful of associates were preparing the Bay of Pigs operation to liberate Cubans from what the Americans believed was Fidel Castro's communist tyranny. The pipe-smoking, Yale-educated Richard Bissell would never be mistaken for the black-clad Western gunfighter Chris Adams, but their missions bore striking similarities.

In *The Magnificent Seven*, the American filmmaker depicted the villagers as childlike in their deference toward the American gunfighters. Richard Bissell's boss, Allen Dulles, the director of Central Intelligence, concluded, "The new Cuban officials had to be treated more or less like children."[1] For Americans, Calvera and Castro became the bearded embodiments of the tyrannical extremist. Just as Adams and the other gunfighters trained the peasants in the use of weapons to aid in their own liberation, Bissell and his crew were training Cuban exiles in paramilitary tactics to liberate their homeland. And in the end both groups would turn to violence in the hopes of saving Latin Americans from what the Americans would describe as the forces of evil.[2] In fact, from the Cuban invasion to the U.S. intervention in the Dominican Republic in 1965 and the CIA's hunt for Che Guevara, who attempted to spark a revolution in Bolivia in 1967, the use of violence became a continuing pattern in U.S.–Latin American relations. As leftist political leaders and revolutionaries challenged the U.S. mission of modernization and the inequities in their own societies, U.S. leaders resorted to interventionist tactics, which while more sophisticated than simple gunboat diplomacy, harkened back to the methods of the imperialist mission of the early twentieth century. Counterinsurgency and covert operations had now joined productivity and anticommunism as fundamental tenets of the American mission of modernization.

☙

At the time of John F. Kennedy's election, the New Deal political alliance among Democrats, big business, and big labor continued to function effectively, and the American design for a U.S.-dominated, open world economy had taken concrete form through multilateral organizations such as the World Bank and the IMF. His election also brought to power a new generation of the American elite trained in the imperial traditions personified by Henry L. Stimson, who had brokered the peace agreement in Nicaragua in the late 1920s and later served as secretary of war and secretary of state. Kennedy and advisors such as McGeorge Bundy had been educated in exclusive eastern boarding schools that instilled in them a sense of belonging to an elite brotherhood marked by a masculine code of conduct that stressed physical courage and unselfish service to defending the American empire. They were in a very real sense the intellectual and spiritual heirs of Teddy Roosevelt and Henry L. Stimson. Kennedy and his advisors saw themselves as aggressive, heroic males dedicated to defending the empire from challenges emanating from the Soviet Union and the third world, especially Vietnam and Latin America. And while Kennedy's successor Lyndon Johnson had endured economic hardship growing up in Texas where he attended public schools, he too would assume the trappings of this warrior elite and consistently seek to demonstrate his commitment to that manly cause in his own foreign policy decisions.[3]

Despite assuming leadership in a period of continuing postwar economic prosperity and U.S. global dominance, John F. Kennedy and Lyndon Johnson perceived an increasing threat to U.S. power from the Soviet Union and feared that the United States's economic boom and relative social calm might soon come to an end. As a result, both presidents pursued an aggressive anticommunist foreign policy combined with efforts to stimulate the national economy while expanding social welfare benefits at home.

The concern for social stability grew out of the mounting campaign by African Americans to overcome institutionalized discrimination. Their struggles also helped expose the deep divide that separated rich and poor in American society. Building on the New Deal legacy, the state responded to these challenges with an expanded program of social welfare exemplified by Lyndon Johnson's plans for a "Great Society." At the same time, U.S. leaders ramped up military spending, hoping to counter a new threat they perceived in the third world as scores of nations emerged from the disintegration of European colonial empires, and Soviet Prime Minister Nikita Khrushchev sought allies among these newly created states. A Soviet challenge in the third world threatened U.S. economic interests as American multinationals poured increasing amounts of capital into these countries. Washington's commitment to combat what it perceived as Soviet-inspired wars of national liberation drew the nation ever more deeply into a series of confrontations in the third world, most notably in Vietnam. Yet policies designed to ensure domestic stability and continued U.S. international dominance contributed to mounting difficulties on both fronts.

The Democratic Party's support of the civil rights movement alienated middle- and working-class elements of its base constituency, who began to perceive the movement as the creature of a single special interest group. At the same time, the struggles of African Americans helped prompt new liberation movements among a broad array of groups including Hispanics, women, and gays. As U.S casualties in Vietnam mounted after Washington began committing combat troops in 1965, the nation became increasingly polarized over the war.[4] For much of this turbulent time, Latin America exemplified for U.S. policymakers both the promise of their policies of social and economic engineering and the threat of social instability and communist revolution in the third world.

The challenge of revolution became a reality in January 1959 when Fidel Castro's guerrilla forces marched into Havana. Castro's triumph represented an intersection of historical actors and events that had strongly influenced U.S.–Latin American relations. The revolution had erupted on the island where General Leonard Wood had attempted to create a version of his own Anglo-Saxon republic. Castro had challenged and defeated Cuban dictator Fulgencio Batista, who had once allied himself with Sumner Welles to end Cuba's 1933 revolution—events that helped define the parameters of the noninterventionist strategy of the Roosevelt administration. Castro's close ally as he battled Batista from the mountains of eastern Cuba was Che Guevara, the young Argentinean who had witnessed the U.S.-engineered overthrow of Guatemalan president Jacobo Arbenz. In 1957 when reports circulated that Castro had died, *New York Times* reporter Herbert L. Matthews trekked into the Cuban mountains to check out the story. As a young man, Matthews had idealized Richard Harding Davis, who had dramatized the Cuban independence struggle with his depiction of Adolfo Rodriguez's stoic heroism. Matthews found Castro very much alive and in a series of articles depicted him as a heroic young

revolutionary.[5] But Castro's expropriation of U.S. corporate investments and his increasing ties to the Soviet Union quickly convinced
U.S. leaders that he represented the most serious threat that they had
ever faced in Latin America.

The Cuban Revolution shook the U.S. foreign policy establishment
to its foundations. More than half a century of intense U.S. involvement
in Cuba had ended in a revolution that took on an anti-American tone,
nationalized more than $1 billion in U.S. investments, and drew ever
closer to the Soviet Union. The revolution also infused popular mobilizations in Latin America with new energy, offering a far more radical
alterative than the prescriptions of populist politicians. The revolution
not only prompted the Bay of Pigs operation; it also led to a commitment by the U.S. government to wage a wide-ranging war against what
was believed to be the threat of communist insurgencies throughout
Latin America. President Kennedy launched the Alliance for Progress,
a program of economic aid to relieve the poverty and social inequality
believed to fuel communist insurgencies. Yet despite the grand design
of the alliance, one nation after another seemed to flirt with the possibility of radical revolution.

≈

At the beginning of the 1960s the economic prospects of Latin America
seemed as bright as those of the United States. The larger economies such
as Brazil, Argentina, Mexico, and Chile were fully engaged in Import
Substituting Industrialization, with multinational corporations playing
an important role in the development of their manufacturing sectors.
During the decade, the Latin American economies averaged healthy
annual growth rates of 5.4 percent. And yet, as in the United States, these
positive economic signs were more than matched by negative developments. Population growth rates in the region pushing 3.0 percent annually meant that effective per capita economic growth was less than half the
5.4 percent figure. The ever-increasing commercialization of agriculture drove hundreds of thousands of now landless peasants into
urban settings with limited job opportunities, contributing to high
levels of unemployment and underemployment and straining social
services. Despite economic growth, the disparities between rich and

poor persisted and even worsened. The poorest 20 percent of Latin Americans accounted for only 3.4 percent of national income, while the richest 20 percent continued to capture as much as 60 percent of that income. These continuing gaps between rich and poor despite growing economies, combined with the continued concentration of political power in a relatively few hands, gave rise to new waves of unrest in the region.[6]

Latin Americans increasingly tested the limits of populist politics that had promoted the formation of multiclass political movements and sought reform within existing political institutions. As doubts arose over the unfulfilled promises of populist leaders, some Latin Americans sought more radical solutions to social and economic inequities. In addition to the upheaval in Cuba, guerrillas stalked the jungles of Colombia and Peru while Brazilian peasants mobilized and demanded land. Although the Communist Party remained extremely small except in Cuba and Chile, Fidel Castro and Che Guevara became living symbols of revolutionary liberation to millions of Latin Americans. A variety of leftist and populist political movements captured support by denouncing the deep-seated inequities that persisted in their societies despite the onrushing process of modernization. Furthermore, Latin American intellectuals constructed a new paradigm to explain the persistent underdevelopment of their economies and societies.

Dependency theorists, such as the Brazilian sociologist Fernando Henrique Cardoso, argued that Latin America's plight stemmed from its position as a peripheral region exploited throughout the centuries by a core of capitalist countries, most recently the United States. In alliance with Latin American elites, foreign capitalists had crafted structures that kept Latin America dependent on the production and export of raw materials and the infusion of foreign industrial goods and capital. In the process foreigners had strengthened a traditional elite that thrived on its interests in the export sector and the plentiful supply of cheap foreign imports while discouraging self-sustaining economic development.

Dependency theorists provided a powerful critique of the dominant U.S. position for political movements covering a broad spectrum of ideologies. The theorists argued that the powerful U.S. presence in the region prompted not only economic underdevelopment but also facilitated the survival of a conservative elite and the highly inequitable structures of political and social power that underpinned their position. The theory also illustrated a fundamental difference between Americans and Latin Americans regarding the concept of democracy. Americans increasingly saw democracy as the freedom to consume guarded by political institutions that insured orderly transfers of power. While American campaigns for democracy certainly resonated among Latin Americans, they also brought to the forefront the struggle between elite liberalism and popular demands for social and economic democracy and the restructuring of power relations that obstructed such democracy. Clashes over these very different agendas had roiled the region throughout most of the nineteenth century and contributed to Latin America's democratic resurgence at the end of World War II. As events during the 1940s had demonstrated, there was little doubt which side Washington would choose to support. Little wonder that Presidents Kennedy and Johnson believed Latin America to be an increasingly dangerous environment, where communism threatened to undermine a half-century of U.S. hegemony. In response, Washington launched a series of covert interventions to counter that threat. The growing concern of U.S. leaders with creating a rigid regional social stability reflected not only a heightened concern with communism but also the increased vulnerability of American multinationals.

Protecting U.S. business had at one time, with the rare exceptions of the Mexican Revolution and the 1933 Cuban Revolution, been a relatively simple matter. Gunboats and marines could be dispatched to suppress unrest against American fruteras, or as in the case of Peru in the 1930s, local governments could be pressured to crack down on militant workers. But in that earlier era, U.S. investments consisted largely of mining and agricultural export enclaves, where threats from workers, peasants, small planters, and merchants could be easily targeted and crushed. By the 1960s, conditions had changed dramatically. Threats to extractive industries came not simply from local strikers or demonstrators, but from the economic policies of elected national governments. Furthermore, manufacturing industries, the fastest-growing segment of U.S. investment, were integrating themselves into national economies, drawing on local suppliers and credit networks, and relying on the growth of local markets for their success. It would not take a direct threat to such corporations to do them serious harm. Social unrest that disrupted a national economy, or the failure of a state to curtail inflation, could be just as damaging as labor actions directed at a specific company. At the same time, Import Substituting Industrialization had enabled members of the domestic elite in the larger Latin American economies to build substantial positions in their own manufacturing sectors, making them equally vulnerable to threats of systemic instability. In light of these conditions, Washington, anxious to protect U.S. corporations and its Latin American allies, would show zero tolerance for social mobilization. That became apparent in the execution of the Alliance for Progress.

The Alliance for Progress

On Tuesday, April 18, 1961, in the hours before dawn broke over Playa Larga on Cuba's Bay of Pigs, Erneido Oliva led his men in a pitched battle against the advancing tanks and troops of the Cuban Army. Although Oliva's forces succeeded in halting the army's advance, they only briefly delayed the collapse of the invasion by fourteen hundred Cuban exiles, which Richard Bissell had carefully planned and orchestrated.[7] Much like the ill-fated Narciso López more than a century earlier, the planners of the Bay of Pigs operation assumed that a small-scale invasion would trigger a massive popular uprising on the island—an uprising that never took place. The invaders were attempting to halt a revolution whose policies of expropriating U.S. assets and wealth redistribution represented a repudiation of the American mission and whose historical roots could be traced at least as far back as the 1933 revolution. But rather than humbling President Kennedy, the Cuban fiasco made him even more aggressive in confronting Castro and the more general threat of communism in Latin America.

In the months after the Bay of Pigs, the CIA renewed earlier efforts to assassinate Castro and disrupt the Cuban economy. Seeking help from the Soviet Union, Castro convinced Nikita Khrushchev to install nuclear-tipped missiles on the island. Washington's nineteenth-century concern that a foreign power might use the island to challenge U.S. interests in the region had reemerged as a contemporary nuclear nightmare. The Soviet weapons installations triggered a confrontation between the United States and the Soviet Union known as the Cuban Missile Crisis. With the two superpowers teetering on the brink of nuclear conflict both sides sought a compromise, and the crisis ended with the withdrawal of the missiles and a commitment by Kennedy not to invade the island. But even before the failure at the Bay of Pigs, Kennedy had launched a broad new initiative to promote economic development and social reform that he hoped would deter the rise of communist insurgencies elsewhere in Latin America. The program took on new urgency in light of Kennedy's failure to roll back the Cuban revolution.[8]

❧

On March 13, 1961, President Kennedy formally announced the launching of the Alliance for Progress. Reminiscent of Franklin Roosevelt's Good Neighbor Policy, the Kennedy administration envisioned a broad development program that would in effect make the United States and Latin America partners in progress. Almost simultaneously the president also created the Peace Corps, a program designed to send thousands of young American volunteers to assist in development projects in the third world. That same year the Kennedy administration created the Agency for International Development (AID), which consolidated foreign aid activities that had previously operated under programs such as Point Four. The Alliance for Progress specifically called for the infusion of increased U.S. economic aid totaling $20 billion to boost Latin American nations into the "takeoff stage" of self-sustaining development. At the same time the alliance linked such assistance to Latin American efforts to create more just and equitable societies. Kennedy hoped the alliance, by spurring economic development and more open societies, would offer a capitalist alternative to socialism. In theory at least, the alliance tied the protection of U.S. interests to bettering the lives of impoverished and disenfranchised Latin Americans. In practice, the United States would not stray far from its long-standing alliance with Latin American elites and its desire to protect its economic interests in the region.

Kennedy's programs were rooted in the ideas of American modernization theorists. In fact modernization scholars such as W. W. Rostow and Lincoln Gordon assumed critical roles in his administration. The alliance's architects viewed Latin America as a series of traditional societies impeded on the path to progress by a variety of obstacles such as a

lack of individual initiative and insufficient emphasis on rational problem solving. Modernization theorists believed that they could design
efficient, relatively low-cost programs that would overcome these difficulties. At the same time, these approaches reflected the paternalistic
attitudes that had long characterized U.S. policies toward the region.
More importantly, as in the past, American planners stressed the need to
maintain social stability as these transformations took place. The preservation of the existing power relationships in the region would be essential to protecting the closely linked interests of the United States and its
allies, the Latin American elites.

In the minds of U.S. policymakers it was precisely at the time that
societies were experiencing the rapid changes of modernization that they
were most susceptible to communist influence. In 1957 Walt Rostow and
his coauthor Max Millikan had stressed the importance of this problem
for U.S. foreign policy. They emphasized that the United States must
start "steering the world's newly aroused human energies in constructive
rather than destructive directions."[9] The need for the United States to
combat the inevitable link between modernization and social instability was explained in great detail in 1962 by Irving Tragen, the American
labor attaché in Caracas. Tragen described how Venezuela's oil boom had
shaken its traditional order, as well as the role U.S. programs would play
in the process of modernization and the maintenance of social order:

> The new social order created massive social problems, which
> an underdeveloped governmental system was not prepared to
> meet. The lack of trained technicians and administrators made
> government ineffectual in meeting rising popular demands for
> adequate housing, public health, social security and spiritual
> satisfaction. A society in transition lacked the human resources
> to channel constructively the fruits of economic transformation.
>   In this environment, the exotic doctrines of Marxist
> ideology became the medium of intellectuals for espousing
> utopian solutions for complex problems. . . .
>   The challenge of any program for social development in
> Venezuela is the formulation and execution of programs which
> will effectively facilitate the adaptation and fitting of the masses
> into the new social order.

For this, a program must be designed primarily to educate and train—both in the narrow sense of learning needed skills for incorporation into modern economic society and in the broader sense of assimilating the knowledges [sic] and discipline needed for effective and constructive participation in civic life. Those who live on the fringes of society become the most susceptible to violent change; those who have no stake in society are indifferent to its maintenance.[10]

As events would soon prove, the maintenance of stability far outweighed concerns about development and social justice. But initially the planners of the Alliance for Progress shaped a program that reflected their conviction that they could rapidly modernize Latin America while maintaining order. Furthermore, they would find allies for their cause in Latin America, especially among middle-class political movements such as Venezuela's Acción Democrática (AD), which built its political project and indeed sought to shape national identity around a set of themes, most notably, nationalism, economic development, democracy, and social justice that were compatible with the goals of the Alliance for Progress.[11]

Under the Alliance for Progress, U.S. leaders called for the infusion of $20 billion in aid to be supplemented by considerably larger sums from Latin Americans and U.S. business interests. Washington committed itself to a series of laudable goals, including raising the rate of economic growth, improving and expanding education and health services, agrarian reform, and improved agricultural productivity, as well as encouraging liberal democracy. During the 1960s the United States in fact funneled some $18 billion into the region, largely through AID and multilateral organizations such as the newly created Inter-American Development Bank (IDB) and the International Bank for Reconstruction and Development. During that time, the IDB alone made $600 million in loans for agrarian reform and development throughout Latin America. To address problems created by the explosive growth in urban populations, AID and the IDB loaned $500 million for low-cost housing projects in the region. In addition, the United States provided $157 million in direct assistance to education programs.[12] And yet after a decade of such assistance, even early supporters of the alliance confessed that it had largely failed to fulfill its promise.

The Kennedy administration had sought to raise per capita economic growth rates to 2.5 percent annually, but actual rates hovered around 1.5 percent. There had been no widespread redistribution of land to peasants, and agricultural production and per capita food production had fallen. The alliance effectively abandoned its housing programs, and the number of children who were receiving no formal education had actually risen.[13] A variety of factors help explain these failures. The "Best and the Brightest," as the leading figures in the Kennedy administration were known, had been wildly optimistic in their projections of what targeted development and reform programs could achieve. Much of the money funneled into the region went not to promote economic growth or reform, but to meet exploding payments due on earlier foreign loans. Many of Kennedy's advisors also argued that under Lyndon Johnson the alliance had taken a distinctly conservative turn, robbing it of its focus on social and economic justice. Yet in the end, the simple truth was that the alliance represented no more than a permutation of earlier policies designed to ensure stability for U.S. interests while promoting modernization.

Chile emerged as a showcase for the Alliance for Progress and U.S. policy in general, receiving more aid per capita than any other Latin American country. Chile appeared to provide an ideal opportunity to prove the viability of U.S. programs. The nation had a long tradition of political stability. Although by no means a full-fledged democracy, the franchise was gradually being extended to an ever-larger portion of the population. And while Chile suffered from slow economic growth and inflation, its problems seemed eminently solvable in comparison to the acute levels of underdevelopment that plagued many other Latin American economies. Furthermore, during the early years of the alliance, an ideal political partner seemed to be emerging in the person of Eduardo Frei, leader of the Christian Democratic Party (PDC). The Christian Democrats stressed a technocratic approach to achieving modernization while adopting a fairly conservative stance on social issues. Frei and his PDC colleagues were just the type of cautious, moderate modernizers that Washington sought. They also might be able to blunt the growing popularity of a communist-socialist coalition led by Dr. Salvador Allende Gossens. Taking no chances on the latter front, the CIA funneled $20 million into the 1964 presidential campaign. CIA assistance and the decision of conservative voters to choose Frei in order to avoid an Allende presidency provided a comfortable victory margin for the Christian Democratic candidate.

Once Frei took office, the United States made every effort to ensure the success of his programs for reform and modernization. The Frei government sharply increased state spending on education and succeeded in dramatically reducing the number of children not receiving any formal schooling. Washington made certain to publicize its support of these programs. The Sociedad de Santiago School, which received U.S. aid, flew both the Chilean and U.S. flags. Its students wore a JFK logo on their uniforms and learned the principal facts of the U.S. president's life. Such initiatives and the positive publicity they generated might justify the tens of millions of dollars that the United States provided in education assistance.[14] But elsewhere the record of the Chilean-U.S. partnership proved far less impressive. Frei had promised to settle one hundred thousand peasants on their own land during his six-year term of office. But while the United States provided millions of dollars in assistance for resettling peasants, the Chilean government distributed land to only about twenty-one thousand individuals. In terms of economic growth, the per capita rate of growth slipped into negative numbers during the last three years of Frei's presidency, unemployment fluctuated between 20 and 25 percent, and inflation continued to eat away at the average Chilean's standard of living.[15] The failure of Frei's development programs helped pave the road to victory for socialist Salvador Allende in his run for the presidency in 1970.

The eventual failure of Frei and the Christian Democrats stemmed in no small part from their development and reform program that so closely mimicked the U.S. plan for Latin America's future. That plan included a continuing dominant role for U.S. business in the nation's economy and reform programs that were extremely conservative in their approach to achieving social justice, stressing instead the importance of accelerating economic efficiency. The PDC sought to avoid the course of action promoted by Allende and supported by most Chileans—the outright nationalization of the U.S.-dominated copper industry that accounted for more than 50 percent of Chile's annual exports. Instead Frei called for the Chileanization of the copper industry, a process in which the Chilean government would buy part ownership in the U.S.-dominated sector.

The Kennecott Company, one of two U.S. corporate giants that controlled 90 percent of Chile's copper wealth, embraced Frei's program with an astute strategy. It offered Frei the 51 percent share that he desired while at the same time borrowing $110 million from the EXIM Bank to finance part of a $257 million expansion program for its El Teniente mine. Kennecott then took the Chilean government's payment of $80 million for its share in the company and loaned it back to itself and insured that loan through an AID guarantee program. In short, the Alliance for Progress served to finance a dramatic increase in the size and value of Kennecott's operations in Chile, while the involvement of the EXIM Bank and AID meant that any attempt at nationalization would bring on a direct confrontation with the U.S. government.[16] In the end, the new arrangement actually led to reduced returns to the state from copper, and it failed to still the popular demand for all-out nationalization.

In the area of agrarian reform Frei proved unwilling to aggressively push a process, which would anger Chile's landowning elite. Before the end of Frei's presidential term, the leader of the PDC's principal agrarian program led his frustrated peasant supporters out of the PDC and into Allende's leftist coalition. Such developments hardly fazed Washington because while policymakers had recognized the need for land reform, they had no desire to promote mass mobilization or class conflict in the Chilean countryside. As in the 1950s, agricultural productivity represented the leading concern for the United States. Despite ideal agricultural conditions in Chile's Central Valley that made it the South American equivalent of California's San Joaquin Valley, Chile was unable to feed itself, and food accounted for 20 percent of the nation's total imports by 1967.

American policymakers saw agrarian reform less as a force for social justice and more as an important means of enhancing productivity improvement. U.S. support for agriculture focused on commercial farmers, not agrarian reform. Of the $28 million the IDB loaned to Chilean agriculture, $10 million went to small commercial farmers, $10 million for infrastructure improvements, only a portion of which would help reformed areas, with only the last $8 million spent on peasant resettlement. In short, the alliance's main thrust in agriculture built on Albion Patterson's model of assisting commercial farmers to increase productivity and production in order to provide cheaper food for what was hoped would be an expanding industrial workforce.[17] Ultimately, the U.S. initiative in Chile hued to a highly conservative modernization model that continued to promote U.S. economic dominance while encouraging increased economic efficiency, especially in agriculture, and avoiding serious challenges to the deep-seated inequities in Chilean society. In the end that model could not save the PDC or U.S. interests. Meanwhile, in Brazil, Washington employed the alliance to actually combat social mobilization.

Unlike Chile, Brazil certainly did not appear to be a potential showcase for the Alliance for Progress. Although Brazil had strengthened its economic ties to the United States after the Roosevelt administration agreed to fund the Volta Redonda steel plant, and Brazilian troops had fought alongside U.S. forces in Italy, it could scarcely be considered a shining example of democracy or a nation making major strides on the road to social equality. From 1930 to 1945, Getulio Vargas had ruled the nation through an authoritarian populist regime that created a state-controlled network of unions to manage labor unrest and pressed forward a nationalist program of industrialization, which nonetheless welcomed foreign investment. Military officers, who had long acted as regulators of the civilian political process, ousted Vargas in 1945, setting the stage for the election of one of their own as president, only to see Vargas return to power in 1951 for a brief, ill-fated term of office that ended in his suicide.

As of 1960, Brazil continued on the trajectory that Vargas had set in the 1930s, that is, an accelerating process of industrialization staffed by an urban labor force under the supervision of state-controlled labor federations. But for Brazilian peasants these developments offered little in the way of help or hope. The country's large rural population eked out an existence on tiny subsistence plots or as low-wage workers on the large estates of the elite. Brazil's rural northeastern region, consisting of nine states, was considered one of the poorest areas in Latin America.

During the early 1960s the dynamics of authoritarian populism began to change. Peasants in the northeast had been organizing Peasant Leagues to fight for their rights, and some labor leaders were showing a new independence from the state-run system of unions. The abrupt resignation of President Jânio Quadros in August 1961 left his vice president, João Goulart, in charge. Washington came to view Goulart, a

Vargas protégé, as an opportunistic populist willing to make alliances with dangerous leftists such as his brother-in-law Lionel Brizola, the governor of the state of Rio Grande do Sul.

For the Kennedy administration, Brazil emerged not so much as a showcase, but as a must-win situation for the Alliance for Progress. As the largest country in Latin America, sporting a well-advanced process of industrialization but troubled by highly imperfect democratic institutions and an increasingly mobilized peasantry and working class, Brazil emerged as a critical test case of the United States's ability to promote modernization, while avoiding the radical course now being pursued in Cuba. From the outset, the United States made security against communist inroads rather than development the top priority in Brazil and throughout Latin America. During the period 1961 through 1964, U.S. military aid to the region increased by an average of 50 percent over the levels reached during the Eisenhower administration. Kennedy envisioned Latin American militaries as particularly appropriate agents of the U.S. mission. Scholars such as John J. Johnson of Stanford University argued that military officers were themselves members of the middle class, who no longer represented the interests of the elite and who wanted to promote industrialization and efficiency. U.S. assistance focused on promoting counterinsurgency programs to assist the military in thwarting guerrilla uprisings. Such programs would include civic action initiatives in which the military would win the hearts and minds of the local population by undertaking projects such as building schools and roads. In addition, AID began a massive police-training program in Brazil and other countries to ensure that urban police forces could suppress riots and other forms of unrest that might contribute to destabilization.[18] These short-term concerns about the political future also permeated the larger projects of the alliance.

The Brazilian government, well aware of the acute underdevelopment of the northeast, created the Superintendency for the Development of the Northeast (SUDENE) in 1959. Under the leadership of its director Celso Furtado, SUDENE designed and began implementing plans for infrastructure projects that would promote industrialization and thereby long-term development. Given the fact that Brazil had already created a professional development agency for the region, the northeast appeared to be an ideal location to launch alliance initiatives that would be professionally managed and effective. However, the U.S. embassy had become increasingly concerned by the radical pronouncements of Francisco Julião, the leader of the Peasant Leagues. Julião, himself a major landowner with populist political ambitions, was being marginalized in national politics and faced growing competition from peasant unions sponsored by the Catholic Church. But U.S. diplomats took his demands for immediate land reform seriously and insisted that aid to the northeast must be in a form that would have the short-term political effects of blunting Julião's presumed influence and assisting conservative candidates for governorships in the 1962 elections.[19]

Driven by short-term political concerns, U.S. aid for the northeast flowed into education and health projects, specifically the building of schools and clinics that would hopefully have a positive political impact by convincing the poor of the region that the United States was sincerely committed to bettering their lot. Although state governors eagerly accepted the opportunity to expend U.S. dollars to buy political support and funnel funds to their backers, the end result was medical clinics without the professionals to staff them and the construction of only a fraction of the planned school buildings. The one AID-funded educational initiative that enjoyed visible success was the literacy program directed by Brazilian philosopher and educator Paulo Freire. Freire's program emphasized dialogue between student and teacher and the encouragement of a sense of personal responsibility by the student. But the program nurtured that sense of responsibility by promoting discussions of contemporary events including local and national problems. Although AID's modernization schemes sought to encourage self-reliance, the Americans criticized Freire's methods as highly politicized activities that fomented social unrest. As a result, the United States cancelled funding for the literacy program in January 1964.[20] On the national level similar political concerns had become particularly intense for the CIA as the 1962 elections approached.

In 1959 the CIA set up the Brazilian Institute for Democratic Action (IBAD), a front organization ostensibly created by Brazilian military and business leaders. The CIA used the organization in an effort to influence the 1960 presidential election, which resulted in Jânio Quadros's brief tenure as president. The IBAD also provided a Brazilian face to American criticism of Brazilian policies. In late 1961, the CIA through the IBAD encouraged and helped fund the creation of a private research organization known as the Institute of Research and Social Studies (IPES). The military and business figures who led the IPES were united by a militant anticommunism and used the institute to gather intelligence information on communists and other suspected subversives. During the 1962 elections for state governors and congress, the CIA funneled at least $5 million through IBAD and to a lesser extent IPES to back hundreds of conservative candidates for state and federal offices. Although the elections did little to alter the political profile of Brazil, the United States would continue its efforts to influence and even destabilize the Brazilian political system.[21]

From the moment he became president after Jânio Quadros's resignation, Jão Goulart's grip on power was tenuous at best. Conservatives had only acquiesced to Goulart's assuming office after passing a constitutional amendment that severely limited his powers. Goulart spent much of his brief time in office trying to rally support for a 1963 plebiscite that would restore full powers to the presidency. That proved no easy task because leftists, who were his logical allies, remained highly suspicious of Goulart's populist politics. Furthermore, his courting of the left incensed the Kennedy administration and finally convinced Washington to seek his ouster.

During the course of 1962 a number of issues stoked U.S. animosity toward Goulart—his signing of a profit-remittance bill that would limit the ability of U.S. corporations to send their profits back to the United States, a general strike and food riots in early July, Leonel Brizola's expropriation of ITT's assets in Rio Grande do Sul, and the American and Foreign Power Company's insistence that the government buy out all its Brazilian assets.[22] From these disparate events, most of which Goulart had little control over, the Kennedy administration concluded that Goulart was hostile to U.S. business and willing to ally himself with communists. From Washington's perspective, Brazil appeared to be emerging as the worst-case scenario for Latin America's future. The national regime seemed open to leftist influence and tolerated policies inimical to U.S. business interests while allowing social ferment. Such developments created serious additional risks for U.S. multinationals that had embedded themselves in Brazil's social and economic system, leaving them vulnerable to domestic instability.

In December 1962, the National Security Council, composed of the president's principal advisors on national security issues, dispatched Attorney General Robert Kennedy to Brazil to lecture Goulart on such issues as ITT and the profit-remittance law. At the same time the council decided on a tactic later dubbed the "Islands of Sanity" policy that would direct future aid away from the central government and toward regional anti-Goulart political forces.[23] During the course of 1963, Washington viewed events in Brazil with mounting concern as the plebiscite restored full powers to the presidency. In addition, a new labor law authorized agricultural workers to form unions—rapidly accelerating the mobilization of the rural poor. With their own efforts to destabilize Brazil underway, U.S. policymakers anxiously awaited a military coup to topple Goulart. Well aware of preparations for a coup by March 1964, the U.S. ambassador requested an assistance package including petroleum, small arms, and the dispatch of an aircraft carrier task force to Brazil. With that aid on its way, Washington cancelled the operation on April 2 because the Brazilian military had already overthrown Goulart. Although the new military regime arrested thousands of Brazilian intellectuals, students, and union and peasant leaders and proceeded to impose a harsh dictatorship, the Johnson administration would shower it with economic assistance.[24] The perceived threat from popular mobilization exposed the fact that social and political instability far outweighed economic development concerns when it came to U.S. priorities in Latin America. Brazil also created a blueprint for another, more focused destabilization program by the United States less than a decade later in what had been the showcase nation of the Alliance for Progress. Meanwhile, the threat to U.S. economic interests loomed ever larger.

PARTNERS IN PROGRESS

The ten years that followed the triumph of Fidel Castro in 1959 seemed to bring nothing but bad news for U.S. businesses in the region. Castro's land reform program led to the expropriation of hundreds of thousands of acres owned by American firms such as United Fruit and the King Ranch. The Cuban government ordered the GE subsidiary, AFP, to cut rates and refused to let it make dollar remittances to the United States. Its revenues falling and unable to make payments on its loans, the corporation might have welcomed its expropriation in 1960. But the bonds it was to receive in compensation were tied to Cuban sugar exports to the United States, which Washington was cutting off. The wave of nationalizations swept away $1 billion in U.S. investments including corporate giants like GE, ITT, and United Fruit. Fulfilling the worst fears of U.S. officials, the Cuban actions appeared to set off a series of nationalizations across Latin America.[25] During the mid-1960s, the American and Foreign Power Company faced the takeover of its operations in Brazil and Chile. In 1969 the highly nationalistic military government of Peru expropriated the entire $190 million assets of the International Petroleum Company (IPC), a subsidiary of the Standard Oil Company. Yet even as these expropriations proceeded, U.S. investment in the region nearly doubled.

Direct U.S. investment, which totaled slightly more than $8 billion in 1960, climbed to nearly $15 billion by 1970. A number of factors help explain this surge in investment, even as expropriations seemed to spread like wildfire. First, with the exception of the Cuban takeovers, the expropriating governments usually provided compensation to the companies, in many cases with provisions that the payments be reinvested in their national economies.[26] In addition, the alliance between the state and multinational corporations forged during the New Deal was now functioning at maximum efficiency with Washington providing considerable legislative and financial support for corporations investing overseas.

Although the EXIM Bank had been designed to promote exports, the bank also facilitated foreign investment by providing low-cost loans for companies to buy capital goods that they used to build overseas subsidiaries. Since the 1950s the government had also been offering insurance against expropriation for companies investing in developing countries. During the 1960s, AID administered the program and then spun it off as a separate institution, the Overseas Private Investment Corporation (OPIC).[27] AID also administered the P. L. 480 program that took some of the foreign currency earned from sales of surplus agricultural products and lent it to U.S. companies investing in developing countries.[28] In addition, Congress passed the Hickenlooper Amendment in 1962, which required a cutoff of foreign aid to any country that expropriated U.S. investments without prompt and adequate compensation.[29] Finally, most expropriations zeroed in on extractive industries, including petroleum, mining, and public utilities, which had long been targets of nationalist ire. And while these sectors were struggling with nationalization, manufacturing rapidly became the cutting edge of U.S. foreign investment. Manufacturing investments soared during the 1960s, accounting for nearly one-third of all direct U.S. holdings in the region by 1970. That trend continued throughout the next decade with manufacturing reaching $16 billion, or more than 41 percent of total U.S. investments.[30]

General Electric's early initiatives in Latin America had centered on the development and control of power grids, largely through its subsidiary American and Foreign Power Company. That strategy allowed GE to create a market for its power generation equipment while maintaining tight control over the valuable technology it represented. But as early as the 1920s, the company had begun selling consumer products such as light bulbs and radios. By the beginning of the 1960s the firm had joined the movement toward creating factories for its products in the region's largest economies such as Brazil and Mexico. Like other manufacturers, GE would need to integrate itself ever more deeply into local economies and societies. The company created a credit network that incorporated retailers and consumers. Because GE required highly skilled and disciplined workers, it provided technical training as well as incentives to ensure regular attendance. In Brazil the company offered assistance to universities and shaped their curricula to create a steady supply of qualified engineers. It also responded to the nationalist protests of the populist era, and by the 1960s, its local supervisory and technical staff were almost all Brazilians. GE relied on mass advertising campaigns to promote demand for its products and to introduce consumers to the wonders of new technologies such as refrigerators.[31]

Much like General Electric, Coca-Cola had been an early entrant in the Latin American market. However, prior to World War II, it had enjoyed little success outside of the clusters of American expatriate communities in the circum-Caribbean. But with the outbreak of the war, the company launched an intense marketing effort with a particular focus on Mexico, where it spent half of its $350,000 Latin American advertising budget in 1942. Through newspapers, radio, and wall posters, the company initiated a multifaceted campaign. In keeping with the U.S. government's stress on hemispheric partnerships, Coke incorporated slogans about solidarity of the Americas along with an emphasis on the high quality of its product. It sponsored radio programs featuring

Mexican music to create an image of Coke as a "Mexican" product, while also sponsoring raffles that helped imprint its slogans on the minds of Mexican consumers.[32]

In Brazil, the company downplayed its U.S. image by contracting with prominent Brazilians as its franchisees, and it established exclusive purchasing arrangements with them to ensure the dominance of its soft drinks.[33] By the 1960s, Coke faced intense competition from Pepsi-Cola, which sought to tap into the social unrest among Brazilian youth by recasting the marketing slogan "Pepsi Generation" as the "Pepsi Revolution." By choosing the "new" Pepsi over the "old" Coke, Brazilian youth could supposedly express their social and generational discontents. The beverage companies were helping to establish a common value of modern consumer societies, namely, that personal identity can be defined by the material goods and services that an individual consumes.[34] These messages for a wide range of U.S. consumer products and the promotion of the ideas of a consumer society were now being spread not only through films and radio but also television.

When episodes of *I Love Lucy* were flickering across Latin American TV screens in the mid-1950s there were only about six hundred thousand sets in the entire region. However, by 1968 the number of sets was approaching ten million with more than two hundred stations bracketing the area. This explosive growth in a medium, which brought a dizzying array of images directly into the homes of millions of Latin Americans, represented rapidly growing market opportunities for U.S. businesses on several different fronts. First, American television networks, especially ABC, began acquiring interests in networks throughout Latin America. Although the presence of U.S. firms in the region's broadcast infrastructure would soon crest and subside, the leading U.S. networks would still be supplying 80 percent of all programming for Latin American television as of the early 1970s. In addition, television rapidly became the fastest-growing and most important medium for advertising in most of the region. Corporate America could now transmit its messages about the quality of its products and the ideals of consumerism directly to Latin Americans on a daily basis.[35] Cognizant of the power and growing pervasiveness of the medium, U.S. advertising agencies made television a major focus of their campaigns. Unlike the 1930s, when J. Walter Thompson stood out as a Latin American pioneer among large firms,

there was now a field crowded with more than a dozen major U.S. advertising agencies. Thompson continued to lead its competitors with more
than $60 million in billings in 1960; however, McCann-Erickson was a
close second and conducted business in sixteen Latin American countries, more than twice as many as the Thompson agency.[36]

Although the American state focused on creating positive opinions about U.S. foreign policy rather than specifically promoting U.S.
products and consumerism, it mimicked corporate efforts by employing
television as a major tool in conveying its message. The United States
Information Service provided a wide array of television programs and
series to local stations with this purpose in mind. The service produced
some of the series, such as *Enfoque las Americas*, which publicized the
Alliance for Progress, while in other cases USIS acquired documenta-
ries produced by the major networks for distribution in the region. The
service set up 110 stations or offices in Latin America that maintained
libraries and distributed books to schools and universities while also
supplying news copy to local television stations—all with the intention
of disseminating a positive American image among Latin Americans.[37]
Although the state had provided various forms of support to corporations and worked along parallel courses to theirs in communications,
it played a far more dominant role in the Latin American activities of
American labor unions.

ORIT, the AFL-CIO's Latin American labor federation, had proved
an effective weapon against the leftist labor federation CTAL during the
1950s. But AFL-CIO officials became increasingly dissatisfied with ORIT
as some of its affiliated unions demonstrated nationalistic leanings that
clashed with U.S. interests. One such controversy erupted in Cuba where
the leaders of the CTC, the ORIT affiliated labor federation, rejected Fidel
Castro's calls for a general strike against the Batista dictatorship. Protests
against the no-strike policy by union members led to purges of the unions
and set off conflicts within the CTC.[38] Such problems and the challenge
of the Cuban Revolution led the AFL-CIO to create a new instrument for
its international policy with the establishment of the American Institute
for Free Labor Development (AIFLD) in 1961. Although ostensibly an
independent labor institution, the AIFLD received 90 percent of its funding from the U.S. government, funneled to it through the CIA and then
increasingly through AID. J. Peter Grace of Grace and Company chaired

its board, and other board members represented such corporations as Anaconda, United Fruit, Merck and Company, as well as the Rockefeller interests.[39] In effect, the institute became a policy instrument jointly managed by representatives from organized labor, the state, and large corporations. From the outset, its activities reflected the shared anticommunist ideology of its creators and managers.

AIFLD created anticommunist unions and labor federations, and it trained labor leaders in the principles of what it termed "democratic labor organizing." The institute brought more than five hundred Latin American labor leaders to the United States for training at its Font Royal, Virginia training facility, and thirty thousand others received training at AIFLD offices in Latin America between 1962 and 1968.[40] Most of this training dealt with issues of combating communism as opposed to techniques of labor organizing. AIFLD personnel usually initiated organization of unions and federations to counter the growing influence of what they considered to be leftist labor movements.

In Brazil, AIFLD operated two stations, one in Recife in the volatile Northeast and the other in São Paulo, the industrial center of the country. Potential labor leaders received scholarships for three months of local training, with a few sent on for three more months of work in the United States. They then spent another nine months on the AIFLD payroll practicing what they had learned. Although the AIFLD director later boasted that these trainees had played a critical role in the 1964 coup, it is unclear whether they did in fact have a major impact. Indeed, AIFLD seemed to have relatively little success organizing anticommunist unions among Brazilian workers, who were more concerned with the bread-and-butter issues that AIFLD claimed to promote in its unions than with the strident anticommunist message of the AIFLD station personnel.[41] Central America also loomed large in the activities of the institute.

AIFLD established the Central American Institute for Labor Studies (IESCA) in 1963 to sponsor labor management conferences in the region. The institute then created the Central American Confederation of Workers to coordinate activities among regional AIFLD unions. Eventually the institute worked to organize rural associations for small farmers that encouraged their members to produce exportable crops as a counter to more militant campesino movements that demanded land reform. Typical of AIFLD's efforts was its creation of the National

Association of Agricultural Workers in Honduras. The association urged its members to work through the existing land reform law rather than adopt the tactics of other groups that engaged in illegal seizures to satisfy campesinos' land hunger. However, even AIFLD's very conservative approach to organizing workers and peasants proved too radical for the right-wing dictatorships in Guatemala and El Salvador where AIFLD was either expelled or chose to abandon its activities during the 1970s.[42] At the same time, another partner in progress was taking a different approach to the problems of peasants.

By the 1960s, the effects of the Rockefeller Foundation's Mexican agricultural programs were spreading through most of Latin America and the rest of the third world in a process commonly termed the Green Revolution. In the abstract, the Green Revolution represented the perfect embodiment of the American modernizing mission. U.S. experts would apply technologies to a fundamental development obstacle thrown up by traditional societies, obliterating the roadblock to economic advancement while leaving unaddressed larger issues of inequalities in economic and political power, assuming they would dissolve as these societies proceeded down the road of development.

The Rockefeller project, which began in the 1940s, offered a seemingly straightforward technological solution to Mexico's lack of self-sufficiency in food production. The foundation would send experts to develop hybrid versions of corn and wheat that would dramatically increase production of both crops. Despite the recent strains on U.S.-Mexican relations due to the nationalization of the oil industry, U.S. and Mexican elites could strongly support a project that promised to end hunger in Mexico, burnish the image of the United States as a humanitarian power, fend off Nazi and later communist exploitation of the poor and hungry, and facilitate industrialization by supplying cheap and abundant food to urban workers. And the results of the project seemed just short of miraculous. By 1956 Mexico achieved self-sufficiency in wheat production, and in 1964 the country exported half a million tons of the staple crop. The foundation soon sought to spread the benefits of hybrid seeds throughout the region, establishing the Inter-American Food Crop Improvement Program in 1959 and creating the International Center for Tropical Agriculture in Colombia in 1967. But despite the impressive numbers that the hybrid programs consistently produced, serious problems underlay the whole process.[43]

Although the foundation's agricultural experts conceived of themselves as impartial and objective, they in fact harbored serious biases regarding the peasants, who comprised the overwhelming majority of Latin America's rural populations. One officer observed at the beginning of the program that "it would probably be wholly impossible to introduce hybrid corn on a significant scale to an unorganized, largely ignorant peasantry."[44] Foundation scientists claimed to be the impartial purveyors of technology, and yet one of them commented in retrospect that "from a national standpoint, it would have been better if the food production had been in the hands of the more intelligent people and the large land owners who could operate on a bigger scale. . . . But the Mexicans preferred the poverty and freedom to operate the land themselves."[45] It was not simply a matter of personal prejudice, for the technology itself was embedded with a bias that favored the economically better off in rural society.

The Green Revolution did not simply rely on the creation and dissemination of higher-yield grain types. The new high-yield grains required fertilizer, machinery, irrigation, and the application of pesticides to achieve their impressive increases in output. Furthermore, producers who chose to plant hybrid seeds would need quality transportation and marketing systems to ensure that their crops could be sold at remunerative prices. All these requirements meant that the programs of the Green Revolution favored agriculturists with substantial landholdings and access to capital. For the vast majority of subsistence peasants with small holdings and little or no capital, the hybrid seeds represented significant risks. Peasants had long assured their survival by planting a range of crops, avoiding the risks of a single crop that could easily fall victim to disease or extremes of weather. Within the Green Revolution, they would have to go into debt, hope that marketing and transportation systems proved adequate, and take the very high risk of single-crop production for commercial markets where prices could fluctuate dramatically.[46]

The Mexican state, following the logic and biases built into the Green Revolution, pumped money into the northwestern states to support commercial wheat farmers. The government rehabilitated the railroad systems, built new farm-to-market roads, invested heavily in irrigation, and supported the development of fertilizer factories. In contrast, the *ejiditarios*, who worked communal holdings farther south, found themselves starved of fertilizer and credit by the state. Not surprisingly, their productivity rapidly fell behind that of commercial farmers using hybrid seeds.[47] By the 1960s, foundation personnel recognized the disparities created by their Green Revolution and began programs directed at small farmers. But despite one such program in Colombia's Cauca Valley, the technological advantages of large-scale farms producing sugar and corn had effectively eliminated small-scale producers in the area by the beginning of the 1970s.[48] Some peasants, who could no longer support their families due to competition from the Green Revolution farmers, would find work on these commercial ventures. But the capital and technological intensity of the new farms limited such opportunities. The Green Revolution for all its accomplishments in food production advanced the capitalist development of agriculture that accelerated the disintegration of peasant societies and contributed to the growing stream of impoverished rural residents, who flocked to urban centers in a futile search for decent-paying jobs. Rural to urban migration was one of many problems arising from modernization, which the foundations hoped could be managed by a new generation of technocrats.

The foundations initiated a two-prong strategy to ensure the training of social scientists, who could serve as a technocratic elite to manage the modernization of their own societies and to ensure that the American concept of modernization would serve as their development model. First the foundations targeted specific universities for assistance, counting on them to serve as catalysts that would influence other academic institutions in the same country. The field staff of the foundations worked closely with administrators and faculty to create or enhance social science departments and institutes. They also cooperated with AID and the World Bank as both these institutions often provided additional funding for the targeted universities. Although a latecomer to Latin America, the Ford Foundation would emerge as the leading financial supporter of social science research in Latin America during the 1960s. And while their support indicated that foundation officials expected that most future leaders of Latin America would be trained in local universities, both Ford and Rockefeller selected hundreds of outstanding students for fellowships that sent them to elite institutions such as Chicago, Harvard, and Stanford. One particularly notable joint government-foundation effort to upgrade academic departments occurred in Chile, where the

University of Chicago worked closely with the Catholic University to train a new generation of economists who would have a profound influence on the nation's economy after the military seized power in 1973.

Albion Patterson, the Nelson Rockefeller protégé who designed the agrarian development program for southern Chile in the 1950s, had not restricted his ambitions to reshaping Chilean agriculture. Patterson's experiences as a U.S. technical advisor in Latin America convinced him that a key obstacle to the successful implementation of U.S. aid programs in the region was the absence of well-trained Latin American social scientists, especially economists, who could work effectively with U.S. experts to implement reforms. That belief was reinforced in a meeting with Professor Theodore W. Schultz of the Department of Economics at the University of Chicago. Led by such figures as Milton Friedman, Chicago's economics department had become a bastion of neoclassical economic thought, or what is now generally referred to as neoliberalism. Schultz's particular contribution was his argument that education, rather than simply constituting an act of consumption, represented investment in human capital that contributed significantly to economic growth. In his conversations with Schultz, Patterson discovered a theoretical underpinning for his interest in promoting higher education in the region as a means of accelerating development. Placing such a project in the hands of the Chicago economists would mesh perfectly with U.S. development strategies that promoted free markets, a larger role for foreign investment, and countered Marxist ideology and the protectionist strategies of Raul Prebisch.[49]

Thanks to Patterson's dogged determination, the University of Chicago, Chile's Catholic University, and the Point Four Program (later USAID) reached an agreement to train economists in 1956. With the U.S. government offering initial funding of $350,000, the members of the University of Chicago faculty would set up a graduate program in economics at the Catholic University. That process included training twenty-six Chilean students in Chicago's graduate program, many of whom returned to the Catholic University as faculty members in the new program.[50] Eventually, both the Rockefeller and Ford Foundations would provide significant financial support to the project. AID funded a similar undertaking by the University of Chicago in Argentina and another such initiative in Colombia with the assistance of the Rockefeller

Foundation. The Chicago faculty later extended their influence to Mexico and Panama. The Ford Foundation provided more than half a million dollars in support to a Chicago project to train graduate students from all over Latin America. Between 1965 and 1975 the university's Latin American program produced twenty-six PhDs and seventy-four MAs in economics. The Ford Foundation did not allocate its support along strict ideological lines. It provided even more aid to the University of Chile, where social scientists emphasized state-driven development policies. But the joint efforts of AID and the University of Chicago created a cadre of highly trained economists who were dedicated to the principle of free-market economics.[51] Given the lengthy gestation periods of professional careers, the full impact of these programs would not be apparent until the closing decades of the twentieth century. The foundations' higher-education project also sought to train leaders in the United States, who would have expertise in third world societies, including Latin America. By the mid-1960s the Ford Foundation had allocated $138 million for training foreign area specialists in the United States, and between 1959 and 1963 Ford dispersed $26 million to develop foreign area studies programs. Ford also funded the Foreign Area Fellowship Program, which between 1953 and 1965 funded the work of more than twelve hundred young scholars carrying out research overseas. Not all the young scholars who received these fellowships during the 1960s and '70s adopted the capitalist modernization theories that the foundations sought to promote—in fact some became proponents of dependency analysis.[52] But many others would provide their expertise to government and corporations as academic scholars or policy analysts.

Much like their counterparts in Washington, foundation bureaucrats expressed concern that third world countries enduring the social turbulence that they associated with modernization would be prime targets for communist infiltration. Part of their interest in the development of the social sciences in areas like Latin America was to provide a capitalist counter to communist ideology. The striking similarity between their concerns and those of Washington policymakers was hardly a coincidence. During the period of 1952 to 1971, three secretaries of state, John Foster Dulles, Cyrus Vance, and Dean Rusk, assumed their government posts after resigning from high-ranking positions in the Rockefeller Foundation.[53] But the concerns about the social sciences went beyond a simple anticommunism. Officials of the Ford Foundation, who had established their first Latin American offices in 1961, noted that one other reason for focusing on the social sciences was that "the theories of development and social change that had originated in North America and Europe were increasingly challenged by Latin Americans during the 1960s."[54] They were referring to the emergence of dependency theory that was having a profound impact on ideas about development.

Drawing on Marxist ideas about class conflict and imperialism, dependency theorists described Latin America's relationship with developed economies as one that was inherently exploitative. While these scholars might share some of the views of modernization theorists about the stages of economic growth, they directly challenged the central belief of people like Walt Rostow that infusions of foreign capital and expertise were essential to modernize traditional societies. Dependency advocates argued that true development only occurred in the region when its dependent relations with the developed world were frayed as during the Great Depression. Most dependency theorists asserted that socialism provided the only long-term policies, which would ensure economic development and social equality.[55] It is hardly surprising that foundation officers were anxious to combat the influence of dependency theory by shaping the development of social science departments in Latin American universities. At the same time, some members of the missionary movements that had once inspired secular philanthropists were seeking more radical solutions.

The social and political mobilizations that addressed the issues of poverty and inequality in Latin America during these decades soon engulfed Protestant churches. By this time, the vast majority of Protestant congregations counted themselves as thoroughly national in their membership and leadership. Many Protestants became increasingly concerned about the strife that afflicted their societies. Those concerns found expression among progressive Protestants, who felt that their Christian faith called them to relieve social injustices. Their efforts ranged from those who provided charitable assistance to the poor to theologians who engaged Marxists in dialogue. At the same time members of the Catholic clergy were also stirred to social action.

The hierarchy of the Catholic Church, which had long maintained a close identification with the ruling elite in most Latin American countries, found itself challenged by new ideas as a result of the papacy of John XXIII and the ideas generated at the Second Vatican Council (1961–65). The concept of a church committed to social activism drew support from the conference of bishops held in Medellín, Colombia, in 1968, and in the subsequent writings of Peruvian theologian Gustavo Gutiérrez, who coined the phrase Liberation Theology. The ideas of Liberation Theology, which called on the clergy to actively identify with the poor in their struggle for economic and social justice, resonated strongly among many church leaders, especially those in Brazil who had organized Base Ecclesiastical Communities (BECs) that sought to create communities of the faithful who would take an active role in their own liberation.[56] Liberation theology that also influenced activist movements in Protestant denominations sought to inspire a revolutionary mobilization of the disenfranchised to confront acute social and economic inequalities. But its challenges to the established order would help trigger massive repression in the region.

🙟

In the years after the Cuban Revolution, the New Deal coalition that guided U.S. foreign policy gave full vent to the American mission of modernization in Latin America. The Kennedy administration's Alliance for Progress embodied the idea that the powerful American technocratic state could, with infusions of public and private capital, reengineer Latin America's traditional societies and propel them toward full economic development, while promoting the growth of democratic institutions. Corporations, unions, philanthropic agencies, as well as multilateral institutions worked in close cooperation with the state in this project. But the mission of modernization suffered from a fundamental internal contradiction. Determined to defend its position and that of Latin American elites, the United States insisted that the process of modernization must not disrupt the existing power relations in the region. Overshadowing the goal of development was the concern with the need for development within a stable social environment. Ultimately anticommunism and the insistence on stability to protect foreign and domestic corporate interests led to U.S. policies that incited and supported military intervention and to the creation of repressive regimes in the region.

This increasingly aggressive policy that employed both covert and overt forms of intervention came easily to a generation of leaders who were heirs to the "manly" traditions of the American imperial brotherhood. Such an approach was not unwelcomed by corporate leaders, who, in an increasingly competitive global economy, were seeking the sort of offshore manufacturing platforms with low labor costs that military regimes such as the one in Brazil helped pioneer. But not all the initiatives of the coalition would meet with success, nor were they the only forces influencing interactions between Americans and Latin Americans.

The attempts of U.S. labor leaders to fashion anticommunist worker and peasant organizations dedicated to collective bargaining often failed to resonate among working people struggling to maintain subsistence in highly repressive political environments. While Washington promoted a form of democracy focused on the freedom to consume and regularized transfers of political power, most Latin Americans aspired to forms of democracy that sought more equitable distributions of wealth and political power. Other American influences were more complex in terms of their effects. American foundations, while seeking to promote economic development through the Green Revolution and the training of Latin American technocrats, also proved as anxious as ever to ensure social stability for American corporations investing in the area. And while the principal thrust of mainstream Protestant churches' missionary efforts had faded by the 1960s, Liberation Theology gave new vigor and social purpose to Christian clergy. But their activism and that of the political left would soon be crushed by a series of military regimes that enjoyed the backing of the United States.

CHAPTER EIGHT

DICTATORSHIP AND
REVOLUTION,
1970–1979

ON THE MORNING OF SEPTEMBER 10, 1973, ELEMENTS OF THE CHILEAN Navy left Valparaiso, the country's main port, ostensibly to rendezvous with U.S. naval forces and conduct joint maneuvers. However, by nightfall the Chilean vessels were steaming back to the coast. At that same time, several dozen military officers believed to still be loyal to President Salvador Allende's government were being rounded up. By the early morning of September 11, the Chilean Navy had seized Valparaiso, and Concepción, the country's third-largest city, was also under military control. Learning of the unfolding coup d'etat, President Allende left his residence and went to the Moneda, the presidential palace. Having rejected offers by the coup plotters to fly him into exile, Allende delivered a dramatic radio message declaring, "I am ready to resist by any means even at the cost of my life." By noon the Chilean Air Force was bombing and strafing the Moneda. During the attack Allende either took his own life or was killed in the attack. During the next several days the military suppressed scattered resistance and carried out summary executions. Tens of thousands of people were rounded up and held at local sports stadiums. The final total of victims of the coup remains unclear even today, but at a minimum three thousand people were killed during and after the coup.[1] Later, exiled members of Allende's government were assassinated by the Chilean secret police, and thousands of Chileans found themselves subjected to intimidation and torture. Chile's experiment in democratic socialism had ended in violent repression. In fact, the administration of President Richard Nixon had taken a very direct role in promoting the military coup when Chile's citizens turned their backs on American modernization policies by electing a Marxist president. The events in Chile typified an era in which Washington looked to repressive military regimes to preserve its interests in Latin America.

During the 1970s domestic political turmoil and persistent economic problems troubled American society. The Vietnam War tore at the political fabric of the nation as popular support for the conflict declined and demands for a complete U.S. military withdrawal mounted. Even when the war wound down as Washington withdrew more and more troops during the early 1970s, a new domestic debate erupted when President Richard Nixon's increasing fear of the war's opponents and his own political rivals led him to engage in illegal activities that triggered the famed Watergate scandal and finally led to the president's resignation. The attempt to fund both expanded social programs and an aggressive foreign policy, combined with the shock of rising oil prices in the 1970s, triggered a prolonged period of high inflation, high unemployment, and slow growth. In 1974 inflation topped 11 percent while unemployment began a rise that would take it from 6 to more than 8 percent in two years.[2] Furthermore, the economies of Western Europe and Japan were now challenging the global dominance of American corporations in sectors such as automobile manufacturing. These years were also marked by mounting suspicions of American youth culture, especially the recreational use of controlled substances. Conservative social commentators and the Nixon administration issued dire warnings about the threat drug use posed to the fabric of American society. Once again Washington identified Latin America as the root of its problem, declaring a "war on drugs" that would seek to impede the drug trade and suppress the production of controlled substances in Latin America. It is not surprising that under these conditions, U.S. policymakers seemed to operate from a siege mentality.

During these troubled years, American foreign policy was dominated by President Nixon and Henry Kissinger, who served as national security advisor for Nixon, and later as secretary of state to Presidents Nixon and Ford. Neither Nixon nor Kissinger fit the mold of the eastern establishment elite who had long dominated U.S. foreign policy. Nixon had grown up under difficult economic circumstances in California and attended Whittier College. Defining himself as a self-made man, he had nothing but contempt for the eastern establishment. Kissinger's family had fled Nazi Germany, and while he received an Ivy League education and attached himself as an advisor to Nelson Rockefeller, that paragon of the eastern foreign policy establishment, Kissinger worked diligently to distance himself from those connections as he sought entry into Nixon's inner circle.

Both men saw themselves as offering a corrective to what they viewed as the weak, even effeminate eastern elite that was no longer up to the task of protecting the empire. As a young congressman, Nixon had made his reputation as a tough anticommunist weeding out alleged subversives within the federal government. As president, Nixon would present himself as a no-nonsense statesman willing to confront communist challenges whether from the Soviet Union, Vietnam, or Latin America. Kissinger envisioned himself as following in the realist diplomatic tradition of European figures such as the nineteenth-century German chancellor Otto von Bismarck. Kissinger saw his mission as that of preserving the global dominance of the United States in the face of the rising power of the Soviet Union and the People's Republic of China. In Kissinger's world vision, Latin America represented a U.S. sphere of influence that must be protected from Soviet penetration. To achieve that goal, Kissinger and Nixon were quite willing to confront challenges to the U.S. position in Latin America and ally themselves with repressive military regimes.

In 1969 Nelson Rockefeller, who had loomed so large in the Americas for more than a quarter of a century, agreed to undertake a study mission to Latin America on behalf of President Nixon. Much like Richard Nixon's visit a decade earlier, mass demonstrations and repeated denunciations of Rockefeller and U.S. policies marred the trip. Rockefeller's diagnosis and prescription for the sad state into which inter-American relations had fallen grew directly out of his earlier experiences in the region. He argued that one of the most serious problems was the continued belief that U.S. investment represented nothing but exploitation of the region's riches by the United States. Rockefeller felt it essential that both sides work to open up their economic relationship by lowering trade and investment barriers.[3] He also picked up on a theme that had found resonance in government circles during the previous decade—that the military now represented a middle-class perspective and could be a source of reformist initiatives. Rockefeller described the new officer corps in glowing terms:

> Increasingly their concern and dedication is to the eradication of poverty and the improvement of the lot of the oppressed, both in rural and urban areas.
>
> In short, a new type of military man is coming to the fore and often becoming a major force for constructive social change in the American republics. Motivated by increasing impatience with corruption and inefficiency, and a stagnant political order, the new military man is prepared to adapt his authoritarian tradition to the goals of social and economic progress.[4]

Rockefeller clearly presented the military as an attractive alternative to elected civilian governments for solving the social and economic problems of the region. By the time of Rockefeller's trip, the Alliance for Progress had effectively ceased to function as a meaningful policy. Beyond the fact that the alliance had largely failed to produce signs of developmental progress, Washington had made clear through its actions in Brazil and the Dominican Republic that it focused on security and the protection of U.S. business interests, not development or liberal political institutions. These trends in U.S. policy during the 1960s opened the way for Rockefeller to reassert a vision for the region that he had long promoted while incorporating the support for military regimes of the Kennedy-era modernizers. Both of Rockefeller's recommendations would be prominently reflected in U.S. policy during the remaining decades of the twentieth century. Even with the election of President Jimmy Carter, who promoted human rights as a central feature of his foreign policy, Washington would continue to support the established power structures as they were challenged by radical domestic insurgencies. These policies first became apparent in the U.S. reaction to developments in the region involving U.S. multinationals.

THE CHILEAN CHALLENGE

On November 5, 1970, Salvador Allende, the newly inaugurated president of Chile, delivered an address to a gathering of foreign dignitaries in which he recalled with pride the sacrifices of an earlier Chilean president, José Manuel Balmaceda (1886–91). Balmaceda had championed a greater Chilean role in the British dominated nitrate industry and had clashed with congress over the control of state resources. In the civil war that ensued between the chief executive and congress, Balmaceda's forces suffered defeat and the president took his own life.[5] Allende himself would soon begin nationalizing more than $1 billion in U.S. investments and radically reshaping his country's social and economic contours. Those policies led to bitter conflict with centrist and right-wing groups and finally the military coup on September 11, 1973, that cost Allende his life.

Allende's path to power at the head of Unidad Popular or Popular Unity (UP), a leftist coalition dominated by the Communist and Socialist Parties, and the subsequent collapse of democracy in Chile, grew in part out of the experiences of the Frei administration. Despite significant financial backing from the Alliance for Progress, Frei had fallen far short of his agrarian reform goals, and by the end of the 1960s economic growth was falling behind population growth while inflation was advancing at a rapid rate. The shortcomings of moderate reforms pushed Chilean voters to both the left and the right. But more was transpiring in Chile than simply a political reaction to failed economic policies.

The Chilean middle class and the organized working class had first gained a significant voice in the state at the end of the 1930s through a center-left coalition known as the Popular Front. However, the elite's acceptance of political power sharing rested on a tacit understanding that centrist and leftist political parties would not disturb the elite's grip on rural society and its peasant population, which continued to provide a vital voting block for the ruling class.[6] Cracks in this historic compromise had begun to appear as early as the 1950s, and by the 1960s the parties of the center and the left were busily recruiting supporters in the countryside. Indeed, while Eduardo Frei made limited headway in terms of turning land over to peasants, he could point with pride to the fact that newly legalized peasant unions sported membership lists totaling 150,000. As the historic compromise began to crumble, political conflict began to rise with bombings carried out by the far left in 1968 and an abortive military coup in 1969.[7]

Salvador Allende believed that his nation's recent history of political compromise and the increasing enfranchisement of its citizens represented a "Chilean way" that would enable him to peacefully convert Chile into a socialist society. But Allende's ambitious program to transform Chile rapidly accelerated the social and political polarization that had emerged during Frei's presidency. The new government planned on creating an economy that included both public and private sectors with the public sector consisting of large domestic and foreign corporations that would be expropriated by the state. This development would be coupled with a sharp redistribution of wealth to benefit the lower half of income earners. Government planners believed this strategy would allow them to break the hold of monopolistic corporations and increase production as well as efficiency in response to what was certain to be rapidly rising demand.

The president's supporters hoped that these policies would accelerate development and build political support among the most marginalized groups in society. An intensification of agrarian reform comprised an important part of the program. In its first year, the Allende administration expropriated nearly as many properties as the Frei government had in six years. By mid-1972 the government had achieved its initial goal of expropriating all holdings larger than 80 hectares (32.4 acres), and by September 1973 it had taken over four thousand properties. Not surprisingly, these seizures infuriated large landowners, and illegal occupations prompted by militant groups aligned with the government spread doubt about the survival of modest-sized properties.[8] Chilean capitalists reacted with equal fury when the regime took over dozens of large domestic corporations, while growing labor militancy challenged those industrialists who retained ownership of their enterprises. Small businesses began to battle increasing government regulation and what they feared was the undermining of the principle of private property. As private investment declined while domestic demand grew, the government found it impossible to control inflation, which surged to more than 300 percent by 1973, further dividing Chileans over the Allende government and its policies. While much of the growing animosity and the economic problems can be attributed to inevitable class conflicts and poor planning by the government, the United States was doing all that it could to destabilize Chile economically and politically.[9]

In July 1971, the Chilean Congress unanimously approved the nationalization of the U.S. copper giants, Kennecott and Anaconda. Although Allende's Popular Unity coalition held only a minority of congressional seats, the nationalist measure enjoyed near universal support in the country. The two U.S. companies valued their investments at $600 million, but the government claimed that the corporations owed Chile $700 million in excess profits that it alleged the copper companies had earned during their decades of operation in the country. The Allende government deducted those excess profits from the estimated worth of the copper mines, leaving the two corporations with no compensation. The regime went on to seize virtually all U.S. corporate holdings, including those of the Bank of America, General Motors, and ITT. While most of these companies would receive some compensation, the copper giants had been left empty-handed, and ITT anticipated that it would receive only a fraction of the value of its investments.[10] Neither the companies nor the U.S. government would stand idly by as the Popular Unity government proceeded with these nationalizations.

For the Nixon administration, the Allende government represented a variety of threats. Allende was nationalizing more than $1 billion in U.S. investments, much of it without compensation. President Nixon saw Chile's Marxist government as a second communist front that when combined with communist Cuba threatened to destabilize South America from both the north and the south. And there was the unsettling image of a freely elected Marxist government coming to power in what had been the showcase of the Alliance for Progress. The Nixon administration had developed a two-track strategy to deal with the looming threat. The first track employed political tactics designed to prevent Allende's election and, failing that, to remove him from power.

The second and increasingly important strategy focused on destabilizing the country to force a military coup. Long accustomed to intervening in Chilean elections, the CIA expended at least $1 million supporting Allende's opponents. When Allende garnered more than 36 percent of the vote to lead his two principal competitors, the CIA then attempted to influence the Chilean Congress, which had routinely selected the leading vote getter as president in previous elections. These efforts to win congressional support for the second-place finisher collapsed. The CIA then tried to convince the military that Allende's election was triggering anarchy that must be suppressed. The agency backed an attempt by extremists to kidnap the commander of the armed forces. But the kidnapping effort ended in the murder of the commander, General René Schneider, and was soon exposed as a right-wing conspiracy.[11]

Undaunted by these setbacks, the CIA proceeded to expend $8 million during the next two and a half years to destabilize Chile and topple its government. The agency supported opposition newspapers, TV, and radio stations in a barrage of attacks on the government, including rumors designed to prompt panic among the public. It bankrolled right-wing paramilitary groups that pursued economic sabotage and assassination, as well as provided funding for a strike by truck owners between October and November 1972 that paralyzed much of the economy. That action represented a shift in tactics by the agency away from its focus on opposition political parties to the *gremialista* movement, a coalition of professional associations that controlled much of the country's economy.

Gremios were professional organizations that represented different sectors such as industrialists, landowners, truck owners, and various professionals. The agency came to see these groups as the holders of real power in the country, capable of paralyzing the economy as they did during the 1972 strike. In addition, Washington initiated an economic blockade, cutting off lending from national and multilateral agencies such as AID, the Inter-American Development Bank, and the World Bank. U.S. private enterprise joined in this effort. Kennecott brought suit in a number of European countries seeking the seizure of Chilean copper, which seriously dampened market demand for the Chilean product, while Anaconda schemed to lower world copper prices to shrink government revenues. ITT emerged as the most vociferous corporate opponent of the government. John McCone, an ITT executive and former director of Central Intelligence, offered the agency $1 million to prevent Allende from coming to power. Although the CIA rejected the offer, ITT executives continued to consult regularly with officials in the Nixon administration on strategies to topple the Chilean president.[12]

When the military under General Augusto Pinochet finally intervened in a bloody coup on September 11, 1973, the primary motivating force was the class conflict, which had torn Chilean society apart as a result of Allende's socialist experiment. But no one doubted that the United States had played a significant role in destabilizing the country by fueling political combat and launching a multifront assault on the national economy. In the aftermath of the coup, the United States embraced the new military regime that instituted a reign of terror leading to the deaths of thousands of Chileans, closed down the civilian political process, rolled back land reform, and welcomed U.S. corporations back to the country. In June 1976, Secretary of State Henry Kissinger met with Pinochet to assure him that a speech on human rights he was about to give at an OAS meeting was strictly to appease domestic critics in the United States. Kissinger was also quick to silence State Department officials who criticized human rights abuses in Chile and neighboring Argentina where the military also held sway.[13]

By the time of the coup in Chile most people in South America, including Brazilians, Argentineans, Uruguayans, Bolivians, and Peruvians, lived under military regimes. Unlike military dictatorships of the past that rested on the charismatic leadership of a single officer, these regimes represented rule by the military as an institution. In one sense academics such as John Johnson and members of the elite such as Rockefeller had correctly described the emergence of a new officer class. Latin American military leaders had appropriated much of the American model of modernization with its emphasis on capitalist economic development. But given their own authoritarian environments and the U.S. emphasis on internal security, these officers looked to political models that were radically different than the American vision of liberal democracy. Most of these regimes pursued harsh repressive policies designed to crush the mass mobilizations that had threatened the established order and planned on long-term military rule designed to transform the state into a stable authoritarian force. Explicitly or implicitly many of these officers envisioned a corporatist political model rooted in the region's colonial past that would organize society in a series of vertically integrated interest groups representing landowners, industrialists, the middle class, workers, and peasants. These hierarchal organizations would supposedly integrate the interests of groups at all levels of society and thus preempt the class conflicts that had become a common feature of modern and modernizing societies.[14] At the same time these regimes would seek partnerships with foreign corporations as a part of their development plans.

MILITARY AND CORPORATE MODERNIZERS

American corporations had faced a series of challenges to their interests during the early 1970s. In Chile, the socialist government nationalized more than $1 billion in U.S. investments. In 1974 the nationalistic military regime that ruled Peru expropriated the holdings of the U.S.-owned Cerro de Pasco Corporation that had long dominated the Peruvian mining sector. Finally, in 1976 Venezuela, a leading supplier of petroleum to the United States, seized the entire oil industry, valued at $1 billion.[15] Political risk assessment now became the mantra of corporate executives investing in Latin America. Many U.S. corporations seemed obsessed with threats of nationalization; restructuring their assets to avoid expropriation and, in the cases of Brazil and Chile, supporting military coups to preempt or undo such seizures. Even in countries where expropriation did not loom as a serious threat, policies of economic nationalism challenged U.S. interests. In Mexico, for example, corporations such as the Ford Motor Company found themselves pressured by the government's strategy of Mexicanization, that is, Mexican majority equity ownership of companies.[16] And yet, in the midst of this seemingly relentless assault on American companies, total U.S. investments in Latin America were increasing at a vigorous pace thanks in no small part to the new economic policies being pursued principally by the region's military regimes.

Although the specific strategies varied, military rulers (along with civilian governments such as in Mexico) concluded that their domestic markets were simply insufficient to sustain the industrialization process previously pursued under Import Substituting Industrialization (ISI). They turned away from the reliance on protected domestic markets and toward models based on the promotion of exports. In Brazil, the dictatorship fashioned a partnership between foreign corporations, domestic capitalists, and state enterprises to encourage industrial production for both export and domestic markets. To encourage industrial exports the state provided favorable exchange rates, tax rebates, and subsidized credit. As a further attraction to both foreign and domestic investment, the military froze wages and outlawed strikes. These tactics were also part of a larger strategy to increase domestic demand for consumer goods by shifting increasing portions of national income toward the elite and upper middle class, creating an expanding demand for consumer durables such as automobiles. In Brazil, the new policies produced a sharp increase in industrial exports and annual growth rates of 10 percent by the late 1960s.[17]

The Chilean dictatorship, following the advice of the American economist Milton Freidman and his disciples, pursued a program very similar to the liberal economic policies of the late nineteenth century. The protectionist barriers of ISI that had shielded domestic industry were torn down, opening the economy to the forces of world markets and promoting the growth of mineral and agricultural exports that would pay for the imports that would now replace the production of inefficient domestic industries. Again, the repression of labor activity that helped to drive down real wages and serve as an incentive for domestic and foreign investment played a key role in this strategy. Although these various approaches to development were not entirely welcoming to U.S. investment—Brazil, for example, limited foreign investment to certain economic sectors—they nevertheless represented a radical departure from the massive nationalizations and increased regulation of foreign investment that had typified the years since the Cuban Revolution.[18] For American business, they presented a golden opportunity to rapidly expand investments in Latin America.

The new economic policies pioneered by the Brazilian military regime and later emulated by both military (Argentina) and civilian governments (Mexico) gave new momentum to the rapid growth of U.S. corporations. Between 1967 and 1976 total U.S. investment in Brazil soared from $1.3 billion to $5.4 billion, accounting for more than 56 percent of the total increase in U.S. investment in all of Latin America.[19] The dictatorship's muzzling of labor unions and enforcement of low wages, along with its deliberate shifting of income toward the upper-income groups to deepen the domestic consumer market, and the elimination of restrictions on repatriating profits prompted this surge in U.S. corporate investment. American companies now achieved a prominent role in such sectors as automobiles, pharmaceuticals, electrical equipment, and machinery. The Institutionalized Revolutionary Party (PRI) that had governed Mexico through a one-party system since the revolution pursued similar policies to attract foreign investment in manufacturing, while the state continued to limit or exclude foreign capital from critical areas such as petroleum. One mechanism the state employed to attract foreign manufacturers was the *maquiladora* program initiated in 1965.

The maquiladora system provided for the creation of bonded manufacturing zones where foreign companies could import free of duty but under bond goods for assembly or processing within Mexico. When the manufacturer reexported the finished products, a duty would be paid only on the value added in Mexico. For U.S. companies facing an ever-more-competitive world market, the opportunity to assemble products with low-wage overseas labor without paying import duties proved irresistible. From 72 plants on the Mexican border in 1967, the U.S. commitment to maquiladoras grew to 665 facilities in 1974. By that latter year, these companies exported $450 million in added value to the United States.[20] Similar export processing zones, which did not include a bonding requirement, would sprout up elsewhere in the region during the 1970s as governments sought to attract foreign manufacturing investment. To improve their competitive advantage among a group of economies that all offered cheap labor, Latin American governments often suspended national labor codes such as minimum-wage requirements in the zones.[21]

Chile's military dictatorship followed a different economic plan than the one pioneered by the Brazilian military, opening its economy up by slashing import duties and encouraging nonmanufactured exports such as fish, flowers, and forestry products. At the same time, the regime opened wide the door to foreign investment, excluding only the previously nationalized copper mines for which it paid Kennecott and Anaconda $300 million. But even in this sector it encouraged new foreign investment so that by the end of the 1970s Standard Oil, the U.S. petroleum giant now known as Exxon, had already invested nearly $100 million in Chilean copper mines and was being joined in that sector by Getty Oil and Phelps Dodge. Meanwhile other U.S. companies were entering nontraditional export sectors such as forestry products.[22] American banking provided another example of this rapidly expanding commitment to Latin American investments.

The Great Depression seemed to sound the death knell for American banking in Latin America. During the frenzied borrowing of the 1920s, U.S. financial institutions had arranged loans that were funded through the purchase of bonds by private American investors, but every Latin American country except Haiti had defaulted on its debt by 1933. By 1935 the debtors had stopped payments on $1.6 billion out of the $1.9 billion in loans represented by those bonds. The debt problem had largely been resolved by 1952, through years of renegotiating interest rates and maturities, as well as drastic drops in the market value of the original bonds. But neither individual investors nor the banks were anxious to reenter the Latin American market. The number of U.S. bank branches in the region had dropped from seventy-seven in 1930 to forty in 1945, while the market for Latin American bonds effectively disappeared. During the 1950s and '60s, the U.S. government and various multilateral agencies such as the World Bank provided the major source of loans. In 1958 when government lending reached a high point for the decade at $562 million, private lending amounted to only $66 million. Although private lending picked up during the 1960s, it still totaled less than $1.4 billion compared to $3.4 billion by state sources.[23] But almost as if in response to Nelson Rockefeller's call for greater private sector involvement, this imbalance shifted dramatically during the 1970s as private lending increased twentyfold while the level of government financing flattened out.

The explosive growth in private loans to Latin America actually stemmed from changing realities in the global economy. Rising prices for oil led petroleum-rich countries to make large deposits in U.S. banks at the same time that both the U.S. and European economies were experiencing recession. U.S. banks now competed intensely to find profitable loan opportunities. Latin American countries that were anxious to secure international credits to fund new export promotion strategies quickly emerged among the banks' favorite customers. At the same time, U.S. financial institutions such as Bank of America, Citibank (previously National City Bank), and Chase increased the number of their branches and acquired local banks. In 1979, when this lending frenzy reached its peak, U.S. banks loaned nearly $6 billion to Latin America. The flood of financing would propel economic growth, but the eventual consequences would prove almost as disastrous for the region as the lending spree of the 1920s.[24] Meanwhile, U.S. manufacturers were surging ahead with new initiatives.

Between World War I and the Great Depression the leading U.S. automakers, Ford, General Motors, and Chrysler, had established assembly plants in the region, taking advantage of low labor costs and escaping high tariffs imposed on imports of fully assembled vehicles. However, the companies proved reluctant to participate in government-sponsored programs to develop local automobile manufacturing in Brazil, Argentina, and Mexico during the late 1950s and early 1960s. By the mid-1960s the companies adjusted their strategy to changing conditions. As the great postwar boom in domestic auto sales faded, the leading automakers realized that they would need to look overseas in order to boost revenues. But by this time, the recovery of the German and Japanese economies had led to the emergence of formidable international competitors in the form of Volkswagen and Toyota. Furthermore, Volkswagen had already established itself as the leading car manufacturer in Brazil. The Big Three now rushed to meet the competitive challenge. First in Mexico, then in Brazil and Argentina, the U.S. automakers threw themselves into building factories and taking over local car manufacturers.

By 1973, the Big Three accounted for 40 percent of automobile production in Latin America with most of the rest in the hands of German and Japanese multinationals.[25] As the auto giants' investments created global production platforms, the manufacturers had to ensure that these plants would achieve the levels of productivity necessary to compete in the world market. That meant creating a far more disciplined workforce than those that had been laboring in U.S.-run mines and plantations during the past century. To ensure that workers adapted efficiently to the rigors of continuous process production, or assembly-line manufacturing, the companies utilized strategies termed Fordism after the U.S. auto magnate Henry Ford. The firms offered high wages to attract workers to the monotonous production line and subjected them to intense supervision and ever-present threats of dismissal to discipline them to the speeding up of the production process.[26] But the impact of auto manufacturing emanated far beyond the factory floor.

From their experience in the U.S. market, the Big Three were well aware of the need to promote a market for replacement vehicles by whetting consumer appetites for new models that might incorporate only minor modifications in the actual vehicle. The automakers addressed this issue as they had at home: with massive advertising campaigns designed to establish their products as symbols of power and success in the minds of consumers. These campaigns not only boosted sales but also encouraged shifts in local infrastructure development from public transportation to private vehicles.[27] Meanwhile the U.S. government and the AFL-CIO were working to further enhance conditions for U.S. multinationals.

Between 1962 and 1972, AIFLD, the organization created by the federal government, large unions, and corporations to shape the development of the Latin American labor movement trained nearly nine thousand potential labor leaders in its Chilean seminars and selected seventy nine for further training in the United States. Despite this substantial effort, the institute hardly put a dent in the power of Chile's leftist national labor federation. That lack of success became particularly worrisome with Salvador Allende's election in 1970. AIFLD now changed its focus, helping to form the Confederation of Chilean Professionals (CUPROCH) in May 1971. The confederation became a key actor in the 1972 gremialista strike, and AIFLD almost certainly used it as one conduit through which it could funnel CIA monies to fuel the strike designed to oust Allende. That same year, the gremialista movement organized an umbrella organization, the National Command for Gremio Defense, which also played a key role in the strike. AIFLD invited its director to Washington shortly after the strike ended.[28] A second strike by the gremios that began in August 1973 helped set the stage for the coup that toppled Allende on September 11.

The overthrow of the Popular Unity government actually illustrated some of the limitations of AIFLD strategies. Its success in Chile came not with unions but with professional associations that represented not workers but owners of capital from large landowners and industrialists to more modestly endowed truck owners. Given the gross disparities of wealth and power, and the reluctance of most regimes to enact or enforce land reform and labor laws, AIFLD's focus on anticommunism and its emphasis on labor management negotiations usually failed to rally significant support among workers and campesinos. One of the most telling examples of those limitations came in Central America where the institute had devoted so much energy. By the early 1960s, United Fruit, a charter member of AIFLD and one of the corporations the institute had sought to protect, recognized that its declining profits resulted in no small measure from increasing costs in the form of rising wages and losses due to labor actions in the region. The company rapidly divested itself of many of its direct investments in production and refashioned itself into a banana-marketing firm. Although the shift in strategy still left the company as an extremely powerful force in Central America, it also demonstrated its inability, and the inability of AIFLD, to effectively control the militancy of workers and campesinos.[29] Nevertheless, the state, corporations, and the labor elite would continue to cooperate within the institute and pursue its aggressive tactics, especially when revolution threatened the region at the end of the 1970s. Government, corporate, and labor leaders' vision of modernization was increasingly marked by a concern with stability that led them to subvert movements for mass mobilization and support dictatorial regimes. A similar need for social control in the domestic sphere found expression in Washington's "war on drugs."

DRUG LORDS, PREACHERS, AND TOURISTS

The youth culture of the 1960s, along with mounting frustrations with the war in Vietnam, helped spur a surge in drug use in the United States by the latter part of the decade. During the 1970s social conservatives in the United States responded with increasing criticism of recreational drug use. Marijuana, once a seemingly innocuous symbol of youthful rebellion, took its place alongside cocaine, heroin, and other substances as a direct threat to American values such as hard work. It was argued that if young people were allowed to slip into the lethargy of habitual drug use then the dynamism of America's society and economy would soon dissipate. The Nixon administration responded by declaring a "war on drugs" in 1971.

New laws harshly punished drug dealers and created the Drug Enforcement Agency (DEA) out of several older agencies that had dealt with controlled substances. With marijuana serving as the signature drug of youth culture, Washington, as it had in the 1930s, began looking south of the border for a solution to the nation's growing drug habit. Envisioning Mexican drug lords as the unprincipled exploiters of American youth, the administration reverted to the punitive interdiction policies that had been pursued in the past toward Latin America. It launched Operation Intercept that required a detailed inspection of every vehicle crossing the border with Mexico. In the few weeks that it lasted, the program managed to slash Mexican farm exports and the spending of U.S. tourists in Mexico. In light of the economic consequences for both countries, the United States cancelled the program in exchange for a Mexican commitment to pursue drug dealers more aggressively. A more successful U.S. effort came with pressure on the Mexican government to spray marijuana fields with herbicides. However, Colombian dealers soon made up for the decrease in Mexican supply. And when the United States managed to reduce shipments from Colombia, domestic growers filled the gap. In light of the United States's own billion-dollar domestic marijuana crop, Latin American leaders found U.S. pressure on them to stem the drug flow hypocritical. The policies pursued by the Nixon administration not only harkened back to the past by stressing interdiction and demonizing Latin Americans as drug dealers and ineffectual political leaders, but also established important precedents for the drug war that the United States would wage in the decades ahead.[30] In contrast to the negative connotations of the U.S. "war on drugs" in Latin America, foundation officials sought to counteract some of the effects of the militarization of U.S.–Latin American relations.

In 1978 the Ford Foundation, which had devoted much of its energy and capital to improving higher education in Latin America, provided a sad commentary on the increasing repression in the region, noting that it had "to try to protect and sustain portions of the intellectual communities of countries in which human rights and intellectual freedom, in our judgment, are adversely affected." In other words in countries such as Brazil and Chile, Ford was helping scholars who had to flee their countries or those who remained behind but were denied the resources to carry on their work.[31] That repression was also being felt by Christian activists. Military regimes destroyed or dispersed many of the Liberation Theology groups and other Christian activists by the mid-1970s. By then another powerful movement was influencing Protestantism in Latin America.

In postwar America, the Reverend Billy Graham pioneered a revivalist, fundamentalist form of Protestantism that relied heavily on the mass media to reach its audience. By the beginning of the 1960s, Graham took his message to the Caribbean, Central America, and Mexico, and local movements, heavily influenced by Graham's approach, were spreading through the region. These groups diverged sharply from the ideas and practices of progressive Protestantism of the early twentieth century. For these Evangelists, the crisis of Latin America stemmed not from social and economic injustice, but from the rebellion of individual souls against God. Salvation lay not in social reform or revolution, but in the rescuing of individual souls. They denounced revolutionary violence and vehemently condemned communism. That message found a receptive audience among the military dictators of Latin America, who welcomed the Protestant Evangelists much like Liberal dictators had welcomed missionaries a century earlier. But unlike those earlier rulers, who saw Protestantism as a progressive force, these twentieth-century dictators welcomed the new religious preachers as a force for social demobilization. By the 1970s, this movement received new reinforcement from televangelical groups such as Pat Robertson's PTL Club, whose television programs supported the sale of U.S. weapons to military dictatorships and vehemently denounced leftist political movements.[32]

Pentecostal sects formed the fastest-growing element of the Protestant movement. In the countryside, Pentecostalism, with its millenarian visions of the final days and the Second Coming of Christ, offered a powerful vision often compatible with folk magic and religious beliefs that offered consolation to rural residents whose subsistence communities faced disintegration from the penetration of market forces. In rural villages, subsistence agriculture had for centuries underpinned communal values and practices that ensured survival and limited the disparities between rich and poor. Catholicism with its array of saints and holy days had given new legitimacy to these practices in the aftermath of the conquest. But in the second half of the twentieth century, population growth and market forces placed increasing pressure on this way of life.

Peasants with the greatest resource endowments, as well as those who encountered increasing difficulty in wrenching subsistence from their small plots, were anxious to shake off customs that limited wealth accumulation. These rural residents found in Pentecostalism a set of values stressing individual salvation and individual initiative that offered an alternative framework as a solution to their problems. For peasants, who sought escape from rural poverty in urban centers only to face equally harsh material conditions and the seemingly ever-changing values of modern society, Pentecostalism also offered solace. Its rigorous requirements to abandon drink and other vices provided believers an opportunity to conquer evil, not in the larger and enigmatic world around them but in their own souls. Furthermore, the emphasis on self-denial provided a moral code for self-improvement and hopefully advancement in a free-market economy. At the same time, much like the anticommunism of Pat Robertson, these Pentecostal movements carried a powerful message of social demobilization. Their followers sought to win the battle over evil in their own souls not by massing in the streets of Latin American cities demanding fundamental change.[33] Meanwhile, other Latin Americans found the promise of rising from poverty embodied in Americans clutching cameras and trudging behind tour guides.

Although modernization theory had shunted aside the images of primitive races embedded in the civilizing mission, it still conceived of Latin American societies as traditional and therefore imbued with many of the same qualities attributed to primitive societies. Much like their forbears of the eighteenth and nineteenth centuries, twentieth-century Americans would go in search of the exotic in Latin America. In the 1960s, Americans had come to view Latin American folk culture as truly "authentic" in contrast to what they imagined as the artificial, manufactured character of their own modern culture. In Latin American folk cultures American tourists hoped to experience and purchase such authenticity. Many Latin Americans concerned with national development or simply earning a livelihood were willing to manufacture such authenticity for their guests.

American tourists had become a common sight in the proximate locations of Cuba and Mexico by the 1940s, but it was the postwar boom in commercial air travel that gave the most important boost to international tourism. In 1954, Americans departed on one million overseas trips. That number had risen to two million by 1960 and approached five million in 1968.[34] That surge brought millions of U.S consumers to Central and South America during the 1960s and '70s. A further incentive came in the form of U.S. government assistance to promote tourism during the Alliance for

Progress. American planners were concerned that despite the past popularity of Mexico and Cuba, most Americans still looked to Europe and Asia as exotic tourist havens. They hoped to change that perspective and use tourism as a means of rapidly generating foreign exchange for Latin American economies. Furthermore, given Latin America's close economic ties to the United States, officials were confident that American tourist dollars spent in the region would be recaptured much more quickly by the U.S. economy than similar outlays in Europe or Asia.[35]

Much like American travelers in Cuba in the 1940s, tourists once again came to Latin America drawn by the promise of experiencing the exotic in a relatively safe environment. Traveling by air, staying in hotels designed to meet their expectations in terms of amenities, and by participating in packaged tours, Americans found security and reassurance. By contrast, unlike the risqué appeal of Havana's nightclubs and Tijuana's casinos, the new element of exoticism was the mystery of folk cultures. American tourists could enjoy the comforts of home while experiencing and acquiring the authentic cultures of the region. At the same time, such trips were portrayed not only as pleasurable leisure-time activities but as people-to-people encounters that would enhance hemispheric understanding.

Modernizing elites in countries such as Mexico had for decades promoted folk culture as a means of providing a common national identity rooted in their country's pre-Conquest past. In the postwar era, Latin American technocrats came to view folk crafts as a spur to tourism that represented a potentially low-cost development initiative. Using the people, locations, and handicrafts of their own society, planners calculated that tourism would require much lower start-up costs than development projects like factories and power stations. At the same time, tourism would have a multiplier effect on local economies, increasing income and employment at hotels, transportation facilities, travel agencies, restaurants, retailers, and so on. But of course tourists were not anthropologists who would travel to remote villages to study the local social environment. Folk culture would have to be presented to tourists in readily consumable forms. For that, training and organization, as well as some capital investment, would be needed.

In the Andean highlands of Ecuador, the drive to develop tourism had significant effects by the 1960s. During the 1950s, the government secured support from the United States and the United Nations to provide technical training in weaving to Otavalan Indians, who had been making textiles for centuries. The state also began promoting the Otavalans' Saturday morning market as a tourist attraction. By the 1970s, the Peace Corps had helped create textile cooperatives and was advising Otavalans on the development of new styles that would find a market among tourists. The Otavalans themselves exhibited considerable entrepreneurial initiative in developing new types of woven products with ethnic motifs. Meanwhile other changes, with their roots in the 1950s, helped draw tourists into the area.

The *hacendados*, or large landowners of the region who controlled peasants' labor by providing them with subsistence plots on which to raise crops, found their system of control under increasing stress with the enactment of a land reform law and the growing tensions resulting from population growth that was straining already scarce land resources among peasants. Fearing either expropriation under the new law or land occupations by desperate peons, some hacendados sold off most of their land and converted their manor houses into *hosterías*, or country inns, designed to attract tourists.

One landowner went a step further; he contacted the owners of a new luxury hotel in the capital of Quito and suggested they hire a number of Quimseñas, the Native American women who worked on his estate. Dressed in "authentic" costumes, the women would bring a distinctive identity of "Indianness" to the hotel. The Quimseñas soon established a monopoly in the staffing of the hotel while relieving the landowner of the need to support at least some of the Native Americans on his estate. The authentic Indian culture that tourists were exposed to at the hotel had of course been refined to appeal to preconceived notions about folk culture and the exotic. The authentic everyday dress that the women wore on duty at the hotel consisted of sumptuous costumes that they would normally wear only on festive occasions. At the same time their tasks at the hotel actually replicated the sort of domestic duties they had been required to carry out in the hacendado's home as fulfillment of their families' labor obligations.[36]

During the 1960s and '70s the production and sale of folk art and the creation of tourist venues decorated with symbols of "authentic" Indian culture proliferated in Latin America as elites promoted tourism as an engine for economic development and as Americans came in search of the exotic and the authentic in their consumption of folk crafts. In the process, local cultures, whether in the form of handicrafts or local inhabitants, were refined to fulfill the preconceived notions of Westernized elites and the demands of tourists. Tourism indeed became a fast-growing segment of most Latin American economies; at the same time, elites, tourists, and the producers of these cultural products reacted to each other to shape these "authentic" artifacts. Aside from the manufacture or reinvention of local culture to meet consumer demand and the impact on economic growth, the effects of the process proved complex.

Although trumpeted as promoting international understanding, the tourist trade usually placed tourists in positions of power in their interactions with locals, who served subservient roles as hotel staff, drivers, tradespeople, and artisans. Intermediaries such as retailers often exploited the labor of local inhabitants to produce inexpensive artifacts for tourists. At the same time, the higher incomes of successful folk craftsmen increased wealth disparities in rural communities. Those who successfully entered the craft trade often exhibited an unwillingness to take on the sponsorship of communal festivals that drew resources from individuals to benefit the community. By contrast, craft makers at times used their additional income to preserve a way of life centered on subsistence agriculture. Many of the crafts that they fashioned gave expression both to long-held aesthetic values as well as new self-images. For the Otavalans, their expanding involvement in commercial weaving led them to acquire skills that better equipped them to deal with the dominant Spanish-speaking society and expanded their own sense of identity beyond the individual village to the larger ethnic group. So, too, the Quimseñas found liberating elements in their experience as professionals working in a modern urban environment as opposed to their roles in a patriarchal rural setting. What is certain is that the demands of U.S. consumers, the goals of modernizing elites, and the efforts of rural people to adjust to the mounting pressure on the peasant way of life combined to create a tourist-driven cultural product presented as an authentic expression of a pre-Hispanic way of life.[37] But while Latin Americans were quite willing to engage Americans in the tourist marketplace, they remained unwilling to accept the continuation of U.S. hegemony in the region.

CHALLENGES IN CENTRAL AMERICA

The Panama Canal, the most compelling physical symbol of U.S. power, became a contentious issue during the 1960s as Panamanian nationalists staged a series of demonstrations to protest continuing U.S. control of the canal and the territory around it. Despite efforts by both governments to reach an accord, the issue remained unresolved when President Jimmy Carter took office. Determined to make Latin America a showcase for his human rights policy, Carter took up the issue of the canal. His administration succeeded in crafting two treaties with the government of strongman Omar Torrijos. The first provided for the termination of U.S. control on December 31, 1999, and a series of payments to be made to Panama in the interim. The second defined the continuing rights of the United States to defend the canal. Although Carter managed to secure ratification of both treaties, his success was vilified by American conservatives like Ronald Reagan, who once noted of the canal, "We bought it, we paid for it, it's ours and we're going to keep it." For many Americans the treaties represented one sign of a weakening of U.S. global power in the aftermath of Vietnam. Meanwhile, another challenge to U.S. power emerged just a few hundred miles from the canal.[38]

By the late 1970s, revolution had erupted in Nicaragua. For those knowledgeable in the history of American empire the struggle in Nicaragua bore eerie reminders of the past because a revolutionary movement known as the Sandinista National Liberation Front had launched a guerrilla insurgency against the heir to the Somoza dynasty. After the assassination of Augusto Sandino in 1934, Anastasio Somoza García had seized power in 1936 and proceeded to rule Nicaragua directly or through surrogates until his assassination in 1956. Much like the character Michael Corleone in *The Godfather*, Somoza's son Luis, who succeeded him, concluded that in the family's best interest it would be wise to withdraw from their principal business—in this case, dictatorial politics. Luis launched a program of liberalization hoping to leave a carefully structured political process that would allow the family to focus on its considerable business interests instead of dynastic politics. However, Luis's demise in 1967 left his brother Anastasio Somoza Debayle, or "Tacho," to inherit the mantle of power. Much like "Sonny" Corleone, Tacho reverted to his father's reliance on force—the repressive power of the National Guard to maintain the family's monopoly on power. In the postwar years the country enjoyed spurts of economic growth based on coffee exports and rapid development of cotton production.

By the 1970s declining prices for coffee and cotton caused severe economic setbacks. Furthermore, the growth of agribusinesses such as cotton plantations had driven a growing number of peasants from the land and had left others to scratch out an existence on the output from tiny plots supplemented by seasonal work on coffee or cotton plantations. In the urban sector, workers labored under a state system that offered them little protection while the owners of microbusinesses such as bicycle repair shops and tiny groceries suffered heavy taxation and abuse from Somoza's National Guard. In the early 1960s a small group of former university students founded the Sandinista movement, drawing inspiration from the Nicaraguan revolutionary and from Fidel Castro. For the next decade the Sandinistas, who drew much of their support from the adult children of urban shopkeepers and microentrepreneurs, struggled to mobilize peasants and workers with minimal success. As of the mid-1970s, the young revolutionaries still found themselves a poor match for the National Guard and Somoza, who continued to enjoy strong support from Washington. But mounting economic difficulties, increased popular support for the Sandinistas, and Somoza's heavy-handed repression of all forms of opposition gradually undermined the dictator's position. By 1978 the guerrillas were enjoying increasing success against the regime's forces. Furthermore, the assassination of Pedro Joaquin Chamorro, the leading figure in the opposition Conservative Party, in January of that year exhausted the Nicaraguan elite's tolerance of the Somoza regime.[39]

As the Sandinistas mounted new attacks on the Nicaraguan dictatorship, the Carter administration became concerned that Somoza would not survive the challenge from the revolutionaries. Initially it pressured Somoza to resign, hoping that his resignation would deflate popular support for the rebels. When the dictator refused to resign, the United States attempted to negotiate an agreement between Somoza and his more conservative political opponents for a plebiscite that would determine future control of the presidency. When those efforts also failed, Washington eased its pressure on the dictator in early 1979, believing that he might still manage to crush the insurgency. However, by June a new Sandinista offensive made it clear that the dynasty's days were numbered. Washington appealed to the OAS for approval of a peacekeeping force that would preempt a Sandinista victory. But an overwhelming majority of Latin American states rejected the U.S. call for intervention, and on July 17 the victorious Sandinistas entered the capital of Managua.[40] Two decades after Fidel Castro's rise to power and after twenty years of modernization policies, covert interventions, and counterinsurgency policies, Marxist revolution had come to another Latin American nation that had decades earlier served as a model of the American civilizing mission.

The Sandinista victory marked the beginning of a decade of dramatic developments in the relations between the United States and Latin America. In the years ahead, Washington would launch a war against the Sandinista regime and seek to suppress Marxist revolutionaries in neighboring El Salvador. At the same time, the lending binge by U.S. banks would end in an international financial crisis that threatened to topple the global financial system just as the American coalition that had promoted the mission of modernization since the days of the New Deal was fracturing.

❦

During the 1970s the United States seemed to be besieged at home and abroad. The war in Vietnam, the growing power of the Soviet Union, the election of a Marxist president in Chile, and the increasing economic rivalry offered by Western Europe and Japan all offered challenges to the global dominance that Americans had become accustomed to since the end of World War II. At home protests against the war, rising drug use, slowing economic growth coupled with rising inflation, and the national political crisis created by the Watergate scandal shook Americans' confidence in a social order that they had long considered a model for the rest of the world to emulate.

In this environment Richard Nixon and Henry Kissinger envisioned themselves as tough male leaders who would overcome the failings of the weak-kneed eastern elite whose policies had led to this state of affairs. They would challenge the Soviets and roll back third world threats such as the Allende government in Chile. Their policies in Latin America also reflected the paternalistic attitudes that American leaders had often exhibited toward the region's people. In justifying U.S. intervention in Chile, Henry Kissinger had argued, "I don't see why we need to stand by and watch a country go Communist due to the irresponsibility of its own people."[41] As with past generations of American statesmen, Kissinger simply presumed that the United States had the right to direct the course of events in Latin America to its own benefit. In their role as protectors of American interests, U.S. policymakers aided by domestic elites subverted the elected government of Chile, supported repressive military regimes in Latin America, and sought to preempt the Sandinistas' rise to power. Washington also placed the responsibility for its growing drug problems on Latin American nations and took coercive actions such as Operation Intercept against them. But developments in Latin American were not entirely negative for U.S. interests.

U.S. multinationals found a welcoming environment in Latin America under military regimes that were promoting export-oriented industrialization. The multinationals also enjoyed the support of the AFL-CIO through AIFLD's policies of encouraging business-friendly unions and fighting leftist labor organizers. Meanwhile, the rapidly growing Pentecostal movements encouraged their followers to turn away from social activism that challenged the established order. As in the past, the relationship between Latin Americans and the United States was not a one-sided affair. Latin Americans and American tourists engaged in a complex interplay of American desires for "authenticity" and the refashioning of Latin American folk cultures to meet those needs in the context of a market economy. As the decade ended, major new revolutionary challenges to U.S. dominance appeared in Central America.

CHAPTER NINE

INSURGENCY AND
INSOLVENCY, 1980–1992

ON THE EVENING OF DECEMBER 2, 1980, DOROTHY KAZEL, AN URSULINE
sister, and Jean Donovan, a Catholic lay worker, arrived in a van at San
Salvador's main airport to pick up Maura Clarke and Ita Ford, two
Maryknoll nuns who were returning from a conference in neighboring Nicaragua. Soon after the four women left the airport their van was
waylaid at a roadblock. Their captors raped and murdered the women,
tossing their bodies into a shallow grave. Americans were outraged
to learn that members of the U.S.-financed and -trained Salvadoran
National Guard had planned and carried out the murders of these
deeply religious women, who worked among El Salvador's poor.[1] These
Americans were only four of tens of thousands of innocent victims who
perished in the course of two decades of civil wars as the U.S. government
sought to crush the guerrilla insurgency in El Salvador and to topple the
Sandinista government of Nicaragua. Decades of poverty and dictatorship had triggered widespread upheavals in Central America, which now
threatened to undermine the U.S. domination of this region that had

endured since the days of Smedley Butler. The Central American insurgencies were not the only challenges to U.S. hegemony in Latin America during the 1980s. Only two years after the murders in El Salvador a Latin American debt crisis threatened to topple some of the most powerful banks in the United States and undermine the entire Western Hemisphere's economic order. American leaders would respond aggressively to both threats.

❧

Ronald Reagan's election in 1980 did not mark the immediate emergence of a major political realignment as occurred under Franklin Roosevelt, but it did signal the disintegration of the New Deal alliance, leaving the state and corporate America as the principal members of the coalition that now directed U.S. international policies. One reason for this change was the inability of capital-intensive businesses to sustain the social pact with labor that ensured rising standards of living in return for union support of continuous reshaping of the workplace to achieve higher productivity. The ever-more-competitive international economy required American multinationals to drive down labor costs, whether that meant reducing real wages of domestic labor or creating offshore production platforms such as the maquiladoras in Mexico. At the same time, labor-intensive industries remained as protectionist as ever and sought relief from labor costs as well as government regulation. The new Republican administration offered something for both these groups with tax cuts, reductions in environmental and other regulations, and the reduction of such labor benefits as cost-of-living increases. These policies reflected the growing influence of neoliberal economists, who challenged the New Deal model of state activism to ensure economic growth and address social problems. In its place, neoliberals urged reducing state power especially in the areas of economic and social policy and strategies that would give free rein to market forces. The administration's foreign policy reflected some of these same neoliberal influences. Drawing on selected elements of the mission to Latin America that stressed the role of U.S. corporations and free trade, and then combining them with the neoliberal emphasis on downsizing the state, the United States promoted a process of globalization. Washington pressed for trade liberalization and drastic reductions in the economic role of third world governments, while it fueled a rapid buildup of its own military. These policies would allow the United States to serve as the unchallenged world power, with a commitment to creating a true global market, thus avoiding the emergence of distinct regional trading blocs. These strategies appealed to both protectionists determined to reduce labor costs and government regulation and to capital-intensive multinationals anxious to secure offshore production facilities and expand opportunities in a truly global market.[2] But despite its new neoliberal elements, U.S. foreign policy also carried forward elements of what Robert Dean has termed the "ideology of masculinity," which had guided generations of foreign policymakers.[3]

Much like Lyndon Johnson and Richard Nixon, Ronald Reagan was no scion of an elite family. He had grown up in Illinois, the son of a hard-drinking shoe salesman. As a student at Eureka College he embraced the rituals of young American manhood by joining a fraternity and earning a spot on the football team. Making his way up the economic ladder as a radio announcer, Hollywood actor, GE spokesperson, and eventually governor of California, Reagan cultivated an image as a plain-talking, no-nonsense individualist, much like the cowboys he had sometimes portrayed in the movies. In his run for the presidency, Regan made clear that he would bring a renewed assertiveness to U.S. foreign policy, which he believed had been undermined by the Vietnam War and the weak policies of the liberal elite. Much like past presidents, whatever their social origins, he too had set out to prove himself a fearless male leader ready to take military action to defend the American empire and confront its enemies.

An important part of the Reagan strategy involved a powerful challenge to the Soviet Union, including confrontations in third world battlegrounds much like those that had occurred during the 1960s and '70s. In addition to funding an Islamic insurgency against the Soviets in Afghanistan, the administration undertook a large-scale paramilitary effort to topple the Sandinistas in Nicaragua and poured military aid into El Salvador to combat a Marxist-inspired rebellion. But with the collapse of the Soviet Union in 1989, the anticommunist justification for intervention in Latin America was robbed of its urgency. Nevertheless, Washington found a new reason to militarize its relations with Latin America in the explosive growth of cocaine use in the mid-1980s. The U.S. "war on drugs" came to possess literal truth as the Bush administration drew on the military to interdict drug flows into the United States and suppress production in Latin America. Washington depicted Latin American drug lords as the embodiment of evil. Envisioning Latin America as the source of the drug problems that plagued the streets of America's cities resonated in a society where many people still viewed Latin Americans as untrustworthy. But during the 1980s the most important group influencing U.S.–Latin American relations was not guerrilla fighters or drug dealers, but international bankers.

When Mexico found itself unable to meet its foreign debt obligations in August 1982, it set off a crisis that shook the global financial system. Even while the debt crisis left governments, banks, and multilateral agencies scrambling to salvage international financial mechanisms, it also created an opportunity for the United States to pursue its neoliberal economic strategies in Latin America. Multilateral agencies such as the IMF pressed Latin American governments to institute neoliberal reforms as a part of agreements for the restructuring of their debts. Those reforms included downsizing of the state by reducing social-welfare spending and privatizing state-owned enterprises, reducing protectionist barriers to trade and investment, and dismantling state guarantees for labor such as minimum-wage laws. Neoliberal policymakers argued that these strategies would accelerate exports that had been slowed by protectionism and make Latin American economies more attractive to foreign investors. In the short term, these policies, which bore striking resemblances to the liberal strategies pursued at the beginning of the twentieth century, were designed to ensure that Latin American nations would be able to pay their debts. The architects of this new strategy also believed that their policies would finally propel Latin America into full-fledged development. But the process was not simply the product of foreign pressure and foreign experts. Latin American technocrats trained in U.S. universities or in local academic institutions whose curricula had been heavily influenced by American foundations and universities had thoroughly absorbed the principles of neoliberalism and were anxious to implement these new approaches. The crisis also contributed to another sweeping change, this one in the political sphere.

The dark night of military dictatorship that had engulfed much of South America began to lift during the 1980s. Leaders of the armed forces proved to be no more competent than their civilian counterparts in coping with the debt crisis that plunged the region into a "lost decade" of economic decline. Those failures combined with mounting popular demands for a return to democracy led the generals to cede power to civilian politicians. In 1982 the Argentine military, after seeking to distract the public from a disintegrating economy with a disastrous attempt to seize the British-occupied Malvinas Islands, agreed to national elections the following year. The Brazilian military, unable to cope with runaway inflation and popular unrest, allowed the selection of a civilian president. The Pinochet regime faced rejection in a 1988 plebiscite and proceeded to return the country to civilian rule. And yet the return to democracy tended to depoliticize conventional Latin American political institutions and practices.

In the aftermath of long-term domestic repression and the collapse of Eastern Bloc socialism, many leftist political parties abandoned ideological stands and moved toward ideas of social democracy. National political leaders of various ideological leanings began to adopt an approach that echoed the ideas of American consumer society. They defined freedom as the freedom to consume, especially to consume foreign-made goods that would be far more readily available under new liberalized trading systems. Individual ambition would lead to individual successes and advancement, which would be rewarded by the cornucopia of goods available in the deepening consumer economy that through the miracles of consumer credit now extended down to the poorer levels of society. People would look to individual competition in the marketplace rather than membership in groups such as political parties to achieve social and economic mobility. The state would no longer serve as a key engine of development nor would it intervene extensively to ease social and economic inequities. Ultimately modernity itself would be redefined. Achieving modernity would no longer mean national projects for infrastructure development and industrialization. Instead, modernity would be conceived of as the widespread availability and consumption of consumer goods produced in industrial economies. Consumption would become identity.[4]

MILITARIZATION

Many of the same social and economic conditions that gave birth to the Nicaraguan Sandinista movement helped stir insurrection in its neighbor, El Salvador. After an export boom in the 1960s, the Central American economies faced mounting problems triggered by recession in developed countries that reduced demand for many of their agricultural products and the jump in oil prices beginning in 1973 that dramatically increased fuel prices and the cost of fertilizers. Furthermore, expanding agribusinesses were wresting control of increasing amounts of land from small peasant producers even as the rural population continued to grow. Only 12 percent of El Salvador's peasants had been landless in 1960; that figure rose to 40 percent by the middle of the 1970s. Meanwhile, urban workers faced rising unemployment and inflation rates that undermined their standard of living.[5] When Salvadoran peasants and workers mobilized to defend their interests during the 1970s, they found themselves facing repression from regimes unwilling to seek democratic solutions to pressing national problems.

In El Salvador, the military intervened to overturn elections held in 1972 and imposed a dictatorship. Facing violence from their own government, many Salvadorans joined guerrilla organizations that eventually merged to form the Farabundo Martí Front for National Liberation (FMLN). Meanwhile civilian opposition parties formed the Democratic Revolutionary Front (FDR). During the course of 1980, military-and government-sanctioned death squads carried out a counterinsurgency campaign that killed nearly nine thousand people, most of them noncombatants. The Carter administration attempted to rein in the worst human rights abuses, while at the same time pumping millions of dollars of aid to the armed forces to prevent an insurgent victory like the one it had so recently witnessed in Nicaragua. The aid helped buoy the military, but it did little to stop the murder of unarmed civilians. With the Salvadoran armed forces facing a large-scale offensive by the guerrillas in January 1981, the United States authorized $10 million in new military aid. The struggle in El Salvador itself provided a justification for intervention in neighboring Nicaragua.

In Nicaragua, the Reagan administration's publicly stated goals differed dramatically from what the United States actually sought to accomplish. The administration pointed to Sandinista support for the FMLN as the reason it needed to intervene in Nicaragua. Ostensibly, U.S. efforts were designed to interdict alleged arms flows to El Salvador and to pressure the Sandinistas into abandoning all support for the insurgents. At times Washington would have to go to great lengths to undermine commitments from the Sandinistas or proposals by international groups that would in fact ensure the end of all such assistance. For the Reagan administration, the real goal of its intervention in Nicaragua was the overthrow of the Sandinista government. The administration wanted to roll back what it believed to be a communist revolution as a part of its larger strategy to confront the Soviet Union and to reassert U.S. preeminence in the circum-Caribbean and the world. But that strategy would require a massive effort whose cost and dimensions far exceeded those of earlier interventions in Cuba and Chile.

At the heart of the U.S. effort stood the Nicaraguan Democratic Front (FDN), an exile organization formed by the CIA to oversee a paramilitary force commonly referred to as the "contras" (short for "counterrevolutionaries" in Spanish). Although this CIA-trained army would come to number fifteen thousand troops, it would have a difficult time winning support in Nicaragua because it drew its officer corps largely from former members of Somoza's hated National Guard. At various times the contras would try guerrilla warfare, conventional combat tactics, and then economic sabotage with much of their military effort geared toward the destruction of Nicaragua's economic infrastructure. But Washington did not expect the contras to succeed strictly on their own. They convinced Honduras's military rulers to allow their country to serve as a base of operations from which the contras could launch their forays across the border into Nicaragua. The U.S. military staged a series of joint military maneuvers with the Honduran Army that allowed the United States to construct barracks, airfields, and roads for use by the FDN's forces. Washington also maintained a flotilla of naval vessels off both coasts of Nicaragua. These ships and the exercises in Honduras were designed to keep the Sandinistas preoccupied with the possibility of an all-out U.S. invasion and to provide monitoring of Sandinista communications in order to supply intelligence information to the contras. The CIA also funneled money to opposition political parties and media outlets in Nicaragua. In addition, the administration cut off the economic aid program launched by President Carter, convinced U.S. allies to reduce their aid funds, pressured multilateral lending agencies to reject Nicaraguan loan applications, and reduced the Nicaraguan sugar quota by 90 percent. The administration deescalated its efforts in the run up to the 1984 U.S. presidential election but soon resumed and intensified its attempts to topple the Sandinistas.[6] Washington also turned to its longtime allies in organized labor to battle Central American insurgents.

The American Institute for Free Labor Development (AIFLD), which had worked closely for two decades with the U.S. government to combat communism in Latin America, had devoted considerable attention to El Salvador. Beginning in 1962 AIFLD had provided support to a government-sponsored labor federation and worked to undermine the left-leaning General Confederation of Salvadoran Workers. AIFLD gave particular attention to problems in the Salvadoran countryside, well aware that the growing number of landless peasants represented a potential social powder keg. During the 1960s, AIFLD jointly sponsored campesino training programs with the government and the Catholic Church. To counter the influence of a leftist peasant federation, the CIA, U.S. military advisors, and AID formed a competing peasant organization, the National Democratic Organization (ORDEN). Oddly enough, the Salvadoran National Security Agency supervised this erstwhile peasant organization. AIFLD did its part by organizing a campesino federation, the Salvadoran Communal Union (CUS), under the guidance of AIFLD organizer Michael Hammer. Despite the fact that the CUS promoted a highly conservative philosophy of self-help aimed at small farmers, the Salvadoran elite became increasingly suspicious that AIFLD efforts were stirring up the rural population, and in 1973 El Salvador's military ruler expelled the institute from his country. But by 1979 with peasants joining guerrilla organizations, the military felt compelled to summon AIFLD back in the hopes that its efforts could quiet an ever-more-turbulent countryside.[7]

Meanwhile, ORDEN had revealed a far more menacing character than that of a campesino organization. Under the army's supervision, ORDEN functioned initially as a rural surveillance network, identifying and spying on peasant organizers. As social conflict escalated into guerrilla insurgency, ORDEN became the source of death squads that murdered militant peasants. In its efforts to disrupt peasant organizations, it was reportedly assisted by the AIFLD-funded CUS. When AIFLD returned to El Salvador it was to take control of CUS and help chart a course for agrarian reform, which hopefully would pacify the countryside. But even AIFLD's minimalist activities were too much for some members of the elite and the military. Right-wing gunmen assassinated Michael Hammer while he was working on the reform program. Yet AIFLD's reform efforts and its formation of a new labor federation, the Popular Democratic Unity (UPD), served several useful purposes for the United States. They helped temporarily increase popular support for the government, and by giving the impression that a political center still existed in El Salvador, they reassured U.S. congressmen concerned about continuing to fund a violent regime. Those effects proved especially useful to the Reagan administration, which pursued a highly aggressive strategy in both El Salvador and Nicaragua.[8]

Convinced that El Salvador and Nicaragua represented further steps in a series of communist challenges in the third world, the Reagan administration committed itself to crushing the insurgency in El Salvador and toppling the Sandinista government of Nicaragua. Military aid to El Salvador rose steadily, reaching a peak of $196 million in 1984 while annual economic aid rose to an astounding $343 million, seven times as much as Carter had dispersed each year. The United States sent teams of military advisors and assisted the armed forces with sophisticated intelligence gathering technologies. To pacify critics in Congress and a skeptical public, the administration backed the political ambitions of José Napoleon Duarte, the head of the Christian Democratic Party. Duarte's 1983 campaign for the presidency was assisted by the efforts of the UPD, which received generous funding from the AIFLD and AID. Once in office Duarte backed away from the UPD, and the federation even found itself abandoned by its American creators. But AIFLD itself had no problem securing financial support from its own government.

Despite the probusiness leanings of the Reagan administration, Washington still had allies among the leadership of the AFL-CIO, due in no small part to the federal government's generous funding of their overseas initiatives. As a result, AIFLD continued organizing federations to counter leftist labor and peasant organizations. In 1986 the institute received a three-year, $7.9 million commitment from AID for its programs in El Salvador, demonstrating the importance of AIFLD's efforts to combat militant labor organizations and to provide Washington with evidence that reforms were working in El Salvador. The Reagan administration also had other allies in its fight against Marxism in Central America.

In a Salvadoran stadium in March 1987, American preacher Jimmy Swaggart brought roars of approval from his followers as he declared, "I'm not going to promise you better times, but it doesn't matter, because you're going to a better place anyway!"⁹ Swaggart had been personally welcomed to El Salvador by President José Napoleon Duarte, and as a part of the same tour Swaggart visited Chile where he praised General Augusto Pinochet's overthrow of the Allende government as "one of the great acts of this century."¹⁰ In an interesting new convergence of American Protestant missionary efforts and U.S. government policy, televangelists like Swaggart and Pat Robertson became militant supporters of U.S. counterinsurgency efforts in Central America. Robertson denounced Congress's cutoff of aid to the Nicaraguan contras as a "craven submission of our leaders and Congress to the demands of communism." Later the American preacher visited a contra training camp in Honduras and stated, "If we can do something to help these men fight for freedom, I think it is perfectly in God's plan." Robertson was as good as his word, raising millions of dollars in contributions to aid Nicaraguan refugees along the Honduran border, many of whom were contra fighters.¹¹

The preaching of U.S. televangelists such as Jimmy Swaggart had a powerful influence on millions of Latin Americans, especially Central Americans, during the 1980s. With Central Americans facing harsh military repression in Guatemala and El Salvador, Pentecostalism enjoyed a highly favorable environment. Its message emphasizing individual conversion and salvation as opposed to addressing larger social and economic evils proved compatible with the efforts of the military to demobilize its own citizens. That environment was further enhanced when General Efraín Ríos Montt, a Pentecostal convert, seized power in Guatemala in 1982. Pentecostalism enjoyed a surge of conversions during the 1980s, which earlier Evangelicals like Cameron Townsend of the Summer Institute of Linguistics could only have dreamed of.¹² But the influence of the U.S. preachers faded at the end of the decade due to the scandals involving televangelists Jimmy Swaggart and Jim Bakker.¹³ Meanwhile, Washington hardly enjoyed a free hand in carrying out its plans. It faced serious hurdles both at home and abroad to its intervention strategy.

Part of the Reagan administration's problem stemmed from the lingering effects of the American debacle in Vietnam. During the 1950s and '60s a cold war consensus in which Congress and the American people essentially gave carte blanche to the executive branch in conducting a war against communism had been shattered by the disaster in Vietnam. The public and legislators were now far more willing to question the appropriateness of U.S. foreign policy, even when the president justified his actions in terms of countering the Soviet threat. Despite Reagan's rhetoric suggesting that Nicaragua could serve as a Soviet military base close to America's borders and that the Sandinistas wished to spread revolution throughout Central America, most Americans had a hard time envisioning the tiny country as a serious threat to U.S. security. Members of Congress echoed those sentiments and expressed concerns about human rights abuses by the contras as well as their ties to drug traffickers. As a result, the legislature proved a less-than-reliable source of funding for the operation. The 1982 Boland Amendment prohibited the use of U.S. funds for the purpose of overthrowing the Nicaraguan government. The president's men found ways to evade the provisions of the amendment, but these restrictions further complicated the task of trying to oust the Sandinistas. After approving $24 million for the intervention in fiscal year 1983–84, Congress voted to cut off funding for the following year only to turn around and approve $27 million for 1985–86 and $100 million for 1986–87. The erratic pattern of support prompted the administration to swap arms for money with the Islamic Republic of Iran in order to funnel funds to the contras. A direct violation of U.S. law, the so-called Iran Contra scandal led Congress to limit support for the contras to "nonlethal" aid for 1987–88.[14] And even as it jousted with Congress, the administration had to contend with international efforts to resolve the conflict peacefully.

The greatest international thorn in the side of the administration was the Contadora Group, consisting of Mexico, Panama, Colombia, and Venezuela. These nations worked together to draft the terms of a treaty that would meet the security concerns of the United States and pave the way for a peace agreement. Caught off guard when the Sandinistas announced their unqualified acceptance of a Contadora-proposed peace treaty in June 1984, Washington raised a series of objections to the agreement and pressured El Salvador, Honduras, and Guatemala into not signing the accord. But in 1987 when the presidents of Costa Rica, El Salvador, Honduras, and Guatemala formulated a new peace agreement known as the Arias

Plan after President Oscar Arias of Costa Rica, Washington made only half-hearted efforts to sabotage the accord. Weakened by the Iran Contra scandal, aware that the contras could not defeat the Sandinistas militarily or politically, and facing an ever-more-recalcitrant Congress, the administration grudgingly abandoned its scheme for toppling the Nicaraguan government. Yet this course of events hardly signaled an outright victory for the Sandinistas.

The contra war had inflicted enormous damage on the Nicaragua economy and forced the Sandinistas to devote more than half the national budget to defense. Those problems and failed Sandinista economic policies had sent the economy plunging downward. For the regime, agreeing to negotiate with the contras and hold internationally supervised elections represented a gamble to secure peace and hopefully rebuild the country. In March 1988 the Sandinistas and contras accepted a cease-fire that was followed by national elections in February 1990. Running against President Daniel Ortega was Violeta Chamorro, an outspoken critic of the Sandinistas and widow of the slain conservative leader Pedro Joaquin Chamorro. Leading a multiparty coalition backed by U.S. funding, Chamorro captured the presidency and a majority of seats in the Congress. Yet ultimately the coalition, whose member parties ranged from far right to far left, proved incapable of governing, and Chamorro forged a working partnership with the Sandinistas, who remained the single largest political party in the country. Meanwhile peace had also come to neighboring El Salvador, thanks again largely to international efforts.

Despite the Reagan administration's staunch support for the Salvadoran armed forces, the war at first did not go well. By 1983, the FMLN controlled about one-third of the country. In the course of the next two years, new tactics and a quadrupling of the armed forces' size to fifty thousand stemmed the guerrillas' advance, and by 1986 the war had stalemated into a series of offensives and counteroffensives. Despite the 1984 electoral victory of José Napoleon Duarte and the Christian Democrats, they proved unable to control the death squads and failed to fulfill their promise of a negotiated solution to the war, which continued unabated when Duarte left office in 1989. By that time the death toll in the Salvadoran war exceeded seventy thousand.[15] Finally in 1991 the FMLN and the Salvadoran government signed a UN-brokered peace accord that provided for an internationally supervised process in which the guerrillas would gradually disarm and the government would purge and downsize the armed forces. Although the United States promised large infusions of economic aid to assist in the recovery of the war-torn economies of Central America, those promises remained largely unfulfilled.

At enormous cost in money and lives, the United States had fought the final battles of the cold war in Latin America. Washington succeeded in diminishing the power of the Sandinistas and had prevented the FMLN from taking power in El Salvador. In so doing, it gave vent to the Reagan administration's aggressive approach to combating communism and reasserted U.S. domination of Central America. And yet these cold war interventions came just as the struggle with the Soviets was ending. After the collapse of the Soviet Union in 1989, the very idea that a guerrilla insurgency in Latin America might represent an extension of Soviet power into the Western Hemisphere became meaningless. As these events unfolded, Washington's military allies in South America were losing their grip on power.

DEMILITARIZATION

After the coup in 1964, the Brazilian military denounced and arrested the educational reformer Paulo Freire, whose literacy program had been deemed subversive by the United States. After more than fifteen years of exile, Freire returned to his homeland where he found a growing audience for his ideas about empowering the poor. Freire's opportunity to return to Brazil resulted from a very gradual liberalization that the moderate faction of the military regime had undertaken beginning in 1974. These military moderates envisioned a slow and tightly controlled opening for civilian political participation as the most effective way to preserve national stability. Nevertheless, the hard-line faction within the military resisted this policy, and even the moderates were leery of any full-fledged return to democracy. But the military faced a growing challenge from an array of social groups and institutions.

The progressive wing of the Catholic Church became an early critic of the dictatorship and provided institutional shelter for both rural and urban labor movements. With the new regime largely ignoring the needs of the urban poor, they began forming grassroots organizations to demand basic services from municipal and state governments. But the most energizing force for liberalization proved to be the labor movement. The dictatorship's economic miracle promoted a rapid growth in the industrial working class, especially in the city and state of São Paulo. Most notably, metal workers in the burgeoning auto industry shaped a new and militant labor movement under the leadership of Luís Inácio Lula da Silva, known simply as Lula.

The regime's draconian form of modernization increased wealth disparities as it imposed work speed-ups employing American-style assembly-line methods without the wage increases that normally accompanied those processes. In response, workers drew away from the traditions of state-managed unions and populist politics that had characterized their activities in the decades before the coup. Meanwhile, the economic miracle deteriorated into economic crisis as surging oil prices in the late '70s struck a staggering blow to the Brazilian economy, followed by the Latin American debt crisis.

Beginning in 1978 the autoworkers launched a series of strikes that eventually spread to other sectors of the economy, marking the return of the labor movement as a significant force in Brazilian life. Freire's ideas about empowering the disenfranchised took on a special meaning for these workers. They also served as the guiding philosophy of the Partido dos Trabalhadores (Brazilian Workers Party), which relied initially on Lula and the metalworkers for much of its strength. Mounting opposition from an array of mass movements and the maneuverings of traditional political groups finally led to the selection of a civilian president in 1985 and the continuation of the liberalization process. Seventeen years later, Lula would be elected president of Brazil. Meanwhile in Chile, a similar effort by popular forces had restored at least a limited form of democracy to that nation.[16]

The Pinochet dictatorship in Chile had devastated organized labor and its political allies, the socialists, communists, and Christian Democrats. Union leadership had been purged, and workers were forced to accept low wages that rarely sufficed to support their families. The Catholic Church survived as the only viable national institution that stood in opposition to the dictatorship. But the 1981–82 economic crisis, the worst since the Great Depression, shook the regime as well as its supporters and triggered new dynamism in the labor movement. Rather than focus simply on union issues, workers demonstrated in May 1983 to demand the restoration of democracy. Their actions would help trigger more widespread protests. Shantytown dwellers began to join the cause, engaging in direct confrontations with the police. Despite signs of economic recovery by 1985, an increasingly discontented middle class joined in the protests. Finally in 1988 the regime agreed to a plebiscite that would give voters a yes or no option on extending Pinochet's rule for eight more years. Chileans rejected the Pinochet option, and in 1989 they elected Patricio Aylwin, a Christian Democrat and head of a center-left coalition, as their new president. Democracy, although limited by the provisions of Pinochet's 1980 constitution, had been restored in Chile.[17] Despite the developments in Brazil and Chile and the unseating of dictatorships elsewhere in the region, the United States had already found new reasons for military involvement.

THE WAR ON DRUGS

Washington's long-standing identification of Latin America as a major cause of its drug problems continued to influence U.S. policy when the cocaine epidemic erupted in the 1980s. Cocaine consumption that ranged between 19 and 25 tons in 1978 had soared to between 71 and 127 tons in 1984. By 1986 the spread of cheap, smokeable crack cocaine seemed to threaten the very social fabric of the country. The Reagan administration responded by intensifying existing programs that stressed interdiction and eradication. Annual spending on such programs had averaged $437 million between 1976 and 1980 but now soared to $1.4 billion. By the time President George H. Bush took office, the drug problem had become a national obsession. During the Reagan years the military had been called on in very limited ways to assist in the drug war, but now under Secretary of Defense Dick Cheney there was an all-out effort to militarize the antidrug campaign. The U.S. armed forces would both assist with interdiction along the country's borders and provide reconnaissance and training support to foreign nations as well as aid in nation-building programs designed to wean peasants away from growing coca leaves.[18] This strategy targeted Latin American countries that produced or transshipped 80 percent of the cocaine and 90 percent of the marijuana smuggled into the United States.

With a particular focus on Bolivia, Peru, and Colombia as producers and marketers of cocaine, the United States, much as it had done in the

1930s, sought to shape the drug policies of these countries. On the one hand, Washington pressured the three nations to accept military aid and teams of U.S. advisors to conduct their internal drug wars while at the same time it promised increased economic aid designed to shift peasants to the production of alternative cash crops. As a part of this strategy, the United States began a process of annually certifying the progress of these countries' efforts to reduce the drug business. Failure to receive certification could mean a cutoff of U.S. economic aid.[19] Peru became one major target of these policies. In the midst of a deepening economic crisis in the early 1980s, peasants had migrated to the Huallaga Valley to plant coca in an effort to survive. Although Washington placed restrictions on aid to Peru because of what it perceived as failure by the Peruvian government to actively pursue eradication plans, the United States soon threw new resources into the country, dispatching advisors, helicopters, and other equipment to aid in drug interdiction and eradication in the Huallaga Valley.[20]

Drug use in the United States did decline significantly by the early 1990s. But that decline had little to do with the eradication and interdiction programs that were intended to reduce usage in the United States by creating scarcity and causing prices to soar. While eradication made headway in marijuana growing, it failed to reduce the coca crop. Coca-leaf production in fact increased from 291,000 metric tons in 1987 to 333,000 tons by 1992. And when the United States stepped up efforts at interdiction off the coast of Florida and in the Caribbean, the Colombian drug cartels simply began shipping more of their product through Mexico.[21] By that time the militarization of the drug war had gone beyond simply providing military assistance to Latin American countries to include the outright invasion of one of them.

General Manuel Antonio Noriega maneuvered himself into control of Panama's armed forces and then the entire country by the early 1980s. In that position, Noriega made himself a valuable ally of the United States. With close ties to the CIA, Noriega allowed the United States to use his country as a staging ground for efforts to assist the contras in Nicaragua, and he supplied intelligence information to the agency while maintaining close ties to Fidel Castro. Noriega also had a hand in drug trafficking, allowing Colombian dealers to use Panamanian banks to launder money and to seek refuge within Panama when they were being pursued by Colombian authorities. But in early 1988, with the U.S. effort against the Sandinistas starting to unravel, federal prosecutors charged Noriega with a series of offenses including money laundering and protecting members of the Medellín drug cartel. With Noriega's usefulness in Central America rapidly declining, he came to personify the sort of corrupt, conniving Latin American political leader whom American officials believed had stymied their efforts to suppress drug trafficking. Washington began openly supporting Noriega's domestic opponents and cut off all Panama Canal payments to his government.

A series of incidents involving U.S. military personnel in Panama prompted President Bush on December 20, 1989, to initiate a full-scale invasion of Panama, which quickly overwhelmed the Panamanian armed forces and compelled Noriega to surrender. Eventually the United States put the Panamanian strongman on trial and sentenced him to forty years in jail, but these actions failed to have any measurable impact on drug trafficking in Panama. In the meantime, the invasion set off a firestorm of criticism by Latin American leaders. Latin Americans had already become incensed over U.S. eradication programs that challenged the sovereignty of Latin American governments. Now as a part of that same drug war, the United States had invaded a Latin American country without consulting regional leaders. But for most Latin Americans the drug issue had been largely eclipsed during the 1980s by the economic trauma of the international debt crisis that had erupted in 1982.

DEBT CRISIS

Latin American countries carried out heavy borrowing from foreign, especially U.S., banks throughout the 1970s with few signs that their debt burdens were becoming excessive. Low interest rates made borrowing inexpensive, and Latin America's rising export totals were earning the foreign exchange needed to service the loans. At the same time bankers in the developed world were more than anxious to lend out the sea of dollars that flooded their coffers as oil-producing nations sought safe investment havens for the profits earned from high petroleum prices. However, this fortuitous set of circumstances changed radically at the beginning of the next decade. To battle high inflation, the U.S. Federal Reserve ratcheted up interest rates. That policy and soaring oil prices sent the U.S. and European economies into a deep recession, forcing loan rates ever higher and dramatically reducing the demand for imports. The average interest rate on Latin American foreign debt rose from 10 percent in 1978 to 18 percent by 1981. At the same time, the growth in export income for Latin American economies slowed. As debt-service payments ballooned and income to pay them flattened, Latin American governments and foreign bankers engaged in a frenzied round of new borrowing to ensure that current debt-service payments could be made. As a result, the region's debt rose from $184 billion in 1979 to $314 billion in 1982, finally creating a regionwide financial crisis.[22]

With Mexico on the verge of defaulting on its debt, U.S. Treasury Secretary Donald Regan summoned his Mexican counterpart, Jesús Silva Herzog, to an urgent meeting in Washington on August 13, 1982. Silva Herzog's hasty visit to Washington reflected the dire nature of the crisis, not only for Latin American governments unable to meet their debt obligations but also for international and especially U.S. banks that had loaned extraordinary sums that might never be repaid. The nine largest U.S. banks, most notably Citibank (later Citigroup) and Bank of America, had loaned $26 billion to the region's two largest debtors, Mexico and Brazil, with Citibank alone holding $5 billion in Brazilian debt.[23] A total default on such enormous sums could topple leading American banks and drag the entire international banking system down with them. Much like the Bankers Committee set up in the 1920s to deal with Mexico's debt after its revolution, leading U.S. financial institutions created an advisory committee to deal with the immediate crisis in Mexico. But during the 1982 debt crisis, multilateral lending agencies, especially the IMF, played an important role in arranging new financing for Mexico, while negotiations proceeded to reschedule its foreign debt.

Initially bankers and government policymakers believed that the crisis represented a short-term liquidity (cash flow) problem as opposed to a structural fault involving the fundamental solvency of national economies. Both bankers and Latin American leaders assumed that if the Latin American debtors could be sustained over the short term, low prices for exports and other such difficulties would correct themselves and would solve the debt problem over the long term. Operating on that assumption and with the assistance of the IMF, the bankers and Latin American leaders managed to patch together short-term rescue packages that included new lending and radical reductions in imports by Latin American countries in order to use the savings in foreign exchange to service their debts. These tactics avoided the collapse of banks and defaults by Latin American governments. But with the region's foreign debt still growing and its economies slowing, it became apparent that fundamental restructuring would be necessary if Latin America was ever going to return to reasonable levels of growth.

In 1989, U.S. Secretary of the Treasury Nicholas F. Brady initiated a program that offered a variety of options that lenders and borrowers could pursue to achieve debt relief. The options included having creditors accept new bonds at low interest for their existing Latin American debt, or receiving bonds with higher rates of interest, but accepting a reduction in the face value of the debt. In the end, the reduction in the debt burden resulted less from write-downs of the old debt and more from increasing economic growth and export revenues. That economic rebound was widely attributed to what was termed the "Washington consensus."

Policymakers in Washington and multilateral institutions had come to the conclusion that the debt crisis stemmed in fact from structural problems in Latin American economies derived from protectionist Import Substituting Industrialization policies. They asserted that these policies had, over the decades, led to poor export growth and thus robbed Latin America of the revenues needed to sustain foreign borrowing. The solution according to this consensus lay in a three-pronged strategy of reducing import restrictions, downsizing the state, and encouraging the growth of the private sector. According to these policymakers such an approach would shrink the cost of external inputs for Latin American economies, reduce deficit spending by such measures as selling off state-owned enterprises, and improve economic efficiency by allowing domestic and foreign corporations a freer hand in the economy. By the early 1990s most Latin American governments had embraced some version of this strategy not merely as a debt-reduction plan but as a regionwide experiment in neoliberal development.

❧

Under President Ronald Reagan, Americans envisioned themselves as a reinvigorated world power fully recovered from the humiliation of the

Vietnam War. During the 1980s the United States pursued interventionist policies in Latin America against social revolutions and drug trafficking while coping with the threat of a regional financial collapse. These events seemed to hark back to the imperialist tactics of the early twentieth century and the interventionism of the midcentury cold war while offering haunting reminders of the Great Depression. Yet while U.S. policies in Central America may have forestalled the triumph of leftist revolutionary movements, the end result in both Nicaragua and El Salvador also revealed the limitations of U.S. strategies. The Central American wars made it clear that the American public would no longer support direct U.S. intervention or long-term military involvement in the region in response to claims of a looming communist threat. The days when the United States could simply dictate the political future of Central America had come to an end. Furthermore, the U.S. banking system had been placed at serious risk by the debt crisis that erupted during the decade. But during the 1990s the images of violent conflicts would fade, and the debt crisis would actually be turned to the advantage of the United States and its neoliberal economic policies.

CHAPTER TEN

GLOBALIZATION AND ITS DISCONTENTS, 1993–2006

On January 1, 1994, a band of masked and armed insurgents entered the outskirts of the town of San Cristóbal de las Casas in Mexico's southern state of Chiapas. Within a few hours the guerrilla column and several others like it had seized government buildings and radio stations in San Cristóbal and four other towns, proclaiming themselves to be the Zapatista National Liberation Army (EZLN). Their appearance could easily prompt memories of the Fidelistas, who had fought their way to victory out of Cuba's Sierra Maestra some thirty-five years earlier. But despite the resemblance, this was not a classic guerrilla army determined to oust a tyrant and seize power by force of arms. As the Zapatistas' spokesman, sub-Comandante Marcos, exclaimed, "This isn't about Chiapas—it's about NAFTA and [Mexican President Carlos] Salinas' whole neoliberal project." The targets of the guerrillas' ire were the North American Free Trade Agreement, designed to lower trade and investment barriers among Canada, the United States, and Mexico, and neoliberal policies aimed at unleashing market forces and downsizing the state's role in achieving social and economic equality. In fact, the neoliberal project had become the central issue in both the region's domestic affairs and U.S.–Latin American relations. Furthermore, despite their weapons, these new insurgents did not rely on force for achieving their ends. The Zapatistas used the modern media to wage a national and international campaign, initiating a broad popular dialogue regarding the onrushing process commonly termed globalization. They used effective communication techniques including launching their insurgency on the very day NAFTA took effect, and they worked to involve the larger population as activists in shaping the future.[1] The Zapatista insurgency testified to how dramatically Latin American societies and their relationships with the United States had changed since the beginning of the 1980s when the United States had pursued military strategies to crush guerrilla insurgencies in Central America.

∞

The closing decades of the twentieth century appeared to mark the triumphant completion of the American mission in Latin America. Although the sweeping economic and social changes of the period could not be simply attributed to the century-long effort by Americans to transform the region, many of these changes did bear striking resemblances to the goals of American modernizers. And there was little question that a variety of American agents worked energetically to encourage and support the neoliberal agenda in Latin America. Yet as the Zapatista insurgency made clear, many Latin Americans were continuing, as they had for more than a century, to both reject as well as appropriate elements of the American mission. If Latin Americans were embracing modernity, they were doing so within the context of their own cultures and histories. Furthermore, a number of developments challenged the influence of the United States in the region by the end of the century.

U.S. domination of the global economy since World War II was being eroded by Japan and the European Union and challenged by China in the 1990s. Although the U.S. effort to protect its strategic interests from the threat of communism had resonated strongly among Latin

American elites whose own interests were threatened by the political left, the anticommunism that underpinned this alliance evaporated with the collapse of the Soviet Union. The U.S. wars on terror and drugs found a far less receptive audience among Latin Americans, who did not perceive the same threat level in these problems as did Americans. As in its earlier iteration, the policy of trade and investment liberalization tied Latin American economies closely to the global market and made them extremely vulnerable to sharp changes in commodity prices and the shifting strategies of multinational corporations. It also became painfully apparent that neither neoliberal economics nor civilian political regimes had yet solved the problems of widespread poverty and social inequality that had so recently triggered armed revolutionary struggles and that had prompted an ever-rising tide of Latin American migration to the United States. By the early years of the twenty-first century, the American war on terror offered a new reason to view immigrants from Latin American with suspicion and to continue to militarize relations with the region.

Overseeing the era of globalization were two presidents from distinctly different backgrounds. Bill Clinton, raised by a single mother in Arkansas, had utilized his intelligence and charm to become a Rhodes scholar and a crafty politician. George W. Bush, the grandson of a wealthy U.S senator and son of a president, had grown up in the heart of the American elite and bore all its trappings, including a degree from Yale University. Clinton and Bush faced a common challenge of how to preserve the paternalistic role that the United States had defined for itself and that for nearly half a century had been legitimized in terms of the United States protecting Latin America from communism. For Clinton, while certainly a classic macho male in terms of his personal life, political legitimation rested on leading the war on drugs and fostering globalization through multilateral trade agreements. Texan George W. Bush, who despite his Yale pedigree adopted many of the same cowboy mannerisms as Ronald Reagan, found legitimation for U.S. dominance in the 9/11 terrorist attacks on the United States. The wars on terror and drugs reflected the president's stress on aggressive military solutions to these threats to U.S. interests even if they required unilateral action. In the Western Hemisphere, the Clinton/Bush redefinition of U.S. paternalism faced significant challenges as many Latin Americans questioned the effects of neoliberal economic policies as well as the militarization that Washington promoted as a solution to the threats of drugs and terrorism.

DRUGS AND TERRORISM

Much as it had done since early in the twentieth century, Washington pursued a highly aggressive drug-control strategy based on the premise that a principal source of its own drug problem lay in the failure of Latin Americans to suppress the drug business in their countries.[2] Even before the U.S. invasion of Panama in 1989, the Medellín cartel had demonstrated its boldness by assassinating Colombian Senator Luis Carlos Galán, a leading presidential candidate, in August of that same year. The Colombian government declared an all-out war on the drug lords, who responded in kind with a bombing campaign designed to rattle the state and force political leaders to accept a temporary truce. The first President Bush quickly joined in the fray with a $65 million emergency aid package. U.S. efforts once again stressed military solutions. The Colombian government eventually did achieve striking successes in its war against the cartels: in 1993 Colombian police killed Pablo Escobar, the head of the Medellín cartel, and in 1995 the Rodríguez Orejeula brothers, leaders of the Calí cartel, were arrested. But in their place emerged the Norte del Valle cartel in southwestern Colombia. As the Colombian government turned its attention to this new drug enterprise, it also faced the reality that an increasing portion of the drug business was passing into the hands of leftist guerrillas and right-wing paramilitary organizations linked to the Colombian Army.[3]

In Washington, the Clinton administration announced it would budget $13.2 billion for the drug problem in fiscal 1995 and shifted the emphasis from interdiction to eradication. This shift in emphasis became apparent in Colombia where the government began eradication programs involving aerial spraying of coca crops with herbicides such as Monsanto's "Roundup." The United States launched a similar program in Bolivia. Washington linked these eradication projects to economic aid designed to promote the growing of alternative cash crops by peasants. After the expenditure of $3.2 billion, the eradication program in Colombia appeared to make considerable headway, reducing coca cultivation 21 percent by 2004. But in 2006 the U.S. government announced that coca cultivation in Colombia had actually risen by 26 percent between 2004 and 2005. Much of the increase was attributed to newly discovered coca-growing areas. It was clear that the Colombian government's goal of reducing coca cultivation by 50 percent between 2000 and 2006 was far from being met.[4] The most compelling evidence that the eradication program had failed was the fact that the price of cocaine in the United States remained low. Supplies remained ample because despite eradication efforts, the production of cocaine remained at least at the same levels achieved in the 1990s, which were more than sufficient to meet demand in the United States. Colombian growers had adapted by abandoning large-scale production units for small plots that were difficult to eradicate with aerial spraying and by cultivating higher-yield varieties of coca leaves.[5] Much like the attacks on the marketing networks of the cartels, the eradication process had served to decentralize drug activity rather than eliminate it. These projects also contributed to destabilizing these societies.

The eradication program led to intensifying warfare between guerrilla forces and militias, pushing Colombia to the brink of civil war. In January 2000, President Clinton announced "Plan Colombia," a new $1.3 billion aid package to combat drug trafficking. Most of the money was earmarked for military hardware and the crop-eradication program. By 2003 annual expenditures on Plan Colombia exceeded $700 million a year, despite warnings from the CIA that if successful the project would further disperse the actual growing of coca leaves into neighboring countries. Meanwhile in Bolivia, the eradication program prompted violent protests by tens of thousands of organized growers and eventually contributed to the toppling of President Gonzalo Sánchez Lozado in 2003. Latin American leaders became increasingly critical of U.S. eradication strategies that contributed to human rights abuses by the military in these countries and that seemed only to spread the drug business into new areas.[6] Meanwhile, the U.S. war on terror provided yet another rationale for militarizing relations with Latin America.

In March 2004, General James Hill, the head of the U.S. Southern Command that oversees U.S. military interests in the southern half of the Western Hemisphere, told a congressional committee that the United States faced a real threat from terrorism in Latin America and must therefore take assertive actions, including strengthening other militaries in the region. Stressing the importance of his command in the war on terror, which was attracting massive funding from Congress, Hill painted a picture of an area stalked by thousands of terrorists. Hill's definitions of terrorists included drug traffickers, criminal gangs, and even populist politicians. As distorted as Hill's images may have been, they were not merely the posturing of a bureaucrat anxious to secure funding for his agency. Eight months later, Secretary of Defense Donald Rumsfeld met with Latin American defense ministers and stressed the need for closer cooperation to combat the twin threats of terrorism and drug trafficking. He specifically urged his audience to create closer links between military and police activities. That latter suggestion met with a cool reception from representatives of nations, which had so recently endured decades of harsh military dictatorship. Furthermore, Latin American leaders consider the drug trade a serious problem, but terrorism is not believed to be a significant threat in any of their societies.[7]

Nevertheless, Washington had been offering and Latin American governments had been accepting an increasing amount of military aid, much of it linked to the wars on drugs and terrorism. In 2003 that aid amounted to $860 million compared to $921 million in economic and humanitarian assistance the United States provided that same year. Even during the cold war, American military assistance had amounted to less than one-third of U.S. economic aid to the region. The Bush administration was also stressing the doctrine of "effective sovereignty," which bore a striking resemblance to Teddy Roosevelt's Big Stick policy. Washington now asserted that states that failed to maintain effective sovereignty over their own territory presented a real threat to the United States by creating ungoverned areas where terrorists could potentially operate. That perspective could provide a justification for preemptive intervention, or more probably, a justification for increases in military assistance and a larger role for Latin American militaries in their nation's affairs. Yet neither drugs nor terrorists offered the sort of rallying cry that anticommunism had provided when it had stirred Latin American elites and the middle class to embrace U.S. policies in the 1950s and '60s. In striking contrast to its drug and terrorism policies, the principal strategies employed by the United States during much of the late twentieth century focused on international trade and investment. In these areas U.S. policy seemed to enjoy exceptional success.[8]

NEOLIBERALISM AND GLOBALIZATION

As Latin American regimes accepted the terms of the Washington consensus that the region's economies had to reduce state regulation and open themselves more to the global marketplace, they placed particular stress on the idea of free trade, believing it would boost exports and improve economic efficiency as cheaper, better foreign imports replaced the products of inefficient, protected domestic industries. A part of that strategy was the creation of regional trading blocs that would lower trade barriers between their members. In 1991 Argentina, Brazil, Uruguay, and Paraguay, guided by a new generation of free-market technocrats, agreed to move toward the creation of a common market as a part of their trading arrangement known as MERCOSUR. In 1994 the launch of NAFTA created a regional free-trade zone. In fact, NAFTA's greatest importance was less the reduction of what were already modest tariffs and more the impulse it gave to foreign investment in Mexico. For Mexico, greater access to the U.S. market meant increased investments from Japanese and European companies seeking low-cost access to that market. For U.S. corporations, Mexico more than ever became a site for low-wage production of their goods for sale in the international economy and a location that now offered even easier access back to their home market.[9] The move toward free trade marked a radical reversal of the protectionist strategies that had dominated Latin American economic policymaking for half a century.

Why did Latin American governments embrace neoliberal policies promoting free trade, a downsized state, and increased foreign investment, rather than reasserting the protectionist policies adopted during the earlier debt crisis of the Great Depression? First, this debt crisis was regional in scope and did not involve the sort of worldwide economic collapse that had left creditor nations unable to offer alternatives to default in the 1930s. Second, sources of support for statist economic policies were disappearing as the Soviet Union disintegrated and China adopted a strategy of state capitalism. But perhaps most telling was the simple fact that many Latin American technocrats in government bureaucracies had been trained in the concepts of neoliberalism and now found an ideal opportunity to offer their ideas as the solution to the crisis. Many of those technocrats were products of earlier U.S. attempts to shape higher education in Latin America.

Despite Albion Patterson's enthusiasm and the resources of AID and private foundations, the University of Chicago's project to train neoliberal economists appeared at first to have little impact in Chile itself. The free-market ideas of the "Chicago Boys," as the new economics faculty came to be known, found little resonance in the Frei and Allende administrations, whose technocrats put emphasis on the role of the state in economic development, and in the process of creating a more equitable society. But the military dictatorship that replaced Allende put the Chicago Boys in control of economic policy, and they pursued this opportunity with a near-religious zeal. They ended price controls and privatized most state-owned corporations as well as the social security system; they established market-based interest rates and launched an offensive against labor unions, radically reducing their power, which contributed to a free fall in real wages. The drastic measures dramatically cut inflation and restored economic growth.[10] However, in 1981 a financial crisis triggered a string of corporate bankruptcies and sent the gross national product plummeting. A combination of short-term foreign loans that temporarily fueled growth but carried a high cost and unfettered activities by corporate conglomerates freed of state supervision had triggered the collapse. Although a variety of unorthodox policies eventually salvaged the situation, neoliberal economics remained the ruling ideology of the military regime.[11] Furthermore, the neoliberal technocrats had a vision, which encompassed more than just economics.

The basic principles of neoliberalism emphasized the importance of market forces in the economic sphere as the most efficient mechanism for determining prices, resource allocation, and so on. To release market forces, the economy must be freed of regulation, international trade and capital flows must be facilitated, and the role of the state in the economy had to be radically reduced. The efficacy of these ideas received powerful support from the performance of the Chilean economy after it weathered its own financial crisis during the early 1980s. During the 1990s the country's gross domestic product grew at an impressive average annual rate of 6.5 percent. For the neoliberals, however, free markets were not merely excellent economic mechanisms: they also represented the ideal environment for human freedom and rational decision making. They wanted to remove decisions about such issues as social welfare and problems of economic and social equality from politicians and place those decisions in the hands of technocrats, imbued of course with the same neoliberal philosophy. Even after the end of the dictatorship, the political regimes that followed in Chile continued to vest technocrats with broad-ranging authority to make such decisions, and most technocrats, whatever their ideological inclinations, came to accept the importance of market forces in shaping policy. Mexico proved to be another case where neoliberal strategies played a pivotal role in policymaking.

The election of Carlos Salinas de Gotari as Mexico's president in 1988 brought to power a true technocrat as opposed to the party bosses who had long occupied the position. A Harvard-trained economist, Salinas had served as minister of planning and budget. Operating within the environment created by Mexico's revolutionary history, Salinas could never act with the single-mindedness of the Chicago Boys, but he did dramatically alter Mexico's long-standing economic and social policies. By 1992, 85 percent of the country's state-owned corporations had been privatized. Even prior to the negotiations that led to NAFTA, which Salinas had ardently promoted, the president had eliminated almost all import permits and reduced remaining import duties to a maximum of 20 percent.[12] These measures were part of Salinas's larger strategy to integrate Mexico fully into the global economy. Because NAFTA was designed not merely to promote trade but also to attract foreign investors seeking an inexpensive gateway to the U.S. market, the president attacked powerful union leaders to ensure a low-wage environment for foreign and domestic corporations.

Although the influence of U.S.-trained technocrats was not as pervasive in other Latin American countries, neoliberal technocrats achieved significant influence in many regimes. Politicians in other nations might not wholeheartedly embrace neoliberal doctrine, but they were well aware that these ideas reflected the thinking among bankers, multilateral agency bureaucrats, and corporate investors. Simply the appointment of such technocrats to powerful positions could stabilize local economic conditions, restore investor confidence, and ease negotiations for international loans. Even Fernando Henrique Cardoso, the noted dependency theorist, had accepted the basic premises of free-market economics by the time he became the president of Brazil in 1995. At the same time, not all technocrats were U.S. trained or influenced, nor did they all adhere to the pristine neoliberalism of the Chicago Boys. Nevertheless, Albion

Patterson's Chilean experiment did indeed come to have a profound influence on economic policymaking and the functioning of the state in Latin America. One notable outcome of that influence was the very positive effect such policies had on U.S. investment in the region, especially as a result of the neoliberal push for privatization of state corporations.

Privatization was not merely a tactic within the new orthodox economic strategy; it was also often set as a condition by the IMF for extensions of credit to Latin American nations that were staggering under the enormous debt burdens that had nearly bankrupted them in the 1980s. In Argentina alone, foreigners invested more than $4.7 billion in newly privatized public corporations including petroleum, petrochemicals, telecommunications, electricity, and railroads between 1990 and 1993.[13] Throughout Latin America many of the state enterprises created since the Great Depression to protect the national patrimony in sectors such as raw materials and utilities went on the auction block to both domestic and foreign capitalists. Investors showed particular interest in the telecommunications sector with its opportunities for rapid growth in high-tech areas such as cell phones. Between 1991 and 1995 Argentina sold off nearly all its publicly held telecommunication companies to private interests. During the 1990s the sale of Latin American utilities to domestic and foreign companies generated $220 billion of capital inflows into these areas. In many instances privatization meant upgraded technologies and improved services. Unfortunately, Latin American governments put most of the billions generated by the sales of the utilities into their general revenue funds, meaning that little of the money actually went to improving the delivery of public services to the poor.[14]

This new era of liberalization also led to yet another surge of U.S. corporate activity in the rapidly growing manufacturing sector and into areas such as petroleum and finance where U.S. corporations had long been unwelcome.[15] In 2001, Citigroup (formerly Citibank), the United States's largest financial conglomerate, purchased Mexico's second-largest bank, Grupo Financiero Banamex Accival, for $12.5 billion, making it the largest foreign acquisition ever by a U.S. bank. Acquiring Banamex made Citigroup, which already had holdings in the country, the largest financial institution in Mexico. Much of the influx in foreign investment came in the form of mergers and acquisition, and much of that resulted from privatizations. In Brazil in 1999, acquisitions resulting from privatizations accounted for 28 percent of new foreign direct investment in the county. Although Latin American states continued to play a far larger role in their economies and the regulation of foreign corporations than could have been imagined a century earlier, the new era of internationalization bore a striking resemblance to the liberalism of the late nineteenth and early twentieth centuries. Initially, neoliberal economic policies enjoyed impressive success in Latin America.

During the 1980s most Latin American economies regularly experienced annual inflation rates between 20 and 50 percent. During the 1990s inflation in the region dropped to less than 20 percent. Between 1990 and 1998, annual U.S exports to Latin America soared from $53.9 billion to $142 billion, while imports from Latin America climbed from $67 billion to $142 billion. U.S. direct investment more than tripled from $70.7 billion in 1990 to $223 billion in 1999. Investments in finance alone more than quadrupled to $124 billion, and holdings in the manufacturing sector doubled to $51 billion.[16] Meanwhile, the North American Free Trade Agreement initiated a series of reciprocal tariff reductions among the United States, Mexico, and Canada during a fifteen-year period, which had a positive effect on the trade between the United States and its southern neighbor. From 1994 to 2000, agricultural trade between the two countries increased by 55 percent, reaching $11.6 billion annually. Overall trade between Mexico and the United States increased from $100 billion in 1994 to $170 billion in 1998.

However, the long-term impact of NAFTA was hotly debated in all three nations. Critics charged that hundreds of thousands of jobs had been lost in the United States and that increased agricultural trade largely benefited multinational agribusinesses rather than small farmers. Supporters claimed that the treaty shifted low-wage jobs to Mexico to produce inputs such as car engines that would be exported to the United States to form part of finished products assembled by high-wage labor. As for the agricultural trade, NAFTA advocates argued that the agreement lowered food costs in both countries.

At times the enthusiasm of Latin American elites for extending the agreement to the entire region seemed to outpace that of U.S. leaders. As the governor of the Argentine province of Jujuy noted in 1998, "Look, it's simple; there is an Americanization of the world. We cannot go in the opposite direction. At last we are going to make America here."[17] In fact, free-trade advocates sought to make NAFTA the basis for the regional free-trade zone envisioned by Nelson Rockefeller in 1969. In April 2001, thirty-four Western Hemisphere leaders met in Quebec City, Canada, for the Summit of the Americas. President George W. Bush gave strong backing to the creation of the Free Trade Area of the Americas (FTAA), which would include a free-trade pact encompassing 800 million consumers in the Western Hemisphere. The summit members called for the establishment of the FTAA by 2005. But the U.S. effort to expand the NAFTA model to the entire hemisphere faced difficult going.

GLOBALIZATION AND ITS DISCONTENTS

Part of the opposition to the FTAA model stemmed from regional industrial powers such as Brazil and Argentina, which feared that their manufacturers would wither under competition from the United States. Brazil also insisted that it must receive access to the highly protected U.S. agricultural sector. Brazilian president Fernando Henrique Cardoso considered the growth of Brazilian exports as essential to the nation's continued development. Without such concessions, Brazil would be unwilling to approve any FTAA agreement. As one Brazilian legislator put it, "If the United States can pull out of the Anti-Ballistic Missile Treaty because that doesn't suit its interests, why shouldn't we pull out of negotiations [on FTAA] that are not going to be of any benefit to us?"[18] Indeed, Argentine President Nestor Kirchner and Brazilian President Luiz Inácio Lula da Silva met in June 2003 and agreed to politically integrate MERCOSUR, the southern common market, which included their nations as well as Paraguay and Uruguay. That move was intended in part to shape a united front on the terms under which they would enter the FTAA. At the same time, Latin American countries sought increased trade with other developed nations to provide further leverage in any dealings with the United States. Most notably, China's trade volume with Brazil, Argentina, and Chile in 2003 reached $14.6 billion as the Chinese tapped the region's natural resources to feed their fast-growing industrial economy. Not only was trade with China growing rapidly, but also the Chinese were investing billions of dollars in the region to facilitate the production and export of its raw materials.[19] Despite the successes attributable to neoliberal economic policies, many Latin Americans were expressing their opposition to free-trade policies.

Free-trade agreements, which did little to protect workers and the environment, helped trigger a growing antiglobalization movement around the world. Indeed, the heads of state who met in Quebec drew the attention of thousands of antiglobalization demonstrators. But most importantly, millions of Latin Americans began to express mounting doubts about the panacea of prosperity, which free-trade advocates had argued would flow from aggressive neoliberal policies. There were growing concerns about whether trade liberalization could in fact bring self-sustaining economic development and relieve the region's deep-seated poverty.

Unemployment rates in Latin America rose during the 1990s, real wages fell, and income distribution worsened. As a result, during that decade, 35 percent of the region's people remained trapped in abject poverty—just as they were a decade before. With their economies growing at rates of 3 or 4 percent annually, Latin American nations did not generate the kind of increases in national wealth that would lift the majority of their populations beyond the level of mere subsistence. In fact, these rates fell considerably below the 5.5 percent growth rate that the region's economies averaged during the state-driven development decades of the 1950s and '60s. Meanwhile, years of hyperinflation, bankruptcies, and the slashing of government social spending devastated the middle and working classes.[20] As one expert succinctly put it, "In the twenty-five years of the Washington Consensus, the Latin American economies have experienced their worst quarter century since the catastrophic second quarter of the nineteenth century."[21]

The neoliberal model for growth that became the standard for development policy in Latin America in the closing years of the twentieth century was strikingly similar to the liberal development schemes of the nineteenth century. Much like nineteenth-century liberals and twentieth-century modernization theorists, neoliberal economists had failed to confront the problems of gross inequalities in political, social, and economic power that would prevent the emergence of free-market economies with greater equality in wealth distribution.[22] In addition, proponents of the neoliberal approach encouraged third world nations to embrace the world marketplace by expanding export-led growth focused on products in which they enjoyed a comparative advantage. For industrializing countries like Brazil and Mexico that has meant the growth in exports of manufactured goods from shoes to automobiles. But this strategy also suffered from some of the same flaws as its nineteenth-century predecessor. In particular, the liberalization of trade encouraged currency outflows that weakened exchange rates as consumers rushed to acquire foreign-produced goods made cheaper by reduced import duties. More importantly, many countries had been encouraged to find their place in the new world economy much as they did in the old world economy, that is, by emphasizing the export of mineral resources and agricultural products. As in the past, this approach increased these economies' vulnerability to the inevitable price gyrations that occur in these products. These fundamental problems of gross internal social and economic inequities and increasing exposure to the erratic price swings in global markets for primary products reared their heads once again.

Coffee prices began dropping precipitously at the end of the 1990s, leading to widespread suffering among coffee growers in the first years of the new century. As one of the main cash crops of Latin America, the sharp decline in the price of coffee visited acute suffering upon millions of small farmers in Brazil, Peru, Colombia, Ecuador, Mexico, and throughout Central America. Exacerbating the problem was the fact that a handful of companies controlled the international market for coffee. Six multinationals accounted for 40 percent of the worldwide trade, while in the United States, four corporations, Procter and Gamble Company, Philip Morris Companies Inc. (now Altria Group), Sara Lee Corporation, and Nestle controlled 60 percent of the retail trade in coffee. Against such massive international powerhouses, small coffee farmers were powerless to influence the prices for their beans. As Santiago de la Rosa, a Guatemalan coffee grower explained, "The problem is that coffee sells at high prices there [U.S.]. But here we suffer."[23] As a result small farmers like de la Rosa survived on $2.00 a day.

Conditions for workers on Guatemala's large coffee plantations were even worse. With prices falling, plantation owners pressed workers to provide more labor including the work of young children. Planters easily crushed efforts by workers to gain better living conditions and payment of the legal minimum wage of $2.48 per day. When workers on Guatemala's Nueva Florencia plantation fought for such rights, the owner fired them, blacklisted them with other plantation owners, shutoff power and water to their homes, and banned their children from the plantation school. Even Chile, the poster child for neoliberal reform, was not immune to such problems. By the year 2001, the world recession had driven copper prices down more than 25 percent. Dependent on copper sales for 40 percent of its annual exports, the country suffered a sharp economic slowdown. As was the case more than a century earlier, opening the Latin American economies to the world market also made them increasingly vulnerable to the vicissitudes of world commodity markets and left them with a limited industrial base to offset the effects of setbacks in their commodity export economies.[24] Furthermore, little had been done by Latin American governments to create more equitable distributions of power within their societies, assuring that setbacks in the international economy would fall most heavily on those least able to absorb them. Popular responses to these problems became increasingly militant during the closing years of the twentieth century. One of the most striking early reactions came in the Zapatista rebellion in the Mexican state of Chiapas.

Chiapas is a state rich in natural resources and the vibrant culture of its Mayan Indian population. Until the last quarter of the twentieth century, the Indian communal villages continued to produce their staple crop of corn while also providing labor for the coffee and sugar estates of the region. Thanks to peasant agitation and government land reform, more than 50 percent of the land in Chiapas remained under the control of indigenous communities. But dramatic changes began in the 1970s. The rapid spread of cattle ranching led to the illegal occupation and renting of communal lands. World Bank programs encouraging peasants to engage in cattle raising actually left many of them under the control of local cattle barons. At the same time, the rapid development of petroleum production in the state triggered high rates of inflation and substandard living conditions in the new oil patch. The thousands of Chiapas peasants who migrated to the oil fields to find work endured a lack of social services and decent housing, as well as skyrocketing prices for basic consumer goods.

Social unrest would accelerate rapidly during the regime of President Carlos Salinas de Gortari (1988–94) as the new regime rolled back the reform programs of previous administrations. To comply with the terms of NAFTA, the government reduced subsidies for corn in Chiapas and throughout Mexico to allow the import of cheaper corn from the United States. The liberalization of the corn trade allowed government subsidized agribusinesses in the United States to flood the Mexican market with their product, driving down Mexican corn prices by 48 percent between 1994 and 1996. Most of Mexico's three million corn farmers, including those in Chiapas, worked fewer than five acres of land. In the face of falling prices they increased production by tilling less fertile lands in an attempt to counter falling prices with increased output. The effort drove many of them to the point of economic ruin. In addition, in 1992, the government made changes in Article 27 of the Mexican Constitution, which had served as the legal underpinning of agrarian reform since 1917.[25] The changes allowed for the buying and selling of communal lands, placing them at the disposal of large landowners and accentuating the disintegration of peasant communities. Large commercial planters and ranchers could now expand their operations and exploit the new opportunities for exports under NAFTA. Large cattle ranches alone now occupied 30 percent of the total land area of the state of Chiapas. The deteriorating position of the Mexican peasantry led the Zapatistas to charge that NAFTA "is the death certificate for the Indian peoples of Mexico."[26] Mexico was not the only society to suffer severe disruptions from its increasing inclusion in the world economy.

In July 2001, a lawsuit was filed in the United States on behalf of the Colombian labor union that represented Coca-Cola workers, charging the corporation and its subsidiaries and affiliates with murdering, torturing, kidnapping, and threatening union leaders at Coke's bottling plants in Colombia. The accusations brought out in dramatic fashion the fact that the raging conflict in Colombia, in which the United States was now directly involved, arose in part from that country's increasing adoption of policies based on neoliberal orthodoxy.

In the past century Colombia's civil society has been shattered by violent conflict during three different epochs, the War of a Thousand Days (1899–1901), La Violencia (1946–65), and most recently a period of renewed strife that has enveloped the county since the mid-1980s. The most recent era of violence was usually characterized as a war against drug lords, reflecting Colombia's emergence as a leading distributor and then producer of cocaine for the U.S. market. But the violence in Colombia stemmed from more than a battle over drug trafficking. As with the country's two earlier episodes of civil conflict, the most recent period of violence involved a struggle over the control and exploitation of the nation's resources.

Colombia's natural endowments include emeralds, gold, coal, oil, and rich agricultural land. In the new era of free-market economics, liberalization of markets in Colombia spurred an influx of foreign capital to exploit those resources. At the same time, consumption of imports surged while domestic manufacturers found themselves hard-pressed to compete with imports. Between 1997 and 1998, five thousand small factories closed in Colombia. In addition, new labor legislation made it easier to lay off workers. These developments helped exacerbate social conflicts in several different arenas. Peasants fought to protect their land from expanding commercial ventures and from the incursions of oil companies, while urban workers battled to protect jobs and working conditions. Violence against labor leaders escalated with 128 killed in the year 2000. Three thousand people were murdered each year in Colombia, most of them in the key economic zones containing the country's leading natural resources. The civilian population became the target of a multifaceted conflict between the state, the military and affiliated death squads, leftist guerrillas, and drug dealers.[27]

President Bill Clinton's $1.3 billion Plan Colombia aid package, while ostensibly designed to reduce the drug trade, was strongly supported by American multinationals, who saw it as a means of stabilizing the investment climate in the country. This was especially true of U.S. oil companies such as Occidental Petroleum that along with other foreign energy ventures had been targeted by leftist guerrillas. Occidental jointly managed the 481-mile Cano Limon pipeline with the national oil company Ecopetrol. The guerrillas had repeatedly attacked the pipeline beginning in 1986. In 2001 alone, rebels bombed the pipeline 170 times. The connection between these interests and Plan Colombia became apparent in February 2002, when the Bush administration announced that it would provide $98 million in assistance to the Colombian military to protect the Cano Limon line. The reverberating effects of American-led globalization also became apparent in Argentina.[28]

In the closing days of December 2001 demonstrators took to the streets of Argentina's leading cities, carrying out violent protests that left twenty-eight people dead and led to the resignation of President Fernando de la Rúa. Four years of economic recession and the increasing possibility that the country would default on its $155 billion public debt had finally prompted the popular uprising. Only a few years earlier

Argentina appeared to be a neoliberal economic success story. During the 1990s, under President Carlos Menem, the government had fixed the foreign exchange rate at one peso to one U.S. dollar. After years of double- and even triple-digit inflation, the newfound currency stability drove average annual inflation down to less than 6 percent during the closing years of the twentieth century. The Menem regime also opened new opportunities to foreign trade and investment and privatized much of the state sector of the economy, policies that helped to spur economic growth. But these measures proved to be a double-edged sword.[29]

The new strength of the Argentine peso, combined with more liberalized import policies, encouraged middle- and upper-class Argentineans to engage in an import-spending spree, utilizing their dollar-pegged pesos to buy everything from Brazilian toothpaste to U.S. beef. Meanwhile, the Menem regime fueled a public-sector spending spree including stunning levels of corruption by government officials that sent the public debt soaring. And while foreign imports might be cheap, Argentinean exports became increasingly expensive as the country's trading partners such as Brazil devalued their currencies. Furthermore, world prices for Argentina's agricultural export products slid downward in the late 1990s, creating new problems for the troubled export sector. The national economy began shrinking, and wages in manufacturing fell by 20 percent between 1998 and 2001. Resentment mounted in particular against foreign-owned service companies and banks that continued to collect payments in dollars and against large foreign corporations that were seen as driving many smaller Argentine-owned businesses from the economy.[30]

After President de la Rúa's election in 1999, he attempted to deal with the mounting debt crisis through austere measures that contributed to economic contraction while failing to resolve the debt problem. Normally in such circumstances currency devaluation would be a logical and relatively painless solution to the problems of high-priced exports and mounting debt. A cheaper peso would make Argentine exports less expensive on the world market. But with the peso pegged to the dollar, devaluation would have had a devastating effect on individual Argentineans' economic well-being because many of them had contracted loans and mortgages payable in dollars. A devalued peso would make it all that much more expensive for people to buy dollars to pay their debts.

These desperate conditions finally triggered the popular protests that toppled the de la Rúa administration.[31]

In the aftermath of the government's collapse, Argentina officially defaulted on its debt, and the new regime under President Eduardo Duhalde took steps to devalue the currency while protecting the average Argentinean from at least some of the impact of devaluation. But with bank accounts frozen and faith in government economic policies disintegrating, many Argentineans turned to bartering goods and services in order to survive. The descendants of European immigrants, who had migrated to Argentina as a land of opportunity, now claimed citizenship in European countries in order to emigrate to homelands they had never known. When Duhalde's regime faltered, yet another election brought Néstor Kirchner, a little-known provincial governor, to power. Although the new president reached an agreement with the IMF on the debt problems, he also pursued policies that gave primacy to promoting economic recovery over debt repayment. Defying IMF orthodoxy, Kirchner managed to spark a national economic recovery by 2004. Kirchner was not the only elected leader who challenged the policies of globalization and the dominant role of the United States in the region.[32]

In 1998 Venezuelans elected Hugo Chávez, a former paratrooper, as their new president. Chávez came to office with a clear populist agenda and soon complemented that with a foreign policy that brought close ties to Fidel Castro and Cuba. He also voiced opposition to Washington's proposed Free Trade Area of the Americas, as well as Plan Colombia. With the source of 13 percent of U.S. oil imports now under the control of a populist critic of U.S. foreign policy, the Bush administration made clear its growing disenchantment with Chávez through its support for his highly vocal opponents.

Seemingly ascribing to Marx's thesis that history repeats itself first as tragedy and then as farce, Washington pursued policies reminiscent of its actions against Salvador Allende three decades earlier. Resorting to past practices, the AFL-CIO became involved through its American Center for International Labor Solidarity (ACILS), created in 1997 to replace the array of international operations of the labor federation. The ACILS was headed by a former staff member of the American Institute for Free Labor Development. Like AIFLD, the ACILS received millions of dollars in annual funding from AID and other government sources. The ACILS channeled money to Carlos Ortega, president of the Confederation of Venezuelan Workers, and arranged for him to visit government officials in Washington. In turn, Ortega was organizing antigovernment strikes and working closely with Pedro Carmona Estanga, the leader of the national business federation, to organize massive anti-Chávez demonstrations. Then on April 11, 2002, a military coup ousted Chávez and installed Carmona Estanga as head of the country. The White House attributed Chávez's demise to his suppression of popular unrest, only to see Chávez restored to power a few days later. Undaunted, AID pumped additional money into opposition groups promoting a demand for a national referendum on whether Chávez should be allowed to complete his term of office. On August 15, 2004, 58 percent of Venezuelan voters backed Chávez, leaving the Bush administration looking for ways to repair relations with one of the nation's leading oil suppliers. Meanwhile, antiglobalization protests continued to shake the politics of other Latin American countries.[33]

If the dark night of dictatorship and the influence of neoliberal technocrats combined to depoliticize state systems, opposition to the larger process of American-promoted globalization provided a cause around which diverse segments of Latin American societies could rally for political action. Latin Americans were particularly sensitive to privatization of public utilities and natural resources. They demonstrated against the higher prices of privatized utilities and the loss of control over the national patrimony. Peruvian protestors from small-businesspeople to workers and peasants made a direct connection between their woes and the increased globalization of their economy. In July 2002 popular protests in the southern city of Arequipa forced the national government to cancel plans to sell off the local power-generating system to a Belgian company. These protests followed on the heels of nationwide demonstrations against the privatization of the Mantaro hydroelectric complex and the Talara oil refinery.[34]

In neighboring Bolivia, thousands of peasants, miners, and workers staged protests against President Gonzalo Sánchez de Lozada's plans for a $5 billion pipeline to export the country's natural gas to the United States and Mexico. For most Bolivians the plan was the latest iteration of free-market reforms that had failed to improve the lot of the two-thirds of Bolivians who still lived in abject poverty. Sánchez de Lozada's cooperation with the U.S. war on drugs had already alienated peasant growers, and when police killed eighty demonstrators, the president resigned and plans for the pipeline were suspended.[35] Foreign investment fell in countries such as Bolivia and Peru where protests had halted privatization schemes. Political risk assessment of an earlier time came back into vogue among corporate planners. Yet even broad popular protests against globalization did not hinder the continuing penetration of U.S. consumer industries into Latin America.

CONSUMERISM

Although American television broadcasters no longer dominated local networks or program content as they had at the dawn of the television age, U.S. programming still played a central role in the Latin American television industry with Mexico offering the most striking example. The United States produced nearly 24 percent of Mexican broadcast television programs, but more importantly U.S. productions accounted for nearly half of all prime-time programming. Even if U.S. programs did not dominate television as they once had, local television entertainment now carried many of the same messages about consumer society that both U.S. and national elites promoted. Although Brazilians preferred telenovelas over U.S. programs, those locally produced soap operas depicted idealized Latin American societies characterized by the harmony and easy upward social mobility that supposedly typified modern capitalist countries. A common story line concerns a lower-class individual's journey from being an uneducated nonconsumer to an educated consumer. Even for the large number of impoverished viewers who could only dream about such a consumer paradise, the telenovelas offered the opportunity to symbolically share in the abundance of modern society. Both domestic and foreign corporations were alive to the possibilities of product placement on these series. When the soap opera *Gabriella* featured a local bar serving only drinks manufactured by the national firm Antarctica, Coca-Cola secured a place on the series *Duas Vidas* (Two Lives) as the only beverage drunk by the main character. Other U.S. multinationals such as General Motors and Levi's regularly secured placements for their products on telenovelas.[36]

In the film market, American movies accounted for 80 percent of films available in video stores. In Mexico and other leading markets in Latin America, Hollywood enjoyed a similar monopoly of cinema screens, with American movies accounting for 80 percent of box office receipts.[37] Less clear was the extent to which audiences absorbed the symbols and ideas of U.S. cultural products, the degree to which they may have internalized U.S. values, and whether such influences served to undermine Latin Americans' sense of national identity. What was clear was that Latin Americans responded to the icons and messages of American consumerism in subtle and highly complex ways.

Much as they had done with U.S. corporate domination of key economic sectors and efforts to transform the workplace, Latin Americans offered a variety of reactions to the spread of American consumer society. They have engaged in an intricate cultural interaction, adopting products such as Coca-Cola but often adapting those symbols to their own purposes, giving these icons of American consumerism new meanings never dreamed of by their creators or promoters.

The era of neoliberal trade liberalization and privatization allowed American capital, goods, and ideas to penetrate ever more broadly and deeply into Latin American societies. American consumer products spread beyond the major urban centers and into the remoter regions of Latin American countries such as the hot and arid northwestern portions of Argentina. With its seasons reversed from those in North America, Christmas falls during a period of intense heat. Celebration of the holiday had long followed European traditions with gift giving reserved for January 6, the Day of the Kings, and revolved around the story of the three wise men who had visited the Christ child. But increasingly, Christmas Day replaced the Day of the Kings for exchanging presents. The most common image of the gift giver was that of Santa Claus dressed for the snow in his fur-trimmed coat and pants and of course his leather boots, mimicking the version of the Santa Claus image popularized as an advertising icon during the 1930s by Coca-Cola. The first American-style shopping center opened in Tucumán, the region's largest city, in 1994. The center's name Paseo Shopping blended the Spanish term for a leisurely walk with the American expression for consumer activity. The word shopping had replaced the more mundane Spanish expression *hacer compras*, meaning to make purchases, because it conveyed an idyllic American image of consumers selecting from a cornucopia of attractive products that would enhance their daily lives. But the first American-style mall was soon overshadowed by the Hipermercado Libertad (the Liberty Hypermarket) that mimicked similar superstores in the United States, with vast collections of everything from food products to consumer electronics and toys. The market's logo, the Statue of Liberty, suggested to Tucumán's consumers that the true meaning of American democracy was the freedom to shop.[38]

Perhaps no product has better symbolized the penetration of American consumer goods and the values attached to them than Coca-Cola. The Coca-Cola Corporation has long associated its product with fundamental American ideals and cultural practices—the idea of freedom as the freedom to consume, the belief that human happiness is derived directly from such forms of consumption, and the sheer pleasures of leisure-time activities and the prosperity that makes them possible. Inevitably the ultimate American consumer good has made its way to northwestern Argentina where cafes, restaurants, and billboards proudly broadcast the wonders of Coca-Cola. In an arid region where water has both vital practical importance and deep cultural significance as the very source of life, Coca-Cola and related products have co-opted that image of a life-giving liquid. At the same time, soft drink cans have become the leading form of consumer refuse on the streets of provincial towns. And yet the success of Coke, and for that matter other American consumer products, does not signify a simple and universal acceptance of American values by Argentineans or other Latin Americans.

Many people in Latin America believe that Coke is in fact a national product of their own society. In the Argentinean Northwest, offerings of water are brought to the shrine of a local saint in soft drink bottles. In Haiti, Coke was believed to revive the dead, and in Chiapas, Mexico, it has been used to rid victims of evil spirits. In other Latin American countries it is mixed with local alcoholic beverages to make such national drinks as Cuba Libres.[39] In other words, as much as the consumption of these goods may at times signify buying into certain American values, it is also true that these goods are integrated into local cultures, thereby giving them new meaning. The reaction to consumer goods is simply one example of how Latin Americans have integrated but also reshaped cultural inputs from the United States. A similar process has unfolded as U.S. Pentecostal missionaries brought new versions of their faith to the region.

PENTECOSTALS AND TOURISTS

In the final decades of the twentieth century, Protestantism underwent explosive growth in Latin America, but almost all of it occurred in its Evangelical and especially Pentecostal branches. At the beginning of the 1980s, 18.6 million Latin Americans identified themselves as Evangelicals. By 1997 that number had soared to 60 million, with Pentecostals accounting for two-thirds of that total as Pentecostal movements enjoyed particular success in Brazil, Guatemala, Chile, and Argentina. As in the past, the most recent surge in Protestantism also enjoyed a degree of U.S. inspiration.[40]

One U.S. influence came in the form of neo-Pentecostalism that preached a "health and wealth gospel," arguing that Christians were entitled not only to spiritual but material well-being and that material deprivation is a sign of insufficient faith. Temporal rewards could in effect be achieved through prayer. In Brazil, this form of Pentecostalism also drew on practices common to the popular religion Umbanda and African Brazilian religious practices with elaborate, emotion-filled ceremonies devised to collectively drive out evil spirits.[41] Despite the obvious influences from the United States, most of the initiative for the explosive growth of Pentecostalism came from within Latin American societies. Yet Pentecostalism also represented a response to the effects of American-led globalization.

While religious conversion is a highly complex phenomenon, there appeared to be strong links between the process of globalization and this religious revival in Latin America. Most of the converts in recent decades have come from among the urban poor of the region whose lives have been dramatically altered by the events that have shaken Latin America as the twentieth century gave way to the twenty-first. The lost decade of the 1980s that caused economies and incomes to shrink, the harsh repression of military dictatorships, the curtailing of state social services under IMF mandates, and the influence of neoliberal policymakers created appalling living conditions for the urban poor. The apparent inability of their own state systems to protect them from these wrenching dislocations led many of these people to lose faith in politics and political ideologies. At the same time, they found themselves exposed to challenging and often contradictory experiences and ideas—the power of market forces, the compelling logic of consumerism, and yet the seeming impossibility of partaking in the human happiness that appeared to be embedded in material goods, the strains on family and community from harsher and more demanding work conditions, and the prolifera-tion of vice and violence. These conditions created daunting challenges for urban dwellers seeking to locate themselves and shape their iden-tity amid a startling array of changes. For many, traditional religious practice whether Catholic or Protestant, political ideologies, and even community and family values sometimes failed to address very real needs arising from poverty, or to satisfy their efforts to construct an identity that could accommodate a globalized environment. For many people Pentecostalism helped mediate between themselves and the larger soci-ety as they sought to adapt to an increasingly globalized culture.

For Pentecostals, their conversion marks an event that profoundly changes them. Yet at the same time, Pentecostalism does not mean a total rejection of their past life. Pentecostal practices, for example, incorporate ideas such as the power of sacred objects that are familiar to Catholics and ideas about evil spirits common to African-based religious practices. Furthermore, rather than completely rejecting their past life and relation-ships, Pentecostalism allows believers to see them in a different light—their own lives as part of a sinful past and unconverted family members as those in need of salvation. Pentecostalism also addresses the immediate needs of converts through faith healing and moral proscriptions against such prac-tices as drinking and smoking that exacerbate the evils of poverty. At the same time, it allows them to engage the world and yet not be a part of it.

Pentecostals envision themselves as part of a war against evil while recognizing that the evil of the world can still bring sorrow into their lives and that as a part of that evil their lives may not be ones of material comfort promised by consumerism. Pentecostalism allows believers to construct an identity that can reconcile their past with the rapidly changing present in which they live. An American-inspired religion has taken root in Latin America and evolved into a faith that helps many Latin Americans engage a globalizing culture driven in no small part by more than a century of U.S. influence.[42] At the same time, other Latin Americans have found other sources of hope amid the grinding poverty that enveloped so many of the region's people at the beginning of the twenty-first century.

In 2000, tourists spent more than $36 billion while visiting Latin American countries, and U.S. citizens accounted for most of this spend-ing, with more than 20 million Americans attracted to the region's six largest markets: Mexico, Brazil, Argentina, Peru, Venezuela, and Colombia. Mexico accounted for the lion's share of this traffic, welcoming nearly 19 million U.S. travelers. The continuing growth of commercial airline traffic drove much of the tourist business in Latin America as 12.3 million passengers traveled between the United States and Mexico alone in 1999. Although the state-developmentalist mode of the 1960s and '70s had given way to the neoliberalism of the 1980s and '90s, Latin American governments spent nearly $7.5 billion in 1999 promoting tourism with the free-market justification that tourism helped promote entrepreneurship and small-business development. Aside from visiting ancient ruins and urban colonial sites, a growing ecotourist business at the beginning of the twenty-first century offered visitors chances to raft rivers in Mexico, traverse rain forests in Central and South America, scale Andean volcanoes, and marvel at glaciers at the southern tip of South America. Such ventures were deemed sustainable forms of environmentally friendly development, unlike mining and oil exploration that exhausted natural resources while scarring and polluting the land. Yet tourism in both its old and new iterations still enshrined stereotypes that Americans found appealing while cloaking continuing inequalities in Latin America in a garment of market equality.[43]

Nestled in the southern Andean region between the ruins of Machu Picchu and the former Inca capital of Cusco, the town of Pisac frequently appears among the attractions of ecotours that offer the adventurous an opportunity for a high-altitude climb to the ancient ruins of the Pisac citadel. Yet the main attraction for most tourists remains the market in the town itself, typically described as a "picturesque Andean village." Indeed Pisac, with its cobblestone streets, stucco walls, tile-roofed buildings, and inhabitants dressed in colorful traditional costumes for the Sunday market, is a tourist's picture-perfect image of an Andean town. In addition to woven goods such as sweaters and a plethora of ceramic goods from pots to ashtrays, shoppers can also buy strings of hand-painted beads with a distinctive llama motif. Here tourists seemingly make equal exchange of their dollars for the authentic artifacts of this timeless community. Yet these exchanges and the images that surround them are in fact the creation of tourists and residents alike.

The production of the "traditional" handicrafts for tourist consumption began in the 1960s as a result of training provided by government programs promoting tourism and are fashioned to appeal to the tastes of tourists and their images of what constitutes indigenous culture. Furthermore, the seemingly equal exchange between tourists and artisans, who are supposedly separated only by their respective "modern" and "traditional" cultures, masks the very modern entrepreneurial activities of the artisans and the very real material gulf that separates well-heeled U.S. tourists from the modest circumstances of Andean villagers. The seeming changelessness of Pisac's tourist image also cloaks growing disparities in wealth between townspeople in the tourist trade and those outside it, as well as disparities in wealth and power between townspeople who control the trade and villagers in the surrounding area, who often provide their handicrafts for sale in Pisac.[44]

In environments such as Pisac, tourists and residents have created images that preserve American stereotypes of Latin America's traditional culture while masking inequalities as simply part of the cultural differences that separate the modern and the traditional. At the same time, ecotravellers, who join guided tours of the rain forest, can relive the "wild, untamed" Latin America that New England sailors once experienced while sheltered by the knowledge that they are bringing dollars to the region in an ecologically friendly form. At the same time, tourism continues its contradictory effects of drawing individuals into the global economy and encouraging entrepreneurship, while giving those who participate in tourist businesses the material means to preserve much of their existing community life. As a growing number of Americans visited Latin American tourist sites, increasing numbers of Latin Americans headed north, but not for purposes of tourism.

PURSUING THE AMERICAN DREAM

In the spring of 2004 in the Pacific waters off of Ecuador, 250 passengers sat crammed into the hold of the small fishing vessel, the *William*. The ship's captain, Héctor Segura, kept them belowdecks, fearing that the authorities might spot them and recognize that the true purpose of his voyage was not fishing, but the smuggling of human beings. His passengers had paid thousands of dollars each to be transported from the northern coast of Ecuador across more than one thousand miles of ocean to Guatemala. There they would begin a long and perilous journey across Central America and Mexico, only to risk their lives once again to cross the desert into the United States. With Washington intensifying border security in response to 9/11, more and more Latin Americans turned to smugglers to help them reach the United States. Between 2000 and 2004 as many as 250,000 people may have departed Ecuador on this dangerous voyage, which for some would end in death by drowning or at the hands of criminals. Yet their numbers continue to swell. By 2004 the U.S. Border Patrol was detaining as many as 110,000 people per month along the Mexican border as they tried to cross into the United States.[45] But such measures had hardly stemmed the tide. As of 2001 it was estimated that approximately 7.8 million undocumented immigrants resided in the United States, with Mexicans comprising 4.5 million of that total and Central Americans another 1.5 million.[46]

A number of factors fed the rising tide of undocumented and documented Latin American immigration into the United States. U.S.-backed wars in Nicaragua and El Salvador during the 1980s sent hundreds of thousands of Central Americans fleeing north. By 1984, 500,000 Salvadorans had arrived in the United States with the Salvadoran population of Los Angeles alone soaring from 30,000 in 1979 to 300,000 by 1983.[47] Many of them were the children of death-squad victims, but the U.S. government refused to recognize them as political refugees and attempted to send them back to their war-torn homeland. By contrast, since the 1960s the United States had welcomed Cuban immigrants fleeing the Castro regime, but this policy became a problem when in 1980 Castro permitted about 125,000 émigrés, some of them criminals, to leave the island for the United States. In 1994 another wave of Cuban immigrants began arriving, prompting the Clinton administration to initiate a policy of turning back the immigrants while they were still at sea and admitting only those who somehow managed to reach the shores of the United States. Haitians meanwhile continued to be subject to an even harsher policy that turned them back at sea and deported those who managed to reach land.

In no small measure, U.S. policies have contributed to this mass migration. As one author has described it, these immigrants are "the harvest of empire."[48] U.S. counterinsurgency programs in Central America and the effort to bring down the Castro regime through economic isolation have prompted part of this mass exodus of Latin Americans. Furthermore, despite the fact that regional population growth had fallen to 1.5 percent at the end of the twentieth century and despite some economic successes in the 1990s, the globalization of Latin American economies encouraged by the United States failed to improve the lives of the poor. The growth of large-scale commercial agricultural enterprises, encouraged and supported by the U.S.-sponsored Green Revolution, had driven ever more peasants from the land. The draconian economic policies pressed on the region by the United States and the IMF during the lost decade of the 1980s, as well as the economic downturn that set in by the turn of the century, left as many as 40 percent of the region's people living in abject poverty. Even as heady dreams of consumerism penetrated ever more widely and deeply in Latin America, the real possibility of achieving those dreams was receding for tens of millions of its citizens. Imbued with the promise of the American dream but denied the chance to achieve it in their homelands, increasing numbers of Latin Americans sought the dream's fulfillment in the land of its origin. In doing so they were profoundly altering the birthplace of that dream.

In the year 2002, the 38.7 million Hispanics who lived in the United States comprised more than 13 percent of its total population, and their numbers were projected to reach 88 million in 2050, when they would account for one-quarter of all Americans. Although most of this growth can be traced to U.S.-born Hispanics, immigrants made up 37 percent of the Hispanic population in 2000.[49] With Americans often identifying Latin America as the source of their drug epidemic, and with immigrants comprising an ever-larger portion of the U.S. workforce, hostility toward Latino immigration mounted during the last two decades of the twentieth century. With the cocaine epidemic raging, Richard Lamm, the former governor of Colorado, wrote a book describing Latin American immigration as a "time bomb." In 1992 Pat Buchanan became the first prominent presidential candidate to run on a platform that included an anti-immigrant plank. New immigration laws in 1996 subjected legal residents to deportation if background checks revealed even minor criminal records. The war on terror provided an opportunity for opponents of immigration to argue that unauthorized immigration from Latin America offered an opportunity for terrorists to infiltrate the United States. The issues of illegal drugs and undocumented immigrants fused in a policy of militarizing the border with

Mexico as Washington dispatched National Guard troops to intercept both drugs and immigrants.[50]

In 2004, Harvard Professor Samuel P. Huntington asserted in his book *Who Are We?* that Hispanic immigrants have failed to assimilate American culture and the Anglo-Protestant values that underpin it. Huntington's argument seemed to hearken back to nineteenth-century ideas concerning the existence of an Anglo-Saxon race, tempered by twentieth-century concepts that translated race differences into distinctions in cultures. He argued that at the core of American society lay an Anglo-Protestant culture distinguished by such characteristics as the English language, Christianity, individualism, the work ethic, and a belief that humans can create a heaven on earth. Huntington went on to assert that unlike earlier immigrants, Hispanic, and especially Mexican immigrants, have shown a low propensity to intermarry outside their group and seek naturalization, while exhibiting a high propensity to retain their native language through succeeding generations. Huntington claimed that these alleged characteristics of Hispanic immigrants demonstrated their disinclination to absorb the United States's Anglo-Protestant culture, raising the possibility of the United States emerging as a bifurcated society with two different languages and two distinct cultures.[51]

Despite the near hysteria sometimes attached to the immigration issue, Latino immigrants made progress as a 1990 court decision overruled the Immigration and Naturalization Service's denial of asylum to one hundred thousand Central Americans.[52] Furthermore, their growing numbers and their activism forced the major political parties to court Hispanic voters more intensely. Latino influences in American culture including music and sports became even more prominent as the twentieth century gave way to the twenty-first. Latino pop stars such as Jennifer Lopez and Marc Antony attracted diverse, nationwide audiences while Latino influence had become even more significant in art, literature, cuisine, and fashion. In addition Latin American, and especially Mexican, cinematic productions began to enjoy unprecedented success with films such as *Like Water for Chocolate* and *Amores Perros*, which ranged in perspective from neoromanticism to harsh contemporary realism. Not only in their numbers but also through hard work and talent, Latin Americans were gradually transforming the birthplace of the American mission.

By the beginning of the twenty-first century, the revolutionary upheavals that wracked Central America in the 1980s had subsided and along with them the leading justification for direct U.S. intervention. Compared to the anticommunist campaign of the cold war, the wars on drugs and terror proved far less effective in rallying Latin American support for U.S. policies. Most striking of all was the apparent triumph of the American mission to Latin America as most Latin American nations embraced U.S.-promoted strategies of free-market development and the ideals of consumer democracy, accepting a dramatically increased role for U.S. business in their economies while many Latin Americans turned to American-inspired Pentecostalism for spiritual uplift. Such a turn of events seemed to mark the fulfillment of the dreams of the agents of the American mission from the colonial jurist Judge Sewall to twentieth-century missionaries of modernization such as W. W. Rostow and Nelson Rockefeller. Yet such a conclusion would represent a far-too-simple reading of these events.

Part of the problem for U.S. leaders in maintaining U.S. dominance in the region was reconfiguring its own identity as the protector of Latin America. Eventually the promotion of globalization and the wars on drugs and terrorism failed to resonate with the same power as the crusade against communism. Both Chile and Mexico refused to support the U.S. position on Iraq in the UN Security Council. Washington had to face the fact that in the hemisphere, only circum-Caribbean regimes supported its 2003 invasion of Iraq. Even if Washington could still command the allegiance of circum-Caribbean governments, similar support it once relied on from other Latin American states was slipping away. In addition to the populist challenge from Hugo Chávez, Latin Americans resisted attempts by the United States to militarize the wars on drugs and terror. They continued to see controlled substances as a problem rooted in U.S. consumption, while they considered terrorism to be a negligible threat to their own societies. Latin American states also gave a cool reception to Washington's campaign for a hemispheric free-trade agreement. They preferred to sign regional agreements among themselves and expand trade relations outside the hemisphere, thus strengthening their hand in any future negotiations with the United States. And in terms of foreign investment, the U.S. stake in the four largest economies in Latin America exceeded that of the European Union in only one—Mexico.

As for the triumph of the American globalization mission, that achievement has been of dubious economic benefit to most Latin Americans. Although modernization theorists and neoliberal economists might differ on the precise role of the state in developing economies, both groups had pressed on Latin America schemes for free-market development with little or no concern for the gross social and economic inequalities that existed in Latin America that would prevent the emergence of more equitable societies.

As with past iterations of the American mission, Latin Americans have responded in a complex, sometimes contradictory fashion to the latest efforts of the United States to transform their societies. Although they largely abandoned the protectionist economic policies of the past, they have also shown vehement resistance to many aspects of globalization, especially those policies that threaten their own social welfare and challenge national sovereignty. In fact the threats from globalization have served as a catalyst, triggering cohesive, militant political action from diverse social groups despite the fragmentation of their societies by globalization and the depoliticization of conventional politics after decades of military dictatorship. Although Latin Americans have embraced various forms of American consumerism from Hollywood films to sportswear and tourism, they have also reshaped and reinterpreted many of these icons of consumerism to fit their own values and needs. So, too, the American-inspired Pentecostal movement now takes its primary inspiration from Latin American concerns and aspirations. Finally, the future of the American homeland itself will be shaped in no small measure by Latino immigrants and their descendants, whose presence in the United States is in part a product of the American mission in Latin America.

CONCLUSION

IN THE COURSE OF MORE THAN TWO CENTURIES, THE PEOPLES OF THE United States and Latin America have increasingly interacted with one another to shape their respective histories. In that process, the people of the Americas have not only profoundly influenced the course of history in the Western Hemisphere; they have also created a dynamic interplay of economic and social forces, cultural values, and political ideas that is now influencing the course of global history.

For more than two hundred years, North Americans have pursued a mission of transformation. Confident that their Christian faith, capitalist economy, and republican form of government constituted an ideal society worthy of emulation, Americans set out to reshape their neighbors in their own image. Although Latin Americans would adopt certain aspects of North American culture, they would also challenge the aggressive U.S. policies of territorial expansion, civilizing imperialism, and the missions of modernization and globalization. Despite the apparent triumph of the American mission at the end of the twentieth century, Latin Americans by that time were charting an independent course in international diplomacy, reshaping American cultural icons even as they incorporated them into their daily lives, and profoundly influencing the future of the United States itself.

The American sense of mission stretches from Cotton Mather and his friend Judge Samuel Sewall who envisioned a "New Jerusalem" in

Mexico, to the acolytes of Milton Friedman who spread the faith of neoliberalism among Latin Americans in the closing decades of the twentieth century. As the ambitions of these individuals suggest, the American sense of mission has evolved significantly over the course of two centuries. Early American dreams of creating a reborn Christianity in the Western Hemisphere were complemented by merchants like Richard Cleveland who sought to spread the ideas and the institutions of American republican government to Latin America. Prior to the Civil War, Americans, confident that they represented a superior Anglo-Saxon race, believed their "Manifest Destiny" lay in occupying and "civilizing" the northern territories and inhabitants of Mexico. By the early twentieth century the mission had been transformed into an imperial paradigm. The civilizing mission now justified outright U.S. intervention in the circum-Caribbean and the imposition of wide-ranging reforms that included American-influenced constitutions, reconfigured legal systems to support free enterprise and foreign investment, large-scale investments by U.S. corporations, public works projects, and American-designed educational systems.

The mission that was marked in the early decades of the twentieth century by overt imperialism and racism underwent considerable modification in the second half of the twentieth century as social scientists developed modernization theory that explained the perceived "backwardness" of third world societies as a product of traditional cultures that could be recrafted under the tutelage of American technocrats. Yet the ideas of modernizers like Walt W. Rostow retained several key features of the old imperial paradigm. Much like Teddy Roosevelt, modernization theorists saw the international endeavors of the United States as a male-centered paternalistic mission to developing countries in need of American technocratic expertise. President John F. Kennedy and his successors envisioned themselves as members of a tough-minded brotherhood dedicated to preserving the dominant position the United States had achieved regionally and globally. Modernization theory also reflected a long-held American belief that infusions of American capital, technology, and values would generate substantial new wealth in developing nations that would be shared to a significant degree by groups at all levels of society. Radical redistributions of economic and political power would thus be unnecessary and, in fact, adamantly opposed by the

United States. A further modification in the American mission occurred in recent decades as policymakers largely abandoned the idea of state crafted solutions in favor of a complete embrace of neoliberal policies.

In the aftermath of the 1982 Mexican debt crisis, virtually every major Latin American government embraced some neoliberal ideas about free trade and dramatically reduced the economic and social roles of the state. Part of the willingness to embrace globalization stemmed from demands by private as well as multilateral lenders that Latin American governments promote exports, slash social spending, and sell off state-owned corporations as ways of reducing their indebtedness. Yet these policies also had influential domestic advocates among a generation of economists trained in neoliberal economics in the U.S.-sponsored program at the Catholic University of Chile and similar initiatives launched elsewhere in the region. The joint effort by Washington and private foundations to reshape higher education paid an important dividend in the scores of highly placed technocrats anxious to pursue neoliberal strategies. Beyond economic policies, these experts promoted the idea of depoliticizing policymaking in the state, leaving decisions on issues such as social welfare to the supposedly impartial decision making of technocrats. But as important as these shifts have been, the American mission has never been strictly a matter of technocratic policymaking.

The American mission, especially since the Great Depression when the Democratic Party, capital-intensive corporations, and big labor fashioned a new domestic political consensus and foreign strategy, had always been more than a foreign policy of the U.S. government. It has involved the activities of big business, big labor, major philanthropies, and religious organizations. These various groups have never marched in lockstep fashion as agents of a centrally designed and directed mission. There have often been serious disagreements between these groups from early Protestant missionaries' criticisms of American businessmen to labor leaders critical of neoliberal economic policies of globalization. Yet these distinct elements of American society have all embraced the idea of the transformational power of American culture from its republican political institutions to free-enterprise economics and consumerism. That shared belief has frequently led them to cooperate or to pursue compatible strategies in an effort to shape the future of their neighbors in the Americas. The AFL-CIO has long been a partner in this process, encouraging business-style unionism in the region and combating labor proponents of Marxist, socialist, or simply statist alternatives to free-enterprise policies. Philanthropic institutions have promoted a capitalist order marked by social reform and social stability. Protestant missionaries in the late nineteenth and early twentieth centuries instructed their students not only in the specifics of their Christian faith but also in the wonders of the free market and skills and values they believed would assure their students success in such a system. But the American mission has never been strictly a phenomenon of American-imposed change.

From the vehement denunciations of the U.S. war with Mexico to the rise of a new generation of nationalist populist leaders at the dawn of the twenty-first century, Latin Americans have been active participants in a process of encounter with their North American neighbors. Those encounters have encompassed the range of human experience and have had widespread effects on both the United States and Latin America.

From the Mexican guerrillas who harassed invading U.S. troops in the 1840s to Augusto Sandino, Fidel Castro, Salvador Allende, to the Zapatista National Liberation Army, Latin Americans have vehemently resisted what they have viewed as American economic and political domination. Reagan-era policymakers may have interpreted the end of the Central American insurgencies as a reaffirmation of U.S. regional dominance, made all the more secure by the collapse of the Soviet Union. Yet such views offered a highly simplistic picture of reality. The military solutions pursued in Central America angered Latin Americans and encouraged them to seek alternative solutions. Much to Washington's chagrin, the peace settlements were the result of multilateral initiatives. Furthermore, the fall of communism removed a powerful justification for direct U.S. intervention. At the same time, American initiatives since the wars in Central America have reignited Latin Americans' long-standing suspicions of U.S. motives and intentions. For Latin Americans, U.S. proposals to more closely coordinate police and military functions in the region to combat terrorism immediately sparked reminders of the U.S.-backed military regimes of the 1960s and '70s and their war on human rights. In the international arena, the United States at most could now rely on the smaller circum-Caribbean states for consistent support, as most Latin American nations charted a more independent course in international diplomacy and trade negotiations.

Meanwhile, American foreign policy stirred other areas of conflict with Latin Americans.

The United States has long cast its drug problems in terms of a war on evil Latin American drug dealers. Even as the international financial crisis of the 1980s and the embrace of neoliberal economics dominated U.S.–Latin American relations, Washington resorted once again to military force to combat the drug traffic flowing from the Andean region. The drug problem and September 11 provided new justifications for the United States to militarize its borders and to intensify its attempts to stem the northward flow of Latin American immigrants. But the wars on drugs and terrorism provided poor justifications for intervention and failed to rally Latin American elites to the American cause as the anti-communist crusade once did. In fact, U.S. attempts to find military solutions to these problems have had a minimal impact on the smuggling of drugs or the desperate flight of human beings. But the interplay between the United States and Latin America often occurs at more subtle levels than simply exchanges over official policies such as the drug war.

The 1982 debt crisis, the collapse of the socialist bloc, and the decades-long effort of the U.S. government and private foundations to train a generation of neoliberal technocrats prompted a near-universal embrace of at least some form of neoliberal policies by Latin American governments. Meanwhile, American consumerism seemed to penetrate to every level of Latin American society and every corner of the region's geography. The dramatic growth in U.S. consumer industries in Latin America in the past half-century, the increasing influence of American media forms, and the adoption of free-market policies in the region helped spread consumerism throughout Latin American societies. From the bustling streets of their great urban centers to the smallest rural villages, Latin Americans from all social and economic levels have embraced American consumer products. Yet the success of the American mission has not been nearly as all encompassing as many contemporary observers believed.

Even some advocates of neoliberal policies have come to realize that their strategies failed to take into account the existing inequalities in Latin America reinforced by social, economic, and political institutions that have prevented the lower strata of Latin American societies from sharing in any meaningful way in what economic growth did occur. The persistence of gross social and economic disparities has in turn prompted an antigloblalization movement as neoliberal forecasts of robust economic growth proved illusory. Furthermore, although many Latin Americans have embraced the idea of material consumption as a source of human happiness, they have not simply accepted the array of American values that are imbedded in such products. Latin Americans often reimagine these material goods as items of national origin and put them to uses—such as spiritual cleansing—never imagined by their creators. In the tourist trade Latin Americans and U.S. visitors have created a version of folk culture that meets the needs of Americans hungry for authenticity and of artisans finding their way in a market economy. Complex responses have also marked the Latin American reaction to Protestant missionaries.

Although the missionary zeal of conventional Protestant sects has faded over the past half-century, evangelical and especially Pentecostal movements have flourished. Unlike their Methodist and Episcopalian predecessors, these proselytizers do not share the ideals of the Social Gospel, which so closely aligned early missionaries with the reformist strategies of government technocrats, businessmen, and philanthropists. But they offer values and world visions that assist the urban poor in adjusting to a complex and conflicted globalized environment that dazzles with its consumer treasures while leaving those rewards achingly far from the grasp of the many slum dwellers, who now flock to Pentecostal services. Furthermore, although Pentecostalism's origins are thoroughly American, its Latin American leadership is now thoroughly local. An American religious phenomenon has been incorporated and reconfigured by Latin Americans. Nor do all these interactions take place in a Latin American environment.

U.S. efforts to reshape Latin America have often disrupted Latin American societies, contributing to the waves of migration from the region. The millions of Latin Americans who have made the United States their home and the generations of their descendants are changing the face of America and providing new, richly varied contributions to its culture. Ironically, the American mission that has sought to transform Latin America has contributed to the decision by millions of Latin Americans to migrate to the United States. Those immigrants, who have come in search of the American dream, may alter and enrich their new homeland more pervasively than anything the agents of Americanization dreamed of for Latin America. Contemporary events reflect the fact that this complex process of engagement continues as intensely as ever in the twenty-first century.

In 2005 with the numbers of undocumented Latin Americans in the United States on the rise, immigration once again became a flashpoint of American politics. Largely ignoring the fact that immigrants were not only being attracted to the United States by economic opportunity but being pushed by neoliberal strategies that undermined the viability of peasant agriculture and downsized state social spending in Latin America, Americans fearful of the immigrants' influence demanded stronger border security. The Minute Man Project organized protests along the border with Mexico and demanded action. Congressman Tom Tancredo of Colorado, echoing the conclusions of Samuel Huntington, implied that the immigrants represented a threat to the national identity of the United States. He and other conservative congressmen like James Sensenbrenner of Wisconsin pressed for legislation that would make undocumented immigration a felony. In response, Latinos organized mass demonstrations against that type of legislation. Once again Americans plunged into an emotional debate about the role of immigrants in shaping the future of the United States. Meanwhile, Latin American populist/nationalist leaders offered new challenges to the United States.

President Hugo Chávez of Venezuela continued to berate the United States as an imperialist power and promoted policies antithetical to U.S. interests such as his unsuccessful call in June 2006 for the Organization of Petroleum Exporting Countries (OPEC) to reduce production quotas at a time when oil prices were already climbing sharply. In a scene reminiscent of Richard Nixon's ill-fated visit to the country half a century earlier, Chávez supporters pelted U.S. Ambassador William Brownfield's motorcade with eggs and tomatoes. In Bolivia, Evo Morales became the country's first indigenous citizen to be elected president. Morales made it clear that he would not support U.S. strategies to suppress the growing of coca leaves, and in May 2006 he ordered the nationalization of the country's natural gas industry that had been privatized during the heyday of neoliberalism in the 1990s. It is important to note, however, that these events do not simply mark a repetition of the populist/nationalist strategies of the 1930s and '40s, which had been conceived in an international environment marked by global depression and world war. The new generation of populist/ nationalist leaders is operating in a world shaped by rapid spurts of globalization. Latin American nationalists are not advocating or implementing a simple return to policies of the past. Evo Morales, for example, has made clear his intention to work with foreign energy companies in the natural-gas sector. At the same time Morales, Chávez, and other Latin American leaders have reasserted the importance of the state in the economy, especially in dealing with foreign corporations. They have also made clear the need for the state to address problems of poverty and social injustice. Most leaders in the region, whatever their specific political leanings, seem to be seeking a middle ground between neoliberal measures of the present and the socialist/statist strategies of the past. These contemporary events reflect the intricate process of interaction by which the people of the Americas have shaped their history. That process offers important insights into the making of the globalized world.

The evolving American mission in Latin America during the past two hundred years has profoundly influenced the course of the region's history. The American mission has, on one the hand, brought the extraordinary productivity of American capitalism, the wonders of consumerism, and the promise of democratic institutions and individual rights. On the other hand, Americans have frequently harbored disparaging attitudes toward Latin Americans, opposed progressive changes in the political order, and frequently sought to impose their ideas on the people of the region. Latin Americans have not been passive recipients in that process. They have variously embraced, rejected, and reconfigured elements of the American mission and now promise to have a transformational impact of their own in the United States. This history has importance far beyond the Western Hemisphere, because for more than half a century the United States has been pursuing a comparable global mission. There are of course considerable differences between these two projects. The United States has never enjoyed the level of dominance in regions such as Asia and the Middle East it achieved in Latin America for much of the twentieth century. So, too, the cultural differences that separate many of these societies and the United Sates are far more profound than those within the Western Hemisphere where its elites share common Western traditions. Yet even with these differences, the similarities between the two missions are striking.

Much like its actions in the Caribbean and Central America during the era of Dollar Diplomacy, the United States after World War II used its growing might to displace England and France as the most powerful Western influence in the Middle East. The American civilizing mission that employed military occupation as a mechanism to carry out nation building in the circum-Caribbean has been repeated in both Vietnam and Iraq. Modernization theory guided not only the Alliance for Progress but also a vast array of U.S. aid projects in third world countries from Africa to Southeast Asia. Pentecostalism has found millions of converts not only in Latin America but in Africa as well. The United States has promoted the interests of its multinational corporations, and they in turn have transformed productive capabilities and spread consumerism around the globe. With the collapse of the Soviet empire, American political scientists flocked to Eastern Europe to share the wonders of constitution writing, much as Joel Poinsett had done a century and a half ago in Chile. So, too, American agents of neoliberalism have been preaching their doctrine throughout the developing world, much like nineteenth-century American merchants promoted free trade and American money doctors prescribed fiscal orthodoxy during the 1920s in Latin America. And like Latin Americans, people throughout the rest of the world have offered complex responses to American influences.

The American mission has challenged deeply held values such as national sovereignty and national identity. Dominating U.S. military and economic power has stirred intense resentments. American efforts to promote development have often been imbued with a sense of American superiority and a dismissive attitude toward other cultures. Not surprisingly the American mission has fostered community and national identities as well as political movements inspired in part by anti-Americanism. And given the American insistence on attempting to foster economic development while stridently opposing redistributions of political and social power, many third world societies much like Latin America have fostered capitalism but within the context of authoritarian states and societies with highly skewed distributions of wealth and power, creating new waves of unrest. As a result, the United States has often found itself mired in conflicts in order to promote and protect its interests from challenges ranging from third world nationalism and Marxism to Islamic militancy. At another level of encounter with the American-promoted process of modernization, people in non-Western societies have embraced American-produced or -inspired consumer goods and values, but they have reconfigured, reinterpreted, and incorporated them into a wide variety of other cultures. From the communist Ho Chi Minh's incorporation of language from the American Declaration of Independence into the Vietnamese Declaration of Independence to India's Bollywood that uses the technology of the American film industry to produce films rooted in the ancient texts of the Rig Veda, American ideas and its material culture have long been adapted and revised as they are incorporated into other cultures.[1] These realities that point to the limits of the American mission first became apparent in Latin America.

Even given the disproportionate power relations between the United States and Latin America, the advantages of physical proximity, and a number of common Western influences, it is clear that there are very real limits to the achievements of the American mission in Latin America. During the 1930s and '40s populist nationalist movements rallied millions of Latin Americans with their demands for an end to U.S. imperialism. Mexico and Cuba, the two nations most intensely affected by the U.S. mission, have experienced revolutions driven in no small measure by intense anti-Americanism. Latin American states have charted an increasingly independent course in diplomatic and economic strategies. The people of Latin America have shaped cultures that while incorporating American influences retain and reinforce their own rich historical traditions. Beneath the apparent triumph of the mission of globalization in the contemporary era there have appeared clear signs confirming what had long been true in the Western Hemisphere—that the United States could profoundly influence but not completely transform its Latin American neighbors. What is unclear is whether in light of their experiences in Latin America, the people of the United States and their leaders possess the wisdom to appreciate the limits of their powers to transform the globe and a respect for the ability of people in other cultures to shape their own destinies.

Notes

Introduction

1. Hunt, "Long Crisis in U.S. Diplomatic History," 115–16.

2. Rosenberg, *Spreading the American Dream*; Roseberry, *Anthropologies and Histories*.

3. O'Brien, *Revolutionary Mission*; Cueto, *Missionaries of Science*.

4. Bederman, *Manliness & Civilization*, ch. 5; Kaplan, "Black and Blue on San Juan Hill," 219–36; Renda, *Taking Haiti*; Pérez, *On Becoming Cuban*.

Chapter One

1. Stephens, *Incidents of Travel*, p. 6.

2. Ibid., p. 92.

3. Ibid., p. 80.

4. Ibid., pp. 154–55.

5. Ibid., pp. 183, 195.

6. Ibid., p. 245.

7. Ibid., p. 250.

8. Ibid., p. 338.

9. Bernstein, "Some Inter-American Aspects of the Enlightenment," p. 64.

10. Stackpole, *Sea-Hunters*, pp. 152–53.

11. Whitaker, *United States and the Independence of Latin America*, pp. 14–17; Coatsworth, "American Trade," pp. 243–66.

12. Pereira Salas, *Los primeros contactos*, pp. 20, 269.

13. Quoted in Bernstein, "Aspects of the Enlightenment," p. 55.

14. Cleveland, *Voyages and Commercial Enterprises*, pp. 162–76; Nichols, "Shaler," p. 73.

15. Cleveland, *Voyages and Commercial Enterprises*, p. 175.

16. Nichols, "Shaler," p. 74.

17. Pérez Vila, *Simón Bolívar*, p. 98.

18. De Onís, *United States as Seen by Spanish American Writers*, p. 88.

19. Adams, *Writings of John Quincy Adams*, pp. vii, 443.

20. Whitaker, *Independence*, p. 148, n. 12.

21. Pérez Vila, *Bolívar*, pp. 98–99.

22. Nichols, "Shaler," pp. 85–95; Whitaker, *Independence*, pp. 95–96.

23. Rippy, *Joel R. Poinsett, Versatile American*, chs. 4, 8, and 9.

24. De Onís, *Spanish American Writers*, pp. 65–67.

25. Ibid., p. 31.

26. Jacobsen, *Mirages of Transition*, pp. 121–48.

27. Weeks, *Building the Continental Empire*, pp. 53–58.

28. Burns, *Poverty of Progress*, passim; Stern, *Resistance, Rebellion and Consciousness*.

29. See, for example, Johnson, *Shopkeepers' Millennium*; Prude, *Coming of the Industrial Order*.

30. Gates, *Landlords and Tenants*, p. 56.

31. Reichstein, *Rise of the Lone Star*, pp. 20–29, 42, 69.

32. Ibid., pp. 110–12.

33. Horsman, *Race and Manifest Destiny*, pp. 9–228.

34. Quoted in Pike, *United States and Latin America*, p. 99.

35. Quoted in Horsman, *Race and Manifest Destiny*, p. 217.

36. Pike, *United States and Latin America*, pp. 5–11.

37. Quoted in Brack, *Mexico Views Manifest Destiny*, p. 96.

38. Ibid., pp. 88–111.

39. For this interpretation, see Levinson, *Wars Within War*.

40. Brown, *Agents of Manifest Destiny*, pp. 33–37.

41. Quoted in May, *Southern Dream of Empire*, p. 7.

42. Ibid., pp. 59–67.

43. Brown, *Agents of Manifest Destiny*, pp. 222–43.

44. May, *Dream of Empire*, p. 96; Brown, *Agents of Manifest Destiny*, pp. 174–218, 266–313.

45. May, *Dream of Empire*, pp. 126–31.

46. Fabens, *Story of Life on the Isthmus*, p. 10.

47. Ibid., p. vii.

48. Manning, *Diplomatic Correspondence of the United States II*, pp. 48–64, 85–86.

49. www.trainweb.org/panama/history1.html

50. www.trainweb.org/panama/history1.html; Chen Daley, "Watermelon Riot," 90–100.

51. *U.S. Naval Astronomical Expedition to the Southern Hemisphere*, vol. I, p. 416.

52. www.trainweb.org/panama/history1.html

53. Chen Daley, "Watermelon Riot," pp. 85–88.

54. Pérez, *On Becoming Cuban*, pp. 17–37, 75–80.

55. Hart, *Revolutionary Mexico*, pp. 108–12.

56. Reed, *New Orleans and the Railroads*, pp. 68–69; Roeder, *Juárez and His Mexico*, vol. I, p. 232; Hart, *Revolutionary Mexico*, pp. 117–21.

57. Fifer, *United States Perceptions of Latin America*, pp. 20–52; for a detailed account of Wheelwright's activities, see Alberdi, *Life and Industrial Labors of William Wheelwright*.

58. Fifer, *Capricorn*, pp. 6–11.

59. Ibid., p. 21.

60. *U.S. Naval Astronomical Expedition to the Southern Hemisphere*, vol. I, pp. 156–58.

Chapter Two

1. Licht, *Industrializing America*, pp. 102, 133; Tuttle and Perry, *Economic History*, p. 276.

2. Tuttle and Perry, *Economic History*, pp. 304, 363.

3. On the creation of the U.S. commercial empire, see LaFeber, *New Empire*.

4. On the intersection of concepts of manliness, race, and civilization, see Bederman, *Manliness & Civilization*.

5. Atkins, *Sixty Years in Cuba*, pp. 1–13.

6. Ibid., p. 95.

7. Ibid., p. 96.

8. U.S. Bureau of the Census, *Statistical History of the United States*, pp. 903–4.

9. Wilkins, *Emergence of Multinational Enterprise*, pp. 39, 50, 57, 64.

10. O'Brien, *Revolutionary Mission*, pp. 50, 116.

11. Wilkins, *Emergence of Multinational Enterprise*, pp. 47–48; www.atlantic-cable.com/CableCos/CSA/index.html; Britton and Ahvenainen, "Showdown in South America," pp. 1–27.

12. For a classic study of United Fruit, see Kepner and Soothill, *Banana Empire*.

13. Butler, *Mexico in Transition*, p. 281.

14. Baldwin, *Protestants and the Mexican Revolution*, pp. 18–19; Butler, *Mexico in Transition*, p. 300.

15. Case, *Thirty Years with the Mexicans*, pp. 282–83.

16. Butler, *Mexico in Transition*, pp. 286–87.

17. Rosenberg, *American Dream*, pp. 28–29.

18. Pérez, *On Becoming Cuban*, pp. 55–60.

19. Butler, *Mexico in Transition*, pp. 301–2; Baldwin, *Protestants and the Mexican Revolution*, p. 25; Pérez, *On Becoming Cuban*, p. 57.

20. On this subject, see LaFeber, *New American Empire*; Langley, *American Mediterranean*, ch. 6.

21. Langley, *American Mediterranean*, pp. 81–101.

22. Ibid., pp. 152–63.

23. LaFeber, *New American Empire*, pp. 210–83.

24. Pérez, *Cuba*, pp. 119–28.

25. academic2.american.edu/~wjc/ wjc4/Death%20of %20Rodriguez.html

26. LaFeber, *New American Empire*, pp. 383–90; Atkins, *Sixty Years in Cuba*, pp. 248–93.

27. Pérez, *Platt Amendment*, p. 24.

28. LaFeber, *New American Empire*, pp. 388–89.

29. Pérez, *Platt Amendment*, pp. 29–31.

30. Kaplan, "Black and Blue on San Juan Hill," pp. 219–36.

31. Bederman, *Manliness & Civilization*, ch. 5.

32. Lane, *Armed Progressive*, pp. 83–86.

33. Wood, "Military Government of Cuba," p. 182.

34. Lane, *Armed Progressive*, pp. 96–97; Hitchman, *Wood*, p. 50.

35. Healy, *United States in Cuba*, pp. 179, 181; Hitchman, *Wood*, p. 50.

36. Portell Vilá, *Historia*, pp. 92–96.

37. Pérez, *Platt Amendment*, p. 72; Hoernel, "Sugar and Social Change," pp. 223, 230.

38. Quoted in Lane, *Armed Progressive*, p. 110.

39. Pérez, *Platt Amendment*, pp. 44–45.

40. Quoted in Lane, *Armed Progressive*, p. 112.

CHAPTER THREE

1. Venzon, *General Smedley Darlington Butler*, p. 122.

2. Quoted in Wilson, "Plotting the Border," p. 346.

3. Walton and Robertson, *History of the American Economy*, p. 401.

4. Watts, *Order Against Chaos*.

5. Williamson, *Crucible of Race*, pp. 333–69.

6. Bederman, *Manliness & Civilization*, ch. 5.

7. Quoted in Britton, *Revolution and Ideology*, p. 28.

8. Reed, *Insurgent Mexico*, pp. 170–71.

9. Beals, "With Sandino in Nicaragua." On the activities of progressive writers in the revolutionary environments of Mexico and Central America, see Britton, *Carleton Beals*; Britton, *Revolution and Ideology*; and Delpar, *Enormous Vogue of Things Mexican*.

10. O'Brien, *Revolutionary Mission*, pp. 38–40; Bergquist, *Labor in Latin America*, passim.

11. See, for example, Mallon, *Defense of Community*, passim.

12. McCullough, *Path Between the Seas*, pp. 559–65.

13. Ibid., pp. 543–47.

14. Franck, *Zone Policeman 88*, pp. 27, 43.

15. McCullough, *Path Between the Seas*, pp. 579–82.

16. Gilderhus, *Second Century*, pp. 29–30; Leonard, *Central America*, p. 57.

17. Pérez, *Platt Amendment*, pp. 110–15.

18. Bermann, *Under the Big Stick*, pp. 151–63. O'Brien, *Revolutionary Mission*, pp. 60–66; Schmidt, *Maverick Marine*, pp. 41–42.

19. Bermann, *Under the Big Stick*, pp. 157–61.

20. Plummer, *Haiti and the Great Powers*, pp. 90–95; Schmidt, *United States Occupation of Haiti*, pp. 161–65.

21. Pike, *Myths and Stereotypes*, p. 212.

22. Calder, *Impact of Intervention*, pp. 4–66.

23. Taft to Leonard Wood, March 12, 1911, Augusta, Georgia, vol. 13, Philander C. Knox Papers, Library of Congress, Washington DC.

24. Frank Vanderlip to James Stillman, New York, August 15, 1913, B-I-5, Frank A. Vanderlip Papers, Butler Library, Columbia University.

25. Pérez, *Platt Amendment*, p. 44; "Notes for Arguments in Favor of Honduras and Nicaragua Loan Convention," vol. 9, Philander C. Knox Papers.

26. Hart, *Revolutionary Mexico*, pp. 290–302, O'Brien, *Revolutionary Mission*, p. 263.

27. O'Brien, *Revolutionary Mission*, pp. 34–35, 216; O'Brien, *Century of U.S. Capitalism*, p. 37.

28. O'Brien, *Century of U.S. Capitalism*, pp. 39–40.

29. Brown, *Oil and Revolution*, pp. 13–165; Philip, *Oil and Politics*, pp. 13–27.

30. O'Brien, *Century of U.S. Capitalism*, p. 45.

31. Bastian, *Historia*, p. 102.

Chapter Four

1. William Garrity to Secretary of State, La Ceiba, August 19 and September 3, 1920, 815.5045/11/25, General Records of the Department of State Record Group 59 (hereafter RG59), United States National Archive (hereafter USNA).

2. George P. Waller, "Political and Economic Conditions in La Ceiba, March 1, 1925," 815.5045/58, rl. 33, M-647, RG59, USNA.

3. Allen Plummer to Senator W. B. Bankhead, La Ceiba, June 22, 1923, 315.11/25, RG 59, USNA.

4. McGovern, *Anatomy of a Lynching*, pp. 2–11; Chalmers, *Hooded Americanism*, pp. 28–33.

5. Wiebe, *Search for Order*, pp. 111–95; Blocker, *Retreat from Reform*; Kobler, *Ardent Spirits*.

6. Leach, *Land of Desire*.

7. Pérez, *Platt Amendment*, pp. 223–30.

8. Calder, *Impact of Intervention*, pp. 119–20.

9. Renda, *Taking Haiti*, p. 14.

10. A. L. Lindberg to B. L. Jefferson, Managua, August 5, 1916, 817.51/828, rl. 76, M-632, RG 59; Pike, *Myths and Stereotypes*, pp. 210–11.

11. Calder, *Impact of Intervention*, pp. 123–32; Pike, *Myths and Stereotypes*, p. 213.

12. Renda, *Taking Haiti*, pp. 131–81.

13. Johnson, "Self-Determining Haiti II," pp. 266–67.

14. Plummer, *Haiti and the United States*, p. 71.

15. Balch, *Occupied Haiti*, p. 36; Knight, *Americans in Santo Domingo*, p. 101.

16. Gilderhus, *Second Century*, p. 31.

17. Calixto, "Rubén Darío," pp. 57–61.

18. Klarén, *Modernization*, pp. 107–9.

19. Sobel, *I.T.T.*, pp. 89–91.

20. O'Brien, *Century of U.S. Capitalism*, p. 45.

21. Delpar, *Enormous Vogue of Things Mexican*, pp. 169–70.

22. Chomsky, *West Indian Workers*, pp. 17–59.

23. Mallon, *Defense of Community*, pp. 222–25.

24. O'Brien, *Century of U.S. Capitalism*, p. 49.

25. Klubock, *Contested Communities*, pp. 62–64; O'Brien, *Revolutionary Mission*, pp. 258, 275.

26. Chomsky, *West Indian Workers*, pp. 89–104.

27. Quoted in Chomsky, *West Indian Workers*, p. 57.

28. O'Brien, *Century of U.S. Capitalism*, pp. 126, 144.

29. Radosh, *American Labor*, pp. 349–53; Snow, *Pan-American Federation of Labor*, pp. 41, 46–47.

30. Bastian, *Protestantismo*, p. 126. Pérez, *On Becoming Cuban*, pp. 247–59.

31. Delbert Haff to Walter Douglas, Mexico City, September 5, 1929, File 2013, Box 1371–0331, Phelps Dodge Papers.

32. Berman, *Influence of the Carnegie, Ford and Rockefeller Foundations*, pp. 16–17.

33. Cueto, *Missionaries of Science*, p. xi; Solorzano, "Rockefeller Foundation," pp. 51–71.

34. Cueto, "Visionaries of Science," p. 16.

35. Rosenberg, *Financial Missionaries*, pp. 15–24.

36. Ibid., pp. 151–65.

37. Ibid., pp. 9, 23–24.

38. Ibid., pp. 34–35.

39. Ibid., p. 39.

40. On the strike, see 814,504/4–9, reel 20, microfilm-655, RG59, USNA.

41. Hart, *Revolutionary Mexico*, pp. 64–68.

42. Cueto, "Visionaries of Science and Development," pp. 13–18.

43. Ingersoll, *In and Under Mexico*, pp. 116–17.

44. O'Brien, *Revolutionary Mission*, pp. 88–89, 220–21; Kluboch, *Contested Communities*, pp. 31–48.

45. O'Brien, *Revolutionary Mission*, pp. 116–17.

46. Smith, *Revolutionary Nationalism in Mexico*, pp. 207–13.

47. O'Brien, *Revolutionary Mission*, pp. 268–75.

48. Andrews, *Shoulder to Shoulder?*, pp. 82–91; O'Brien, *Revolutionary Mission*, pp. 268–75.

49. Calder, *Impact of Intervention*, pp. 183–237.

50. Quoted in Schmidt, *United States Occupation of Haiti*, p. 189.

51. Ibid., pp. 189–206.

52. Bermann, *Big Stick*, pp. 178–90.

53. Schroeder, "Sandino Rebellion Revisited," pp. 208–32; O'Brien, *Revolutionary Mission*, pp. 74–79.

54. Schroeder, "Sandino Rebellion Revisited," pp. 221–51.

55. William W. Cumberland to Secretary of State, Managua, March 10, 1928, 817.51/1921, rl. 89, M-632, RG 59, USNA.

56. Salisbury, *Anti-imperialism*, pp. 119–23; Rosenberg, *Financial Missionaries*, 233–37.

57. Quoted in Schmidt, *Maverick Marine*, p. 2.

Chapter Five

1. Gellman, *Roosevelt and Batista*, pp. 8–9; Thomas, *Cuba*, pp. 596–98.

2. Hobsbawm, *Age of Extremes*, pp. 97–102.

3. Hobsbawm, *Age of Extremes*, pp. 88–97; Tuttle and Perry, *Economic History*, p. 616.

4. Ferguson, "From Normalcy to the New Deal," pp. 113–72.

5. Maier, "Politics of Productivity," p. 614.

6. Ibid., pp. 613–15.

7. Bulmer-Thomas, *Economic History*, pp. 196–209.

8. Bermann, *Big Stick*, pp. 214–17.

9. O'Brien, *Revolutionary Mission*, pp. 137–53.

10. Ibid., pp. 213–39.

11. Pérez, *Platt Amendment*, pp. 310–17.

12. Pérez, *Platt Amendment*, pp. 330–32; Gellman, *Roosevelt and Batista*, pp. 44–50, 114.

13. Lawrence Duggan, memorandum, Washington DC, July 15, 1938, 825.00/1041, RG 59, USNA.

14. Hataway, "Economic Diplomacy," pp. 294–95; O'Brien, *Revolutionary Mission*, pp. 300–301.

15. Joseph Daniels to Secretary of State, Mexico City, August 12, 1938, RG84, USNA.

16. Hataway, "Economic Diplomacy," p. 292.

17. Ibid., p. 317.

18. McCann, *Brazilian-American Alliance*.

19. Rosenberg, *American Dream*, pp. 206–90; Moreno, *Yankee Don't Go Home*, pp. 63–78.

20. Rosenberg, *American Dream*, pp. 222–23.

21. Hal Sevier to Secretary of State, Santiago, March 25, 1933, 825.6374/1132, RG 59, USNA.

22. Wilkins, *Maturing of Multinational Enterprise*, p. 182; Rippy, *Globe and Hemisphere*, pp. 61–70.

23. O'Brien, *Century of U.S. Capitalism*, pp. 90–91.

24. Wilkins, *Maturing of Multinational Enterprise*, pp. 183, 197–98, 224; O'Brien, *Century of U.S. Capitalism*, pp. 109–15.

25. Kluboch, *Contested Communities*, pp. 81–85.

26. Wilkins, *Maturing of Multinational Enterprise*, pp. 251–60; Rosenberg, *American Dream*, p. 199.

27. Wilkins, *Maturing of Multinational Enterprise*, p. 283.

28. Marchand, *Advertising the American Dream*, pp. 1–4; Woodard, "Marketing Modernity," pp. 257–90.

29. O'Brien, *Revolutionary Mission*, pp. 244, 292; Moreno, *Yankee Don't Go Home*, p. 70.

30. Delpar, *Enormous Vogue of Things Mexican*, pp. 73–75.

31. Taylor, "Wild Frontier Moves South," pp. 204–29.

32. Delpar, *Enormous Vogue of Things Mexican*, pp. 57–58; Pérez, *On Becoming Cuban*, pp. 165–218.

33. Woll, *Latin Image*, pp. 53–63.

34. Cueto, *Missionaries of Science*, pp. ix–xv, 126–32.

35. Fitzgerald, "Exporting American Agriculture," pp. 72–96.

36. Bastian, *Protestantismo*, pp. 118–26.

37. Bastian, *Protestantismo*, p. 127; O'Brien, *Revolutionary Mission*, pp. 135, 285, 293, 315.

38. Bastian, *Protestantismo*, p. 128; Colby, *Thy Will Be Done*, pp. 66–74.

39. Bastian, *Protestantismo*, pp. 129–32; Andrew R. Chesnut, *Born Again in Brazil*, pp. 25–34.

40. Caulfield, *Mexican Workers*, pp. 71–74; Radosh, *American Labor*, pp. 352–57.

CHAPTER SIX

1. Nixon, *Six Crises*, p. 217.

2. Nixon, *Six Crises*, pp. 218–25; Rabe, *Eisenhower and Latin America*, p. 39.

3. Green, *Containment of Latin America*, p. 176.

4. *Foreign Relations of the United States 1950*, vol. II, pp. 603, 609.

5. Nationalism is consistently listed ahead of communism as a U.S. concern in documents in *Foreign Relations of the United States* for the 1950s. See, for example, the relevant volumes of *Foreign Relations* from 1950 through 1954.

6. Haines, *Americanization of Brazil*, p. 31.

7. Bethell and Roxborough, "Postwar Conjuncture in Latin America," pp. 1–32.

8. Baily, *Development of South America*; Rabe, *Eisenhower*, p. 21.

9. Immerman, *John Foster Dulles*.

10. Quoted in Rabe, *Eisenhower*, p. 32.

11. Rosenberg, *American Dream*, 176–201.

12. Baily, *Development of South America*, pp. 54–79.

13. Latham, *Modernization as Ideology*, p. 92.

14. Latham, "Introduction," pp. 1–22; and Gilman, "Modernization Theory," pp. 47–70.

15. Latham, *Modernization as Ideology*, pp. 53–55.

16. Albion W. Patterson to Roy M. Hill, Santiago, February 5, 1954, Records of the Foreign Assistance Agencies, 1948–1961, Record Group 469 (hereafter, RG 469), USNA. See also Albion W. Patterson to Roy M. Hill, Santiago, July 7, 1953, RG469, USNA.

17. "Brazil Country Narrative FY 1952," 832.00TA/921 LM119 General Records of the Department of State, RG 59, USNA.

18. "The Zona de Mata," American Consulate General and United States Agency for International Development, Recife Pernambuco, June 1971, Records of the Agency for International Development, Record Group 286 (hereafter RG 286), USNA.

19. Vance Rogers to Rollin S. Atwood, Mexico City, June 18, 1956, enclosure: Memo by Ben Stephansky, "Notes on the Labor Situation in Mexico," RG 469, USNA.

20. Kofas, "Stabilization and Class Conflict," pp. 352–85.

21. "USIS Mexico Country Plan," Mexico City, June 19, 1958, RG 469; "USIS Country Plan" Mexico City, June 21, 1960, RG 306, USNA.

22. "Community Development Programs and Methods," by Carl C. Taylor, June 1954, RG 469, USNA.

23. "Community Center Project at Chonin Brazil," by Kalervo Oberg and Jose Arthur Rios, Rio de Janeiro, March 29, 1954, RG469, USNA.

24. Maddox, *Technical Assistance*, pp. 20–26.

25. Austin Sullivan to Harry W. Yoe, Washington DC, September 24, 1954, RG 469, USNA.

26. Maddox, *Technical Assistance*, pp. 102–8.

27. Chesnut, *Competitive Spirits*, pp. 25–44.

28. Bastian, *Protestantismo*, pp. 135–42.

29. Bucheli, *Bananas and Business*, pp. 50–64.

30. Wilkins, *Maturing of Multinational Enterprise*, pp. 310, 330.

31. Taylor and Lindeman, *United States Business Performance Abroad*, pp. 34–36.

32. Ibid., p. 39.

33. Ibid., pp. 41–45.

34. *Annual Report of the Creole Petroleum Company*, pp. 13–14.

35. Geiger, *The General Electric Company in Brazil*, 70–82.

36. Wood and Keyser, *United States Business Performance Abroad*, pp. 37–38; Moreno, *Yankee Don't Go Home*, pp. 185–86.

37. Caulfield, "Mexican State Development Policy," pp. 53–63.

38. Vance Rogers to Rollin S. Atwood, Mexico City, June 18, 1956, enclosure: Memo by Ben Stephansky, "Notes on the Labor Situation in Mexico," RG 469, USNA.

39. "Concrete Effectiveness Report," Mexico City, September 13, 1955, Records of the United States Information Agency, Record Group 306 (hereafter RG 306), USNA.

40. "USIS Semi-Annual Report," Mexico City, August 12, 1955, RG 306, USNA.

41. Romauldi, *Presidents and Peons*, p. 329.

42. "Country Plan for USIS Santiago FY 1960," Santiago, June 26, 1959, RG 306, USNA.

43. "Country Plan for USIS Santiago FY 1961," Santiago, August 20, 1960, RG 306, USNA. Emphasis added.

44. Kirstein, *Anglo over Bracero*, pp. 2–14, 103.

45. Bajarkman, *Baseball with a Latin Beat*, pp. 25–35, 385–86.

46. Woll, *Latin Image*, pp. 83–103; Pérez, *On Becoming Cuban*, p. 217.

47. See Bethell and Roxborough, *Latin America Between the Second World War and the Cold War.*

48. Bulmer-Thomas, *Economic History of Latin America*, pp. 309–13.

49. *Foreign Relations 1950*, vol. II, p. 611.

50. Rabe, *Eisenhower*, pp. 36–37.

51. Barnard, "Chile," pp. 66–91; Klubock, *Contested Communities*, pp. 256–73.

52. *Foreign Relations 1952–54*, vol. IV, p. 193.

53. Forster, "'Macondo of Guatemala,'" pp. 191–228; American and Foreign Power Financial Reports 5/30/53 and 6/30/54, Box 0152370, Electric Bond and Share Company Papers, Boise, Idaho; Gleijeses, *Shattered Hope*, passim; Meza, "Historia del Movimiento Obrero en Honduras," pp. 158–95.

CHAPTER SEVEN

1. Pérez, *On Becoming Cuban*, p. 490.

2. This section is based on ideas contained in Slotkin, *Gunfighter Nation*, pp. 474–86.

3. Dean, *Imperial Brotherhood*, pp. 9–35, 19–52.

4. Isserman and Kazin, *America Divided*, passim.

5. DePalma, *Man Who Invented Fidel.*

6. Bulmer-Thomas, *Economic History*, pp. 308–16.

7. Wyden, *Bay of Pigs*, pp. 272–73.

8. Patterson, *Contesting Castro*, pp. 258–61.

9. Quoted in Latham, *Modernization as Ideology*, p. 56.

10. "Social Development Policy in Venezuela," Irving G. Tragen, Labor Attaché, Caracas, March 22, 1962. 831.40/3–2262, RG 59, USNA.

11. Roseberry, *Anthropologies and Histories*, pp. 72–73.

12. Levinson and de Onís, *Alliance that Lost its Way*, pp. 257, 259, 281.

13. Ibid., pp. 5–16.

14. "Report on a Journey to Chile-Peru-Colombia, August 1965 for General Advisory Committee on Foreign Assistance Programs," NS File, Agency File, Box 1, Lyndon Johnson Presidential Library.

15. Levinson and de Onís, *Alliance that Lost its Way*, pp. 234–36, 301–3; Cockcroft, *Neighbors in Turmoil*, pp. 466–67.

16. O'Brien, *Century of U.S. Capitalism*, pp. 148–49.

17. Levinson and de Onís, *Alliance that Lost its Way*, pp. 234–39.

18. Rabe, *Most Dangerous Area in the World*, pp. 127–32.

19. Leacock, *Requiem for Revolution*, pp. 70–71, 114.

20. Roett, *Politics of Foreign Aid*, pp. 116–40; Levinson and de Onís, *Alliance that Lost Its Way*, pp. 288–91.

21. Leacock, *Requiem for Revolution*, pp. 70, 120–21, 108–13.

22. Ibid., pp. 85–92, 114–16.

23. Ibid., pp. 134–35.

24. Weis, *Cold Warriors and Coups d'etat*, pp. 167–68.

25. O'Brien, *Century of U.S. Capitalism*, p. 153.

26. Sigmund, *Multinationals in Latin America*, passim. Wilkins, *Maturing of Multinational Enterprise*, p. 330.

27. Sigmund, *Multinationals in Latin America*, pp. 313–15.

28. O'Brien, *Century of U.S. Capitalism*, pp. 139–40.

29. Wilkins, *Maturing of Multinational Enterprise*, p. 333.

30. O'Brien, *Century of U.S. Capitalism*, pp. 143, 160.

31. Geiger, *General Electric Company in Brazil*.

32. Moreno, *Yankee Don't Go Home*, pp. 69, 75, 105.

33. Allen, *Secret Formula*, pp. 170–73.

34. Allen, *Secret Formula*, pp. 170–73; Ledogar, *Hungry for Profits*, ch. 8.

35. Wells, *Picture-Tube Imperialism?*, pp. 102–6, 120–21, 185.

36. Woodard, "Marketing Modernity," pp. 257–90.

37. Wells, *Picture-Tube Imperialism?*, pp. 96–98.

38. Scott, *Yankee Unions*, pp. 221–22.

39. Scott, *Yankee Unions*, pp. 223–24; Barry, *AIFLD*, p. 11.

40. Scott, *Yankee Unions*, p. 228.

41. Leacock, *Requiem for Revolution*, p. 187.

42. Barry, *AIFLD*, pp. 15–16, 19, 33, 43.

43. Dahlberg, *Beyond the Green Revolution*, pp. 55–56.

44. Cotter, *Troubled Harvest*, p. 145.

45. Quoted in Cotter, *Troubled Harvest*, p. 189.

46. Pearse, *Seeds of Plenty*, pp. 6–25.

47. Ibid., pp. 36–37, 56–57.

48. Pearse, *Seeds of Plenty*, p. 7; Streeter, *Colombia*; Griffin, *Political Economy of Agrarian Change*.

49. Valdés, *Pinochet's Economists*, pp. 96–114.

50. Ibid., pp. 126–27.

51. Valdés, *Pinochet's Economists*, pp. 181–91; Berman, *Influence of the Carnegie, Ford and Rockefeller Foundations*, pp. 59–60, 79–83.

52. Berman, *Influence of the Carnegie, Ford and Rockefeller Foundations*, pp. 100–103. The author was one of those young scholars who benefited from Ford Foundation funding but became an advocate of dependency theory.

53. Ibid., pp. 62–63.

54. Magat, *Ford Foundation at Work*, p. 157.

55. Packenham, *Dependency Movement*, pp. 7–33.

56. Smith, *Emergence of Liberation Theology*, pp. 14–21; Lehmann, *Democracy and Development in Latin America*, pp. 91–110.

Chapter Eight

1. Sigmund, *Overthrow of Allende*, pp. 240–53.

2. Walton and Robertson, *American Economy*, pp. 635–38; Becker and Wells, *Economics and World Power*, pp. 399–408.

3. Rockefeller, *Rockefeller Report*, p. 89.

4. Ibid., pp. 32–33.

5. Sigmund, *Overthrow of Allende*, p. 130.

6. Loveman, *Struggle in the Countryside*, pp. 115–31, 201–6.

7. Sigmund, *Overthrow of Allende*, pp. 69–87, 124.

8. Kaufman, *Crisis in Allende's Chile*, pp. 70–71.

9. De Vylder, *Allende's Chile*; Roxborough, O'Brien, and Roddick, *Chile*.

10. O'Brien, *Century of U.S. Capitalism*, pp. 157–58.

11. Sigmund, *Overthrow of Allende*, pp. 115–27.

12. Kaufman, *Crisis in Allende's Chile*, pp. 6–27.

13. Kornbluh, "Kissinger and Pinochet"; James, "Kissinger Criticized Subordinates."

14. Schmitter, *Military Rule*; Pike and Stritch, *New Corporatism*.

15. Wilkins, *Maturing of Multinational Enterprise*, pp. 361–62; Rabe, *Road to OPEC*, pp. 184–85; O'Brien, *Century of U.S. Capitalism*, pp. 149–51.

16. John McKee, Regional Manager, Ford Motor Company to Marvin Watson, Special Assistant to the President, Dallas, September 21, 1967, CO, July–December, 1966, Box 6, Lyndon B. Johnson Presidential Library.

17. Evans, *Dependent Development*, pp. 3–100; Bulmer-Thomas, *Economic History*, pp. 326–27.

18. Bulmer-Thomas, *Economic History*, pp. 326–41.

19. Evans and Gereffi, "Foreign Investment," p. 130.

20. Baird and McCaughan, *Beyond the Border*, p. 132.

21. Guarjardo-Quiroga, "Economic Impact of the Maquiladora Industry in Mexico."

22. Kline, *Foreign Investment Strategies*, pp. 49–57, 99–101.

23. Stallings, *Banker to the Third World*, pp. 75–80, 334.

24. Ibid., pp. 94–100, 334.

25. Jenkins, *Transnational Corporations and Industrial Transformation*, pp. 5–82; Jenkins, *Transnational Corporations and the Latin American Automobile Industry*, pp. 17–23; Shapiro, *Engines of Growth*, pp. 2–3; Wilkins, *Maturing of Multinational Enterprise*, pp. 311–13.

26. Humphrey, *Capitalist Control*.

27. Jenkins, *Transnational Corporations and the Latin American Automobile Industry*, ch. 4.

28. Scott, *Yankee Unions*, pp. 245–36; Kaufman, *Crisis in Allende's Chile*, p. 81.

29. Bucheli, *Bananas and Business*, pp. 50–70.

30. Rosenberger, *America's Drug War Debacle*, pp. 19–24.

31. Magat, *Ford Foundation*, p. 159.

32. Bastian, *Protestantismo*, pp. 150–63.

33. Bastian, *Protestantismo*, pp. 164–68; Annis, *God and Production*, pp. 1–12, 140–42.

34. U.S. Department of Commerce, *Business Statistics*, p. 123.

35. Memorandum, United States Department of the Interior, June 20, 1966, Box 5, Lyndon B. Johnson Library, NSF Country File Latin America.

36. Crain, "Negotiating Identities," pp. 125–30.

37. Crain, "Negotiating Identities," pp. 129–36; Chibnik, *Crafting Tradition*, pp. 3–6; Walter, "Otavaleño Development," pp. 319–37.

38. Gilderhus, *Second Century*, pp. 185–87, 204–6.

39. Black, *Triumph of the People*, pp. 28–74: Vilas, *Sandinista Revolution*, pp. 112–19.

40. Bermann, *Under the Big Stick*, pp. 265–74.

41. Hersh, *Price of Power*, p. 265.

Chapter Nine

1. Religious Task Force on Central America and Mexico, "Four Churchwomen: Martyrs in El Salvador."

2. Ferguson, "By Invitation Only," pp. 241–50.

3. Dean, *Imperial Brotherhood*, p. 5.

4. Silva, "Authoritarianism," pp. 51–62.

5. Smith, *Talons of the Eagle*, p. 180; Coatsworth, *Central America*, p. 132.

6. Coatsworth, *Central America*, p. 177.

7. Allan Nairn, "Behind the Death Squads," *The Progressive* (May 1984), pp. 20–28; Barry, *AIFLD*, pp. 32–33.

8. Barry, *AIFLD*, p. 35; Coatsworth, *Central America*, pp. 153–54.

9. *Time*, March 16, 1987.

10. Stoll, *Is Latin America Turning Protestant?*, p. 153.

11. Lernoux, "Fundamentalist Surge."

12. Brouwer, Gifford, and Rose, *Exporting the American Gospel*, pp. 53–62.

13. Smith, "Religion and the Electronic Media."

14. Coatsworth, *Central America*, pp. 183–84.

15. Ibid., pp. 172–76.

16. Stepan, *Democratizing Brazil*; see especially articles by Skidmore, Mainwaring, and Keck; Bentley, "Paulo Freire."

17. Drake and Jaksić, "Introduction," pp. 1–17; Angell, "Unions and Workers," pp. 194–95.

18. Rosenberger, *Drug War*, pp. 26–31.

19. Walker, "Foreign Narcotics Policy," p. 232.

20. Ibid., pp. 240–41.

21. Smith, *Talons*, pp. 365–67.

22. Bulmer-Thomas, *Economic History*, pp. 363–64; Smith, *Talons*, pp. 236–37.

23. O'Brien, *Century of U.S. Capitalism*, p. 162.

CHAPTER TEN

1. Jeffries, "Zapatismo and the Intergalactic Age," pp. 129–32.

2. Smith, *Talons*, pp. 270–75.

3. Bagley, "Drug War in Colombia," pp. 201–9; McDermott, "New Cartel Crackdown in Colombia."

4. www.ciponline.org/colombia/blog/archives/000243.htm

5. "Letter from the Americas: Hide-and-Seek Among the Coca Leaves," *New York Times*, June 9, 2004.

6. Bigwood and Henry, "Drug Wars Part One." On Orjuelas, see BBC News, November 8, 2002, news.bbc.co.uk/2/hi/Americas/2417847.stm; *New York Times*, October 23, 2003.

7. Epstein, "General Seeks Boost for Latin American Armies"; Bachelet, "Rumsfeld, Latin American Officials Discuss Regional Security."

8. Lobe, "U.S. Military Aid to Latin America Grows."

9. Smith, *Talons*, pp. 244–45.

10. Valdés, *Pinochet's Economists*, pp. 22–28.

11. Silva, "Technocrats and Politics in Chile," pp. 393–98.

12. Centeno, *Democracy Within Reason*, p. 201.

13. Chudnovsky, López, and Porta, "New Foreign Direct Investment," pp. 57–58.

14. World Bank Press Release No. 2002/077/LCR, Rio de Janeiro, Brazil, September 10, 2001.

15. UNCTAD Press Release, "Latin America and the Caribbean Attract the Largest Share of Foreign Direct Investment in the Developing World in 1999."

16. Wilkie, *Statistical Abstract of Latin America*, pp. 785, 887; Public Citizen, "North American Free Trade Agreement."

17. "A Region at Risk: Argentine Economy Reborn But Still Ailing," *New York Times*, February 6, 1998, p. A7.

18. Interhemispheric Resource Center, "Brazil Increasingly Unenthusiastic."

19. Rodríguez Yebra, "Kirchner Reorients Foreign Policy"; Harmon, "China Eyes New Turf."

20. O'Brien, *Century of U.S. Capitalism*, p. 166.

21. Coatsworth, "Structures, Endowments and Institutions," p. 137.

22. Ibid., p. 138.

23. "The Coffee Connection Thousands of Miles from Boston's Breakfast Tables and Fast-Food Restaurants, at the End of a Global Trade Network, Guatemala's Farmers are Barely Scraping By," *Boston Globe*, July 29, 2001.

24. "The Coffee Connection," *Boston Globe*, July 29, 2001; *The Economist*, September 29, 2001, and December 1, 2001.

25. Raghavan, "Mexico"; Burbach, "Roots of the Postmodern," pp. 119–26.

26. Quoted in Burbach, "Roots of the Postmodern," p. 126. Land-use statistic from Howard and Homer-Dixon, "Environmental Scarcity and Violent Conflict."

27. Leech, "Coca Cola Accused of Using Death Squads."

28. "Administration Shifts Focus on Colombia Aid," *New York Times*, February 6, 2002.

29. *The Economist*, November 3, 2001, and January 2, 2002.

30. *The Economist*, January 2, 2002; Acosta, "Argentina Atrapada por los Alquimistas."

31. Williams, "IMF May Ease Stance on Argentine Debt."

32. Ibid.

33. Golinger, "U.S. Pays Millions to Overthrow Chavez"; Vann, "AFL-CIO's Role in the Venezuelan Coup."

34. "Still Poor, Latin Americans Protest Push for Open Markets," *New York Times*, July 19, 2002.

35. "Carlos Mesa New Leader in Troubled Bolivia as President Quits."

36. Oliveira, "Brazilian Soaps Outshine Hollywood," pp. 124–28.

37. Lozano, "Media Reception," pp. 160–66.

38. Classen, "Coca-Cola and Hypermarkets," pp. 43–49.

39. Howes, "Introduction," pp. 3–6; Classen, "Coca-Cola and Hypermarkets," pp. 42–43; "Shamans Put Coke to the Test."

40. Moreno "Rapture and Renewal," pp. 31–34.

41. Chesnut, *Born Again*, pp. 45–48.

42. Droogers, "Globalization and Pentecostal Success," pp. 41–61; and Laënnec Hurbon, "Pentecostalism and Transnationalisation of the Caribbean," pp. 124–41, both in Corten and Marshall-Fratani, *Between Babel and Pentecost.*

43. Flores, "What Drives Tourism in Latin America?"

44. Henrici, "Trading Culture," pp. 161–80.

45. "By a Back Door to the U.S.: A Migrant's Grim Sea Voyage," *New York Times,* June 13, 2004.

46. Bean, Van Hook, and Woodrow-Lafield, "Estimates of Numbers of Unauthorized Migrants Residing in the United States."

47. Gonzalez, *Harvest of Empire,* pp. 138–39.

48. See Gonzalez, *Harvest of Empire.*

49. "Hispanic Population in the United States, March 2000," Hispanic Literacy Task Force mexico-info.com; "History of Hispanic Immigration," www2.worldbook.com/wc/features/cinco/html/immigration.htm

50. Gonzalez, *Harvest of Empire,* p. 195.

51. Huntington, *Who Are We?,* pp. xv–xvi, 221–43.

52. Gonzalez, *Harvest of Empire,* p. 143.

CONCLUSION

1. The American mission beyond the Western Hemisphere has become the focus of a growing body of scholarly literature. Some of the notable works include: Zunz, *Why the American Century?*; Agnew, *United States in the World-Economy*; Zeitlin and Herrigel, *Americanization and its Limits*; Nye, *Soft Power*; and de la Garzia, *Irresistible Empire.*

BIBLIOGRAPHY

Archival Sources

Boise Cascade Corporation, Boise, Idaho
Electric Bond and Share Company Papers

Butler Library, Rare Books and Manuscript Library,
    Columbia University, New York
    Frank A. Vanderlip Papers

Library of Congress
    Philander C. Knox Papers

Lyndon B. Johnson Presidential Library, Austin, Texas
    Presidential Papers of Lyndon Baines Johnson

Phelps Dodge Corporation, Phoenix, Arizona
    Papers of the Phelps Dodge Corporation

United States National Archives, Washington DC

    Record Group 59: General Records of the
        Department of State (microfilm)

    Record Group 84: Records of the Foreign Service
        Posts of the Department of State

    Record Group 286: Records of the Agency for
        International Development

    Record Group 306: Records of the United States
        Information Agency

    Record Group 469: Records of United States Foreign
        Assistance Agencies

Newspapers and Magazines

Boston Globe

The Charlotte Observer

The Economist

Houston Chronicle

New York Times

Time

Books

Adams, John Quincy. *Writings of John Quincy Adams*. Ed. Worthington Chauncey Ford. New York: Macmillan, 1913–17.

Agnew, John. *The United States in the World-Economy: A Regional Geography*. Cambridge: Cambridge University Press, 1987.

Agosin, Manuel, ed. *Foreign Direct Investment in Latin America*. Washington DC: Banco Interamericano de Desarrollo, 1995.

Alberdi, J. B. *The Life and Industrial Labors of William Wheelwright in South America*. Boston: W. Williams & Company, 1877.

Allen, Frederick. *Secret Formula: How Brilliant Marketing and Relentless Salesmanship Made Coca-Cola the Best-Known Product in the World*. New York: Harper Business, 1994.

Andrews, Gregg. *Shoulder to Shoulder?: The American Federation of Labor, the United States, and the Mexican Revolution, 1910–1924*. Berkeley: University of California Press, 1991.

Annis, Sheldon. *God and Production in a Guatemalan Town*. Austin: University of Texas Press, 1987.

Atkins, Edwin F. *Sixty Years in Cuba*. 1926. New York: Arno Press, 1980.

Baily, Samuel L. *The United States and the Development of South America, 1945–1975*. New York: Franklin Watts, 1976.

Baird, Peter, and Ed McCaughan. *Beyond the Border: Mexico and the U.S. Today*. New York: North American Congress on Latin America, 1979.

Bajarkman, Peter C. *Baseball with a Latin Beat: A History of the Latin American Game*. Jefferson, NC: McFarland and Company Inc., 1994.

Balch, Emily Greene, ed. *Occupied Haiti: Being the Report of a Committee of Six Disinterested Americans Representing Organizations Exclusively American, Who, Having Personally Studied Conditions in Haiti in 1926, Favor the Restoration of the Independence of the Negro Republic*. New York: The Writers Publishing Company, 1927.

Baldwin, Deborah J. *Protestants and the Mexican Revolution: Missionaries, Ministers, and Social Change.* Urbana: University of Illinois Press, 1990.

Barry, Tom. *AIFLD in Central America: Agents as Organizers.* Albuquerque, NM: Inter-Hemispheric Education Resource Center, 1987.

Bastian, Jean Pierre. *Breve historia del Protestantismo en América Latina.* Mexico: Casa Unida de Publicaciones, 1986.

Becker, William H. and Samuel Wells, Jr., eds. *Economics and World Power: An Assessment of American Diplomacy since 1789.* New York: Columbia University Press, 1984.

Bederman, Gail. *Manliness & Civilization: A Cultural History of Gender and Race in the United States, 1880–1917.* Chicago: University of Chicago Press, 1995.

Bergquist, Charles W. *Labor in Latin America: Comparative Essays on Chile, Argentina, Venezuela, and Colombia.* Stanford, CA: Stanford University Press, 1986.

Berman, Edward H. *The Influence of the Carnegie, Ford and Rockefeller Foundations on American Foreign Policy: The Ideology of Philanthropy.* Albany: State University of New York Press, 1983.

Bermann, Karl. *Under the Big Stick: Nicaragua and the United States Since 1848.* Boston: South End Press, 1986.

Bethell, Leslie, and Ian Roxborough, eds. *Latin America Between the Second World War and the Cold War, 1944–1948.* New York: Cambridge University Press, 1992.

Black, George. *Triumph of the People: The Sandinista Revolution in Nicaragua.* London: Zed Press, 1981.

Blocker, Jack S. *Retreat from Reform: The Prohibitionist Movement in the United States, 1890–1913.* Westport, CT: Greenwood Press, 1976.

Brack, Gene M. *Mexico Views Manifest Destiny, 1821–1846: An Essay on the Origins of the Mexican War.* Albuquerque: University of New Mexico Press, 1975.

Britton, John A. *Carleton Beals: A Radical Journalist in Latin America.* Albuquerque: University of New Mexico Press, 1987.

———. *Revolution and Ideology: Images of the Mexican Revolution in the United States.* Lexington: University Press of Kentucky, 1995.

Brouwer, Steve, Paul Gifford, and Susan D. Rose. *Exporting the American Gospel: Global Christian Fundamentalism.* New York: Routledge, 1996.

Brown, Charles Henry. *Agents of Manifest Destiny: The Lives and Times of the Filibusters.* Chapel Hill: University of North Carolina Press, 1980.

Brown, Jonathan C. *Oil and Revolution in Mexico*. Berkeley: University of California Press, 1993.

Bucheli, Macelo. *Bananas and Business: The United Fruit Company in Colombia, 1899–2000*. New York: New York University Press, 2005.

Bulmer-Thomas, Victor. *The Economic History of Latin America Since Independence*. Cambridge: Cambridge University Press, 1994.

Burns, Bradford. *The Poverty of Progress: Latin America in the Nineteenth Century*. Berkeley: University of California Press, 1980.

Butler, William. *Mexico in Transition from the Power of Political Romanism to Civil and Religious Liberty*. New York: Hunt & Eaton, 1893.

Calder, Bruce J. *The Impact of Intervention: The Dominican Republic During the U.S. Occupation of 1916–1924*. Austin: University of Texas Press, 1984.

Case, Alden Buell. *Thirty Years with the Mexicans: In Peace and Revolution*. New York: Fleming H. Revell Company, 1917.

Caulfield, Norman. *Mexican Workers and the State: From the Porfiriato to NAFTA*. Fort Worth: Texas Christian University Press, 1998.

Centeno, Miguel Ángel. *Democracy Within Reason: Technocratic Revolution in Mexico*. University Park: Pennsylvania State University Press, 1994.

Chalmers, David Mark. *Hooded Americanism: The History of the Ku Klux Klan*. 3rd ed. Durham, NC: Duke University Press, 1987.

Chesnut, Andrew R. *Born Again in Brazil: The Pentecostal Boom and the Pathogens of Poverty*. New Brunswick, NJ: Rutgers University Press, 1997.

———. *Competitive Spirits: Latin America's New Religious Economy*. New York: Oxford University Press, 2003.

Chibnik, Michael. *Crafting Tradition: The Making and Marketing of Oaxacan Wood Carvings*. Austin: University of Texas Press, 2003.

Chomsky, Aviva. *West Indian Workers and the United Fruit Company in Costa Rica, 1870–1940*. Baton Rouge: Louisiana State University Press, 1996.

Cleveland, Richard J. *Voyages and Commercial Enterprises of the Sons of New England*. 1841. New York: Burt Franklin, 1968.

Coatsworth, John. *Central America and the United States: The Clients and the Colossus*. New York: Twayne, 1994.

Cockcroft, James D. *Neighbors in Turmoil: Latin America*. New York: Harper & Row, 1989.

Colby, Gerard with Charlotte Dennett. *Thy Will be Done: The Conquest of the Amazon: Nelson Rockefeller and Evangelism in the Age of Oil*. New York: Harper Collins, 1995.

Corten, André, and Ruth Marshall-Fratani, eds. *Between Babel and Pentecost: Transnational Pentecostalism in Africa and Latin America*. Bloomington: Indiana University Press, 2001.

Cotter, Joseph. *Troubled Harvest: Agronomy and Revolution in Mexico, 1880–2002*. Westport, CT: Praeger Press, 2003.

Creole Petroleum Company. *Annual Report of the Creole Petroleum Company, 1959*. New York: Creole Petroleum Company, 1960.

Cueto, Marcos, ed. *Missionaries of Science: The Rockefeller Foundation and Latin America*. Bloomington: Indiana University Press, 1994.

Dahlberg, Kenneth. *Beyond the Green Revolution: The Ecology and Politics of Global Agricultural Development*. New York: Plenum Press, 1979.

Dean, Robert D. *Imperial Brotherhood: Gender and the Making of Cold War Foreign Policy*. Amherst: University of Massachusetts Press, 2001.

De la Garzia, Victoria. *Irresistible Empire: America's Advance Through Twentieth-Century Europe*. Cambridge, MA: Harvard University Press, 2005.

Delpar, Helen. *The Enormous Vogue of Things Mexican: Cultural Relations between the United States and Mexico, 1920–1935*. Tuscaloosa: University of Alabama Press, 1992.

De Onís, José. *The United States as Seen by Spanish American Writers, 1776–1860*. 1952. Reprint, New York: Gordian Press, 1975.

DePalma, Anthony. *The Man Who Invented Fidel: Castro, Cuba and Herbert L. Matthews of the* New York Times. New York: Public Affairs, 2006.

De Vylder, Stefan. *Allende's Chile: The Political Economy of the Rise and Fall of the Unidad Popular*. New York: Cambridge University Press, 1974.

Drake, Paul W., and Iván Jaksić, eds. *The Struggle for Democracy in Chile*. Lincoln: University of Nebraska Press, 1995.

Evans, Peter. *Dependent Development: The Alliance of Multinational, State and Local Capital in Brazil*. Princeton, NJ: Princeton University Press, 1979.

Fabens, Joseph W. *A Story of Life on the Isthmus*. New York: Putnam, 1853.

Ferguson, Thomas. *Golden Rule: The Investment Theory of Party Competition and the Logic of Money Driven Political Systems*. Chicago: University of Chicago Press, 1995.

Fifer, Valerie. *United States Perceptions of Latin America, 1850–1930: A "New West" South of Capricorn?* Manchester, England: Manchester University Press, 1991.

Franck, Harry A. *Zone Policeman 88: A Close Range Study of the Panama Canal and its Workers.* New York: The Century Company, 1913.

Gates, Paul W. *Landlords and Tenants on the Prairie Frontier: Studies in American Land Policy.* Ithaca, NY: Cornell University Press, 1973.

Geiger, Theodore, with the assistance of Liesel Goode. *The General Electric Company in Brazil.* New York: National Planning Association, 1961.

Gellman, Irwin F. *Roosevelt and Batista: Good Neighbor Diplomacy in Cuba, 1933–1945.* Albuquerque: University of New Mexico Press, 1973.

Gilderhus, Mark T. *The Second Century: U.S.–Latin American Relations Since 1889.* Wilmington, DE: Scholarly Resources, 2000.

Gleijeses, Piero. *Shattered Hope: The Guatemalan Revolution and the United States.* Princeton, NJ: Princeton University Press, 1991.

Gonzalez, Juan. *Harvest of Empire: A History of Latinos in America.* New York: Viking, 2000.

Green, David. *The Containment of Latin America: A History of the Myths and Realities of the Good Neighbor Policy.* Chicago: Quadrangle Books, 1971.

Griffin, Keith. *The Political Economy of Agrarian Change: An Essay on the Green Revolution.* Cambridge, MA: Harvard University Press, 1974.

Guarjardo-Quiroga, Ramon G. "Economic Impact of the Maquiladora Industry in Mexico." PhD diss., Texas A&M University, 1990.

Gwynne Robert N., and Cristóbal Kay, eds. *Latin America Transformed: Globalization and Modernity.* London: Arnold, 1999.

Haines, Gerald K. *The Americanization of Brazil: A Study of U.S. Cold War Diplomacy in the Third World, 1945–1954.* Wilmington, DE: Scholarly Resources, 1989.

Hart, John Mason. *Revolutionary Mexico: The Coming and Process of the Mexican Revolution.* Berkeley: University of California Press, 1989.

Healy, David. *The United States in Cuba, 1898–1902.* Madison: University of Wisconsin Press, 1963.

Hersh, Seymour. *The Price of Power: Henry Kissinger in the Nixon White House.* New York: Summit Books, 1983.

Hewlett, Sylvia Ann, and Richard S. Weinert, eds. *Brazil and Mexico: Patterns in Late Development.* Philadelphia, PA: Institute for the Study of Human Issues, 1982.

Hitchman, James H. *Leonard Wood and Cuban Independence, 1898–1902.* The Hague, Netherlands: Nijhoff, 1971.

Hobsbawm, Eric J. *The Age of Extremes: A History of the World, 1914–1991.* New York: Pantheon Books, 1994.

Horsman, Reginald. *Race and Manifest Destiny: The Origins of American Racial Anglo-Saxonism.* Cambridge, MA: Harvard University Press, 1981.

Humphrey, John. *Capitalist Control and Workers' Struggle in the Brazilian Auto Industry.* Princeton, NJ: Princeton University Press, 1982.

Huntington, Samuel P. *Who Are We? The Challenges to America's National Identity.* New York: Simon & Schuster, 2004.

Immerman, Richard H. *John Foster Dulles: Piety, Pragmatism, and Power in U.S. Foreign Policy.* Wilmington, DE: Scholarly Resources, 1999.

Ingersoll, Ralph M. *In and Under Mexico.* New York: Century, 1924.

Isserman, Maurice, and Michael Kazin. *America Divided: The Civil War of the 1960s.* New York: Oxford University Press, 2000.

Jacobsen, Nils. *Mirages of Transition, the Peruvian Altiplano, 1780–1930.* Berkeley: University of California Press, 1993.

Jenkins, Rhys. *Transnational Corporations and Industrial Transformation in Latin America.* London and New York: MacMillan, 1984.

———. *Transnational Corporations and the Latin American Automobile Industry.* Pittsburgh, PA: Pittsburgh University Press, 1987.

Johnson, Paul E. *Shopkeepers' Millennium: Society and Revivals in Rochester New York, 1815–1837.* New York: Hill and Wang, 1978.

Kaufman, Edy. *Crisis in Allende's Chile: New Perspectives.* New York: Praeger Press, 1988.

Kepner Jr., Charles David, and Jay Henry Soothill. *The Banana Empire: A Case Study of Economic Imperialism.* 1935. Reprint, New York: Russell & Russell, 1968.

Kirstein, Peter N. *Anglo over Bracero: A History of the Mexican Worker in the United States from Roosevelt to Nixon.* San Francisco: R and E Research Associates, 1977.

Klarén, Peter. *Modernization, Dislocation, and Aprismo: Origins of the Peruvian Aprista Party, 1870–1932.* Austin: University of Texas Press, 1973.

Kline, John M. *Foreign Investment Strategies in Restructuring Economies: Learning from Corporate Experiences in Chile.* Westport, CT: Quouram Books, 1992.

Klubock, Thomas. *Contested Communities: Class, Gender, and Politics in Chile's El Teniente Copper Mine, 1904–1951*. Durham, NC: Duke University Press, 1998.

Knight, Melvin M. *The Americans in Santo Domingo*. Reprint ed. New York: Arnos Press, 1970.

Kobler, John. *Ardent Spirits: The Rise and Fall of Prohibition*. New York: Ritnam, 1973.

LaFeber, Walter. *The New Empire: An Interpretation of American Expansion, 1860–1898*. Ithaca, NY: Cornell University Press, 1963.

Lane, Jack C. *Armed Progressive: General Leonard Wood*. San Rafael, CA: Presidio Press, 1978.

Langley, Lester. *Struggle for the American Mediterranean: United States-European Rivalry in the Gulf-Caribbean, 1776–1904*. Athens: University of Georgia Press, 1976.

Latham, Michael. *Modernization as Ideology: American Social Science and "Nation Building" in the Kennedy Era*. Chapel Hill: University of North Carolina Press, 2000.

Leach, William. *Land of Desire: Merchants, Power, and the Rise of a New American Culture*. New York: Pantheon Books, 1993.

Leacock, Ruth. *Requiem for Revolution: The United States and Brazil, 1961–1969*. Kent, OH: Kent State University Press, 1990.

Ledogar, Robert J. *Hungry for Profits: U.S. Food and Drug Multinationals in Latin America*. New York: IDOC North America, 1975.

Lehmann, David. *Democracy and Development in Latin America: Economics, Politics and Religion in the Post-War Period*. Philadelphia: Temple University Press, 1990.

Leonard, Thomas M. *Central America and the United States: The Search for Stability*. Athens: University of Georgia Press, 1991.

Levinson, Irving. *Wars Within War: Mexican Guerrillas, Domestic Elites and the United States of America*. Fort Worth: Texas Christian University Press, 2005.

Levinson, Jerome, and Juan de Onís. *The Alliance that Lost its Way: A Critical Report on the Alliance for Progress*. Chicago: Quadrangle Books, 1970.

Licht, Walter. *Industrializing America: The Nineteenth Century*. Baltimore, MD: Johns Hopkins University Press, 1995.

Loveman, Brian. *Struggle in the Countryside: Politics and Rural Labor in Chile, 1919–1973*. Bloomington: Indiana University Press, 1976.

Maddox, James G. *Technical Assistance by Religious Agencies in Latin America.* Chicago: University of Chicago Press, 1956.

Magat, Richard. *The Ford Foundation at Work: Philanthropic Choices, Methods, and Styles.* New York: Plenum Press, 1979.

Mallon, Florenica. *The Defense of Community in Peru's Central Highlands: Peasant Struggle and Capitalist Transition, 1860–1940.* Princeton, NJ: Princeton University Press, 1983.

Manning, William R., ed. *Diplomatic Correspondence of the United States II.* Washington DC: Carnegie Endowment for International Peace, 1932–39.

Marchand, Roland. *Advertising the American Dream: Making Way for Modernity, 1920–1940.* Berkeley: University of California Press, 1985.

May, Robert E. *The Southern Dream of Empire, 1854–1861.* Baton Rouge: Louisiana State University Press, 1980.

McAnany, Emile G., and Kenton T. Wilkinson, eds. *Mass Media and Free Trade: NAFTA and the Cultural Industries.* Austin: University of Texas Press, 1996.

McCann, Frank D. *The Brazilian-American Alliance, 1937–1945.* Princeton, NJ: Princeton University Press, 1973.

McCullough, David G. *The Path Between the Seas: The Creation of the Panama Canal, 1870–1914.* New York: Simon and Schuster, 1977.

McGovern, James R. *Anatomy of a Lynching: The Killing of Claude Neal.* Baton Rouge: Louisiana State University Press, 1982.

Moreno, Julio. *Yankee Don't Go Home: Mexican Nationalism, American Business Culture and the Shaping of Modern Mexico, 1920–1950.* Chapel Hill: University of North Carolina Press, 2003.

Nixon, Richard M. *Six Crises.* Garden City, NY: Doubleday, 1962.

Nordenstreng, Kaarle, and Herbert I. Schiller. *Beyond National Sovereignty: International Communication in the 1990s.* Norwood, NJ: Ablex Publishing, 1993.

Nye, Joseph S. *Soft Power: The Means to Success in American Foreign Policy.* New York: Foreign Affairs, 2004.

O'Brien, Thomas F. *The Century of U.S. Capitalism in Latin America.* Albuquerque: University of New Mexico Press, 1999.

———. *The Revolutionary Mission: American Enterprise in Latin America, 1900–1945.* New York: Cambridge University Press, 1996.

Packenham, Robert A. *The Dependency Movement: Scholarship and Politics in Development Studies.* Cambridge, MA: Harvard University Press, 1992.

Patterson, Thomas. *Contesting Castro: The United States and the Triumph of the Cuban Revolution.* New York: Oxford University Press, 1994.

Pearse, Andrew. *Seeds of Plenty, Seeds of Want.* New York: Oxford University Press, 1980.

Pereira Salas, Eugenio. *Los primeros contactos entre Chile y los Estados Unidos, 1778–1809.* Santiago, Chile: Editorial Andres Bello, 1971.

Pérez Jr., Louis A. *Cuba: Between Reform and Revolution.* New York: Oxford University Press, 1988.

———. *Cuba Under the Platt Amendment, 1902–1934.* Pittsburgh, PA: University of Pittsburgh Press, 1986.

——— *On Becoming Cuban: Identity, Nationality & Culture.* New York: Harper Collins, 1999.

Pérez Vila, Manuel, ed. *Simón Bolívar: His Basic Thoughts.* Caracas, Venezuela: Presidency of the Republic of Venezuela, 1981.

Philip, George. *Oil and Politics in Latin America: Nationalist Movements and State Companies.* Cambridge: Cambridge University Press, 1982.

Pike, Frederick B. *The United States and Latin America: Myths and Stereotypes of Civilization and Nature.* Austin: University of Texas Press, 1992.

Pike, Frederick B., and Thomas Stritch, eds. *The New Corporatism: Social-Political Structures in the Iberian World.* Notre Dame, IL: University of Notre Dame Press, 1974.

Plummer, Brenda Gayle. *Haiti and the Great Powers, 1902–1915.* Baton Rouge: Louisiana State University Press, 1988.

Portell Vilá, Herminio. *Nueva historia de la República de Cuba (1898–1979).* Miami, FL: Modern Press, 1986.

Prude, Jonathan. *The Coming of the Industrial Order: Town and Factory Life in Rural Massachusetts, 1810–1860.* Cambridge: Cambridge University Press, 1983.

Rabe, Stephen G. *Eisenhower and Latin America: The Foreign Policy of Anti-Communism.* Chapel Hill: University of North Carolina Press, 1988.

———. *The Most Dangerous Area in the World: John F. Kennedy Confronts Communist Revolution in Latin America.* Chapel Hill: University of North Carolina Press, 1999.

———. *The Road to OPEC: United States Relations with Venezuela, 1919–1976*. Austin: University of Texas Press, 1982.

Radosh, Ronald. *American Labor and United States Foreign Policy*. New York: Random House, 1969.

Reed, John. *Insurgent Mexico*. 1914. Reprint, New York: International Publishers, 1969.

Reed, Merl. *New Orleans and the Railroads: The Struggle for Commercial Empire, 1830–1860*. Baton Rouge: Louisiana State University Press, 1966.

Reichstein, Andreas W. *Rise of the Lone Star: The Making of Texas*. Trans. Jeanne R. Wilson. College Station: Texas A&M University Press, 1989.

Renda, Mary A. *Taking Haiti: Military Occupation & the Culture of U.S. Imperialism, 1915–1940*. Chapel Hill: University of North Carolina Press, 2001.

Rippy, J. Fred. *Globe and Hemisphere: Latin America in the Post-war Foreign Relations of the United States*. Chicago: Henry Regnery Company, 1958.

———. *Joel R. Poinsett, Versatile American*. 1935. New York: Greenwood Press, 1968.

Robinson, Mike, and Priscilla Boniface, eds. *Tourism and Cultural Conflicts*. New York: CABI International, 1999.

Rockefeller, Nelson. *The Rockefeller Report on the Americas*. Chicago: Quadrangle Books, 1969.

Roeder, Ralph. *Juárez and His Mexico*. 2 vols. New York: Viking Press, 1947.

Roett, Riordan. *The Politics of Foreign Aid in the Brazilian Northeast*. Nashville, TN: Vanderbilt University Press, 1972.

Romualdi, Serafino. *Presidents and Peons: Recollections of a Labor Ambassador in Latin America*. New York: Funk and Wagnalls, 1967.

Roseberry, William. *Anthropologies and Histories: Essays in Culture, History and Political Economy*. New Brunswick, NJ: Rutgers University Press, 1989.

Rosenberg, Emily S. *Financial Missionaries to the World: The Politics and Culture of Dollar Diplomacy, 1900–1930*. Cambridge, MA: Harvard University Press, 1999.

———. *Spreading the American Dream: American Economic and Cultural Expansion 1890–1945*. New York: Hill and Wang, 1982.

Rosenberger, Leif Roderick. *America's Drug War Debacle.* Aldershot, England: Ashgate Publishing, 1996.

Rostow, Walt W. *The Stages of Economic Growth: A Non-Communist Manifesto.* Cambridge: Cambridge University Press, 1960.

Roxborough, Ian, Philip O'Brien, and Jackie Roddick. *Chile: The State and Revolution.* London: MacMillan Press, 1977.

Salisbury, Richard V. *Anti-imperialism and International Competition in Central America, 1920–1929.* Wilmington, DE: Scholarly Resources, 1989.

Schmidt, Hans. *Maverick Marine: General Smedley D. Butler and the Contradictions of American Military History.* Lexington: University Press of Kentucky, 1987.

———. *The United States Occupation of Haiti, 1915–1934.* New Brunswick, NJ: Rutgers University Press, 1971.

Schmitter, Philippe C. *Military Rule in Latin America: Function, Consequences, and Perspectives.* Beverly Hills, CA: Sage Publications, 1973.

Scott, Jack. *Yankee Unions Go Home: How the AFL Helped the U.S. Build an Empire in Latin America.* Vancouver, Canada: New Star Books, 1978.

Shapiro, Helen. *Engines of Growth: The State and Transnational Auto Companies in Brazil.* New York: Cambridge University Press, 1994.

Sigmund, Paul E. *Multinationals in Latin America: The Politics of Nationalization.* Madison: University of Wisconsin Press, 1980.

———. *The Overthrow of Allende and the Politics of Chile, 1964–1976.* Pittsburgh, PA: Pittsburgh University Press, 1977.

Slotkin, Richard. *Gunfighter Nation: The Myth of the Frontier in Twentieth-Century America.* New York: Atheneum Press, 1992.

Smith, Christian. *The Emergence of Liberation Theology: Radical Religion and Social Movement Theory.* Chicago: University of Chicago Press, 1991.

Smith, Peter H. *Talons of the Eagle: Dynamics of U.S.–Latin American Relations.* New York: Oxford University Press, 1996.

Smith, Robert Freeman. *The United States and Revolutionary Nationalism in Mexico, 1916–1932.* Chicago: University of Chicago Press, 1972.

Snow, Sinclair. *The Pan-American Federation of Labor.* Durham, NC: Duke University Press, 1964.

Sobel, Robert. *I.T.T.: The Management of Opportunity*. New York: Times Books, 1982.

Stackpole, Edouard A. *The Sea-Hunters; The New England Whalemen During Two Centuries, 1635–1835*. Philadelphia, PA: Lippincott, 1953.

Stallings, Barbara. *Banker to the Third World: U.S. Portfolio Investment in Latin America, 1900–1986*. Berkeley: University of California Press, 1987.

Stepan, Alfred, ed. *Democratizing Brazil: Problems of Transition and Consolidation*. New York: Oxford University Press, 1989.

Stephens, John L. *Incidents of Travel in Central America, Chiapas, & Yucatan*. 1841. New Brunswick, NJ: Rutgers University Press, 1949.

Stern, Steve J., ed. *Resistance, Rebellion and Consciousness in the Andean Peasant World, 18th to 20th Centuries*. Madison: University of Wisconsin Press, 1987.

Stoll, David. *Is Latin America Turning Protestant?: The Politics of Evangelical Growth*. Berkeley: University of California Press, 1990.

Streeter, Carroll P. *Colombia: Agricultural Change: The Men and the Methods*. New York: Rockefeller Foundation, 1972.

Taylor, Wayne C., and John Lindeman. *United States Business Performance Abroad: The Creole Petroleum Corporation in Venezuela*. New York: National Planning Association, 1955.

Thomas, Hugh. *Cuba: The Pursuit of Freedom*. New York: Harper & Row, 1971.

Tuttle, Frank W., and Joseph M. Perry. *An Economic History of the United States*. Cincinnati, OH: Southwestern Publishing Company, 1970.

U.S. Bureau of the Census. *The Statistical History of the United States from Colonial Times to the Present*. New York: Basic Books, 1976.

U.S. Department of Commerce, Office of Business Economics. *Business Statistics*. Washington DC: Government Printing Office, 1969.

U.S. Department of State. *Foreign Relations of the United States, 1950 Vol II*. Washington DC: Government Printing Office, 1976.

U.S. Department of State. *Foreign Relations of the United States, 1952–1954 Vol IV*. Washington DC: Government Printing Office, 1983.

The U.S. Naval Astronomical Expedition to the Southern Hemisphere, During the Years 1849–1852. Lieutenant J. M. Gillis, superintendent I. Washington, DC: A.O.P. Nicholson, 1855–56.

Valdés, Juan Gabriel. *Pinochet's Economists: The Chicago School in Chile*. New York: Cambridge University Press, 1995.

Venzon, Anne Cipriano, ed. *General Smedley Darlington Butler: The Letters of a Leatherneck, 1898–1931*. New York: Praeger, 1992.

Vilas, Carlos Maria. *The Sandinista Revolution: National Liberation and Social Transformation in Central America*. New York: Monthly Review Press, 1986.

Walton, Gary M., and Ross M. Robertson. *History of the American Economy*. 5th ed. New York: Harcourt Brace Jovanovich Inc., 1983.

Watts, Sarah Lyons. *Order Against Chaos: Business Culture and Labor Ideology in America, 1880–1915*. New York: Greenwood Press, 1991.

Weeks, William Earl. *Building the Continental Empire: American Expansion from the Revolution to the Civil War*. Chicago: Ivan R. Dee, 1996.

Weis, Michael W. *Cold Warriors & Coups d'etat: Brazilian-American Relations, 1945–1964*. Albuquerque: University of New Mexico Press, 1993.

Wells, Alan. *Picture-Tube Imperialism? The Impact of U.S. Television on Latin America*. Maryknoll, NY: Orbis Books, 1972.

Whitaker, Arthur P. *Latin America and the Enlightenment*. Ithaca, NY: Great Seal Books, 1961.

———. *The United States and the Independence of Latin America, 1810–1830*. 1941. Reprint, New York: Norton & Company, 1964.

Wiebe, Robert H. *The Search for Order, 1877–1920*. New York: Hill and Wang, 1967.

Wilkie, James, ed., and Eduardo Aleman and Jose Guadalupe Ortega, coeds. *Statistical Abstract of Latin America*. Vol. 37. Los Angeles: University of California Press, 2001.

Wilkins, Mira. *The Emergence of Multinational Enterprise: American Business Abroad from the Colonial Era to 1914*. Cambridge, MA: Harvard University Press, 1970.

———. *The Maturing of Multinational Enterprise: American Business Abroad from 1914 to 1970*. Cambridge, MA: Harvard University Press, 1974.

Williams, William Appleman. *The Tragedy of American Diplomacy*. New York: Delta, 1962.

Williamson, Joel. *The Crucible of Race: Black/White Relations in the American South Since Emancipation*. New York: Oxford University Press, 1984.

Woll, Allen L. *The Latin Image in American Film*. Los Angeles: University of California Press, 1977.

Wood, Richardson, and Virginia Keyser. *United States Business Performance Abroad: Sears Roebuck de Mexico, S.A.* New York: National Planning Association, 1953.

Wyden, Peter. *Bay of Pigs: The Untold Story.* New York: Simon & Schuster, 1979.

Zeitlin Jonathan, and Garry Herrigel, eds. *Americanization and its Limits: Reworking U.S. Technology and Management in Post-War Europe and Japan.* Oxford: Oxford University Press, 2000.

Zunz, Oliver. *Why the American Century?* Chicago: University of Chicago Press, 1998.

ARTICLES

Acosta, Alberto. "Argentina Atrapada por los Alquimistas." Based on articles published in *Hoy* (Quito), December 12 and 26, 2001. http://www.gobalizacion.org/argentina/ArgentinaAcostaEconomia.htm

Angell, Alan. "Unions and Workers in Chile during the 1980s." In Paul W. Drake and Iván Jaksić, eds., *The Struggle for Democracy in Chile,* pp. 188–210. Lincoln: University of Nebraska Press, 1995.

Bachelet, Pablo, and Jim Lobe. "U.S. Military Aid to Latin America Grows." October 7, 2004. http://antiwar.com

Bagley, Bruce M. "The Drug War in Colombia." In William O. Walker III, ed., *Drugs in the Western Hemisphere: An Odyssey of Cultures in Conflict,* pp. 201–15. Wilmington, DE: Scholarly Resources, 1996.

Barnard, Andrew. "Chile." In Leslie Bethell and Ian Roxborough, eds., *Latin America Between the Second World War and the Cold War, 1944–1948,* pp. 66–91. Cambridge: Cambridge University Press, 1992.

BBC News. "Gilberto Rodriguez Orjeuela's Drug Cartel." November 8, 2002. news.bbc.co.uk/2/hi/Americas/2417847.stm

Beals, Carlton. "With Sandino in Nicaragua." *The Nation* 126, nos. 3268–74 (1928).

Bean, Frank D., Jennifer Van Hook, and Karen Woodrow-Lafield. "Estimates of Numbers of Unauthorized Migrants Residing in the United States: The Total, Mexican, and Non-Mexican Central American Unauthorized Populations in Mid-2001." Special Report: Pew Charitable Trusts, 2001.

Bentley, Leslie. "Paulo Freire." December 1999. http://www.unomaha.edu/~pto/paulo.htm

Bernstein, Harry. "Some Inter-American Aspects of the Englightenment." In Arthur P. Whitaker, ed., *Latin America and the Enlightenment*, pp. 53–69. New York: Appleton-Century, 1942.

Bethell, Leslie, and Ian Roxborough. "The Postwar Conjuncture in Latin America: Democracy, Labor and the Left." In Leslie Bethell and Ian Roxborough, eds., *Latin America Between the Second World War and the Cold War, 1944–1948*, pp. 1–32. Cambridge: Cambridge University Press, 1992.

Bigwood, Jeremy, and James S. Henry. "The Drug Wars Part One: The CIA Finally Gets One Right! September 2000 Intelligence Report: 'Plan Colombia May Not Work!'" Submerging Markets http://bloodbankers.typepad.com/recent_post_and _pdfs /2004/05/the_drug_wars_p.html

Britton, John A., and Jorma Ahvenainen. "Showdown in South America: James Scrymser, John Pender, and the United States-British Cable Competition." *Business History Review* 78, no. 1 (spring 2004): 1–27.

Burbach, Roger. "Roots of the Postmodern: Rebellion in Chiapas." In Roger Burbach, ed., *Globalization and Postmodern Politics: From Zapatistas to High Tech Robber Barons*, pp. 116–28. London: Pluto Press, 2001.

Calixto, Prieto. "Rubén Darío and Literary Anti-Americanism and Anti-Imperialism." In David Sheinin, ed., *Beyond the Ideal: Pan Americanism in Inter-American Affairs*, pp. 57–65. Westport, CT: Greenwood Press, 2000.

"Carlos Mesa New Leader in Troubled Bolivia as President Quits." *Agence France Press Information Clearing House*. October 18, 2003. www.informationclearinghouse.info/article5000.htm

Caulfield, Norman. "Mexican State Development Policy and Labor Internationalism, 1945–1958." *International Review of Social History* 42 (1997): 53–63.

Chen Daley, Mercedes. "The Watermelon Riot: Cultural Encounters in Panama City, April 15, 1856." *Hispanic American Historical Review* 70, no. 1 (1990): 85–108.

Chudnovsky, Daniel, Andrés López, and Fernando Porta. "New Foreign Direct Investment in Argentina: Privatization, the Domestic Market, and Regional Integration." In Manuel Agosin, ed., *Foreign Direct Investment in Latin America*, pp. 39–104. Washington DC: Banco Interamericano de Desarrollo, 1995.

Classen, Constance. "Sugar Cane, Coca-Cola and Hypermarkets: Consumption and Surrealism in the Argentine Northwest." In David Howes, ed., *Cross Cultural Consumption: Global Markets, Local Realities*, pp. 39–54. New York: Routledge, 1996.

Coatsworth, John H. "American Trade with European Colonies in the Caribbean and South America, 1790–1812." *William and Mary Quarterly* 3d. ser., 24 (1969): 243–66.

———. "Structures, Endowments and Institutions in the Economic History of Latin America." *Latin American Research Review* 40, no. 3 (2005): 126–44.

Crain, Mary M. "Negotiating Identities in Quito's Cultural Borderlands: Native Women's Performances for the Ecuadorean Tourist Market." In David Howes, ed., *Cross Cultural Consumption: Global Markets, Local Realities*, pp. 125–37. New York: Routledge, 1996.

Cueto, Marcos. "Visionaries of Science and Development: The Rockefeller Foundation's Latin American Surveys of the 1920s." In Marcos Cueto, ed., *Missionaries of Science: The Rockefeller Foundation and Latin America*, pp. 1–22. Bloomington: Indiana University Press, 1994.

Davis, Richard Harding. "The Death of Rodriguez." *New York Journal*. February 2, 1897. http://academic2.american.edu/~wjc /wjc4/Death%20of%20Rodriguez.html

Drake, Paul W., and Iván Jaksić. "Introduction: Transformation and Transition in Chile, 1982–1990." In Paul W. Drake and Iván Jaksić, eds., *The Struggle for Democracy in Chile*, pp. 1–17. Lincoln: University of Nebraska Press, 1995.

Epstein, Jack. "General Seeks Boost for Latin American Armies." *San Francisco Chronicle*, April 30, 2004.

Evans, Peter, and Gary Gereffi. "Foreign Investment and Dependent Development: Comparing Brazil and Mexico." In Ann Hewlett and Richard S. Weinert, eds., *Brazil and Mexico: Patterns in Late Development*, pp. 111–68. Philadelphia, PA: Institute for the Study of Human Issues, 1982.

Ferguson, Thomas. "By Invitation Only: Party Competition and Industrial Structure in the 1988 Election." In Thomas Ferguson, *Golden Rule: The Investment Theory of Party Competition and the Logic of Money-Driven Political Systems*, pp. 241–74. Chicago: The University of Chicago Press, 1995.

———. "From Normalcy to the New Deal: Industrial Structure, Party Competition, and American Public Policy in the Great Depression." In Thomas Ferguson, *Golden Rule: The Investment Theory of Party Competition and the Logic of Money Driven Political Systems*, pp. 113–72. Chicago: University of Chicago Press, 1995.

Fitzgerald, Deborah. "Exporting American Agriculture: The Rockefeller Foundation in Mexico, 1943–1953." In Marcos Cueto, ed., *Missionaries of Science: The Rockefeller Foundation and Latin America*, pp. 72–96. Bloomington: Indiana University Press, 1994.

Flores, Fernando. "What Drives Tourism in Latin America?" *Tendecias, Latin American Market Report*. December 2000. tendencias.infoamericas.com/article_archive/2000/1200; www.infoplease.com/ipa/A0778210.html

Forster, Cindy. "'The Macondo of Guatemala: Banana Workers and National Revolution in Tiquisate, 1944–1954." In Steve Striffler and Mark Moberg, eds., *Banana Wars: Power, Production and History in the Americas*, pp. 191–228. Durham, NC: Duke University Press, 2003.

Gilman, Nils. "Modernization Theory, the Highest Stage of American Intellectual History." In David C. Engerman, Nils Gilman, Mark H. Haefele, and Michael E. Latham, eds., *Staging Growth: Modernization, Development and the Global Cold War*, pp. 41–70. Amherst: University of Massachusetts Press, 2003.

Glover, Bill. "History of the Atlantic Cable & Submarine Telegraphy Company." http://www.trainweb.org/panama/

Golinger, Eva. "United States: U.S. Pays Millions to Overthrow Chavez." *Green Left Weekly*. September 15, 2004. www.greenleft.org.au/back/2004/598p16.htm

Harmon, Danna. "China Eyes New Turf: S. America." *Christian Science Monitor*. November 19, 2003. www.csmonitor.com

Hataway, Robert M. "1933–1945: Economic Diplomacy in a Time of Crisis." In William H. Becker and Samuel F. Wells, eds., *Economic and World Power: An Assessment of American Diplomacy Since 1789*, pp. 277–331. New York: Columbia University Press, 1984.

Henrici, Jane. "Trading Culture: Tourism and Tourist Art in Pisac, Peru." In Mike Robinson and Priscilla Boniface, eds., *Tourism and Cultural Conflicts*, pp. 161–80. New York: CABI International, 1999.

"The Hispanic Population in the United States, March 2000." Hispanic Literacy Task Force mexico-info.com; "History of Hispanic Immigration." www2.worldbook.com/wc/features /cinco/html/immigration.htm

Hoernel, Robert B. "Sugar and Social Change in Oriente, Cuba, 1898–1946." *Journal of Latin American Studies* 8 (1979): 215–49.

Howard, Philip, and Thomas Homer-Dixon. "Environmental Scarcity and Violent Conflict: The Case of Chiapas, Mexico." January 1996. http://www.library.utoronto.ca/pcs/eps/chiapas/chiapas1.htm

Howes, David. "Introduction: Commodities and Cultural Borders." In David Howes, ed., *Cross Cultural Consumption: Global Markets, Local Realities*, pp.1–16. New York: Routledge, 1996.

Hunt, Michael. "The Long Crisis in U.S. Diplomatic History: Coming to Closure." *Diplomatic History* 16, no. 1 (winter 1992): 115–40.

Interhemispheric Resource Center. "Brazil Increasingly Unenthusiastic about U.S. FTAA Proposals." Americas Program Analytical Article. February 1, 2002. http://www.americaspolicy.org/briefs/2002 /0202brazil.html

James, Randy. "Kissinger Criticized Subordinates." *Newsday*. October 1, 2004. www.newsday.com

Jeffries, Fiona. "Zapatismo and the Intergalactic Age." In Roger Burbach, ed., *Globalization and Postmodern Politics: From Zapatistas to High Tech Robber Barons*, pp. 129–44. London: Pluto Press, 2001.

Johnson, James Weldon. "Self-Determining Haiti II: What the United States Has Accomplished." *The Nation* (September 4, 1920).

Kaplan, Amy. "Black and Blue on San Juan Hill." In Amy Kaplan and Donald E. Pease, eds., *Cultures of United States Imperialism*, pp. 219–36. Durham, NC: Duke University Press, 1993.

Kofas, Jon V. "Stabilization and Class Conflict: The State Department, the IMF, and the IBRD in Chile, 1952–1958." *International History Review* 21, no. 2 (June 1999): 352–85.

Kornbluh, Peter. "Kissinger and Pinochet." *The Nation* (March 29, 1999).

Latham, Michael E. "Introduction: Modernization, International History and the Cold War World." In David C. Engerman, Nils Gilman, Mark H. Haefele, and Michael E. Latham, eds., *Staging Growth: Modernization, Development and the Global Cold War*, pp. 1–22. Amherst: University of Massachusetts Press, 2003.

Leech, Garry M. "Coca Cola Accused of Using Death Squads to Target Union Leaders." In *Colombia Report* (July 23, 2001). http//www.colombiareport.org/Colombia.73htm

Lernoux, Peggy. "The Fundamentalist Surge in Latin America." June 19, 2004. http://www.religion-online.org/showaricle.asp?/title=927

Lobe, Jim. "U.S. Military Aid to Latin America Grows." October 7, 2004. http://antiwar.com

Lozano, Jose Carlos. "Media Reception on the Mexican Border with the U.S." In Emile G. McAnany and Kenton T. Wilkinson, eds., *Mass Media and Free Trade: NAFTA and the Cultural Industries*, pp. 160–66. Austin: University of Texas Press, 1996.

Maier, Charles S. "The Politics of Productivity: Foundations of American International Economic Policy after World War II." *International Organization* 2, no. 4 (Autumn 1977): 607–33.

McDermott, Jeremy. "New Cartel Crackdown in Colombia." March 5, 2004. http://news.bbc.co.uk/go/pr/fr/-/hi/americas/3535059.stm

Meza, Víctor. "Historia del Movimiento Obrero en Honduras." In Gonzalez Casanova, ed., *Historia del movimiento obrero en América Latina*, pp. 158–95. Mexico City: Siglo Veintiuno, 1985.

Moreno, Pedro C. "Rapture and Renewal in Latin America." *First Things* 74 (June/July 1997): 31–34. www.leadereru.com

Nairn, Allan. "Behind the Death Squads." *The Progressive* (May 1984): 20–28.

Nichols, Roy F. "William Shaler: New England Apostle of Rational Liberty." *New England Quarterly* 9 (1938): 71–96.

Oliveira, Omar Souki. "Brazilian Soaps Outshine Hollywood: Is Cultural Imperialism Fading Out?" In Kaarle Nordenstreng and Herbert I. Schiller, eds., *Beyond National Sovereignty: International Communication in the 1990s*, pp. 116–31. Norwood, NJ: Ablex Publishing, 1993.

Public Citizen. "North American Free Trade Agreement (NAFTA)." www.citizen.org/trade/nafta/index.cfm; www.sumcoc.org/nafta.html

Raghavan, Chakvavarthi. "Mexico: NAFTA Corn Liberalization Fails Farmers and Environment." October 25, 2000. http://www.twnside.org

Religious Task Force on Central America and Mexico. "Four Churchwomen: Martyrs in El Salvador." http://www.rtfcam.org/martyrs/women/women.htm

Rodríguez Yebra, Martín. "Kirchner Reorients Foreign Policy." *La Nación* (Buenos Aires), June 15, 2003. www.worldpress.org

Schroeder, Michael J. "The Sandino Rebellion Revisited: Civil War, Imperialism, Popular Nationalism, and State Formation Muddied Up Together in the Segovias of Nicaragua, 1926–1934." In Gilbert M. Joseph, Catherine LeGrand, and Ricardo D. Salvatore, eds., *Close Encounters of Empire: Writing the Cultural History of U.S.– Latin American Relations*, pp. 208–32. Durham, NC: Duke University Press, 1998.

"Shamans Put Coke to the Test." *El Universal*, April 27, 2004. www.eluniversalgrafico.com.mx/impreso

Silva, Patricio. "Authoritarianism, Democracy and Development." In Robert N. Gwynne and Cristóbal Kay, eds., *Latin America Transformed: Globalization and Modernity*, pp. 51–65. London: Arnold, 1999.

———. "Technocrats and Politics in Chile: From the Chicago Boys to the CIEPLAN Monks." *Journal of Latin American Studies* 23, no. 2 (May 1991): 385–410.

Solorzano, Armando. "The Rockefeller Foundation in Revolutionary Mexico: Yellow Fever in Yucatan and Veracruz." In Marcos Cueto, ed., *Missionaries of Science: The Rockefeller Foundation and Latin America*, pp. 52–71. Bloomington: Indiana University Press, 1994.

Taylor, Lawrence D. "The Wild Frontier Moves South: U.S. Entrepreneurs and the Growth of Tijuana's Vice Industry, 1908–1935." *The Journal of San Diego History* 48, no. 3 (summer 2002): 204–29.

TrainWeb. "The Panama Railroad." http://www.trainweb.org/panama/history1.html

UNCTAD Press Release, tad/inf 835. "Latin America and the Caribbean Attract the Largest Share of Foreign Direct Investment in the Developing World in 1999." February 1, 2000. www.unctad.org/en/press/pr2835.htm

Vann, Bill. "The AFL-CIO's Role in the Venezuelan Coup." May 3, 2002. www.wsws.org/articles/2002/vene-m03.shtml

Walker III, William O. "The Foreign Narcotics Policy of the United States Since 1980." In William O. Walker III, ed., *Drugs in the Western Hemisphere: An Odyssey of Cultures in Conflict*, pp. 229–50. Wilmington, DE: Scholarly Resources, 1996.

Walter, Lynn. "Otavaleño Development, Ethnicity and National Integration." *América Indígena* 41, no. 2 (April–June 1981): 319–37.

Williams, Carol J. "IMF May Ease Stance on Argentine Debt." *Los Angeles Times*, July 19, 2003. http://www.globalpolicy.org /socecon/bwi-wto/imf/2003/0719debt.htm

Wilson, Christopher P. "Plotting the Border: John Reed, Pancho Villa and *Insurgent Mexico*." In Amy Kaplan and Donald E. Pease, eds., *Cultures of United States Imperialism*, 340–64. Durham, NC: Duke University Press, 1993.

Wood, Leonard. "The Military Government of Cuba." *Annals of the American Academy of Political and Social Science* 21 (March 1903): 153–82.

Woodard, James P. "Marketing Modernity: The J. Walter Thompson Company and North American Advertising in Brazil, 1929–1939." *Hispanic American Historical Review* 82, no. 2 (2002): 257–90.

World Bank Press Release No. 2002/077/LCR. "Infrastructure Reform and Privatization Must Help Poor, Promote Growth, Says World Bank." Rio de Janeiro, Brazil, September 10, 2001. http://web.worldbank.org/WBSITE/EXTERNAL /COUNTRIES/LACEXT/BOLIVIAEXTN /0,,contentMDK:20012573~menuPK:322299~pagePK :141137~piPK:141127~theSitePK:322279,00.html

UNPUBLISHED SOURCES

Guarjardo-Quiroga, Ramon G. "Economic Impact of the Maquiladora Industry in Mexico." PhD dissertation. Texas A&M University, 1990.

Smith, Dennis A. "Religion and the Electronic Media in Latin America: A Review." Paper presented at the 2001 meeting of the Latin American Studies Association, Washington DC. September 6–8, 2001.

INDEX

Page numbers in *italics* indicate illustrations.

Peru, 59, 109, 214, 215, 228; cocaine
in, 281–82, 323; coffee crop
of, 300; discontent in, 306–7;
globalization effect on, 306;
Great Depression influence on,
135–36; Indigenista movements
of, 107; war on drugs and, 282;
W. R. Grace and Company in, 58;
YMCA in, 114

Phelps Dodge Corporation, 93, 144,
146, 148, 252; Americanization
and, 119

Philip Morris Companies Inc., 300

Philippines, 116

piecework system, of labor, 118

Pierce, Franklin, 41, 42

Pinel, Gustavo, 98

Pinochet, Augusto, 249, 271, 276,
280, 281

Plan Colombia, 303, 305

Platt Amendment, 73, 103

Platt, Orville, 72, 73

Plummer, Allen, 98

Poinsett, Joel R., 26, 327

Point Four foreign-aid program, 133,
184, 236

Polk, James, 37–38, 40

Popular Democratic Unity
(UPD), 275

Popular Front, 245

Popular Unity (UP), 245, 247;
overthrow of, 255

Populist Party, 53

positivists, 55–56

Prebisch, Raúl, 193–94, 236

PRI. See Institutionalized
Revolutionary Party

privatization, 296–97

Proctor and Gamble, 300

Progressivism, 100, 103, 106, 114–15

Protestantism, 60–62, 93–95, 101, 114,
153, 192, 238, 239, 240, 257, 258,
276, 311, 322, 324; Latin American
youth and, 81–82, 151–52; North
Americans as advocates of, 19. See
also Pentecostalism

PTL Club, 258

Punta Alegre Sugar Company, 92

Quadros, Jânio, 223, 225, 226

Quitman, John, 40, 41

Rabe, Steve, 4

racism, 17, 18–19, 24, 34–35, 39, 44,
99, 104, 130, 193, 202, 206, 320;
in baseball, 200; canal project
reflecting U.S., 86; Haiti, U.S.
and, 89, 123; Latin Americans
reacting to U.S., 106; reform and,
118; in United States, 78

Radio Corporation of America
(RCA), 108, 109

railroads, 18, 44, 53, 59

RCA. See Radio Corporation of
America

Reagan, Ronald, 10, 263, 268, 269, 285,
289, 322; Nicaragua and, 272–79;
war on drugs and, 281

Reconstruction era, 78

Reed, John, 81

Reed, Paul K., 198

Regan, Donald, 284

religious conversion, 310–13;
elimination of racial inferiority
through, 62. See also specific
religions

Renda, Mary, 4

Republican Party, 132; African
Americans abandonment by, 53

Revolutionary Mission (O'Brien), 3

Rig Veda, 328

Rio de Janeiro, 147